ADDINGTON

PHILIP ZIEGLER

ADDINGTON

A Life of Henry Addington,
First Viscount Sidmouth

"an unshaken and inviolable attachment
to the Constitution as established at the
Revolution, and a determination to uphold
it against innovation, as the best security of
our civil and religious liberty."

THE JOHN DAY COMPANY
New York

Library of Congress Catalogue Card Number: 65-25445

Printed in Great Britain

To my father

Illustrations

Acknowledgments

I owe great gratitude to the present Lord Sidmouth, both for allowing me free access to his family papers and for the constant help, advice and encouragement which he has given me over the last few years. Mrs. Marjorie Villiers, Mr. Richard Ollard and Professor Le May of the University of the Witwatersrand have been most patient in working through my manuscript and most helpful and constructive in their comments. Mr. A. E. Smith, of the University of Reading, was good enough to examine my text in the light of his formidable knowledge of the period and subject. The Earl of Donoughmore kindly allowed me to make use of his family papers and I was fortunate enough to be able to consult unpublished theses by Mr. J. G. Rogers and Mr. D. A. Scholfield, and certain studies by Sir Austin Strutt, lately of the Home Office. My debt to the staffs of the British Museum, the Public Record Office, the London Library and the County Archives at Exeter is almost too obvious to require mention. Miss Maspero typed my manuscript with skill and care. Without my wife I could not even have undertaken this work, let alone finished it. I have made use of the works of many historians: it is invidious to single out any one yet I am reluctant not to mention in particular the debt which every student of the period must owe to Professor Aspinall of Reading University.

P.Z.

I

When Anthony Addington, in 1740, decided that in medicine lay his surest road to fortune, his choice, while unusual was neither outrageous nor irrational. The run-of-the-mill apothecary was certainly small beer, no better than his complement the barber-cum-surgeon, an ill-trained and ill-paid drudge who supplemented his pitiful income by peddling love potions to credulous yokels and attending to the wants of cows and horses. But this was not at all what Addington intended. As a graduate of Oxford his way was clear to become a fellow of the Royal College of Physicians and it was in this company that he knew fame and wealth was to be found.

A fellow of the Royal College was a very considerable member of society. There were few houses in which he might feel that he had strayed above his station; noblemen might sometimes treat him with the affable condescension due to a superior kind of servant but by the country gentry he was usually held to be different in species but broadly similar in status. Dr. Jernegham, himself the son of a baronet, actually married the daughter of a viscount; Dr. Freind became a Tory Member of Parliament; Sir Edward Hulse built a stately home in the New Forest and founded a dynasty of country gentlemen. And if the standing of the Society was ever in doubt, it ceased to be so when the great Duke of Montagu, in 1717, craved the honour of being admitted as a Fellow and often took the trouble to dine among its members.[1]

For the *élite* of the profession, the financial rewards were equally impressive. As early as 1700 Dr. Radcliffe, favourite doctor of William III, was earning a steady £7,000 a year. Dr. Mead, his successor in fashionable esteem, averaged between five and six thousand. And Dr. Warren, Addington's contemporary and rival, died leaving a fortune of £150,000.[2] For a young man, confident in his own abilities but without the support of an

13

important family, medicine must have seemed to offer prospects surer than the Bar and more remunerative than the Army or the Church.

For the Addingtons, though in their small way worthy and well respected, were in no position to give their progeny a helping hand into high society. They were a family of yeomen farmers, settled since the sixteenth century near Fringford in Oxfordshire. The barrier between yeomen and country gentlemen was never well defined but the first Addington who unequivocally crossed it was Anthony Addington's father Henry. Henry Addington had a talent for acquiring legacies, married two wives, both of small but acceptable fortune, was officially styled gentleman and sat on the Grand Jury for Oxfordshire. Of his eight children only three survived infancy and two of these were girls. A comfortable proportion of the family fortune was thus available for the education of Anthony and for launching him on his career.[1]

Winchester was felt to be the school best suited to his talents. His career there was unexceptionable though he achieved no very noteworthy distinction and did not get the scholarship to New College which then as now confirmed the good Wykehamist as an established member of the society into which he had been baptised a few years before. Instead Addington went to Trinity, Oxford and graduated in 1739. He was ill, off and on, throughout his Oxford career and nearly died in 1740. The experience seems to have impressed him deeply: both by the inadequacy of the treatment given him and the disproportionately great rewards demanded by his doctors. He was not slow to draw the moral and, shortly after his recovery, announced to his family that he had decided to read for the degree of bachelor of medicine.

Addington first practised as a doctor at Reading in 1745. He was by then thirty-two and looking about him for a suitable wife. He found her in Mary Hiley, the daughter of the Headmaster of Reading Grammar School. She was described as "a lady of small fortune and great beauty"[2] but the fortune, £3,000, was not as small as all that and, combined with his father-in-law's influence in the town, must have done much to smooth Dr. Addington's path to success. Most important of all, it gave him the chance to look beyond the drudgery of a provincial practice to the specialised spheres in which fame and fortune were most likely to be found. He opted for mental illness, on which sur-

14

prisingly little recent work had been done. The choice was a shrewd one. Few ailments were more fashionable than insanity. If he could once achieve acknowledged mastery in his field then Dr. Addington was assured an entry into the best houses in London. Let him but bide his time indeed and even the royal palaces must fall within his sway. As a first step he opened a private lunatic asylum next door to his house in Reading. Quickly its reputation was established as a resort for the richer members of local society who wished to rid themselves of their imbecile relations while assuring themselves that all possible was being done on their behalf.

His first published work, however, was an "Essay on the Scurvy, with the Method of Preserving Water Sweet at Sea." Like most of Dr. Addington's professional work it was sensible and cautious; bearing all the marks of serious study while lacking any trace of inspiration or even the spirit of scientific inquiry.[1] It contained much helpful advice, such as keeping the ship clean by throwing dead men overboard, but there seems no reason to suppose that it contributed to saving the life of even a single sailor. It was, however, well received by the Lords of the Admiralty to whom it was deferentially dedicated and achieved its primary purpose of making the name of Dr. Addington known in medical circles of the metropolis.

The first time that the general public ever heard of him was also in circumstances far remote from his chosen field of study. In 1751 a certain Mary Blandy was persuaded by her lover to put pills into her father's porridge. The pills were euphemistically described as Scotch pebbles: she claimed to think they were a potion intended to make her father approve her marriage; in fact they contained a lethal dose of arsenic. The murder trial that followed was one of the *causes célèbres* of the eighteenth century, and Dr. Addington's evidence was instrumental in sending Mary Blandy to the gallows.

Encouraged by this notoriety and by a solid reputation among the inhabitants of Reading, Addington decided the time had come to move to London. The step was essential if he were ever to reach the top of his profession but it was still a gamble. Only those with exceptionally good connections or a lot of luck could hope to earn a living in their first few years and many who were prepared to take the risk found that translation to a higher class

15

of practice called for talents, both social and medical, with which they were not equipped. Dr. Addington, however, furnished with adequate private means and an ineffable confidence in his own powers, did not doubt that he would succeed. He had solid grounds for his self-esteem. He was intelligent if not brilliant; his notebooks[1] show that he worked assiduously at the theoretical side of his craft; he was plausible, dignified, courteous, a master of the lucid and impressive exposition which betrayed nothing of his real opinions or of his not infrequent inability to diagnose the illness. He was, in short, a competent doctor who could reassure even where he could not cure, and leave the bereaved with the comforting conviction that their loved ones' lives had been extended to the uttermost limit of their allotted span.

He quickly won success. The year after his arrival in London he was a candidate for the College of Physicians. The following year he was appointed Fellow and, in 1757, became Censor of the College and was called on to deliver the Gulstonian lectures. By the time that his eldest son Henry was born on 30th May of the same year Dr. Addington had built up a fashionable practice and was becoming a familiar figure in some of the greatest houses of the city.

*   *   *   *   *

Henry Addington's early years seem to have been much like those of any other child brought up in a sedate and comfortable eighteenth-century home. His father, grave, ambitious and absorbed in his work, cared little for small children and asked only that they should be paraded before him, quiet and relatively clean, at suitable moments throughout the week. Later Henry's career and accomplishments were to be the subject of exhaustingly intense inspection but, until his son was seven or eight, Dr. Addington confined himself to a professional concern for his childish fevers. His mother undoubtedly did something to redress this indifference, but Mary Addington was a shadowy figure who lived her life uneasily in the interstices of her husband's prejudices. Her son loved her, welcomed her presence, but forgot her when she was not there. For company Henry looked to his three elder sisters and to his brother, Hiley, two years his junior but his closest companion for the greater part of his life.

Dr. Addington was determined that his son should enjoy all

the advantages to which his parentage entitled him. The son of such a father, he felt, could hardly lack talents. Those talents must be developed without delay. When he was only five years old Henry Addington was despatched to Dr. Gilpin's academy at Cheam. The school, which still flourishes to-day, was opened at the time of the Great Plague when its location was considered so healthy as to defy even the severest epidemic. In the early eighteenth century it had lost some of its repute but Dr. Gilpin quickly regained the lost ground. By the time Addington became a pupil, the numbers had risen from fifteen to eighty and its repute had spread all over England.

It had better claim to fame than most such institutions. William Gilpin was a man of talent and imagination. A clergyman, like most school-masters of the age, he was also a competent draughtsman and water-colourist and a prolific author. As an educationalist he would have seemed advanced at any period. Discipline at Cheam was maintained almost entirely by the boys themselves. A code of rules, with the appropriate punishments for their breach, was read over to the school at stated intervals. If there was any doubt about their application a jury of twelve boys was empanelled to pass judgment on their fellow. Dr. Gilpin claimed never to have found a decision of this court to be patently incorrect. The school was run on the lines of an independent state with Cabinet, Lord Chamberlain and Prime Minister. Dr. Gilpin arrogated to himself the role of King; a constitutional monarch for the most part but with a reserve of Divine Right to be invoked in extreme emergency.[1]

The rules for the observance of bounds were equally original. A certain number of walks outside the school grounds were approved as suitable for the young gentlemen of Cheam. Boys could then either promise to stick to the authorised routes, in which case they were free to take their walks whenever they chose, or refuse to make such a promise, in which case they were confined to the school grounds for the whole term. If those who had refused to give their parole broke bounds and were caught, then the punishment was comparatively light. But if a boy who had promised to stick to the prescribed routes strayed into forbidden territory, his crime was considered most serious and he was fortunate if he were allowed to stay in the school at all.

It would be pleasant to record that this sophisticated treatment always met with success. Certainly failures were few, but failures there were. Dr. Gilpin perhaps met his worst disaster when he boldly accepted a number of boys who had been expelled from a rival school. They took advantage of his leniency to keep a pack of hounds in a neighbouring village and most evenings returned to school drunk after some adolescent debauch. To compound their crimes, they mulcted the smaller boys of half their luncheon so as to feed their hounds and sent the Doctor's food-bills soaring as the victims sought for second helpings to make good their loss. Discovery led to a second expulsion and the school returned to its usual tranquillity. But for Dr. Gilpin the blow was a hard one and, though his methods remained as idiosyncratic as ever, his faith in the essential reasonableness of schoolboys was sadly shaken.

Henry Addington was an adaptable child, friendly, good-natured, too docile to get into serious trouble yet with enough spirit not to be written off as a prig. Though it pained him to be away from his brother Hiley there was little else about his home which he regretted. Indeed he found life at Cheam a great deal livelier and freer than it had ever been in the sober oppressiveness of his father's house. He was of a temperament to enjoy or, at least, make the best of any new experience, and it did not take him long to conclude that school had got a great deal in its favour. Dr. Gilpin was well satisfied with his new pupil. "I have the pleasure to inform you," he wrote to Dr. Addington,[1] "that your little gentleman is extremely well, in all appearance a very happy member of our community. . . . He is indeed an engaging, sweet boy, obliging to every body, and tractable in the highest degree . . ."

His satisfaction was undiminished during the seven years which Henry Addington spent at Cheam. Even before Addington went there he had been given a fair grounding in the elements of learning and his quick intelligence ensured that he more than held his own among the other children. "Harry is a genius," wrote Dr. Gilpin enthusiastically two years after Addington had joined the school,[2] "and I may add, he takes the licence of a genius—he trusts more to his parts than his industry. He is certainly an idle boy; and yet he generally has his lesson as well as any, often the best, of his class, though he is raised among boys who are his seniors much in point of years. . . ." Painstaking application was

18

more the quality for which Dr. Addington was looking. He comforted himself, however, with the reflection that a measure of irresponsibility at the age of seven did not necessarily point the way to a lifetime of frivolity.

It was at Cheam that Addington made the first of the little group of friends who were to remain close to him for the span of their lives. To Addington friendship was something of extreme importance and to all those who qualified he offered absolute trust and loyalty. The sentiment indeed extended to institutions as well as individuals. He was one of nature's Old Boys, vesting his schools and colleges with every merit on slight grounds except that he had attended them. There was little he would not do to help them in after life. The weakness was an amiable one but still hazardous in a Minister of the Crown. Throughout his life his appointments were made with more reference to the claims of old acquaintance than of merit. From Cheam he recruited the nucleus of his government. His brother Hiley, who had followed him to school after two years' delay, was to be a Joint Secretary of the Treasury. John Mitford, Addington's future Chancellor in Ireland, was briefly a contemporary. Nicholas Vansittart, the other Joint Secretary, and Charles Yorke, the Secretary for War, were both at Cheam within a few years of Addington. None of these were fools—it could indeed be argued that all of them deserved their position—but it can hardly be doubted that in Addington's mind one of their most important qualifications was the experience that they held in common with him.

At the age of twelve Henry Addington, accompanied by his brother Hiley, moved on to Winchester. The headmaster at the time was Dr. Warton, a minor poet and indifferent scholar who nevertheless contrived to impress most of those whom he considered important with a sense of his dignity and wisdom. His discipline was so inadequate that three times the boys rose in mutiny against him and Winchester acquired a well-earned reputation for profligacy and vice.

But for Addington the important figure of his years at Winchester was not the headmaster but one of his most junior assistants, George Isaac Huntingford. Huntingford was a clergyman; only nine years older than his new pupil and each season conscientiously rejuvenating himself by total immersion in the stream of youth which flowed through Winchester. Romantic, susceptible, ever hopeful, he was the prototype of all those ardent missionaries who prey like benevolent succubi upon succeeding generations of schoolboys. He loved them with a pure and painful love, worked for them, intrigued for them, was continually disappointed by them and, as continually, pinned his expectations on fresh heroes of whose merits, this time, there could be no doubt. Limited intelligence and imagination and a total lack of intellectual curiosity completed the traditional pattern of the dedicated schoolmaster; a being disliked by some and mocked by many but with it all sincere, conscientious and benign. He did, by and large, more good than harm.

Huntingford arrived at Winchester at much the same time as Henry Addington. It did not take him long to single out the latter as pre-eminent amongst his pupils for virtue, intelligence and manly qualities. Henry was a handsome child, tall for his age with wavy hair, a friendly disposition and ingratiating manners. He sincerely admired Huntingford and made evident both his admiration and his readiness to absorb wisdom from his teacher on any subject that the latter might feel appropriate. Huntingford responded by unleashing on his gratified pupil his formidable capacity for affection and admiration. He built up Addington in his mind as an impossible paragon of virtue and honour and cherished him as the chosen disciple who would one day far outstrip his master.

Within a few months of their first acquaintance Huntingford was seeking to mitigate the pangs of separation by writing long and heartfelt letters to his pupil. "My desire is not that you may be wealthy," he wrote in an early letter,[1] "but that virtue might guide you in all your actions; that faith or rather fidelity may still protect you, and in spite of persecution, preserve in you that love of truth and ingenuity which peculiarly distinguishes and ennobles your mind in your present tender age: that *wisdom* may teach you to resist the impetuosity of *passion*, your greatest and most dangerous enemy." The tone of this epistle, loving, admiring, didactic, was to be struck again and again in all the multitude of letters which Huntingford was to address to Addington over the next sixty years.

But it was not long before a suggestion of the passion which he had deplored in his charge crept into the preceptor's letters. "How shall I boast to call you my pupil," he rhapsodised on one

20

occasion, "how shall I be transported to call myself, my dearest Addington, your tender and most affectionate friend."[1] "I verily believe," he wrote a few years later, "I could die for you with even a degree of pleasure."[2] He took to verse[3] in a vigorous if misguided effort to "stamp with fame my Harry's name" and pleaded with the heavenly powers:

> . . . To make this social bliss for ever last!
> And as the wiser few
> No vulgar themes pursue
> Make me with rapture to commend
> The faith, the virtues of my friend.

The ardent love of a teacher for his pupil is conventionally a subject for sneers and innuendo. No one can say what unpleasant undertones might not be dredged from Huntingford's dreams or most private soul-searchings. But everything in their characters attests that the relationship was one of formidable chastity, conducted on a level of idealism which may sometimes have been enervating to the participants but left not the slightest grounds for the efforts of gossip and scandalmongers.

Innocent or not, the relationship was stiflingly intense. Addington was a sensitive and impressionable child. The extravagant and exacting affection of his master went near to overwhelming him. It is difficult to overestimate the importance of the influence which Huntingford enjoyed over Addington during these critically important years; never in his life indeed did Addington cease to believe in the former's wisdom and good judgment. It is difficult also to exaggerate the mischief which was done.

To Huntingford the virtues which above all contributed to a contented and well-spent life were prudence, discretion, conformity and moderation in all things save in rigid adherence to the established order. In politics, religion and every other field of life he was a narrow-minded and inflexible conservative, a sworn enemy of any kind of non-conformity. He was no fool and did not find it necessary to pretend that all was perfect as it was. Instead he would argue cogently that any alteration might be for the worse and that inactivity must therefore be the better course. Himself a man of honour and virtue, he conceded nothing to the weaknesses of others; a man of decided opinion, he conceded nothing to their doubts and hesitations. His closed and intolerant mind led him to distrust all speculations and inquiry and to inculcate in his pupils blind acceptance of authority and of the traditional patterns of society.

There is not much to be gained by speculating how Addington might have developed if it had not been for Huntingford. The atmosphere of his home was staunchly conservative. From his father he had already learned that prudence and circumspection were cardinal among the virtues and that "progress" was a concept to be viewed with distrust or, more often, out-and-out hostility. His nature had taken happily to such precepts. Probably no education could now have imbued him with reforming zeal. But the blind opposition to any form of change which was increasingly to dominate his private life and his political career can be traced in part at least to the training given him by Huntingford. It is striking how often Addington's attitudes on the leading issues of the day were accurate reflections of his tutor's views. On slavery, Catholic Emancipation, the treatment of dissenters; the policy which Addington adopted throughout his life was closely modelled on the opinions of Huntingford as set out again and again in innumerable letters. Always Huntingford spoke on the side of reaction and immobility. "I hate liberality . . . nine times out of ten it is cowardice, and the tenth time lack of principle,"[1] Addington was to pronounce many years later. It was illiberality and a blind distrust of the different or the unknown which Addington above all else owed to his devoted master.

* * * * *

Although he was no more than ten years old, Hiley Addington accompanied his brother to Winchester. Mrs. Addington entrusted the child's welfare to his elder brother in the breathless style characteristic of all her letters.[2] "You my dear Harry are to lead the way and I hope your brother will follow your example. . . . Oh what misery what stings of conscience would you be liable to when embarked on the wide world were *you* to stray from the right path and were *he* weak enough to copy you." She need have had no fears. Never in his life was Addington to evince any inclination to stray from the right path and he accepted without demur the additional charge of his little brother. It was, indeed, a charge which he had already taken upon himself and which he was willingly to bear for the rest of his brother's life.

Hiley in many ways was the more able of the two to look after himself; less sensitive, sharper of tongue, with only a slight portion of Henry's scrupulousness and solicitude for the feelings of others. Yet the older boy never for a moment doubted that it was his duty, privilege almost, to protect his brother and to ensure that the latter received a fair share of the world's good things. He admired Hiley's quickness, appreciated too the aggressiveness which he so signally lacked himself, deprecated his idleness but found even this weakness endearing.

He was a better scholar than his brother as well as more industrious and the work at Winchester was well within his scope. In sending Dr. Addington the bill for his two sons—£12 10s. to cover board for six months, washing, mending and house expenses of all kinds—Dr. Warton wrote:[1] "Both your sons have been diligent, regular and obedient. They are justly entitled to these three epithets. It is however manifest that the elder makes the more rapid progress." Diligence, regularity and obedience are certainly more the virtues which one would expect to find in Henry Addington than the careless brilliance with which Dr. Gilpin had credited him a few years before.

At Winchester Addington added two more to the group of friends who were to join him in his future Administration. Of these Nathaniel Bond, a Lord of the Treasury, was never more than a sycophantic hanger-on but Charles Bragge quickly became and remained the closest of all Addington's friends and political allies. When in 1788 he married Addington's youngest sister Charlotte it seemed almost as if he were seeking a brother-in-law rather than a wife. He was a worthy and right-minded boy whom even Huntingford considered fit to enjoy the company of his favourite; "an amiable young man" who had "more propriety and decency of conduct than any of your school-fellows."[2]

But Addington still does not seem to have found Winchester altogether to his taste. "I recollect to have been struck," he wrote long afterwards, "by the helpless situation of the boys in junior, both in and out of school."[3] Certainly the prevailing decadence and ill-discipline of Winchester in the 1770s can not have suited him. Huntingford saw him as a schoolboy hero, clean-limbed and incorruptible, battling for the right in a jungle of immorality and ill-will. The truth seems to have been less dramatic. Addington was never a leader among the boys, least of all of a

23

splinter-group battling for the cause of virtue. In the perennial struggle between master and boy he was, very properly, on the side of his contemporaries. But he had no wish to play a major role and, on the whole, was intent to keep out of trouble and pursue the studies which he found more congenial than guerrilla warfare against authority. He was, in short, something of a prig but nothing like so virulent a case as Huntingford believed.

He left Winchester abruptly and a year earlier than was expected. The reason is obscure. Dr. Gilpin[1] claims that he ". . . was so shocked at the wickedness he found at Winchester, that after some struggles with himself, he ran away from school." Dr. Addington took his son's part and told the headmaster that he would only send Henry back if the "vicious boys" were first removed. To this Dr. Warton could not agree, and Henry and Hiley were thereupon removed from the school. But a letter which Huntingford wrote to Addington shortly after the incident[2] suggests that this is not the whole truth:

One person only has enquired your story, from the circumstances he had heard he thought you shamefully treated, and pitied me exceedingly that I could have no friend among so many pupils without exciting jealousy and suspicion. Winton never has seen or will see your equal for virtue, innocence and nobleness of heart. Left as I am alone in my present situation, I reflect more and more on your sudden departure and would do almost anything to recall you . . . let me think upon the loss of you in whatever light I will, it seems one of the greatest afflictions I have ever met with.

It is tempting to read more into this letter than was probably intended. All that can fairly be deduced is that Huntingford's affection for Addington caused trouble and had something to do with the latter's premature departure. The trouble can hardly have been serious. It did no damage to Huntingford's standing at Winchester, of which he was later to become Warden. But at least it seems clear that Addington's withdrawal was not as exclusively in keeping with the principles of schoolboy fiction as Dr. Gilpin appeared to believe.

There was still a year before Addington could go up to Oxford. To ensure that it was profitably passed he and his brother were sent to Ealing to study under Dr. Goodenough, a high-class crammer who later became Bishop of Carlisle. Here at least

Henry and Hiley do not seem to have devoted themselves exclusively to their work. "We are both well and make more use of the bat than ever." Henry Addington wrote to his father[1] in August, 1774: "Quoits likewise are at present a favourite diversion . . ." But the Doctor must not be allowed to think that his sons pursued these activities with no thought but of pleasure. "Indeed I believe you will think it very healthy," Addington continued, "as it must open the chest exceedingly."

Now that his son was capable of intelligent intercourse and already showing signs of being likely to succeed, Dr. Addington took a closer interest in his activities. He himself having successfully made the transition from minor country gentleman to a figure of importance in London society, he now expected his son to carry the family fortunes still further along the road to greatness. His virtues he could reasonably hope that Henry had inherited, but virtues alone were not enough. Of paramount importance, he was convinced, was a knowledge of classical literature. This was the basic arm which equipped the bearer for every situation. The English theologians and philosophers were of substantial but still secondary value. No other studies could be expected to contribute much in the struggle of life. He sought to impress on his son the significance of his academic life and Henry Addington responded willingly. "I think between the evening hours of six and supper time, you may employ yourself very profitably and very agreeably in reading Herodotus, or Aristotle's Rhetoric, or Lock [sic] on the Human Understanding," suggested the father.[2] "I have finished the Electra of Sophocles, and have read two acts of that of Euripides . . ." responded the son, ". . . the former, in my opinion, has all the tenderness and pity of the latter, blended with an almost inconceivable fire and sublimity."[3]

Though fully convinced of his own importance it never seems to have occurred to Dr. Addington that his sons might wish to follow him in his choice of a career. He did nothing to encourage Henry's interest in scientific questions. But if only through a form of intellectual osmosis it was inevitable that the latter should absorb a great deal of medical knowledge or, at least, jargon. The letters between father and son were filled with symptoms and suggested cures. Addington faithfully reported every detail of the functioning of his bowels and the Doctor reciprocated with

blow-by-blow accounts of Mrs. Addington's latest migraine. For
the rest, the principal lessons which Henry Addington could have
learned from study of his father were respect for rank and
authority and an appreciation of the value of well-placed friends
in the career of a coming man. Dr. Addington had perfected for
his dealings with his noble patients a blend of conscious intellectual superiority and unctuous deference. Addington studied
the technique carefully and accepted it as a proper pattern for his
own behaviour.

But Dr. Addington was not the only one anxious to thrust
advice on Henry as he made the final preparations for his life at
Oxford. Huntingford, of course, was quick to proffer his admiring
exhortations and the same note was struck by James Sutton,
Addington's brother-in-law. Sutton, who had married Addington's sister Eleanor in 1771, was considerably older than Henry
and seems to have felt for him as if he had been his own son. He
was a merchant who had made his fortune and then laid out a
large part of it in the purchase of an estate near Devizes. The
property carried with it something close to a controlling interest
in a seat in Parliament. Sutton, who was a man of limited ambition, made small use of his acquisition. He took the seat but
gained little reputation and less pleasure from his time in the
House of Commons. It did not take him long to decide that his
talented young brother-in-law was better qualified to represent
the borough. It was with this in mind that he urged Addington
to hold stoutly to the path on which he was already well begun:[1]

Joy to you my Harry on your black gown and three cornered
cap—as I participate in your pleasures, so should I bear my
portion of pain, should any ills betide you. I may venture
to say that you have hitherto more than answered the expectations of your warmest friends. Consider well, that the
scene in which you now have a trying part to act, is much
enlarged, and temptations of every kind thick sown around
you. Stand therefore on your guard and suffer nothing to
shake those noble principles which your honoured father has
taken so much care to implant in your tender mind.

Addington accepted the advice with courtesy but some tacit
qualifications. The more serious of the temptations referred to
by the earnest Mr. Sutton, he foresaw no difficulty in resisting.
To the venial he intended cheerfully to succumb. Like any young

man of seventeen about to go to a university, his main determination was to enjoy himself. He felt reasonably sure that he would succeed and received the well-meant moralisings of his friends and relations with some impatience. A good deal more to the point was the advice of his mother, whose common sense and good heart more than compensated for her lack of commas:[1] "I hope you don't want money if you really do either of you let me know and I will endeavour to get you supplied if possible. No debts I trust but be open and like yourself and then you cannot greatly offend your father or me."

Brasenose in the 1770s, of which Addington now became a member, was generally held to be a cradle of good scholarship and good order, a college pre-eminently suited for the creation of future Lord Chancellors or eminent divines. "Brazen Nose is, I believe, in a good deal of repute," wrote Bragge to his friend.[2] "I heartily wish you may like it, which you will, I dare say, since you intend to apply, and will not therefore mind a little restraint."

A little restraint Addington was prepared to put up with, but he was still very conscious of his escape from the benevolent but stifling repression of school and family life. He began to drink; not outrageously by the standards of the age but still enough to attract the admiring attention of his fellow-undergraduates. He spent much of his time either on a horse or recovering from the bruises incurred in falling off; for his horsemanship was not the equal either of his courage or his ambitions. He broke bounds and "between the evening hours of six and supper time" often employed his time not "very profitably and very agreeably in reading Herodotus, or Aristotle's Rhetoric" but in wandering with his friends in the meadows or in other forms of mild dissipation. He showed himself capable of skimping his work or even not doing it at all and earned repeated rebukes from his mother for failing to write home at regular intervals.

It would be wrong to build up this modest rebellion into anything of great significance. But in a man whose whole career is stamped with serious purpose, even a flicker of levity is of some moment. At Oxford Addington behaved like an undergraduate. In most people the fact would hardly be worth recording, in his case it was remarkable.

Delighted with his new-found freedom, conscious that he was liked by the other students and well considered by authority, it was not surprising that Addington enjoyed himself at Oxford. "The gownsmen of Brazen Nose are exceedingly kind, which takes off a great deal of the pain one naturally feels in a new situation,"[1] Addington told his father shortly after his arrival. "Everyone allows that Brazen Nose is the only college for study. If I can prove a worthy member of it, I shall be sincerely happy."[2] The pain was probably simulated to please his father. At all events it was soon forgotten. But pleasant though life proved to be, his genuine love of the classics and the satisfaction he derived from work well done ensured that he never degenerated into serious idleness. He remained a conscientious scholar and it was not often that his tutors found it necessary to reproach him.

Before he left Oxford he had entered for and, to the general surprise, won the Chancellor's Gold Medal for an English Essay on "The Affinity between Painting and Poetry in Point of Composition." Addington's entry[3] does not make lively reading. It was a pedestrian piece, sensibly enough argued but weighed down with classical allusions and well-turned statements of the obvious. Patriotically he praised Hogarth as a "more universal genius" than Raphael or Claude Lorraine; otherwise hardly a judgment in the essay rose above the conventional. But with all this he had obviously read and digested many books and looked at large numbers of pictures with some attempt at least at critical appreciation. His effort was a great deal more scholarly and intelligent than most of his contemporaries could have managed.

Addington's best friend and exact contemporary at Brasenose was Benjamin Hobhouse. Hobhouse shared with Addington an uncompromisingly middle-class background, strong affection for the Church and State and a determination to get on in life. The two men liked each other, saw much of each other and began a friendship which was to last for fifty years. It is hardly necessary to say that Hobhouse was among those who found a place in Addington's government, filling the place of Secretary of the Board of Control.

Another intimate at Oxford was William Scott, later to become Lord Stowell. Scott was by birth even less distinguished than Addington, being the son of a successful coal merchant and publican. He was twelve years older than Addington and, by the time they met, was already a Fellow of University College, Camden reader in ancient history and friend of Dr. Johnson. The meeting

28

took place in the Oxford stage coach. After dining liberally on chops and port wine Addington, who had no idea of his new acquaintance's identity, held forth cheerfully on the failings of college Fellows as individuals and as a class. Scott egged him on to fresh indiscretions, then, as he left the coach, remarked benignly: "Well, young gentleman, I have had a very pleasant journey; but the next time you feel inclined to abuse college Fellows, consider that you may possibly have a poor college Fellow in the coach with you."[1] He must have found the journey as pleasant as he professed, for next day he called on Addington at Brasenose and from then on the two saw much of each other.

*　　　*　　　*　　　*　　　*

While Addington had been preparing himself for his entrance into the world, Dr. Addington had been more than playing a father's part by his acquisition of fame, wealth and useful contacts. He was by now one of the most fashionable and, incidentally, expensive doctors of the age; consulted by many of the noble and even some of the royal invalids of London. The most important of his regular patients was William Pitt, Earl of Chatham, and few circumstances can have helped more towards the future prosperity of the Addingtons than the readiness of this nobleman to treat his doctor as a confidant and family friend. Dr. Addington had always been interested in politics. On one occasion he rushed to the house of a dying man and, pausing only to press the hand of the patient's wife in silent sympathy, hurried up towards the sickroom. Twenty minutes later the wife followed him. She found Dr. Addington still on the staircase where he had become engaged in an eager discussion with the Foxite apothecary about the rights and wrongs of the mooted India Bill.

Dr. Addington not only wanted to talk about politics, he craved to play a part himself in the world of great affairs. The patronage of Lord Chatham offered him a chance to gratify his wish. He seems first to have treated Chatham in 1766 or '67 when the latter was suffering from some form of manic-depressive insanity aggravated by life-long gout. Since these maladies were later complicated by Bright's disease and prostate trouble,[2] to be Lord Chatham's physician was in no way a sinecure. The secret of Dr. Addington's treatment lay in wine, partly as a fortifiant but more as a means of driving the illness from the head to the

29

limbs, thus clearing up the insanity, though at the price of aggravating the gout. "I am very glad," runs a typical letter to Lady Chatham,[1] "My Lord has begun to drink old hock; I own I wish him to double his quantity for dinner, i.e. to drink two glasses of plain hock and two glasses of red port every day over and above the Madeira which he drinks unmixed with water and over and above the port which is taken in sago."

Though Dr. Addington was already beginning to be well spoken of by his colleagues in London, his name was still little known to the public when Lord Chatham decided to make use of his services. The choice was generally considered eccentric and the Doctor's prescribed treatment came in for some offensive comment. Horace Walpole wrote[2] that Dr. Addington ". . . originally was a mad doctor. The truth, I believe, is that Addington, who is a kind of empiric, has forbidden his doing the least business . . . Lord Chatham's friends are much alarmed, and so they say is Addington himself; yet what is strange, he calls in no help." No one who knew Addington can have found it strange that he showed no doubt in his own abilities; alarm for his patient he certainly felt but none at all as to his own competence. Nor did Lord Chatham share Walpole's scepticism. He found his doctor's treatment entirely to his taste and continued to put his faith in Addington's skill and wisdom. When George III wrote to advise his former Minister to consult the royal doctor, Lord Chatham replied firmly that he was well looked after already.[3] He was not proved wrong. Whether because of or in spite of Dr. Addington's ministrations, the insanity passed and Lord Chatham, though still a sick man, was able to return to public life.

Part of Dr. Addington's reward was a small share in Chatham's political life; mere confidences at first, then the carrying-out of minor tasks and finally, in 1777, a full-scale negotiating role. It is, in fact, not at all clear how far Lord Chatham chose that Dr. Addington should negotiate on his behalf and how far the Doctor decided that the role became him well and stepped into it without authority. The subject in question was a coalition between Chatham and Bute, the discussions were conducted by Dr. Addington and Sir James Wright, a former Governor of Georgia and close friend of Bute's.[4] The affair was bungled from the start, each party misunderstood the other and accusations of trickery or stupidity were tossed freely from side to side. On the whole it seems that Sir James Wright was the more to blame: certainly Chatham never showed annoyance about the way matters had been conducted or in any way withdrew his confidence from his Doctor.[1]

By this time Dr. Addington was as nearly a friend of the family as the conventions of the age and his own cautiously subservient nature would allow him. Lady Hester Stanhope, who lived much in the Pitt household, was certainly to claim that in her young days doctors, governesses and tutors were all lumped together in uniform obscurity, but Lady Hester's views on the social order, as on many other subjects, were notoriously idiosyncratic. It is quite clear from Dr. Addington's correspondence with Lord, and still more Lady Chatham that they were genuinely attached to him and that his opinion was thought of interest and value on many subjects far remote from medicine. Dr. Addington visited the household almost every day and would often bring his wife and children with him. On one occasion the family watched Lord Chatham's children acting in a play which they had written for themselves; William Pitt, Addington observed to his sister Charlotte, seemed an awkward youth and not much hand as an actor.[2] Another time Lord Chatham made William kneel down and told Hiley Addington to demonstrate on him how Warton flogged the boys at Winchester.[3]

Though Pitt was later to describe himself and Addington as "friends from their childhood,"[4] the two boys in fact do not seem to have made much of each other. Pitt was almost exactly two years younger than Henry Addington. His natural shyness had been exaggerated by Lord Chatham's decision to educate him at home. At the age of fifteen or sixteen he was gauche and uncertain of himself, so much so that Addington treated him with slight condescension. In spite of his father's encouragement and Lord Chatham's affable approval, real friendship did not grow between them until Pitt had emerged into society and the roles of the two men had been reversed.

"Good connections are of the utmost service to young men, especially to such who are to make their futures by their own endeavour." The advice, not surprisingly, came from Huntingford[5] and, though Addington may have paid little attention in the case of William Pitt, in general he took the advice to heart.

His closest friends were not chosen because of their present or potential importance. On the whole he did a lot more to help them than they him and saw nothing to regret in the disproportion. But he still relished grand acquaintances, still knew the importance of influential allies and still set himself assiduously to court those who might be of use. The innermost circle of his intimates was immeasurably more important to him than any of his more brilliant acquaintances, but this did not prevent him deriving much pride and satisfaction from the latter.

At Oxford he made two such friends, William Grenville and Lord Mornington, later Marquis Wellesley. He liked and admired both of them, the latter in particular, but he also recognised them as men certain to go far with whom it would be desirable to keep in touch. They for their part seem to have been well pleased with his company. Both were proud men and there may have been some mental reservations about the degree of intimacy to be allowed to a doctor's son, but if so these were well hidden. Addington could fairly list them among his friends.

Addington graduated in February, 1778. He decided to stay on at Oxford for a further year, nominally to study algebra but as much from disinclination to emerge from the protective cocoon of the university as from a love of learning. It was a happy time. Above all things, Addington wished to be liked. He found it pleasant to be respected and exciting to be admired, but he would willingly have settled for good-natured tolerance, even for a degree of contempt, if by no other way could he feel himself surrounded by friends. In his last year at Oxford, with no particular responsibilities, well-considered alike by authorities and undergraduates, he found himself able to cultivate his friendships without distraction. It was to be the last time in his life that he could afford perfect irresponsibility; he recognised it and savoured the occasion to its full.

One event only spoiled the pleasure of that last year, the death of his mother in November, 1778. Though Mary Addington had neither the character nor the opportunity to have much influence over her son, she nevertheless did something to humanise the bleakly professional atmosphere which surrounded all the doings of Dr. Addington. Her inconsequent and affectionate letters must have come as a relief to her children after their father's measured and dignified exhortations. She had been ill for several months and her husband had long since resigned himself to her approaching death. "The loss to me and my children will be irreparable," he wrote to Lady Chatham.[1] He had been married for more than thirty years and the years had been happy ones. Now the habits of a lifetime had to be refashioned and, at the age of sixty-five, he knew that he would not find the task an easy one.

For Dr. Addington indeed the loss was irreparable. For Henry the immediate pain was probably greater, certainly more unselfish, but the lasting effects were slight. He was on the verge of life; going out to do new work, to meet new people, to live in new places, to become a man. It was small wonder that the figure of his mother, always shadowy, now slipped rapidly into the limbo of rarely recollected memories.

2

It was a feature of Addington's life that he could never take any important step without an accompanying chorus of approval and advice from his devoted friends. There is no reason to believe that this displeased him. Addington's friends, though often sycophants, were rarely fools; their praise was always welcome and some of the advice was good. The weight of their solicitude, indeed, probably falls more heavily on the biographer than it did on the original recipient. There is an awful tedium about the well-turned phrases of Addington's admirers which only the most enthusiastic interest can overcome. He cannot have expected that he would escape such attentions on an occasion so momentous as his entry into fully adult life. Sure enough the letters poured in, bearing congratulations upon his past successes and encouragement for his future career.

Prevailing over the rest was George Huntingford's trumpet call to a God-fearing life. "When you live in London," he exhorted his former pupil,[1] "you will do very unreasonably and of course very wrong not to dedicate one day in the week to the sole service of religion. This practice will be a powerful preservative to you from the unmanly debaucheries with which the thoughtless multitude is deluded." The injunction was unneeded. Addington had too weak a stomach for debaucheries, whether manly or unmanly, and few people can have been more diligent in church attendance. There can be no doubt that he was sincerely religious and that he believed most firmly and fervently in all the tenets of the Church of England. It is doubtful if the state of his soul or his relationship with God occupied much of his thoughts. His mind did not lead itself either to introspection or to philosophical conjecture. But religion was none the less one of the major motive forces in his life. He was to invoke it, without hypocrisy, to justify many of his more questionable opinions and he was

34

consistently to measure his actions against a scale which he believed to be immutably laid down by Christian doctrine. His championship of the Church of England, narrow and bigoted though it might often have seemed in its application, was to his mind no more than a part of his determination to serve his Creator honestly and diligently all the days of his life.

Addington's intention in settling in London was to read for the Bar. He had long ago made up his mind to this career and appears to have been admitted to Lincoln's Inn while still at Winchester.[1] This can hardly have been more than a formality for he certainly did not begin to study law seriously until the autumn of 1780 after a summer spent with his brother-in-law James Sutton at Devizes. Though in later life he was often to refer to his legal training as having been a most valuable part of his education, he does not seem to have shone at his studies or even to have pursued them with special interest. Probably he had already been promised the reversion of Sutton's seat in Parliament and therefore considered the Bar as little more than a stopgap till he could start on his real business.

As if the prospect of Parliament was not enough by itself to distract Addington from his law books, the summer of 1781 provided a fresh disincentive to serious study. It was then that he first met Ursula Mary Hammond, daughter of a prosperous citizen of Cheam and, for perhaps the only time in his life, completely lost his head. It seems to have been only a matter of weeks before Miss Hammond decided that she was as much in love with Addington as he with her. They made up their minds to marry as soon as possible. The decision was a brave one. Miss Hammond was a more than respectable match; co-heiress to her father and already enjoying a fortune of £1,000 a year. But Addington had hardly a penny of his own and could not expect to earn any for several years at least. He was thus dependent on his father and Dr. Addington, who had himself married discreetly late, was unlikely to approve his son's precipitancy. Certainly Henry Addington knew well that his father would expect a deferential request for permission to marry rather than the triumphant declaration of his love which in fact he was bold enough to send.

Dr. Addington's reply was typical of all his dealings with his son; both in its temperate generosity and in the chilly lack of

35

enthusiasm with which he sought to curb his son's exuberance:[1]
"I had the pleasure of your romantic letter on my arrival at Bath.
If there is any fault in it, it is of the hyperbolic kind. I know
love is a passion, but it is not idolatry. Pure love may border on
enthusiasm, but when it once grows unruly, it is hardly ever
permanent and happy. I have no doubt but the violence of your
fever will gradually subside, and that you will conduct yourself
in all its paroxysms with that manly prudence which has adorned
every other situation of your life." Dr. Addington then moved
on to a discussion of the exorbitant cost of the parcel post.

The Doctor followed up this odious letter by making himself
thoroughly difficult over the marriage settlement. He wanted this
to be a provision for the younger children if the husband were to
die, while the Hammonds' solicitor held that in such a case it
should become entirely the property of the widow. This Dr.
Addington stigmatised as[2] "an idea at which humanity revolts
. . ." "I do not say this to put by or retard the match. It is a
connection I must approve of. But I own, it hurts me to see
improper attempts made from time to time to take advantage of
my son's extravagant affection." He sent a copy of this letter to
his son, obligingly hoping that it would not render him uneasy.
His solicitude can have done little to overcome his son's chagrin
at seeing his love turned into a subject for financial chaffering.
Nor can Huntingford's sententious counsel have cheered him.[3]
"Matrimony, if it heightens the joys, embitters the sorrows of
life. Mutual condescension and deference to each other's opinions
prevents a multitude of unnecessary, and sometimes unguarded,
words: and believe me, excepting one's character, and the
character of those we love, there is not a thing in life worth
disputing about."

Eventually financial difficulties were overcome and Henry
Addington was married on 19th September, 1781. The marriage
was an unqualified success and brought great happiness to both
its parties. Ursula Mary was an outstandingly pretty girl and
her character seems to have matched her looks. She was gay,
high-spirited, affectionate, intelligent though with little in the
way of formal education, interested in everything and everyone
around her. She adored Addington but never idolised him, was
conscious of his faults and capable of laughing at him or teasing
him, yet at the same time built up his self-confidence by her love

36

and unfeigned admiration. She made a home where comfort and reassurance were always to be found. Her loyalty to her husband was a byword in London society. By nature easy-going and slow to see or resent affronts, she would put aside all her gentleness and good temper if it was he who was the object of attack. When Addington's interests were in question she became an unabashed partisan; a persistent and vindictive fighter in defence of her husband and her home. When Pitt fell out with Addington in 1804 the King told Rose that Mrs. Addington was far more vengeful than Addington himself could ever be.[1]

She brought into Addington's life a warmth, humanity and gaiety which was strange to his own slow and lukewarm spirit. Her tenderness won from him responses which he had never known existed; there was an innocence and freshness about their relationship which lingered long after familiarity had worn away the more romantic element of mutual discovery. "I shall not forget your kind and affectionate look this morning;" she was writing in 1792[2] "and wish I was a fly on your coat to catch another glance—Do not smile at this, but *above all*, do not read a syllable aloud. I know not why I should fear you, as you generally pay attention to my foolish requests, and this has been made before now."

Addington repaid the happiness she brought him with a complete devotion and fidelity. He accepted from her criticism and rebukes which he could not have borne from any other, even among his intimates. "I shall be impatient till I hear of your journey. Do not hurry yourself and be as merry as possible without much port wine, you will not resent this hint I know . . ."[3] He did not resent the hint or many others of the same nature; indeed he was never to resent any word that came from her or thing she did.

Ursula Mary was never strong and her health was weakened by difficult childbirths. In the first twelve years of married life she had at least two miscarriages, one child died after three days, another aged two months. William, her younger son and third born of the five surviving children, caused her more pain than any of the rest. Addington suffered with her and marvelled at the "wonderful composure of her spirit" and the "sweetness of her disposition."[4] He knew too much of doctoring to delude himself over her danger or the harshness of her pain, yet too

37

little to be able to contribute to her recovery. All that was left him was to watch, pray and hope.

It was Addington's misfortune that, when he wished to express himself, he lacked the means of changing gear. Whether the occasion was one for joy or for dismay, a domestic irritant or a national disaster, the mechanism of his speech and his writing remained inflexible. The words might differ, the mood might swing from solemn satisfaction to stately grief, but the tempo was invariable, the same platitudes ground out, the same lifeless sentences, the same lack-lustre tones. It seemed that neither pain nor pleasure could break through the shroud of his drab verbosity.

Too many people have deduced from this that Addington could not feel, that he was a spiritless fish who cared for nothing save in temperate and strictly rationed portions. The unemotional flatness of his speeches, the bland pomposity of his most private letters, have been taken as proof of superficiality and spiritual lifelessness. This assumption, made by contemporaries as well as posterity, did much to mar his public image. The world wants its heroes to feel as well as to act on a heroic scale, and Addington had little enough to offer. He was not emotional, he was not high-spirited, he loved few people and cared passionately about still fewer issues. But he was none the less a human being, bleeding when pricked and dying when poisoned. Because his feelings were often inarticulate or cloaked under a layer of smothering verbiage, it did not follow that they were insincere or non-existent.

If proof were needed that Addington was capable of feelings as deep as any of those expressed in richer terms by his less reticent contemporaries, it could be found in his relationship with his wife. In that there was no trace of the coldness and shallowness of which he was so often accused; no hesitation, no prudent calculation, no hanging back. The credit might largely be hers but there can be no relationship without two parties. It is impossible to study their life together without feeling some sympathy at least for a kindly, warm-hearted and deeply loving man.

*   *   *   *   *

In English history the party label has seldom been altogether conclusive as a guide to the political principles either of an individual or of a group. At no time can this have been more true than in the second half of the eighteenth century. The traditional appellations of Whig and Tory had largely lost their meaning: they had become more expressions of loyalty towards a group of families or the habits of one's forebears than of any coherent political faith. A handful of old-style Tories still lingered on in their family fastnesses, thinking black thoughts about the Hanoverian succession and believing themselves the sole repository of England's greatness, but long before 1780 these irreconcilables had either been forgotten or dismissed as trivial eccentrics—a flat-earth society in a world of cosmonauts. The Tories in active life, in so far as they used the title, were little more than a splinter group of the old Whig party, differing from the latter in the personality of their leaders rather than in the nature of their beliefs. The great Whig families of the Glorious Revolution still played an important part in politics and still, though with exceptions, tended to act in unison. But as a coherent and dedicated power-bloc the party had lost its momentum and almost its *raison d'être*.

Complacent, prosperous, materialistic England of the mid-eighteenth century had indeed few of the elements which make possible sustained party warfare upon fixed doctrinal lines. The leading statesmen of the age were feudal leaders or manipulators, most often both. By far the most powerful among the former was the King himself. In a sense he was no more than *primus inter pares*, but his power was so much more extensive and more lasting than that of any of his subjects that for all practical purposes he stood alone. The cause of absolute monarchy was lost long before Addington had been born but throughout his political life the strength of the King was such that, deployed with skill and in the absence of an outstanding personality among the politicians, he could exercise something not far from complete control over his country's policies. His main weapons were patronage and the deep-rooted loyalty of the majority of his subjects. It would be over-ingenuous to profess that the second was altogether divorced from the first; the King's role as giver of bounty and fount of honours was inseparable from his right to rule his country. But loyalty to the Crown was not based on greed; the King was honoured, even sometimes loved, by the great majority of his subjects. It took a very considerable cataclysm to convince this docile multitude, ranked solidly behind the squires and the county Members, that he should not be left free to run the country with such Ministers and such policies as he might choose.

The county Member, despite his traditional quickness to resist incursions of central authority into what he regarded as his exclusive preserve, was the bed-rock of royal power as exercised through Parliament. This loyal regiment of squires was more than sufficient to sustain in power any Ministers that the King might choose to put there. Sometimes the King might have no wish to throw his weight behind one faction or another; very occasionally the faithful Commons revolted and refused to tolerate the choice of their monarch; but in general they held that opposition was a dirty game and that the gentleman's part was to give Government such help as it required.

The system reached its apotheosis under Lord North: conscientious, affable, uninspiring and confident in the knowledge that he enjoyed the support of the King. North cared nothing for Whigs, Tories or any other party; all that he asked was to be left in peace with enough support to run the country. His manipulation of the House of Commons was masterly and he might have contrived to rule England until his death but for the calamities of the American Revolution and the European war which shattered his credit and stirred up hostility too deep even for the royal favour to resist.

It was in the closing stages of Lord North's long reign that William Pitt the Younger, in Lord Rosebery's phrase, "went into the House of Commons as an heir enters his home."[1] Rockingham and Shelburne divided Lord North's empire between them. Pitt was offered only a trivial part in the new administration, but Shelburne's reverence for his old leader, Lord Chatham, ensured that he would spare no pains to promote the interests of Lord Chatham's son. Few doubted that he would rapidly force his way into important office.

In 1782 the position of the King was weaker than it had been for many years. George III had committed himself wholeheartedly to Lord North and the American war. Both proved disastrously unpopular, so much so that he had temporarily lost the support of many of his traditional followers in the House of Commons and the country. But that the loss was only temporary should have been evident to anyone with an understanding of English political life. Charles James Fox might pin his faith in the friendship of the Prince of Wales but Pitt knew better. The trust and support of the King was for him always to be the first essential. At the start as a follower of Shelburne, then in his own right, he courted it assiduously.

In July of 1782 the coalition, already close to disintegration, was buried with the corpse of Rockingham. To the chagrin of the latter's followers, Shelburne was offered the succession. Fox and the other representatives of the great Whig houses resigned in dudgeon, leaving Shelburne to take office with Pitt, aged barely twenty-three, as his Chancellor of the Exchequer. He controlled, perhaps, one hundred and forty votes as against North's one hundred and twenty and Fox's ninety. Any one group could hold office only on the sufferance of another; any two groups, so long as they remained in coalition, could govern England.

When Addington settled in London, Lord Shelburne was still precariously in office, depending for his future on the inability of Fox and North to combine against him. There seemed no reason why this should ever end. Throughout the closing stages of Lord North's administration, Fox had denounced the Prime Minister with an enthusiasm and richness of abuse which should have made them life-long enemies. Certainly their hostility was taken for granted by most observers as one of the few fixed points in the parliamentary whirlpool. With almost any other statesmen it would have been. But Fox never took his own invective seriously and North was not the man to nourish a grudge or to allow the insults of others to rankle. The grounds of Fox's opposition had been worn away by time and Fox himself was quite ready to put temporarily to one side his ideas for reform. On these terms the two men soon found that they could agree quite well together.

Early in 1783 therefore the Fox-North coalition brought down the Shelburne Government. The manœuvre earned its leaders the intemperate and lasting hatred of the King. Fox, indeed, he already disliked and considered as the seducer of his son. North now ranked with him in the pantheon of royal enemies. The new partnership was felt by the King to be no more than a temporary evil, a serpent to be scotched as soon as possible. ". . . the most profligate and ungrateful coalition that ever was made in this

Kingdom," he described it to Lord Bathurst,[1] and from this judgment he never deviated.

But the King was not the only one to find the new coalition repugnant. The City of London, the country squire, the Church, the people, with rare unanimity, condemned the alliance as cynical, unprincipled and unfit to rule. Even the Foxite voters of Westminster found this latest gambado of their hero by no means easy to excuse or to understand. All that was needed was a reason to dismiss the Ministers and a leader with the courage to form an alternative Government. King George was already satisfied that he had found the second in William Pitt, he was not going to have to wait long for the coalition to provide the first.

In November, 1783, Fox introduced into the House of Commons his Bill for the reorganisation of the Government of India. The reforms proposed were sweeping and, for the most part, well calculated, but they invested vast powers in the hands of a Board of Commissioners and these Commissioners were nominated in the Bill itself. It did not need an unsympathetic examination of the roster to reveal that most of them were loyal followers of Fox. With their appointment "Carlo Khan" or "the Grand Mogul," as Fox was now dubbed by the cartoonists, would draw into his own hands the vast patronage of the Indian empire.

Not much political skill was needed on the part of the King and Pitt to whip up public anger. The coalition's majority in the Commons seemed impregnable but in the Lords the Government was open to attack. When the India Bill came to be discussed there, George III made it unequivocally clear that "he should consider all who voted for it as his enemies."[2] Ministers were defeated and the King, without even a farewell audience, dismissed them and appointed William Pitt as first Lord of the Treasury. The apparent majority against him was more than a hundred.

The Foxites greeted this simulacrum of a Government with derision. But little by little they saw all the cards which had seemed so safely in their hands trumped as they were played or mysteriously turning up on the other side of the table. The independent Members swung behind Pitt. The followers of North showed a disconcerting readiness to follow their example. Even a few hardened Foxites began to hedge their bets. When

Pitt went to the country in March, 1784, he had already whittled the majority against him in the Commons down to single figures. In the election he shattered what was left of the opposition. A hundred and sixty of Fox's Martyrs lost their seats. In their places appeared a solidly Pittite and royalist phalanx. Among them was Henry Addington.

*   *   *   *   *

Addington in fact owed his seat in Parliament to the favours of his brother-in-law rather than the support of Pitt and the King. Nevertheless the overwhelming influence which these two enjoyed in the country and Parliament was to him the all-important feature of the political scene. Long before the election Addington had declared himself a Pittite and a King's man, secure in the confidence that, so long as his two heroes remained united, little harm could come to England.

Even though its leader had been a stranger to him, all Addington's sympathies would have drawn him into the Pittite camp. But in fact his friendship with Pitt had prospered over the last few years and its importance grew steadily in his eyes. The two men had both read for the Bar and had eaten their dinners at the same inn. They had often been together and enjoyed each other's company. Pitt had few acquaintances when he first arrived in London and depended heavily on relations and old friends. Among these, few were closer to him than Addington. Their association delighted Dr. Addington, who had no doubts about its future value for his son and, anyway, cared sincerely for any member of Lord Chatham's family. He went out of his way to bring them together and took pleasure at every sign of increasing intimacy. "The young gentlemen are just returned from the hall, in good spirits and well," he reported proudly to Lady Chatham.[1] "Last night they were surprised and entertained with a hop of three hours, which was entirely accidental and agreeable."

As Pitt had become better established in London life, so his dependence on Addington had dwindled. His new friends were gayer, more sophisticated and socially more distinguished. He retained his affection for Addington but the relationship was modified. His admiration for Addington's superior worldly wisdom was soon forgotten, his respect for Addington's judgment and integrity was not yet born; in the meantime Addington's role degenerated into that, not so much of poor relation, as of country cousin, a slightly humdrum figure welcome for old times' sake and if no one more stimulating were about but not often actively sought as a companion. The two were always close to each other yet if Pitt at this period had been asked to list his closest friends, the name of Addington might well not have occurred to him. Instead he would probably have mentioned the fellow members of that gay and enterprising fraternity who in 1780 founded a club on the premises of a certain Mr. Goosetree in Pall Mall: Eliot, Arden, Grenville, Wilberforce, Pitt's elder brother Chatham, Robert Smith the banker. Addington was not a member of the Goosetree Club; neither his birth, his purse nor his wit qualified him for such a distinction. Nor indeed would he have wished to be; he would have found the company disquietingly fashionable and have all the time been conscious that he was out of place and doing nothing to add to the enjoyment of his fellows. From time to time he may have gazed wistfully at this brilliant circle but in general he was perfectly content with his own talents and his own friends. He never grudged Pitt his success—he was indeed singularly free from the vice of envy—and though, from time to time, he was a little hurt by his old friend's neglect he seems never to have felt that he was being hardly used.

When Pitt became Chancellor of the Exchequer in Shelburne's administration Dr. Addington hastened to write in congratulation to his mother and to express his pleasure that she should "think another young friend of his not unworthy of such a patron." Among Addington's relations and admirers it was indeed generally accepted that Pitt was likely to offer some job to his old friend. But Shelburne's Government lasted only a few months and the coalition of Fox and North put a temporary end to any hopes that Addington himself might have been nurturing. He continued ostensibly to read for the Bar, comfortably ensconced in a house in Southampton Street which his benevolent brother-in-law Sutton had provided and furnished for him, but his labours, never pursued with much enthusiasm, were now nominal. He knew that Sutton's seat was his at the next election and had no inclination in the meantime to waste his energies on fruitless studies.

When Pitt became Prime Minister in December, 1783,

Addington's friends again began to predict a rapid call to duty. Addington was called to see Pitt on the 28th. "I give you joy of the effects of the interview of last Sunday . . ." wrote Bragge to his friend.[1] "Secretary, either official or confidential, I should wish you; and indeed all the boards are already filled." Addington, recently married, comfortably settled, on the point of gaining a seat in Parliament, was in no particular hurry to seek a job. It could well be that Pitt had nothing sufficiently alluring to offer. At all events, no appointment followed the interview, and Addington continued along the tranquil course of a gentleman of small but independent means.

When the dissolution came in March, 1784, James Sutton duly recommended his brother-in-law to the electors of Devizes. There were less than forty of these gentlemen; the mayor, the recorder, the members of the common council and a few specially created burgesses. It had the reputation of being a cheap borough where local influence could do more than bribery. Sutton's influence, if not overwhelming, was still so great as to make the task of his protégé immeasurably easier. Even so, Addington's easy-going approach to the election imperilled his success. Hiley Addington, who was already playing for his brother the role of election manager and public relations officer which was to be his for life, was sufficiently alarmed to send an urgent S O S.[2] "Your presence is absolutely necessary—Jones has applied to all the Corporation and two or three other candidates are already talked of. Your prospects, however, from what I have been able to learn, are more flattering than when you left New Park . . . I am persuaded that nothing but your appearance here is wanting to ensure your success." Though he does not seem to have been seriously alarmed by his brother's message, Addington duly appeared. His presence was evidently enough to quell the doubts of the electors of Devizes and it was not long before he could report that the seat was his.[3] "Sir James Long is my colleague. Our adversary declined the contest, and went off early this morning for town."

*   *   *   *   *

Addington found much to his taste the overwhelmingly Pittite House of Commons of which he was now a Member. But though the atmosphere was congenial he did not quickly shine or show any particular wish to do so. His parliamentary performance, indeed, threatened to be unobtrusive to the point of invisibility. His rooted dislike of thrusting himself forward, of any action, indeed, likely to place him in the public eye, was based partly on a fear of being snubbed or made to look a fool. He had small confidence in his powers as an orator and still less wish to put his talents to the test. But also he genuinely lacked ambition. He saw political success as mildly alluring but hardly worth the pains of fighting for. If others wished to promote his interests, then he would be well content. But it was quickly clear that, left to his own resources, progress would be slow and the final achievement sadly undistinguished.

Pitt found this lack of enterprise incomprehensible and a little irritating. Constantly he urged Addington to speak in the House of Commons and to make more of a mark for himself in public life. On one occasion, when Addington was justifying his lack of success by pleading his inadequacy for parliamentary battles, Pitt sought to urge him on by quoting from Waller's ode on Henrietta Maria:[1]

> The lark that shuns on lofty boughs to build
> Her humble nest, lies silent in the field;
> But should the promise of a brighter day,
> Aurora smiling, bid her rise and play;
> Quickly she'll show t'was not for want of voice,
> Or power to climb, she made so low a choice;
> Singing she mounts: her airy notes are stretch'd
> Towards heaven, as if from heaven alone her notes
> she fetch'd.

The analogy, though no doubt kindly meant, was startlingly inept. Few people can have had less of the lark than Addington. If a simile had to be culled from natural history it would be more exact to say that he was like a hedgehog: shy and reticent except perhaps with other hedgehogs, prickly when trodden on but otherwise inoffensive, lying extremely low and toning in well with his background. And like the hedgehog in the light of day, Addington's inclination when trapped in a glare of publicity was to run away and hide.

Nor was Addington a fighter; his wish was always to avoid argument or, if argument had to come, to soften the essentials of the dispute. His principles were strongly held and he was ready to defend them if need arose. But no one was happier than he if such a need could be avoided. On all save a few issues he was ready to come more than half-way to meet his interlocutor. Sylvester Douglas, always a shrewd observer where his own vanity was not involved, described Addington[1] as "willing enough to speak freely of men, as well as of political transactions and political questions, but that only when he has ascertained what your opinion is. Not that he is insincere or weak enough to square his own to yours, but if he can he will colour and shade it in to yours if you seem to him to differ from him in some reconcilable degree . . ." This judgment was passed when Addington was already Prime Minister; in 1784 he was still more anxious to agree with others where he in conscience could.

Addington had had too little experience as a public speaker to know much more than that he found it disagreeable. What was already apparent, however, was his slowness in repartee and his small stock of wit. He was certainly not a stupid man nor even a slow thinker, but the expression of his thoughts was at the best long-winded and often inarticulate as well. He had little if any sense of humour, viewing himself and all around him with a painful seriousness which weighed even heavier upon his hearers than upon himself. His occasional jokes were disastrous, causing embarrassment on his behalf even when read a hundred and fifty years later. He was well versed in both French and English literature and had a real love of poetry, in particular that of Robert Burns, yet little of what he read filtered through into his speech and his own prose style remained resolutely flat and unimaginative. He lacked, in short, all the qualities needed for sudden and brilliant success in politics; those he enjoyed, honesty, assiduity, common sense, were neither immediately apparent nor dramatically appealing. Among Pitt's closest friends the one to hold Addington in highest esteem was William Wilberforce; at once more ready to make allowance for a lack of social brilliance and more sympathetic to Addington's substantial virtues.

Though Addington was little noticed during his first sessions in Parliament it did not follow that he was idle. With a professional thoroughness that was to be echoed throughout his public life he set himself to study the rules and practices of the House of Commons. "You are preparing for *your* school," wrote

Huntingford,[1] "and I for *mine*—the humbler of the two," and Addington's preparatory work was indeed assiduous and well directed. He sat on the Downton Election Committee and won a reputation as a sensible and constructive colleague. He worked hard at the traditions and precedents of Parliament and was accepted as something of an expert by those who found such labours ill-rewarding. Conscientiously he widened his acquaintance, in the House, mainly among the Pittites but also, wherever practicable, among the Opposition. Within a year or two he was well known as a friendly and thoughtful Member with no vice about him; unlikely to go far but sure to play a useful and honourable role.

This prudent progress satisfied Addington quite well but to Pitt it seemed ignobly pedestrian. In almost two years Addington had not spoken once in the House. Pitt decided to force his hand by choosing him to second the Address at the beginning of the 1786 session. "I will not disguise," he wrote,[2] "that in asking this favour of you, I look beyond the immediate object of the first day's debate, from a persuasion that whatever induces you to take a part in public, will equally contribute to your personal credit, and that of the system to which I have the pleasure of thinking you are so warmly attached."

Addington undertook the task with some misgivings but, according to Wraxall,[3] "performed with great propriety, in language of elegance, and not destitute of grace and dignity." It was a modest little speech, confined to the blessings of peace, the benefits of trade, the Irish question and, as befitted the occasion, the transcendent virtues of William Pitt. Hiley wrote triumphantly:[4] "My brother infinitely exceeded my expectations —he was *very* little embarrassed . . . His voice and manner I think hardly second to any in the House." The general reception was friendly but less partial; few listeners can have believed that they were witnessing the birth of a new Fox, Pitt or Sheridan. Dr. Addington was closer to the truth when he saw the chief significance of his son's speech in the interest it proved Pitt still took in his career. "Whether he has talents for debate, or not, I cannot tell," he wrote cautiously to Lady Chatham.[5] "If he has, I hope they will appear in proper time; as, I flatter myself, he is possessed of principles which will not disgrace him."

In spite of the tolerable success of his first effort, Addington was not encouraged to intervene more often in debate. It was more than a year before he spoke again and then only for a quarter of an hour and on a technical subject relating to the collection of the horse-tax. Hiley Addington reported that the speech was a triumphant success and that Pitt's countenance expressed great pleasure. No doubt Pitt's pleasure was sincere but one may wonder whether it was induced not so much by what Addington said as by the fact that Addington was on his feet at all.

Addington's reputation at this time was that of a convinced Pittite, a good, safe man, always ready to follow his leader but at times uncertain how close upon his heels it was wise to tread. One of the subjects upon which he felt Pitt was inclined to move too fast and too far was parliamentary reform. In 1785 Pitt asked leave to introduce a Bill which included among its provisions buying out the proprietors of thirty-six rotten boroughs and a widening of the franchise in the counties. Addington accepted the need for such reform in principle but, as soon as it was a question of translating it into practice, became a victim of the gravest doubts. A host of counter arguments, most of them instilled by Huntingford, arose to cloud his vision and disturb his conscience. Would an enlargement of the franchise necessarily lead to better representation? Were the new electors ready for their privilege? Was it wise to upset the existing balance of power between the old families and the new plutocracy? Were the rights of property being adequately considered? Such questions caused Addington much sincere distress and he could not feel that the answers to them were unequivocally clear. So long as any doubt remained, he would feel unable to engage on the dangerous courses of reform. Addington was in London when the vote was taken on Pitt's Bill, yet his name does not appear on the voters' list. It seems at least probable that, when the moment came, he could not bring himself to support a course which he felt to be both hazardous and ill-considered. He was by no means the only Pittite to stand out against reform but, from a supporter as safe as Addington, it must have come as a particularly unkind surprise.

* * * * *

From the moment that Henry Addington had taken his seat in

the House of Commons one of his most urgent desires had been that his brother Hiley should join him there. The affection and loyalty which these brothers felt towards each other and the dependence of Henry on Hiley's advice and support is the more remarkable for the contrast between them. Hiley Addington was sly where his brother was straightforward, brash where his brother was timid, flamboyant where he was sedate; an un-scrupulous and rancorous intriguer who seemed to devote himself to the making of enemies with the same enthusiasm as Henry would put into avoiding them. And yet he was not altogether an unattractive man; he had a certain generosity of nature, he would do much to help those few people for whom he really cared, he had considerable common sense and a readiness to act on his judgment even at risk to himself. His greatest weakness was his inability to foresee the reactions of others; a failure which led him into many pointless quarrels. Uncertain in his own mind whether he wished to be a Fouché or an English country gentle-man, he failed conspicuously to be either; in the country he was considered a parvenu, in the Palace of Westminster a naïve yet malevolent bumpkin. Neither judgment was just yet there was substance in them both.

In spite of a number of calamitous mistakes, Hiley was on the whole an asset to his brother. He understood the mechanics of power, was an ingenious and effective journalist and appeared well content to stay in the background and leave it to his brother to play the starring role. When engaged on a congenial task, such as suborning the Press or vilifying another's reputation, he was capable of great energy and application. But he worked in short bursts; by nature he was lazy and when the impetus failed he would relapse into his habitual state of sluggardly inactivity. In part this can be attributed to his health. His friends laughed him off as a hypochondriac and cited, to prove their point, his prodigious appetite. "He has the stomach of an ostrich," wrote Bragge to Addington.[1] "If I had wanted any additional proof, our last supper . . . would have convinced me, when he ordered a couple of woodcock to succeed half a barrel of oysters, and then quarrelled with the waiter because there were no sausages to succeed, so that he was obliged to finish with nothing higher than ragou'd lobster which he washed down with two tumblers of mixed punch, rich." But the anecdote testified more to the extravagance of his greed than the underlying excellence of his constitution. He continued to eat such meals, he continued to suffer and his friends continued to laugh. It took his death, after a long and painful illness, to convince them that there might be something wrong with him after all.

In July, 1786, Pitt responded to Addington's urging by suggesting that Hiley should stand for Berwick. The seat seemed a moderately safe one and the Addingtons were jubilant, even when they heard that Sir Gilbert Elliot, one of the heavy-weights of the Whig party, was to stand against him. Addington wrote cheerfully to his father of the "zeal and good humour" in Hiley's camp and the panic of the opposition.[1] But a few days later reports became gloomier. Sir Gilbert was said to be sending down thirty voters from London and the morale of the Whigs was rising.[2] In the upshot Hiley lost by forty-five votes. Next year Pitt tried again and asked Lord Falmouth to put him in for Truro. The electors were not delighted by the choice. They accepted it with resignation but demonstrated their disapproval by demanding still larger inducements than they usually felt to be their due. Luckily Hiley had been left a fortune while still a child and sufficient bribes were forthcoming to ensure that he was returned.

With his brother beside him in the House, Addington now had the pleasure of seeing his closest friend become his brother-in-law. In 1788 Charles Bragge married Addington's youngest sister Charlotte. To make it better still, in 1790 he was offered a seat at Monmouth by the Duke of Beaufort. There seemed every reason to hope that he would shortly join his friends in the House of Commons. With Nathaniel Bond and another old acquaintance, Pole-Carew, already there, the kernel was being formed of that devoted circle of mediocrities which was to comprise the Addingtonian interest in Parliament.

Meanwhile Addington quietly built up his own position by assiduous committee work and the cultivation of useful friends. In 1787 a flurry of rumour announced that he was to go to Ireland as Chief Secretary under the Marquis of Buckingham; several friends wrote to congratulate him and Bragge to commiserate with him on his "honourable banishment."[3] Addington himself seems at one stage to have believed the rumours but time passed and he was still in London. He began to take an interest in the

Royal Navy and the conditions of its seamen. At first he probably had little in mind but that it would be good for his reputation to be known as an expert in some popular yet not overcrowded field. But once Addington became involved in a subject he studied it with diligence. With good reason he inveighed against the "usury and scoundrelism" of the Navy agents, by which the seamen were often tricked out of what pitiful wages the Admiralty allowed them, and called for the appointment by Parliament of Commissioners to look after the seamen's interests. His efforts were well received by the Navy and even made some small impression on the general public. He earned a reputation as a loyal Navy man; a fact which helped him to gain the friendship and support of Nelson, Pellew and other naval leaders. He always enjoyed the society of eminent sailors, listened to their words with care and was generally considered by his friends to be extremely knowing on the finer points of naval strategy.

But this new cause did not induce him to speak more often in the House of Commons. Lord Bulkeley must have had him among others in mind when he referred to[1] "Pitt's young friends who never get up to speak." Bulkeley attributed this timidity to fear of Fox, Burke, Sheridan and Grey. Certainly, except for Pitt himself, most of the oratorical big guns were with the Opposition. But it is doubtful whether Addington would have spoken much more often if the Opposition benches had been manned by mutes. It was not until he had gained security from interruption in the Speaker's chair that he acquired a taste for that orotund and contrived verbosity which was to be the hall-mark of his performances in Parliament.

*　　*　　*　　*　　*

Two factors above all were predominant in Addington's rise to power: the friendship of Pitt and the trust of the King. The first he already enjoyed; in March, 1788, by his first audience with the King, he took a small step towards the acquisition of the latter.

There was every reason why Addington should esteem the King. Like most of the subjects of King George III, his view of his monarch was uncritical to the point of blindness. It is difficult to exaggerate the grasp which this slow, sly, obstinate man was gaining upon the affections of his people. "When I forget my

King," ranted Thurlow, "may my God forget me." The words were uttered in a spirit of the purest cynicism but they were echoed with sincerity throughout the land, toasted by country squires, printed on handkerchiefs and stamped on snuff-boxes. Good, honest, Farmer George, the family man, the bluff, jovial champion of his people, was becoming a loved, if mythical, figure in every English home. To the still immense prestige of a reigning monarch he added a lustre of loyal affection won by being patently different from his odious predecessors. To a few sophisticated aristocrats or disgruntled radicals he might be a figure to despise, deride or hate but to the people as a whole he was the very pattern of a King.

Addington, as on almost every issue, was at one with the British people. In his father's house he had long learned to consider the King as the ultimate patron, the invalid whose death-bed no doctor could afford to miss. As a politician he admired the King's toughness, shrewdness and pertinacity. As a suppressed romantic he found in George III a hero whom it was both his pleasure and his duty to adore. He went to his audience with the naïve and rapturous reverence of a child attending his first Communion, resolutely determined to be impressed and moved.

But though Addington might revere the King there seemed no reason to expect that the King would show much esteem for Addington. "Descent from an early enemy or obscurity of birth," wrote Lord Holland,[1] "were in his eyes such offences that, with the exception of Mr. Pitt and Mr. Addington, he was seldom prevailed on to pardon either . . ." In 1788 he had no reason to forgive Addington for being a doctor's son. To the royal mind he was a nobody; a nobody on the right side who therefore deserved a little affable encouragement, but certainly not a man to be considered with attention. He received him with the same offhand courtesy as he would have offered any other servant of respectable but undistinguished standing.

This was quite enough for Addington, who would have accepted the curtest dismissal as a mark of favour. On 29th March he wrote proudly to his father:[2] "On Friday I was introduced to His Majesty who was extremely gracious and on Thursday I kissed the hand of Her Majesty who was equally so." Now that he could feel himself a true associate of the King he pledged himself to serve the royal cause with still greater diligence and to make the furtherance of its interests a first claim upon his parliamentary powers.

It was therefore a severe blow for Addington, both personally and politically, when a note from Grenville on 7th November told him that the King was ill and that his state gave room "for the utmost apprehensions of incurable disorder."[1] George III was, in fact, entirely off his head. He gabbled nonsense, grew hysterical, at times even had to be forcibly restrained. Though Dr. Addington, whom Pitt had called in for old times' sake, was resolutely optimistic, the other doctors either hedged or despaired of recovery.[2] Gleefully the Prince of Wales and his Whig followers accepted the gloomiest forecasts and dismissed Dr. Addington as "eighty six and reckoned an old woman twenty years ago."[3] Pitt knew that his political future depended on the return of the King to at least a semblance of sanity. In the hope that this might eventually happen he fought a skilful rearguard action designed to ensure that the Prince of Wales, even as Regent, should hold only limited powers. It is difficult to believe that Pitt could have made his restrictions hold for long. Mercifully for him, however, old woman though Dr. Addington might be, those years among the lunatics at Reading had taught him how to recognise incurable insanity. His optimism was justified, the King recovered and the Prince of Wales with his Whig courtiers was left bemoaning the paradise which they had so barely missed.

Addington rejoiced with the other Pittites; rejoiced for the recovery of his hero and the vindication of his father's diagnosis as well as for political salvation. "Your opinions and reasons are everywhere quoted," he wrote to Dr. Addington,[4] "and from their proved propriety I must own that I derive no small addition to my exultation . . ." His exultation drove him to verse: a symptom of his satisfaction which had once been a commonplace but which creeping maturity had made more unusual over the last few years:

> When sinks the orb of day, a borrowed light
> The moon displays, pale regent of the night;
> With hungry cries the wolf her coming greets,
> Then Rapine stalks triumphant through the streets;
> Avarice and Fraud in secret ambush lurk,
> And Treason's sons the desperate purpose work.

But, lo! the sun with orient splendour shines,
And scarce observed, the moon's pale orb declines;
Night's guilty spectres own the sovereign sway,
And shrink aghast beneath the eye of day.
Hail source of life and light, all nature cries,
Oh! come resume thy station in the skies,
There long in cloudless glory mayst thou reign,
And distant be the hour when thou shalt set again.[1]

Addington was well satisfied with his effusion and made sure that it was passed from hand to hand. Some word of it must have reached the Prince of Wales, who can hardly have relished the role of pale regency ascribed to him. Still less can his followers have been pleased to figure as Rapine, Avarice and Fraud destined to shrink aghast at the news of the royal recovery.

But in spite of his uninhibited support of the King and Pitt, Addington seems never to have been classed by the opposition among the irreconcilable party men. Rose, Dundas, Arden were ranked with Anti-Christ himself; Addington escaped. Partly the reason for this lay in his conciliatory nature. Except for writing occasional intemperate verses, Addington did little to offend the Opposition. He listened to their arguments with attention, treated them individually with respect and even friendliness and went far out of his way to avoid any clash of personalities. He was a loyal Pittite yet never a partisan. But his protection, too, lay in his very inconspicuousness. His failure to shine earned him in compensation a freedom from jealousy or active dislike. In so far as Sheridan, Fox or Burke thought about Addington at all it was with a slightly condescending friendliness; a man on the wrong side but with no harm in him. This lack of enemies was to stand him in good stead in the next few years.

3

Of all those whom Addington was able to call his friends, the most improbable was William Wyndham Grenville. Grenville's arrogance, his coldness, the exaggerated value he attached to breeding, his total indifference to the sensibilities of others; all these should have ensured that he regarded Addington at the best with indifference, at the worst with unconcealed contempt. Yet in fact he had made a friend of Addington since their time at Oxford, spent days together in his company and consulted him with the air of listening with respect to what was said. Addington was not an intimate of Grenville's—a status almost impossible to attain except for a member or connection of the family—but they got on well together. Not surprisingly the doctor's son remained very much the junior partner. The admiration and affection which he felt for his distinguished friend in fact does much to explain why Grenville found the relationship rewarding.

The admiration, perhaps, was justified; the affection less so. Grenville was efficient, hard-working, conscientious, sometimes even brilliant. He was well worth his place in the Ministry of his cousin Pitt. But he lacked not only the common touch but any sort of human touch at all. "He is not an ill-tempered man," wrote Liverpool,[1] "but he has no feelings for anyone, not even for those to whom they are most due. He is in his outward manner offensive to the last degree." This conventional picture of a cold, proud, capable fish is complicated and, to some extent, falsified by Grenville's own haunting awareness that something was missing in his composition. "I am not competent to the management of men," he confessed to his brother and this well-founded conviction of inadequacy underlaid all the arrogant pride in his family and his talents. Greater self-confidence might have enabled him not only to reach the uppermost place of power but to hold on to it once achieved.

The primary object of every Grenville was to promote the betterment of other members of the clan; their ultimate goal to garnish with a ducal crown the head of their deplorable leader, the Marquis of Buckingham. "A family of cormorants," the Duke of Bedford described them and, indeed, they had much the air of sleek and well-bred birds of prey, circling around the family eyrie at Stowe and bringing home occasional gobbets of office or patronage to enrich the diet of the fat, old patriarch in the nest. William Grenville was more talented than most of his relatives, but when it came to rapacity he was as bad as any.

Addington either did not notice these vices or was too proud of his grand associate to pay them heed. He took great pleasure in Grenville's company and sought it frequently. In August, 1788, Grenville passed a month with him at Lyme; at Grenville's own suggestion, as Addington was careful to point out whenever he told the anecdote in later years.[1] One day when they were visiting a neighbour discussion turned on who was likely to succeed Charles Cornwall as Speaker of the House of Commons. Both politicians agreed that Phelips of Montacute was the most likely choice. "Within twelve months," Addington would conclude the story triumphantly, "we were both Speakers ourselves."

It is difficult to say why Grenville accepted the Speaker's chair. He had no interest in the proceedings of the House of Commons, was temperamentally ill-disposed for any job which involved so large a share of patient listening, and would never have been content with an office which traditionally demanded a lifetime of service with nothing better than a pension at the end. He knew that Pitt destined him for a Cabinet job and possibly thought that the Speakership would provide a convenient means of filling the intervening time. At all events, early in 1789 Grenville was nominated as the Government candidate and returned with a comfortable majority of seventy-one over his Whig rival, Sir Gilbert Elliot. Within five months he was on his way again to replace Lord Sydney as Home Secretary.

There was much indignation in the House of Commons at this incontinent desertion. Was the Chair, demanded Burke, to become "a succession house, a hot bed for statesmen?" To be their Speaker was, in the eyes of the Commons, sufficient glory for any individual. That Grenville should use them as a stepping-stone towards higher office offended their dignity and sense of what was proper.

It may in part have been this indignation which led Pitt to put forward Addington as the next Speaker; a man whose lack of ambition was a by-word and who would have been ready happily to serve the Commons all the days of his life. But this alone would not have been enough. Pitt knew also that Addington had long been an earnest student of the procedures of the House, he knew that he was tactful, persuasive, dignified in manner and sedate in disposition, he knew that he was generally well liked. "He wants only a little more age and being a little more known to be unexceptionable," wrote Grenville to his brother.[1] It was daring on Pitt's part to nominate as Speaker a thirty-two-year-old nonentity with no apparent claim save that of being friend of the Prime Minister. But all those who knew Addington more than superficially were satisfied that the choice was a sound and prudent one and that, once he was in office, rancour at the appointment would swiftly be forgotten.

Sir Gilbert Elliot, Grenville's former rival, stood again for the opposition, not with any hope of success but so as to make it easier to turn out the Tory incumbent when a Whig government eventually took office. He was surprised and offended when he discovered who Grenville's successor was to be. "Pitt could not have made a more obnoxious choice than this one," he complained to his wife.[2] "This is Addington's first parliament. He is the son of Lord Chatham's physician and is in fact a sort of dependant to the family. The Chair has hitherto been filled by persons of quite a different description." Lady Elliot's chief preoccupation was that her husband should be defeated. "I am sure your constitution is by no means equal to the confinement, sedentary life and constant bore of being Speaker to the House of Commons," she had written a few months before. "What is the use of superior talents if you are to sit still and say nothing? Better have nothing than be enveloped in a great wig and state-coach; it would be making an old square-toes of you at once."[3] She had no cause for worry: Addington mustered exactly the same supporters as had Grenville in January, Elliot's vote went down by two, and Addington was safely launched on the career which was to occupy him for the next twelve years. It said much both for his own character and for Sir Gilbert Elliot's that before Addington's

Speakership was run Elliot was to refer to him with some affection as "tho' no genius, . . . cheerful and conversible, and very civil, which always makes good company."[1]

From Addington's friends arose the usual paean of unctuous praise, expressing in a multitude of well-turned phrases the conviction that his promotion was as merited as it was belated and that yet more brilliant things lay ahead for the young Member for Devizes. Gilpin alone struck an idiosyncratic note.[2] "I have only to regret," he admitted, ". . . that such an enlightened countenance as God has given you, should be shrouded in a bushell of horse-hair."

*   *   *   *   *

In the second half of the eighteenth century the Speaker of the House of Commons was not credited automatically with those virtues of omniscience, infallibility and divine indifference to party which to-day he is known to possess. Speaker Onslow indeed, during his long reign, had done much to raise the credit of the Chair. He had held office at a time when party warfare was at a low pitch and made the most of it to parade his impartiality. But with the return of acrimonious conflict to the House of Commons, these standards quickly fell away. Sir John Cust, though respectable, was a weakling "who added little to the dignity of the office and nothing to its development."[3] Fletcher Norton, Speaker from 1769 to 1780, found himself in violent opposition to the Government. He cheerfully announced that "he would treat the resolutions of the House as those of so many drunken porters," and proceeded to do so until evicted in favour of Cornwall. Cornwall was as partial in favour of Government as Norton had been against it. He was a lazy nonentity who diverted the House by keeping a supply of porter underneath his chair and noisily sipping at it during the debates. "Never was any man in public situation less regretted or sooner forgotten," wrote Wraxall sharply,[4] and the judgment does not seem to have been unduly harsh. Finally Grenville, by his contemptuous abandonment of the office as soon as something more interesting offered, did nothing to restore the tarnished credit of the Chair.

With predecessors such as these Addington could hardly have failed to shine. Not much was expected of him. "We were all very sorry to vote against you," Sheridan amiably assured him,[1] but the Opposition on the whole took it for granted that he was Pitt's man and, as such, would lean over backwards to help the Government. When Addington refused an official sinecure—a traditional perquisite of the Speaker—on the grounds that it would impair his independence, Members were impressed but inclined to feel that rectitude so inconvenient was unlikely to withstand the test of time.

Addington was indeed Pitt's man but it is the most remarkable feature of his Speakership that, bitterly contested though debates in the House of Commons were often to be, he never lost the confidence of the Opposition. Few indeed were the accusations of partiality launched against him and of these some at least came from old friends on the Government benches who thought that he was treating them too harshly. His reputation, indeed, stood almost as high among the Whigs as among the Pittites. It was Burke who remarked[2] that Addington had "acted with so much impartiality, attention and diligence, that he had not only answered the expectations of his friends but so far satisfied the House in general as to attach the good opinion of those who had voted for another person to fill the office." It was Tierney who said[3] ". . . the Speaker of the House of Commons is approved by all." And it was another Whig, Sir William Pulteney, who congratulated Addington on conduct which had won him many friends "and, I am persuaded, no one enemy."[4]

Whatever criticisms may relate to the other passages of Addington's career, it would be patent injustice to deny that he was an uncommonly good Speaker. He was patient, diligent, invariably courteous, well versed in the procedures and traditions of the House of Commons and sincerely convinced of their importance. He was a constructive Speaker, deeming it his duty not only to preside at debates but also to act as an intermediary between the various groups and do what he could to conciliate their points of view. As he saw it, to maintain good order and the smooth running of the House was not something which could be done alone by lofty interventions from the Chair. It called for deep knowledge of the issues and individuals concerned and infinite dexterity in the management of prejudices and the soothing of fears or affronted vanity. Work of this kind was particularly attractive to him; his dislike of disagreements, his readiness to see the other person's point of view, his skill in drafting and in finding formulae acceptable to everyone, made him something close to the ideal mediator.

Yet his occupation of the Chair seemed to vest him with a self-confidence and dispassionate firmness which at other periods of his life he sorely lacked. He never lost his temper, never sacrificed politeness; yet was rarely accused of weakness. On the very day that his election was approved by the King, he gently but decisively put down Wilberforce,[1] observing that ". . . if he was not mistaken, the Honourable Gentleman had spoken once or twice already, and that if such a violation of order were acquiesced in from the Chair, the most valuable time of the House would be wasted in desultory debates." Wilberforce was a man of great influence and prestige, at the time perhaps Pitt's closest friend. Addington could feel reasonably sure that he was also too honourable to resent a justified correction, but it showed unexpected courage on the Speaker's part to intervene so firmly while still so new in office.

If proof were needed that the House approved their Speaker's conduct it would lie in the debate of 10th March, 1790. Traditionally the Speaker relied for his income on various fees upon Bills and other proceedings of the House which brought him in about £1,200 a year, certain other lesser allowances and a few extra oddments such as a service of plate weighing four thousand ounces and two hogsheads of claret a year from the King's cellars. This all made up to a handsome total but by no means enough to support the monstrous burden of hospitality which the Speaker was expected to bear. Since Addington had rejected an official sinecure, he seemed to be threatened with privation or bankruptcy.

The idea of a fixed salary for the Speaker had occasionally been mooted in the past but there had been little in the character of the last few incumbents to make the House take up the question seriously. Now a group of Addington's friends, in consort with a few carefully chosen members of the Opposition, proposed that a salary of £5,000 a year should be paid to the occupant of the Speaker's chair. "Another shower of handsome and flattering things has been poured upon your son by the whole House . . ." reported Pole-Carew to Dr. Addington,[2] and indeed the debate was a remarkable triumph for the young Speaker. It would be wrong to read too much into the often formal compliments of the various orators, but the unanimity of their opinion and the warmth of their approval is still impressive. Against the patently insincere opposition of twenty-eight members, all known to be friends of Addington, the figure was increased from £5,000 to £6,000. Only one Member opposed the granting of any salary and he took care to state his belief that Addington was "a gentleman of too upright a mind not to be independent with or without a place."[1] "This is only the beginning of that boy's career,"[2] was Dr. Addington's properly paternal comment on the debate. The Doctor was right, yet it may fairly be held that the years of Addington's Speakership represented for him a high-water mark of popularity and success.

A few years later the grandeur of his office received another boost when the House unanimously voted thanks to the King for his grant to the Speaker of a house in Palace Yard. This house, which had formerly been attached to the post of Auditor to the Exchequer, was destroyed in the fire of 1834. It was not a total success. In spite of the efforts of the Board of Works it was still decidedly damp, and dignity was purchased at the price of gloom and cold. "I had never been ill before or since I lived there," Addington told a friend,[3] "but in Palace Yard I had three fevers and my children were never well." But in spite of this the house was magnificent enough to satisfy a Speaker far more vainglorious than Addington. Its situation, too, was admirable and it became regular practice for Pitt and a few of his close associates to drop in after debate to discuss the future business. Such a habit, agreeable though it was to Addington, was hardly compatible with the strict neutrality that he felt became his position. It was true that, by the time he was established in Palace Yard, organised opposition had almost ceased. But even so his conscience disquieted him. He took advantage of his position to introduce strange figures into the Government circle and Pitt and Sheridan, Pitt and Fox, even Pitt and the Prince of Wales found themselves meeting in intimacy at the Speaker's house.

It was also the custom for Speakers to entertain in the grand manner, a practice to which Addington took with alacrity. Few things pleased him more than to sit at the head of his table and survey the *élite* of the aristocracy and ruling class feasting at his expense. Charles Abbot, one of Addington's successors in the

Chair, has left a description of one of these dinners:[1] "We were twenty in number . . . The whole party full-dressed, and the Speaker himself so, except that he wore no sword. The style of the dinner was soups at top and bottom, changed for fish, and afterwards changed for roast saddle of mutton and roast loin of veal. The middle of the table was filled with a painted plateau ornamented with French white figures and vases of flowers. Along each side were five dishes, the middle centres being a ham and a boiled chicken. The second course had a pig at top, a capon at bottom, and the two centre middles were turkey and a larded Guinea fowl. The other dishes, puddings, pies, puffs, blanc-manges, etc. The wine at the corners was in icepails during the dinner. Burgundy, champagne, hock and hermitage. The dessert was served by drawing the napkins and leaving the cloth on. Ices at top and bottom; the rest of the dessert oranges, apples, ginger, wafers etc. Sweet wine was served with it. After the cloth was drawn a plate of thin biscuits was placed at each end of the table and the wine sent round, viz. claret, port, madeira, sherry. Only one toast was given—'The King' . . ."

It was Addington's habit to give a dinner on this scale for Ministers and their friends on the first Saturday of each session. The first Sunday was reserved for the Opposition and after that he would mix them up as prudence dictated and the mood took him. Every Sunday he would hold a levee, at which all the parliamentary world and its periphery was likely to be found.

This practice of Sunday entertaining was eventually to get Addington into trouble with William Wilberforce, who was conducting a campaign for strict observance of the Sabbath. He called on the Speaker and urged him to join in a general declaration on Sabbatarianism and to give up his own Sunday parties. "He very unreasonably angry——" the reformer commented wistfully in his diary. "I deeply moved and much hurt. Stayed late with him and afterwards could not get to sleep."[2] Three weeks later he took up the subject again. This time he found the Speaker ". . . extremely offended at the declaration, and being asked to change day. 'Personal insult' etc. I told him that it was not so meant. The attempt has failed, but I hope God will accept it."[3]

Wilberforce was rarely diplomatic in pursuit of his ends but in this case he seems to have been more than usually tactless.

He should have realised that, for parliamentary reasons, Sunday was the best day for the Speaker to entertain, that Addington took seriously his duties in this line, and that he would give great offence if he showed that, in his eyes, the Speaker's levees were as much illicit pleasure-making as prize-fighting or public dancing. He made Addington still angrier by discussing the ethics of these Sunday levees with several of the habitual guests before he even mentioned the matter to the host. Addington was always open to argument and more dexterous management by Wilberforce might easily have persuaded him to change his system. As it was the two men had one of the periodic quarrels which disturbed their generally close and mutually approving friendship.

* * * * *

The great parliamentary set-piece before and during the early years of Addington's Speakership was the impeachment of Warren Hastings. This gargantuan inquiry into the activities of Hastings as Governor of Bengal began, in effect, in 1782 with his condemnation *in absentia* by the House of Commons and continued until his acquittal on all charges by the House of Lords in 1795. But for most Englishmen, Addington among them, the story did not begin until Hastings returned to England in 1785 and defied his enemies to pursue their charges. Sheridan, Fox and above all Burke rose enthusiastically to the challenge and the marathon was under way. The debates and trial gave rise to some of the finest oratorical feats of the eighteenth century but such moments were rare and, by the time all was over, the reaction of the public was tedium or even nausea.

Addington strove earnestly to be fair and objective but lacked both the time to sift the evidence and the knowledge of conditions in India which alone could put the Governor's activities into proper perspective. His first reaction was in favour of the accused. "I am convinced Hastings is not blameless," he wrote,[1] "but I think I see enough to satisfy me that, if there is a bald place on his head, we ought to cover it with laurels." But when the debate turned to the spoliation of the Begums of Oudh, those almost legendary ladies whose woes have earned them a martyr's place in the pantheon of every English schoolboy, then Addington found that he could no longer take so benign a view. Sheridan's highly-coloured condemnation of the Governor deeply affected him but it was Pitt's sober summing up which finally decided his verdict. "I am sure you will hear with pain that I felt it to be my duty to be a party in the accusation," he wrote to his father.[1] "Indeed, Mr. Hastings' defence was so completely falsified by *himself* and by witnesses who were known to be well affected to him, and his motives proved to be so wholly incompatible with any principle of justice or humanity, that I must have been insensible to the dictates of both had not my vote contributed to the majority."

After the impeachment, the scene was transferred to Westminster Hall. The task of keeping in touch with the detailed progress of the trial was prodigious and unrewarding. Nor were distractions lacking. In 1789 came the storming of the Bastille: "They have been playing the fool in France," remarked Addington; perhaps the classic understatement of a lifetime dedicated to the avoidance of hyperbole. The Revolution and the war of 1793 turned most people's eyes from the parish-pump problems of the East India Company and their questionably peccant servant. But as Speaker Addington felt himself involved in an impeachment which had been submitted by his House to the House of Lords. He continued to devote painful hours to study of the evidence and conversation with the protagonists.

The trial also gave rise to one of the most important constitutional debates which arose under Addington's Speakership. The problem was whether the dissolution of Parliament could be held automatically to abate an impeachment. The question was of considerable potential importance. If the King were able, by dissolving Parliament, to protect any of his servants whom the Commons had impeached, then one of the main safeguards against absolutism would have been evaded. What was worse, if a group of peers by wilfully dragging out the proceedings in the House of Lords could frustrate an impeachment, the worth of the ultimate weapon of the Commons would be reduced almost to nothing. In the House of Commons Addington ruled that dissolution did not affect the progress of an impeachment. His ruling was challenged and the House went into Committee. It was one of the rare occasions—sixteen times in twelve years—that Addington intervened in debate. His main point was one of common sense rather than constitutional precedent. Since the King had been deemed incapable of granting pardon in cases of impeachment, Addington maintained that he should not be able to achieve the same end by other means. If the rules of procedure did not fit this conclusion, then they must be made to.

Accounts vary as to the effectiveness of his speech. His family and friends were, as always, enthusiastic to the point of idiocy. Elliot reported coldly:[1] "The Speaker made a long speech in defence of the privileges of the House on *our* side. But so very poor in the performance as to have distressed Pitt." Sir Gilbert, as Addington's recently defeated rival, may well have been uncharitable. The speech, though verbose, seems to have been well reasoned and packed with useful matter. The fact that the Speaker had intervened at all and his known mastery of constitutional procedures must have had much influence on the debate. His views, at all events, prevailed by a comfortable majority.

This point out of the way, the impeachment dragged on its apparently interminable course. Gradually Addington became convinced that Hastings had been unfairly accused and that such evil as he had done was venial and more than counter-balanced by the good. As Speaker of the House of Commons he was naturally bound to keep this opinion to himself but he must have found it hard to frame his answer when Hastings' acquittal led to Burke writing to him in passionate disappointment:[2]

I have had the honour and happiness of sitting in parliament under you. I know with how much real dignity you have filled the chair of the House of Commons. It is therefore matter of grief, to me inexpressible, that, without any fault of yours, the greatest disgrace and dishonour which ever has fallen upon that House, and upon your chair, since the time we can trace the existence of a Speaker, or even of an House, have fallen upon both in your time.

You are the first Speaker who has been dismissed from the bar of the House of Lords with the disgrace of a total failure in an object of impeachment by the House of Commons.

Until he received this letter it is doubtful whether it had occurred to Addington that he and his House should feel disgraced. The contention did not for long disturb him. His reaction to the end of the trial was mingled relief that it was over and satisfaction that justice had at last been done. He found his

fellow-members of the House of Commons were quite as oblivious
to their dishonour. Burke's woeful clamour rang out to an unsympathetic world and England turned to more serious matters. With
Hastings Addington became firm friends and their mutual
approval was to endure throughout their lives.

    *   *   *   *   *

Meanwhile, in March, 1790, Dr. Addington had followed the
path along which he had helped so many of his patients. His
father's death can have come as no surprise to Addington; the
old doctor was seventy-six and had been in frail health for some
time. But his sense of loss was still sharp and stirred him to an
unusual parade of emotion.

"When I recollect his participation of all that rejoiced or
grieved us," he wrote,[1] "—the goodness and kindness of his
nature, and those other qualities which made him so beloved and
respected—I feel there is a blank in my happiness which cannot
be supplied till we are restored to each other to part no more . . .
I know that I have lost a prop and a comfort, and am only thank-
ful that I was sensible of their value before they were taken
from me."

There is no reason to believe that these eminently proper
sentiments were insincere. It would equally be surprising if
Addington's grief had been very deep or lasting. Dr. Addington
was not a bad or cruel man. Within the limitations of his tepid
spirit he had been fond of his son and proud of his achievements.
But the bleak and heavy repressiveness which had been his contribution to his son's education had gone far to stifle the power
of feeling which might now have lit Addington's grief into real
life. Dr. Addington had been resolutely benevolent in the last
few years of his life and had done much for the sick and old of
Reading but it is doubtful if, when he died, there was anyone who felt for him more than a generalised and remote
affection.

In spite of the death of its head the family remained closely
united. With Hiley in particular Addington continued his close
partnership. The relationship had its thorns. With Addington's
accession to the Speakership Hiley had begun to adopt the
whining manner of a younger brother whom a trick of birth had
unkindly relegated to the second rank. Addington met his com-

plaints with kindness and forbearance. "If you will view your situation as it really is and estimate it properly," he wrote to Hiley,[1] "you will be grateful for the predominance of your comforts and you will look forward with hope . . . You are happy in your family, in your numerous friends and in the good opinion and esteem of all who know you. Your circumstances, though not affluent, may, I am sure be rendered so by a judicious exercise of the talents you possess, and I am thoroughly convinced that it is still in your power to be an eminently successful and healthy and a happy man." These sage counsels did little to reconcile Hiley to his Jacob's role but at least he kept his grumbles for his family. To the rest of the world the two brothers seemed and indeed were united.

Addington's own children were now of an age where their talents and deficiencies became apparent. Mary Anne, his eldest daughter, was thirteen in 1795, a plain but pleasant child, friendly, intelligent and devoted to her father with whom she was to spend all her life. Henry, the eldest son, was nine. "Of Harry I have great hopes," wrote Addington to Huntingford.[2] "He is very shy, but steady and ingenuous." In August, 1795,[3] Huntingford pledged himself "to give the strongest proof of affection for you, by devoting myself for seven years to the care of your son." He kept his word only too well. Harry was at once more sensitive and less resilient than his father. Stupidity might have saved him from the full weight of Huntingford's attentions or a more contumacious nature helped him to resist them. As it was, he was a docile, even willing victim. "It is evident," reported his tutor,[4] "that your son not only possesses the faculty of versification but has genius and imagination. From his prose . . . I read also a very honest and manly heart." With implacable benevolence Huntingford bore down on the unfortunate child, harrying him into the pursuit of glory. To the father he had already done grave harm, to the son he was to prove totally destructive.

Addington was immensely proud of his eldest son. William, the second surviving boy, born in 1794, he was to find altogether less interesting. To him, and to the three younger daughters who survived his wife's recurrent miscarriages and botched deliveries, he remained kind, thoughtful but somewhat remote; not uninterested but without the time or enthusiasm to follow their progress with close attention.

The family needed a country home and in 1790 Addington bought for four thousand guineas the house and small estate of Woodley in the parish of Sonning near Reading. In rebuilding, laying out of gardens and afforestation he found a soothing and agreeable occupation. The therapeutic effects of country life seem to have been impressive. The dankness of his official house and the strain of constant all-night sittings had done much to damage his constitution. Life at Woodley quickly restored him to his natural condition of extreme good health.

* * * * *

Addington's years as Speaker were marked by his steady growth in stature, if not in the eyes of the general public, at least in those of Pitt and his Ministers. More and more it became the practice to convene him as an honorary member of the Cabinet. Grenville, Dundas, Loughborough and the Speaker composed a kind of inner council, with no direct authority or formal existence but with whom Pitt found it convenient and congenial to discuss his plans. Addington's views were sought in particular whenever financial questions were on the agenda and Pitt can have taken few major decisions in this field without first discussing them with his friend. On military strategy Addington's part was less significant but even here Pitt kept him posted on what was going on.

Addington justified this un-Speaker-like behaviour by the paramount needs of the war. It did not, anyhow, directly affect his conduct in the Chair. A trickle of Whig defectors in 1793 had culminated in 1794 with the Duke of Portland bringing over the bulk of the Opposition to support the Government. Fox and a handful of irreconcilables were all that were left to disturb the harmony of the House. For much of the time they never appeared at all; when they did, their very weakness made it easier for Addington to protect their interests without damage to the cause of Government. Fox disliked Pitt and all things Pittite, but he seems never to have felt that Addington acted improperly in putting his common sense and good judgment at the service of Ministers.

Yet, even if he had felt that he was acting improperly, it is doubtful if Addington could have resisted Pitt's appeal to help him bear the burden of the war. It is difficult to exaggerate Pitt's prestige in Parliament and the country or to over-estimate the compelling power which he enjoyed over the minds of his friends. Addington felt for him an admiration and affection that sometimes seemed not far short of idolatry; the Prime Minister shared with the King the ultimate shrine in his private pantheon but, unlike the King, Pitt was also a personal friend in whose company Addington could feel at ease and with whom he could freely speak his mind. The almost religious devotion of the confirmed Pittite —Rose, Canning, Tomline—to the interests of their master was a strange phenomenon of English political life. Addington yielded to none of them in championship of his glorious friend.

The two men now saw more of each other and with greater pleasure than at any other period of their lives. They dined together, drank together, discussed far into the night together. On one occasion they were almost mobbed together. After a banquet at Canterbury a crowd of hooligans booed them heartily. "A pretty story will this make in the papers," said Pitt. "The Minister and the Speaker dined with the corporation of Canterbury, got very drunk and were hissed out of the town." "The *Morning Chronicle*," reported Addington, "acted more leniently. It only stated that the Chancellor of the Exchequer was observed, in walking to his carriage, to oscillate like his own bills."[1]

Almost every night during the session Pitt would drop in at the Speaker's house for supper, either alone or with a group of friends. Such gatherings were famous as much for the amount drunk as for the high policies discussed. Addington was one of the few people who knew Pitt well enough and was not too much afraid of him to tell him frankly when he drank too much. "Now, Pitt, you shall not have another drop," was a constant refrain at these evenings, but in the end another bottle usually appeared and the drinking would go on to the early hours.[2] Sometimes, however, he could be firm. "Mr. Addington . . . lives about a mile from Holm Park," noted Farington, the diarist.[3] "Mr. Pitt is now with him and has been ten days for the benefit of his health. Sir Walter Farquhar has been down to see him and allows him and the Speaker to drink a bottle between them after dinner but none after supper. Mr. Pitt one night pressed for some, but the Speaker was rigid." In London Grenville, Dundas, Bragge, Arden, Hiley Addington or one of half a dozen others would often join them at port. "Party of *the old firm* at the

Speaker's; I not there," wrote Wilberforce wistfully after a temporary estrangement with Addington.[1] "The old firm" ruled England and there can have been few with any claims to a role in politics who would not have been proud to join them.

Addington's anomalous position as one of Pitt's closest friends and advisers yet not a member of his Government, as well as his independent role as Speaker, gave him a position of peculiar importance among all those who wished well of Ministers but were not of their number. He often found himself consulted about the Prime Minister's intentions or used as an intermediary by those who hesitated to approach the great man directly. Pitt for his part found Addington invaluable as a listening-post outside the Government and a widely trusted go-between expert at dealing with the disaffected. An extreme example of the latter was Lord Mornington, later Marquis Wellesley. Mornington wrote angrily to Addington[2] to protest that he was tired of "creeping on with Rose" and crouching to that "ridiculous animal . . . young Jenky." Not for the last time Addington settled down to soothe his friend's susceptibilities. Nothing could convince Mornington that his transcendent talents were properly appreciated but Addington at least seems temporarily to have persuaded him that they were not ignored altogether.

Towards the end of 1793 Pitt suggested to Addington that he should give up the Speakership and take the place of Dundas as Secretary of State. No details of the full plan are known; most of the evidence lying in letters to Addington from friends whose opinion on the subject he had sought. Huntingford, for once, gave sound advice: "Those who value you as they ought," he wrote, "cannot for your own sake, though they would for that of the public, wish to remove you from the very high, honourable and important station to which the united voice of the Commons has called you."[3] Indeed, anyone concerned for Addington's happiness and reputation would have done well to advise him to let nothing but death or senility remove him from the Speaker's chair. Addington at least was satisfied that he could hardly improve on his situation. He refused Pitt's offer with gratitude but little hesitation.

His junior staff in the House would have been as sorry as anyone to see him go. A considerate and tolerant master, he concerned himself about their conditions of employment with an interest shown by few previous Speakers. He found that Hatsell, the Clerk to the House, was drawing some £11,000 a year while a certain Samuel Gunnel, after twenty-three years in the employ of the Commons, got £20 per annum. Addington asked Gunnel to set out his complaint in writing and found the letter "so artless and affecting that I shall not feel at all at ease in leaving town without being convinced that the distress which occasioned it will be speedily relieved."[1] He got Gunnel a stopgap job with the Committee investigating the Public Records and himself was largely responsible for drafting and piloting through the Commons a Bill to improve the permanent status of the Clerks.

But it was above all the county Member who would have regretted Addington's departure from the Chair. In an article written after he had become Prime Minister the *Gentlemen's Magazine* set out to explain his peculiar attraction to these normally unsusceptible worthies:

His sound, old English principles, which no change of times and scenes—no fancied expediency, could induce him ever to swerve from, his honesty, fearlessness and truth, the sincerity, frankness and dignity of his manners, and his perfect command of temper, the nature also of his conversation and, perhaps, also the similarity of his position in life with their own—this combination of attaching qualities rendered him a peculiar favourite with that class of English gentlemen who constituted a majority of the House over which he presided.

The account is flattering but not grotesquely so. The county Members could follow without difficulty what Addington had to say, he did not bully them or try to make them change their ways, he was invariably polite—a pleasant change after the intellectual arrogance of Pitt or the aristocratic scorn of Grenville. He was not a hero whom they could revere but a man whom they could like and understand. His middle-class and urban background took a little living down but they soon concluded that he had the instincts of a gentleman and were prepared to forget the rest. They were to provide him with a solid body of support and in the end only to desert him in the face of well-nigh irresistible pressure.

Though at this time Addington was unequivocally a con-

Father and son: *above*, Dr. Addington: a portrait on glass at Reading
Hospital; *below*, Henry Addington as a boy

Henry Addington
1774

The House of Commons in 1793 by K. A. Hickel. Pitt is addressing the
House, Addington is in the chair. On the Government front bench, eighth
from left, Lord Liverpool; on his left (wearing sash) Marquess Wellesley.
In the second row, in front and slightly to the right of the pillar nearest the
window, William Wilberforce; on his left, George Canning. On the front
opposition bench Charles James Fox is conspicuous in a hat

Addington in Speaker's robes, by Copley

servative, he had not yet succumbed entirely to the spirit of last-ditch reaction. Hatsell, the Clerk of the House, propounded as a central tenet of his creed that "he would resist all changes, great or small, upon the single reason of their being changes."[1] Addington may have had some sympathy with the principle but he did not allow it to dominate his thinking. He laid down his alternative to Hatsell's dogma when the question was raised whether certain evidence about the slave trade could be heard by Special Committee. "It does not follow," he propounded on that occasion, "that because a mode is new it must therefore be improper."[2] The principle was hardly revolutionary yet nor was it the trumpet call of reaction. He applied it faithfully in all his work as Speaker and, as a result, imported an unusual flexibility into the procedure of the House of Commons.

Nor did he display any of the inveterate determination to impose order even at the expense of justice which marked so much of his career. When Horne Tooke was acquitted on a charge of high treason, he, indeed, took the event far more lightly than many of his colleagues. The Solicitor-General wrote to him to express his dismay. Addington saw no cause for uneasiness or surprise:[3] "It is of more consequence to maintain the credit of a mild and unprejudiced administration of justice, than even to convict a Jacobin."

The reality and yet the limitations of Addington's liberalism were nowhere more clearly shown than in the recurrent debates on the slave trade. To-day this is not a subject which can be viewed except in terms of black and white. Even in 1790 most men of sense were agreed on the cruelty and fundamental injustice of the practice. This Addington endorsed; indeed he voiced such sentiments "with the utmost abhorrence and indignation"[4] every time that the subject was debated. But when it came to following the principle to its proper conclusion—the immediate and total abolition of the trade—then doubts began to arise.

Were the property rights of the slave-owners being remembered? What about the future of the West Indian colonies? Would not the loss of the trade do much harm to our merchant shipping and hence, in time of war, to the Royal Navy? Was there any point in abolishing the trade in England if the only result would be that our continental rivals took it over? Should not the imbalance between male and female negroes in the West Indies first be corrected? Was there not a risk that the conquerors in African wars who to-day sold their captives might in future merely butcher them? It was to Addington's credit that he emerged from this welter of perplexity with the clear conviction that abolition must come. But it should be pursued gradually and with moderation. In the debates of 1792 Addington suggested restrictions and heavier taxes which would lead to the end of the trade within ten years: in the meantime by improvement of conditions and education the slave should be prepared for freedom. Moderation in such a cause drove Fox to fury. "To break open a man's house and kill him, his wife and his family in the night is certainly a most heinous crime and deserving of death, but even this may be done with moderation." By the start of the next debate Addington had reduced his transition period to four years. Even Wilberforce was not dissatisfied by his progress. But for the war with France and the consequential check to all ideas of reform he might well have overcome his remaining scruples.

Even such prudent and qualified support of abolition was more than could easily be stomached by the rank and file of Englishmen. The Earl of Abingdon spoke for many when he declared with loathing that abolitionist agitation must lead to "all being equal, blacks and whites, French and English, shall 'merry companions everyone' promiscuously pig together." And what was the ground for this? "Humanity! But humanity is no ground for petitioning. Humanity is a private feeling and not a public principle to act on." Addington's beloved county Member probably felt that Lord Abingdon had gone a little far but few indeed were prepared whole-heartedly to support Wilberforce. To many of them their Speaker's cautious groping towards reform must have seemed the limit of practical politics. Addington was rarely if ever ahead of his time but in this case at least he can not be said to have conspicuously lagged behind.

*　　*　　*　　*　　*

Addington's years as Speaker destroyed whatever chance there might have been that he would become a competent parliamentary debater. The freedom from interruption, the invitation to pomposity and prolixity, the need for objectivity which went far to rule out any form of dramatic expression or emotional appeal: all these ensured that his delivery remained pedestrian and his matter so displayed as to appeal neither to the imagination nor the intellect. He had in fact incurred the fate which Lady Elliot had predicted for her husband, he had become an old square-toes with neither the will nor the ability to escape.

But even more dangerous was his inability to see when he was making himself ridiculous. A typical if trivial example arose in a debate on the corn shortage in March, 1800, when he "gravely informed the world from his father's notes, that bran was more nutritive than grain, a theory which seemed an emblem by anticipation of that policy which made him first minister in lieu of his friend and patron Mr. Pitt and thus threw away the kernel and juice of the Government to preserve the husk and rind."[1] Lord Holland's mockery would have been still sharper if he had seen Addington's original notes for this speech, mercifully abandoned before delivery, which dwelt lovingly on "the rarefying warmth, the solvent moisture and the grinding action of the stomach."

It never occurred to Addington that a speech of this kind would excite ridicule in the House of Commons whoever made it, let alone when it emanated from someone with the handicap, irresistibly funny in the eyes of the more patrician members, of being a doctor's son. He felt that he had something useful and interesting to contribute and did so without more ado. It was perhaps less typical, though by no means unique, that Addington's view was one which would be shared to-day by almost every dietician and that it was the scoffing Lord Holland who would be considered wrong and out of date.

Such lapses were rare; the aura of dignity which clung around the Speaker's chair ensured that Addington was taken seriously even by his few enemies and critics. The circle of his admirers grew wider while the small nucleus of his closest followers swelled proportionately in numbers and importance. Hiley Addington, Pole-Carew and Bond had already been members of the House of Commons for several years. The election of 1796 brought in some useful reinforcements: Lawrence Palk, a worthy Devonian and old friend of Addington's; his cousin, Vansittart, a future Minister in Addington's administration and another of Dr. Gilpin's old boys; Charles Abbot, a future Speaker who had known Addington well at Oxford; Thomas Powys, later Lord

Lilford, among the most fervent of the country gentlemen in his admiration for the Speaker's wisdom and nobility of character and James Adams, who reinforced his claims to be in the coterie by marrying the sister of Addington's wife. Benjamin Hobhouse, Addington's old friend from Brasenose, did not come in till the following year; a year which also saw Charles Bragge gain a seat on the India Board.

There were no pilgrim souls or fiery spirits among these temperate and well-ordered gentlemen. Few hearts can have quickened to see them in conclave in the corridors of Westminster, few groups gathered to hear the flash of wit as they relaxed in one another's company. But they were not without talents or without influence; they were trustworthy, sensible, prudent, all virtues esteemed by the average Member and the average voter; they made a useful contribution to the work of the House and were generally respected and well liked. Among them Addington was the most eminent. To call him their leader would be to suggest a coherence and unity of purpose which did not yet exist but he it was whom they were most likely to consult in case of doubt and to whose opinion they would attach the greatest weight.

A *sine qua non* for membership of Addington's inner circle was a conviction that the English cause was just and that English arms must finally triumph. Whenever the Speaker was at Woodley, Pitt would send him by courier news of any victory and Addington would then pass on the good tidings by lighting up his house for all the neighbourhood to see. But by 1797 it was a long time since there had been great cause for illuminations. The first coalition had disintegrated by the end of 1795 and Pitt's overtures for peace met little response from the triumphant French. The brilliant naval victory of Cape St. Vincent in February, 1797, did something to redeem the earlier failures but, in the same year, the Austrians were driven to make peace and there were naval mutinies at Spithead and the Nore. Once more Pitt thought of peace, this time ready to accept that France should keep her natural frontiers including the Low Countries. At one moment it seemed that a French offer on these lines might bring the war to an end but in the event hopes of peace proved once more an illusion.

Though Addington disliked the French republican government, he was not one of those fanatics who conceived that no peace could be made unless the monarchy were first restored. But he had few hopes that such a peace could be more than a temporary truce. When Pitt consulted him in October, 1797, about the desirability of coming to terms he replied:[1] "I believe the state of the country as to its interior to be so bad that we cannot, in strict duty, venture to reject the offer, which may at least give us some interval of rest for doing what we have to do at home— an interval longer or shorter as events may happen but long it cannot be." Time, he was convinced, was a commodity of which we had great need and which was worth buying even at a price which many would hold to be extravagant.

During the first few years of the war the rump of the Whig Party and, still more, the Radicals had become increasingly associated in the mind of the public with the cause of France. The association, indeed, did not exist only in the mind of the public. Fox had boasted that he drew inspiration from the events in France; his followers may not actually have hoped for a French victory but certainly they were advocates of peace at any price. It therefore followed that, to the sturdy and Francophobe Englishmen, such people must be unpatriotic, treacherous, bad. Public opinion swung so sharply against them and their few representatives in the House of Commons that, as Steven Watson has pointed out,[2] parliamentary reform would have led to the annihilation of the reformers; only their rotten boroughs preserved their place as members. Under the threat of French invasion Pitt put aside all thoughts of reform and adopted a programme of civil repression in theory as severe as any this country had known. Its execution was rarely as implacable as the letter of the law allowed but societies were suppressed, papers censored and criticism of the Constitution discouraged with a harshness which drove opponents of the Government to helpless indignation.

To preserve the *status quo* by means as kindly and as constitutional as possible was Addington's panacea for England's ills. His initial distrust of reform was vastly reinforced by the carnage in France and finally confirmed when radicalism became inseparably fused in his mind with treason and violent disorder. France stood for revolution, murder, anarchy. The English reformers supported the cause of France. Therefore reform in England must lead to revolution, murder, anarchy. To Addington's eyes the syllogism was demonstrably true. Nothing was ever to shake his belief or to convince him that Robespierre and the Radicals were but a step apart. It was this case of mistaken identity, based upon the abnormal circumstances of the 1790s, which distorted the judgment of a generation of politicians and exaggerated the miseries of the post-war years.

4

As Speaker of the House of Commons Addington found that his part in the conduct of the war lay necessarily in the background. It gave him much satisfaction to know that he was close to the centre of power but still he sometimes hankered after a little of the limelight. In the budget debate of November, 1797, one of his few moments of glory arrived. It seemed clear that the taxes in Pitt's budget would prove inadequate for the needs of a war economy. Addington therefore put forward the concept of a "voluntary contribution" by which anyone who chose could decline to pay his assessed tax and instead make his own— naturally greater—contribution.

For some reason this rather naïve scheme was greeted with enthusiasm. What was more, in its first year it enjoyed remarkable success. In December, 1798, Pitt estimated that the yield would be two million pounds.[1] His mathematics were notoriously optimistic but in this case at least he seems to have been over-cautious for the most authoritative figure for the fruits of the voluntary levy is £2,826,000.[2] The King subscribed £20,000 a year, a third of his privy purse, while Addington, together with Dundas, Pitt and the Lord Chancellor, offered £2,000. Addington told Abbot[3] that he had picked on this sum as being a little over one-fifth of his total income; "the strict fifth would have given too much the appearance of minute *calculation*."

Addington's appeal does indeed seem to have conjured up a surge of patriotic generosity which might otherwise have remained latent. The proposal came at the right time and its justification lay in its success. But it was patently unfair. Grenville wrote[4] with distaste of public supplies raised "by contributions *soi-disant* voluntary, but in reality extorted by popular clamour and prejudice" and there is indeed little to be said for a system which leads to the generous or the weak-willed shouldering a load which should be spread over all the body of tax-payers. In this, and in the diminishing returns which always accrue from any such appeal to conscience, lay the reasons for putting a stop to the voluntary contribution at the end of the following year.

Addington's personal war effort was not confined to his sacrifice of £2,000 a year. Like many citizens of an unmilitary nation one of his secret pleasures was to play at soldiers. The threat of French invasion, which seemed imminent in 1799, provided an unchallengeable excuse for such diversions. "Among its whimsical effects," he wrote to Mornington,[1] "must be mentioned . . . my exchange of the Mace and Wig for a Sabre and Helmet." In April, 1798, Addington had accepted the command of a troop of cavalry to be raised in the neighbourhood of Reading. For more than two years the Woodley Cavalry, as they were always known, occupied almost all the time which Addington did not spend in the Chair or in conclave with Pitt. Its turn-out and efficiency at drill did him much credit; whether this "excellent and respectable troop"[2] would have proved quite as impressive in battle may reasonably be doubted. "You heaths of Bulmarsh, hail!" rhapsodised Henry Pye, the Bard of Faringdon[3] and perhaps the least distinguished poet laureate in all that galaxy of minor talents:

> . . . For you have seen
> Th'embattled sons of Berkshire tread your Green,
> When every hill and dale and verdant plain
> Poured in refulgent arms a gallant train . . .
> And seen the generous Patriot, who presides
> Oer Britain's Senate and its Council guides,
> Now shining in the radiant van, prepared
> Those rights, which freedom gave, by arms to guard.

The finest hour of the Woodley Cavalry came in July, 1799, when the King, the Queen, the Dukes of York and Cumberland and all five royal princesses visited Berkshire to inspect its embattled sons in person. As Addington entertained his royal master on the lawns of Woodley and led him around the little troop of which he was so proud he must have wondered whether, after all, he had not chosen the wrong career. As with many people of prosaic mind and manner Addington secreted within himself an almost schoolboy romanticism. The intoxicating glory of the royal visit must have stirred visions of another, more heroic career, in which he would himself have led Britain's armies to final victory. But like all such visions they withered swiftly. Addington's occasional grasps after the melodramatic were invariably unsuccessful and he would swiftly recoil into humdrum normality. His command of the Woodley Cavalry led him into one of these abject yet poignant failures. In 1803 it fell to him to come to the House of Commons and announce that war had been declared. Determined to do justice to so great an occasion, he made a dramatically late entrance dressed in full uniform. The House would have been ready to find this out-of-character appearance comic at the best of times but, to compound Addington's troubles, the Speaker was in the process of reading the Medicine Act for the second time. Addington's nickname of "The Doctor" was already well established and his bravura entry was greeted with jeers from his enemies and the embarrassed silence of his friends.[1]

＊　　　＊　　　＊　　　＊　　　＊

Pitt, at least, saw nothing ridiculous in his friend's activities. His good opinion of Addington's talents and discretion continued to grow and it was towards the end of 1797 that it seems first to have occurred to him that Addington might succeed him as Prime Minister. Addington's statement that Pitt envisaged him as his successor long before this actually came about has often been dismissed by historians as no more than evidence of ridiculous vanity. But the story is substantiated in the little known and privately printed fourth volume of Tomline's life of Pitt.[2] Tomline was Bishop of Lincoln, formerly Pitt's tutor and private secretary and still one of his closest advisers. His dislike of Addington was notorious and he would have been happy to snatch at any chance of belittling the latter's pretensions. His story, therefore, can safely be accepted. He states that, he believes in 1797:

> it was imagined, though probably without foundation, that the French Government would be more disposed to make peace with a new Minister than with Mr. Pitt; and Mr. Pitt, therefore, entertained some idea of resigning . . . He submitted these circumstances to the King, and had several conferences with His Majesty upon the subject. After much deliberation the plan was abandoned on the ground that a

new, strong administration . . . could not then be formed, and Mr. Pitt remained in office; but the consideration of this business had gone so far that it was settled, in case of Mr. Pitt's resignation that he should be succeeded by Mr. Addington, Speaker of the House of Commons, and this was known at the time to Mr. Addington himself, and to very few other persons.

It is not without importance when considering the surprise caused by Addington's appointment as Prime Minister and the emphasis placed by his critics on his lack of experience that, in his own and Pitt's eyes at least, he had been playing the part of understudy for several years.

In May, 1798, Addington's friendship for Pitt and duties as Speaker combined to involve him in painful and potentially disastrous embarrassment. Tierney, a leading member of what was left of the Whig opposition, was attacking Pitt's Navy Bill. Pitt accused him of wishing to impede the defence of the nation and Tierney appealed to the Speaker for protection against such insults. Addington would have been well advised to call on Pitt to withdraw his words but instead he merely said that any personal imputation by one Member on another was unparliamentary and that Pitt should explain what he had said. He probably calculated that, given a chance, Pitt would so qualify his words as to remove most of the offence. When Tierney allowed Pitt's rather shuffling explanation to pass it seemed that he had been right. Another Member, however, reluctant to give up so promising a means of making mischief, took up the question. In the argument which followed Pitt was provoked into saying that he held by his original words. Tierney then left the House and, later the same evening, challenged the Prime Minister to a duel.

Addington was called from dinner to be given the news. Pitt had just finished making his will and told his friend where the duel was to be. There were those who said that, as Speaker under whose aegis the quarrel had arisen, it was Addington's duty to prevent the two men fighting. But it is hard to see what he could have done. If he had intervened between them, as Lord Chatham pointed out, there would certainly have been some who would have argued that he was Pitt's friend and must therefore be acting at Pitt's secret behest. Such rumours could have destroyed the reputation of the Prime Minister. Addington had missed his chance of preventing the duel when he failed to intervene quickly and firmly in the House of Commons. From that time forward all the irresponsibility can be laid to the charge of Pitt and Tierney.

Next day Addington walked with Pitt down Birdcage Walk to where Pitt's chaise was waiting to take him to Wimbledon Common. The Speaker could not possibly attend but Addington could not bear to stay away. He rode to the top of a nearby hill and there waited till he saw Pitt's chaise leaving the scene of the duel. Two shots had been fired on each side but no one had been hurt. "You must dine with me to-day," Pitt greeted his friend laconically, and the incident was closed.[1] "You must have shuddered when you first heard of the *Rencontre* . . ." Addington wrote to Mornington,[2] "you may however be assured that there was no alternative."

Addington had also been deeply involved in another of Pitt's personal difficulties, his odd, abortive love-affair with Lord Auckland's daughter, Eleanor Eden. So far as Pitt was capable of loving any human being he seems to have loved this handsome and intelligent girl; certainly she cared deeply for him and it was generally believed that they were to marry. Then Pitt began to have doubts. Was he rich enough? Was his position sufficiently secure? Behind them, perhaps, lay torturing uncertainty whether he could bear to share his life with another. He wrote to the Edens, simultaneously to stress his affection and to explain why it could never be consummated; then reported to Addington how the affair now stood.[3] Pellew, Addington's biographer, found the letter among the Sidmouth manuscripts, marked it "Very Delicate" and put it reluctantly to the side.

"The first answer indeed which I received on Saturday, tho' thoroughly kind, was the most embarrassing possible, as it stated the sentiments entertained to be mutual and pressed for explanation and discussion, proposing at the same time any interval of delay in order to take the chance of overcoming the difficulties and desiring me to continue coming in the interval as if nothing had happened. I had then nothing left but to convey in my answer quite explicitly tho' with as much tenderness as I could, that the decision I had felt myself obliged to take was final and that further discussion could only produce increased anxiety and

83

could lead to no good. This was understood and received as I meant it should; and the answer I received last night, considers the thing as over, and proposes to contradict the reports gradually, and with the delicacy which the subject requires. I hope I may collect from the manner in which it is written that the shock has been as little distressful in its consequences to any part of the family, as I could flatter myself. If that hope should be well-founded, I think I can command my feelings enough to bear the rest, and not be wanting either to the calls of public duty or to what yet remains to me of the private relations of life. . . . the recollections of what I owe to your kindness and friendship will I trust always hold a principal place in my thoughts."

Pitt's biographer, Earl Stanhope,[1] describes the affair as ending "most honourably." Perhaps it did, but honour can be bought at too great a price and it is hard to see much difference between Pitt's behaviour and that of any other cold, egocentric and, of course, honourable fish. Certainly Addington, who had married in passion without thought of his prospects, was entitled to feel some scorn at the caution of a friend who did not find the position of Prime Minister of sufficient worldly consequence to justify taking a wife. It is, however, most unlikely that he felt anything of the sort. As with so many of his contemporaries it was hard for Addington to imagine that Pitt could err and it was to take years of dissension before serious criticism of his illustrious friend was to pass his lips.

*   *   *   *   *

At the beginning of 1799 the question of the legislative union between Ireland and England came before the English Parliament. Pitt had long been convinced that such a Union, followed at some not too distant date by full civil rights for the Catholic population, was the only answer to Ireland's endemic unrest. He convinced his Government that the first part of the remedy at least was desirable and Castlereagh, by a systematic and prolonged campaign of threats, bribes and cajolery, induced the Irish Parliament to agree to its extinction. In early February the Bill of Union was discussed by the House of Commons in committee and on 12th February Addington made one of his few and by far the most substantial of his interventions as Speaker.

The speech is of peculiar importance for an understanding of

Addington's political philosophy at the time when he was within two years of becoming Prime Minister. The significance which he himself attached to it is shown by the time he took in its preparation, its inordinate length and the readiness with which he afterwards agreed that it should be printed and circulated to his friends. He wrote to Mornington[1] enclosing a "copy of a publication hardly deserving of your perusal. It is a short and imperfect statement of what I said on the subject of an Union with Ireland. . . . You will readily believe that the publication was occasioned by the wishes of others. I have only to add that it was sent to the press in haste and with very little time for revision." The deprecatory phrases do little to mask Addington's pride in his work; pride which, on the whole, was justified by the interest taken in the speech and the impression it made on its hearers.

After a long and tedious analysis of the existing misery of Ireland and its unhappy relationship with England, Addington turned to the future. He saw three possible remedies: a re-imposition of the popery laws, Catholic emancipation and the proposed Union. The first would have involved harsh legislative disabilities and penalties for the Catholic population of Ireland. The only exceptions would have been "those, if any, whose conduct had been loyal and peaceable." This little band of loyalists would thenceforward be treated as honorary Protestants. "This surely," remarked Addington,[2] "was not a mode of healing the divisions or establishing the tranquillity of Ireland." The second cure, Catholic emancipation unaccompanied by Union, "coupled as it was in general opinion with parliamentary reform," was in Addington's eyes still more objectionable. To accept it would be to "give the influence to numbers, and take it from property, and thus overwhelm the rights of the Protestants of Ireland. . . . Indeed, if the Catholics were true to their conscience and their creed, the Protestant establishment must be exposed by such a change to immediate danger, and the state of its members be rendered worse than that of the Catholics during any period of the last two centuries." Both these courses would therefore be disastrous, for England and for Ireland alike. There remained only the third possibility, complete legislative union of the two countries.

Addington believed that this Union would be of great advantage to the Roman Catholic in Ireland. "Freed, as he already was, from all restrictions affecting the happiness and prosperity of private life, and the regulation of his personal conduct, the Catholic would fully participate in every advantage which the union would bestow generally upon Ireland." But when it came to foretelling whether the Act of Union should ever be followed by the granting of full political rights to Roman Catholic subjects, Addington was resolutely silent. He made it clear that immediate Catholic emancipation would, in his eyes, prove disastrous. He mentioned no arguments which might induce him to change his mind. He implied, indeed, that no such arguments could exist. But he did not quite commit himself, "he would not now offer an opinion as to the expediency, in the event of an Union, of extending to the Catholics of the empire generally a more ample participation in the privileges enjoyed by the Protestants . . ."

Finally the Speaker turned to the fusion of the two Houses. Here he could speak with unique authority and all those who doubted the wisdom of the proposals listened with special attention. He argued cogently and with much learning that no legislative difficulties of particular importance existed to bar the way and that the possible ill-effects of the Union were far outweighed by the certain good. He admitted that he regretted the expansion of the House of Commons which would follow the Union since he was convinced that the House "as at present constituted, faithfully represented the people of England, and accurately expressed their deliberate opinions and wishes." But the union with Scotland had proved that such expansion need not lead to disaster and, anyway, some sacrifices must be accepted to achieve the greater good. The good, however, would be undone if there were any question of coercing Ireland into acceptance; the Union, if it were to come about, must do so without "any other impulse than might derive from their free and unbiased judgment." The resolutions adopted by Parliament must "tend to appease rather than to influence" and "be a pledge of the justice and liberality of Great Britain." On this understanding he would have no hesitation in supporting them.

Addington was known to have had long consultations with John Foster, the Speaker of the Irish House, about the problems of the Union. Members were satisfied that he would support no measure likely to impair the status or the efficiency of the House of Commons. If he believed that a merger of the two Parliaments was both practicable and desirable then they, for the most part, were ready to take his word. The Pittite majority would probably in any case have heeded their master's voice, but Addington's speech did much to satisfy their consciences.

So far as Pitt himself was concerned, he would have preferred to hear a little less from Addington about the perfections of the existing House of Commons. He must also have regretted the caution of his friend's references to Catholic Emancipation. But on the whole he must have been well satisfied and, even on the last point, have seen little reason for worry. Pitt's optimism ranged habitually between the awe-inspiring and the fatuous; now he seems to have had little doubt that, after a year or two's successful Union, King and country alike would see the wisdom of removing the present restrictions on the Catholics. In so believing he showed a lack of understanding of George III astonishing in one who had for so long been his Prime Minister. He also grossly underestimated the tenacity with which Addington and others like him could cling to a principle once they had convinced themselves that it was right.

* * * * *

The two years following this debate saw Pitt once more fix all his hopes on the uncertain capacities of his continental allies. At first the second coalition was reasonably successful. The Austrians and Russians drove the French from most of Italy and turned the thoughts of Napoleon to the possibilities of a compromise peace. On the 25th of December, 1799, he approached King George III with the suggestion that negotiations should begin.

It is doubtful whether Napoleon would have been ready to agree to terms ensuring the minimum needs of British security. Certainly Pitt was justified in his conviction that the First Consul was looking for no more than a truce in which to regroup his forces. But if only to make clear to the rest of Europe that Britain was as anxious as France to explore every possibility of peace, it seemed desirable to return a forthcoming answer to Napoleon's overture. Ministers, however, gave more attention to the dangers of an armistice. "We have felt no difficulty in declining all negotiations *under the present circumstances*," wrote Pitt to Addington,[1] "and have drawn our answer as a sort of manifesto both for France and England, bringing forward the topics which seem most likely to promote the cause of royalty . . ." In fact, Grenville's terse refusal to negotiate was likely to promote nothing except the cause of Bonaparte. His recommendation that the French should restore the Bourbons invited, and duly got, the retort that, in choosing their own ruler, the French were following a most respectable English precedent.

Addington forwarded a copy of Pitt's letter to Hiley.[1] "I will acknowledge to *you* that the terms of the answer do not *entirely* meet my wishes. They are in some parts too caustic and opprobrious, and more appears to me to have been said than was necessary. There is a temper in it which takes from its dignity; and it has not quite enough of the character of moderation. The general tenor of it, or rather its purposed tendency, I must nevertheless say appears to me to be suited to the occasion, and I earnestly hope it will be well received, and produce a good effect both at home and abroad." Reluctantly Addington accepted Pitt's view that "under the present circumstances" it would be unwise to negotiate. But he did not conceal his belief that the circumstances were not likely to endure and that, in the end, we would be compelled at least to try to make peace with the French.

In part at least Pitt's reference to "present circumstances" must have referred to the successes of the Second Coalition and his ever sanguine assessment of the chances of final victory. Once more he was to be disappointed. By mid-1800 the Austrian army had been defeated at Marengo, by the end of the year the work had been completed at Hohenlinden. Pitt had committed his forces to minor forays against Brittany, Minorca, Ferrol and Quiberon Bay. By the time the scale of the disaster in Italy had been realised it was too late to do anything about it. Austria was forced into peace by the Treaty of Lunéville. Russia went over to the French and began to discuss with the Baltic powers a league of armed neutrality designed as a counter-weight to British sea-power. "Within and without the prospect lowers and it will not be owing to our own wisdom and exertions if it does not burst upon our heads," wrote Addington balefully.[2]

For Pitt the disasters without were not half so menacing as the famine and misery within, "for the evils and growing dangers of which I own I see no adequate remedy."[3] Exceptionally heavy rains at the start of the harvest wiped out the crops in large areas of England and damaged them everywhere. The price of wheat rose to more than 120 shillings a quarter and desperate measures of economy could do no more than alleviate the distress. There was rioting in some of the worst afflicted areas and discontent all over England.

Physically and mentally Pitt was near to breaking point. Years of overwork, a confined and unhealthy life, indulgence in alcohol on a scale which would have destroyed most normal constitutions and now the accumulated melancholies of the last few months, had combined to make it almost impossible for him to carry on. In the middle of October he proposed himself as a guest at Woodley where he could recuperate in seclusion yet without losing all contact with the world. "He wants rest and *consolation*," wrote Addington,[1] "and I trust he will find both here. The feelings towards him, not of myself, for of these I say nothing, but of others under this roof, are really not to be described."

Superficially the holiday was a success. After three weeks Pitt was calmer in mind and stronger in body. "Mr Pitt's health . . . is so well established," wrote his host jubilantly,[2] "as to render him fully equal to any exertions that may be required of him." But Addington's verdict reflected little credit on his father. Pitt was still a sick man: psychologically as well as physically ill-equipped to plunge back into his grindingly arduous London life. He slept badly, he tired quickly, he was often in pain and low in spirits, his almost superhuman self-confidence and force of will seemed to have deserted him. In public he insisted on his determination to carry on to final victory, yet within himself he must surely have wondered how much more he could endure.

Addington himself had no thought except that Pitt would continue as Prime Minister and he as Speaker. It was a relationship he had no wish to change. He had already refused the Secretaryship of State and, though he may secretly have cherished still loftier ambitions, his affection and admiration for his friend was far too great for him to wish to rise at Pitt's expense. If he had any serious thought of a change it lay in his own retirement to some less exacting office. Even this was no more than played with. "My own health is not good," he wrote in October,[3] "but so long as I have a tolerable portion of it remaining, and as long as the House of Commons continues to me that degree of support which they have ever shown me, I shall not think myself justified in quitting my present situation, whatever my private feelings and wishes may be." In his eyes at least Pitt's return to London meant that affairs could run again upon their normal course. Neither he nor any of his circle can have foreseen what lay ahead.

*   *   *   *   *

Yet Pitt's return from Woodley was the prelude to a political crisis as pointless and, in sum, as perplexing as any which has disturbed the course of British politics. The bare facts of what happened are in little doubt. Pitt convinced himself that the Union with Ireland must be followed by the grant of full civil rights to the Catholics. He failed to carry with him the King and a certain part of his Government and resigned rather than give up his point, recommending Addington as his successor. The King accepted both resignation and recommendation and Addington found himself translated unexpectedly from Speaker's Chair to Treasury. So much is clear; yet in the forces, conscious or unconscious, which impelled the various participants along their courses and in the inexplicable mistakes in timing and misjudgments of character which stamped the whole affair, there lies a residue of mystery which no historian can hope entirely to resolve.

It is beyond dispute that Pitt, though he might never specifically have promised the Irish Catholics that emancipation would follow Union, still felt morally bound to do all he could to help bring it about. Even if he himself had been prudently vague he knew that Castlereagh had gone much further to raise Catholic hopes[1] and he could not feel that Castlereagh had been acting other than on his behalf. Nor did Pitt delude himself into imagining that Union had a chance of settling the ills of Ireland unless it were swiftly followed by a substantial measure of emancipation. There were thus excellent reasons, in conscience and in common sense, why Pitt should continue to press for Catholic Emancipation and try to educate its opponents into a proper understanding of the issue.

But it is much harder to understand why Pitt, normally so prudent in his internal policies, should have found it necessary to force the issue at a time when the King, the bulk of the ruling party and several members of the Cabinet viewed such a proposal at the best with doubt and more commonly with inveterate dislike. "Is such an enterprise necessary?" Auckland asked Pitt.[2]

'Is it expedient? *Cui bono?* With what view? To what end? Will it convert disaffection to loyalty? . . . Is it consistent with good faith to push forward such a post-script to the Union? . . . I wish this letter to be shown to the Speaker," Auckland concluded. "I am sure it is not fit for any other eye; I do not know that it is fit for his." Addington, if he ever saw the letter, would have added his support to every one of Auckland's doubts.

Pitt must have known how heavily the opposition was massed against him. Left to himself he might never have brought the matter to a head. But second thoughts were ruled out by the activities of the Chancellor, Lord Loughborough. In the hope of eliminating divergencies among his own supporters before taking the hurdle of royal pig-headedness, Pitt had been conducting private discussions with a few trusted intimates. The trust was misplaced. Already, a few years before, Lord Loughborough had secretly advised the King that the repeal of the Test Act would violate his Coronation Oath "to maintain to the utmost of his power . . . the Protestant reformed religion established by law."[1] Now in September, 1801, without a word of warning to the Prime Minister, he showed the King the confidential letters which Pitt had written to him about the need for emancipation. It did not take the Lord Chancellor long to convince the King both that Pitt's ideas were dangerous folly and that he was being monstrously misused. By a few moments' mischief-making he transformed Pitt's quiet diplomacy into an explosive clash between Prime Minister and King.

It is difficult to find motives for Loughborough's actions which are not discreditable. However sincere his dislike of Catholic Emancipation, the way he went to work to check it can only be explained by malign delight in intrigue and possibly also a secret hope that he might replace Pitt as Prime Minister. In acting on the King's mind he seems to have had the help of Lord Auckland and of the Archbishop of Canterbury, Dr. Moore.[2] But whether he laboured alone or in partnership, Pitt was to discover to his cost that the work had been well done.

Meanwhile the Prime Minister was finding it increasingly hard to keep his Cabinet united. Lord Loughborough's opposition was well known, Lord Westmorland and the Duke of Portland seemed to be swinging against the Catholics, even Pitt's own brother Chatham kept discreetly away from the discussions.[3] Only

Grenville, Dundas and Windham were whole-heartedly behind their leader.[1] But Pitt was now unable to retreat. Loughborough's treachery and George III's impatience combined to force the affair on the attention of political England. At a levee on 28th January the King accosted Dundas and broadcast his indignation to all who stood by: "The most Jacobinical thing I ever heard of! I shall reckon any man my personal enemy who proposes any such measure."[2] Dundas mildly replied: "Your Majesty will find among those who are friendly to that measure some whom you never supposed to be your enemies."

So far Addington had lain low. He disapproved of Pitt's proposals, argued against them when he could, but conceived that it would not be proper for the Speaker to become more publicly involved. Now, however, he was to be drawn in willy nilly. After a sleepless night, "very bilious and unwell," the King wrote to his Speaker:[3]

The Speaker of the House of Commons is, I trust, so sensible of the high regard I have for the uprightness of his private character, as well as of his ability and temper in the fulfilling of his public trust, that he will not be surprised at my desire of communicating to him the very strong apprehension I conceive, that the most mischievous measure is in contemplation . . . this is no less than the placing the Roman Catholics of the kingdom in an equal state of right to sit in both houses of parliament, and hold offices of trust and emolument, with those of the Established Church. It is suggested by those best informed that Mr. Pitt favours this opinion. That Lord Grenville and Mr. Dundas do, I have the fullest proof; they have intimated as much to me, who have certainly not disguised to them my abhorrence of the idea. . . .

I should be taking up the Speaker's time very uselessly if I said more, as I know we think alike on this great subject. I wish he would, from himself, open Mr. Pitt's eyes on the danger arising from the agitating this improper question, which may prevent his ever speaking to me on a subject on which I can scarcely keep my temper. . . .

I have adopted this method of conveying my sentiments to the Speaker, as I thought he would not choose to be summoned by me when he could not have assigned the reason of it; but should this ill-judged measure still come forward, I shall then, from the notoriety of the case, think myself justified in setting all etiquettes aside, and desiring the Speaker to come here.

Much though Addington disliked the task which the King had laid upon him, he saw it as his duty to accept. He posted off to Pitt and, judging by a note sent him by the King two days later,[1] reported that he had induced the Prime Minister to change his mind. Possibly he deluded himself, possibly Pitt was half won over but was later over-persuaded by his friends: at all events the Prime Minister proved implacable. On 3rd February, 1801, he wrote to the King to declare that:[2] ". . . the final decision which Your Majesty has formed on the great subject in question . . . and his own unalterable sense of the line which public duty requires from him, must make him consider the moment as now arrived when, on the principles which he has already explained, it must be his first wish to be released as soon as possible from his present situation."

George III's intentions were habitually swathed within such a cocoon of obscurity and double thinking, designed as much to deceive himself as to perplex his subjects, that it is hard ever to be sure what he really meant. But it seems at least possible that by this time he had reconciled himself to Pitt's departure and, indeed, was looking forward with some cheerfulness to a more docile Minister. He sent for Addington with remarkable alacrity and pressed him to form an administration. Addington's first reaction was to say, apparently with complete sincerity, that he would much rather not. He still hoped that Pitt could be induced to shelve the issue of emancipation and, even if Pitt would not, doubted whether he was the man to take his place. "Lay your hand upon your heart," asked the King grandiloquently, "and ask yourself where I am to turn for support if *you* do not stand by me."[3]

Addington for the moment would go no further than promise to visit Pitt and once more try to persuade him to let emancipation rest. He found his friend obdurate and insistent that Addington should succeed him as Prime Minister. "I see nothing but ruin, Addington, if you hesitate."[4] It would indeed have been difficult to find an alternative acceptable at once to the King, Pitt and the country. Some people favoured the candidature of the Duke of

Portland with Addington as Secretary for the Home and War Departments.[1] But neither on the grounds of health nor of capacity was Rosebery's "dull, dumb Duke" a tolerable successor to William Pitt. Addington still hesitated a little longer but his mind must already have been made up. On 5th February he wrote to "express his humble acquiescence in that part of your Majesty's determination which relates immediately to himself." On 10th February, when he called on the King, George III embraced him as he entered, saying, "My dear Addington, you have saved your country."[2] Addington was torn by regrets for the past and doubts about the future. But for so ardent a royalist it must still have been an intoxicating climax to what had been the most exacting fortnight of his life.

*   *   *   *   *

It is doubtful if any professional politician has existed who could have said with complete sincerity that he had no wish to be Prime Minister. Certainly Addington was no exception. But his joy at his promotion was by no means without qualification, indeed the qualifications at times seemed so many and so all pervasive that the joy was forgotten altogether. His sorrow that it was Pitt whom he had supplanted, fears lest few politicians of consequence would be ready to join him, doubts how the difficulties with which Britain was faced might best be overcome, regrets for the security and dignity of the Speaker's Chair: all these combined to make him wonder whether he had decided rightly for England or for himself. Charlotte Bragge's comments on her brother's state of mind read more as if some disaster had struck the family than Addington just acceded to the highest office in the land.[3]

"You may guess how he feels both the arduousness of the undertaking and the sacrifice of private comfort: but what is for the best in the present crisis can be the only consideration. . . . His own struggle is over, and he seems calm and collected and to look forward with confidence, though not without anxiety. The great thing is to keep up his spirits, to carry him through what he feels it his duty to undertake. . . . Mrs. Addington is, he says, a good deal agitated, but on the whole takes it better perhaps than could have been expected."

"Sir, I cannot do as others are doing, give you joy, for I pity you sincerely," said Sir John Anderson after Addington had presided over the House of Commons for the last time. The Speaker's sombre reply was that "It was too late now to look back; he must now go forward, and surmount the difficulties before him."[1]

Addington's greatest regret lay in his resignation of the Chair. In that work he had been successful, he had been popular, he had been admired and respected. Now he was descending from his lofty post above the conflict to a battlefield in which he could expect no quarter from his opponents and, too often, little sympathy from his so-called supporters. His fate can hardly have been clear to him as he peered apprehensively into the future but he would have been less than human and far less than Addington if he had not rejoiced in the warmth of his present friendships and quavered at the prospect of his potential foes. His farewell to the House of Commons as their Speaker rang true in his affirmation that[2] "to enjoy your good opinion was my pride and comfort during my continuance in your service; to experience such a proof of it as has been afforded me upon the present occasion is indeed the highest honour and the most gratifying reward . . . To the House itself I owe every obligation which can bind the duty, veneration and attachment of an individual to the first public body in the world."

Addington would never have undertaken his new task if he had not been convinced that Pitt wished it and intended to give him his full support. Pitt, on his side, made it unequivocally clear to all his followers that he supported Addington's efforts to form a government and wished them to do the same. In a letter which he wrote to his brother urging him to retain his place, he concluded:[3] "I have long been persuaded that, whenever he [the King] might have occasion to do so, the Speaker would be the person to whom he would resort. It has proved so in the present instance, and I am most happy to find that the Speaker feels it his duty, in which I have most strongly and decidedly encouraged him, not to decline the task. I certainly need not add what my intentions are out of office, those of the most uniform and diligent support. . . ."

Not all Pitt's friends were so enthusiastic. Rose and Canning in particular, both unbalanced in their affection for Pitt and resolutely determined to read the worst into any action which threatened the position of their idol, suspected Addington of every kind of treachery. They believed, or affected to believe, that Addington had chosen gleefully "to catch at the situation, without regard to his friends."[1] They hinted that Addington had so abused his position as to stiffen the King's resistance to Catholic Emancipation and to make more difficult any reconciliation between George III and his headstrong Minister.

Canning asked Pitt outright whether Addington had not unfairly grasped at office. "To this question," recorded Lord Malmesbury,[2] "Pitt without hesitation, and in the most unqualified manner, replied, that it was impossible to have behaved with more confidence, more openness, more sincerity, than Addington had done, from the first moment to this; and that the manner in which he had conducted himself, added to his long friendship for him, had raised him higher than ever in his good opinion." In the face of this and his other investigations Canning admitted:[3] "I have no pretensions to maintain my belief . . ."

Pitt promised Addington the most complete support which it would be in his power to give. The two men were already well used to mutual consultation. Neither saw any reason why the practice should not be continued. At the first levee after Addington's appointment the King drew Pitt and his new Prime Minister into a window recess and said: "If we three do but keep together all will do well."[4] He was voicing the thoughts and hopes of all three men.

*　　*　　*　　*　　*

Before Addington could begin to construct his government he had to choose a Speaker to fill his place. Rose[5] states that his first choice was his brother-in-law Charles Bragge but that the King objected. The story seems unlikely; at all events the idea, if ever mooted, was quickly dropped and the offer made to the Attorney-General, Sir John Mitford. Mitford's response was a disturbing presage of events to come. An old friend and schoolfellow of Addington, looked on by most people as one of the new Prime Minister's closest allies and offered a position of independence and dignity, it might have been expected that he would accept with alacrity. Instead, Mitford temporised. He wrote to Pitt to ask his advice.[6] "I feel, upon reflection, a thorough conviction that the administration now forming cannot last. I also

96

feel that if the country remains in its present state, imperious necessity will compel you again to take the lead. I therefore consider you as materially interested . . ."

This nervous curtsy to what was felt to be the real source of power was to be the reaction of many of Addington's future Ministers. So long as Pitt loomed in the background there could be no confidence that Addington's government would last. Each man in turn took care to ingratiate himself with the sun which to-day had set but to-morrow would in all probability rise again. Their caution boded ill for the stability and independence of Addington's administration.

It had been Addington's hope that he would inherit from Pitt the greater part of the previous government. The hope was disappointed. Broadly speaking, members of the late government refused to serve under Addington for two reasons; because they were politically too far committed to Catholic emancipation or because they were emotionally too far committed to William Pitt. The former were by far the more important. Dundas, Spencer, Grenville, Windham had provided the real weight of Pitt's government, the men who had done the work, made the decisions and waged the war. "When the crew of a vessel was preparing for action," remarked Sheridan in derisive comment,[1] "it was usual to clear the decks by throwing overboard the lumber, but he had never heard of such a manœuvre as that of throwing their great guns overboard." Indeed any government deprived of Pitt and this group of Ministers must have worn a singularly denuded and vulnerable air.

The second group, the partisans of Pitt, made up in enthusiasm for what they lacked in stature. Canning, Rose, Long, Lord Granville Leveson-Gower were fanatical devotees, their prime political aim being the retention of Pitt in power. Canning in particular was governed by an obsessive, almost amatory dedication to what he conceived to be the interests of his master. Indeed, his piques, his jealousies, his extravagant declarations of loyalty and equally extravagant recriminations when he felt he was not properly appreciated, remind one more often of an exacting mistress and her lover than of a young politician and his party chief. Canning appealed to Pitt for instructions as to whether or not he should stay in office, then, when they were given, ignored them. Having disobeyed his master, he bewailed the fact that Pitt did not approve his conduct. "It is not at all good fun going out of office . . ." he wrote wryly,[1] "to have a Mr Wollup or Lord Glenbubby come into all my compots instead of me. I never liked anything less, but I think I should have liked myself less, if I could have allowed myself to be prevailed upon by Pitt's arguments or entreaties to let him transfer me to his successor."

Pitt might profess his disapproval but he can hardly have failed to be secretly pleased at this quixotic loyalty. He would not applaud Canning's resignation but nor could he bring himself whole-heartedly to condemn it, any more than he could manage to look more than mildly reproachful when Rose remarked that, for his part, he would as soon consent to the prostitution of his daughter as remain in office.[2] Their hostility proved unrelenting. Even after Canning had accepted that Addington had played fair with Pitt he could not forgive him for being in the latter's place and remained the centre of a rancorous group of dissidents until the eventual fall of the administration.

Addington did his best to part on good terms with all those who wished to leave the Government. Pitt asked him to be kind to Canning but Canning would accept no kindnesses. He tried to placate the Grenvilles by offering to send Lord Grenville's younger brother Tom, to Moscow as Ambassador,[3] made it clear to Dundas that a peerage was his when he wanted it and asked Rose to become a Privy Councillor.[4] But the Grenvilles rejected the offering, Dundas was not yet ready to take to the Lords and Rose said curtly that he had no intention of accepting favours from anyone except Pitt himself. Addington was left uneasily conscious that the best he could hope for from most of Pitt's former colleagues was armed and vigilant neutrality.

But even this embarrassing shortage of material could not induce Addington to look kindly on Lord Loughborough. The Lord Chancellor showed no reluctance to co-operate with Addington, indeed he made it clear that he was happy, even fully determined to remain in office. Abbot told Addington that he must oust the Cardinal de Retz from his Cabinet or he would prove an insidious foe[5] and Addington had seen enough of Loughborough's talents to know that the warning was justified. For a time he considered shifting the former Chancellor to a less responsible position as President of the Council but in the end decided that there was no post in which so malevolent a mischief-maker could be trusted. When Loughborough learned what was envisaged he wrote in dismay to the King urging that Pitt should after all be retained in office.[1] This *démarche* earned him nothing though the courtesies were observed and two months later his dismissal was sweetened by the grant of an earldom.

Lord Loughborough did not so much take his loss of office hardly as pretend it had not happened. When the new Cabinet met, the former Chancellor, to the general surprise, was among the first to arrive. It was assumed that this was merely a somewhat eccentric farewell gesture but, at the next meeting, there he was again. In the end Addington had to make it exceedingly plain that there was no place for him at the council table[2] and even then the Earl of Rosslyn, as Loughborough had become, benevolently assured the Prime Minister that his experience and wisdom would always be at the Government's disposal.

The rump of Pitt's administration was not a satisfactory basis for a Ministry. The Duke of Portland would lend an aura of dignity and probity to any government but little in the way of hard work could be expected from this prematurely crumbling memento of what had once been a statesman of some competence. Westmorland was a hack. Chatham had his value since his presence at least testified to Pitt's support but for the work of government he too was a doubtful asset. Eldon once described him as the ablest man he ever knew in Cabinet[3] but his nickname of "the late Lord Chatham," earned by consistent unpunctuality, reflected better the general view. At least, however, he felt some confidence in his new leader. "If your part is irrevocably taken," he wrote to his brother, "the King could not have acted more wisely than in having recourse to the Speaker."[4]

Such was the not very distinguished core around which a government had to be built. It was obviously not going to be possible for Addington to be unduly selective or to insist on adherence to any rigid code of conduct. On Catholic Emancipation he asked for no pledges nor even any statement of position, "it was enough to be of opinion that now was not the time, nor these the circumstances for entering upon any such change."[5] Apart from this he claimed that he would pay attention to no factors save character, talents and their being his own personal friends.[6]

But personal friends seemed suddenly few and far between, and constant and energetic assistance from Pitt and the King was needed to assemble a government. A typical case was that of Pelham. Several posts were proffered him, culminating in the Home Office. Few statesmen can ever have prized more highly the fruits of office and his natural reaction would certainly have been to hesitate only until it was clear that no better offer was forthcoming. But the Duchess of Devonshire deplored Pitt's idea of "an administration that sets out with all the talents of the opposition on one side and the talents of his administration at best neutral. . . . You are too precious to act under so ridiculous a Chancellor of the Exchequer."[1] Other smart friends took the same line, leaving Pelham torn between avarice and fear of the disgrace that might follow membership of such a gallimaufry. The King came to his rescue, urging him strongly to join the Government. Gratefully Pelham did as he was told; explaining to all who expressed surprise that neither the position nor the salary meant anything to him but that he had felt bound to sacrifice himself in deference to the royal wishes.

Lord Eldon, the new Chancellor, was another who ostentatiously took office at the behest of the King and with the approval of Pitt. Though a close friend of Addington, he never hesitated to rub in the fact that "with respect to the Chancellorship . . . I was indebted for that office to the King himself, and not, as some supposed, to Mr Addington . . ."[2] Addington was later to discover to his cost that loyalty to the King carried with it, in the eyes of the Lord Chancellor, complete liberty to betray the interests of the Prime Minister.

Of the new appointments the most important was Hawkesbury as Foreign Secretary, the eldest son of Charles Jenkinson, 1st Earl of Liverpool, George III's favourite contact man and political fixer. Hawkesbury was sensible, honourable and conscientious, a good orator from a carefully prepared brief and competent as a debater. But his lanky figure, shambling walk and melancholy air "as if he had been on the rack three times and saw the wheel preparing for a fourth,"[3] made him a figure of fun in spite of all his virtues. His expression habitually was one of perplexed arrogance, as if he knew he had something to be proud of but could not quite remember what. He was a most valuable member of Addington's administration but as short of glamour as any other of his colleagues.

Lord St. Vincent, as tough mentally as he was physically, obstinate, aggressive and bigoted, was a strange choice as First Lord of the Admiralty. To bring a popular hero into a weak Cabinet is a traditional form of window-dressing but St. Vincent's popularity with the mob was likely to be more than offset by the irritation he provoked among almost all those who dealt with him officially. He himself had doubts about the wisdom of the appointment: "I have known many a good Admiral make a wretched First Lord."[1] Though his tenure of the Admiralty had its champions, many people would say that his doubts were justified. Unlike most Ministers, who owed allegiance to Pitt, St. Vincent turned to Fox and Lord Lansdowne. The latter approved his acceptance but advised him to limit his participation strictly to naval matters; a counsel to which St. Vincent dutifully adhered.[2]

Amidst so much equivocation it is agreeable to find one Minister at least who accepted office whole-heartedly and with gratitude. Edward Law, later Lord Ellenborough, was a former Whig. He was one of the most lucid and intellectually formidable advocates of the age. Addington, possibly discouraged by his previous rebuffs, seems to have approached him with diffidence. In offering him office as Attorney-General he assured him that he did not expect an immediate answer but would be glad to have one in two days. "Sir," replied Law, "when such an offer is made to me, and communicated in such terms, I should think myself disgraced if I took two days, two hours, or two minutes to deliberate upon it; I am yours, and let the storm blow from what quarter of the hemisphere it may, you shall always find me at your side."[3] He was as good as his word. Often uncouth, always arrogant and intolerant, he stuck to Addington with a loyalty and personal affection which never wavered through years of opposition and unpopularity.

The remaining important posts were filled by the amiable if exigent Hobart as Secretary of State for War, the comatose Lewisham as President of the India Board and Spencer Perceval, soon to make his reputation as one of the best debaters in the Government, as Solicitor General. Lord Hardwicke was Lord Lieutenant of Ireland and his younger brother Charles Yorke, Secretary at War.

Finally came the little band of the faithful; the intimate friends and relations. Brother-in-law Bragge, after a short delay, got the plum; Treasurer of the Navy with £4,000 a year and a house. There were a few offensive murmurs about the advantages of marrying a Princess of the Blood,[1] but in general the appointment was considered reasonable. Vansittart and Hiley Addington were enlisted as Secretaries of the Treasury, Nathaniel Bond as Lord of the Treasury, William Gartshore and another relation, James Adams, as Commissioners of the Admiralty.

It would be untrue to say that any of these appointments were clearly unjustified. There was not such a superfluity of talent that good men were being left outside to make room for Addington's cronies. Bragge and Vansittart were sensible and hardworking while Hiley Addington could on occasion be as astute and energetic as any member of the Government. Nor was it unusual for a Prime Minister to top up his Government with friends and relations; Addington indeed was modest compared with some of his predecessors. But while the hangers-on and poor relations of a North or a Rockingham were likely to be impecunious members of the greater families, Addington's retainers were for the most part as bourgeois as their leader. The minor aristocrat fitted unobtrusively into the traditional pattern of English government, the Bragges and Adams of Addington's circle stood out conspicuously by their very lack of social distinction.

Given all the difficulties, Addington's final Government was by no means unsatisfactory. In Portland, Perceval and Hawkesbury it contained three future Prime Ministers; its law officers were a decided improvement on Pitt's; in administrative ability it was little worse. Its most serious lack was in debating skill. There was not one outstanding parliamentarian in the Government. Hawkesbury was competent and Perceval rapidly improving but there was no one of talent approaching that of Pitt, Fox, Grey, Sheridan, Tierney, Windham or Canning. For the moment most of the big guns were silent or aligned with Government but Addington could never forget their presence or doubt for a moment that if they were to turn their fire on him he would be ill-equipped to defend himself. Addington can hardly be blamed for failing to pick better men, the talent simply was not open to be recruited, but the weakness of the Government in debate was to prove one of his severest handicaps.

In short, the Government was business-like but dull. It appealed therefore to the business-like but dull and was condemned or ridiculed by the brilliant, the turbulent and the merely smart. "The Dumplin' Ministry," said Lady Malmesbury. "The Goose Administration," suggested Canning. "Wretched, pusillanimous, toad-eating . . ." But it was not only sniggers and fishwife abuse. The Opposition objected on the grounds that the new Government would reproduce Pitt's policy without the talents of its predecessors or the solitary grace of an enlightened attitude towards the Catholics.[1] Wellesley asked dubiously:[2] "You know my great value for Addington; from him I should expect much good service in any station; but is he quite equal to that of Commander in Chief?" Even Vansittart, who though a trimmer by nature was still a sound Addingtonian and a member of the Government, remarked that he would willingly go to Botany Bay to bring the former Ministers back again.[3]

In fact Addington's support was substantial but the bulk of it lay among the inarticulate and the stolid. Hookham Frere's story of the Tory Member who thanked God for a Government without one of these damned men of genius in it is probably apocryphal but it does epitomise a widespread feeling in the country that the new Ministers were honest and reliable and could safely be trusted to look to their business without exhibitionist displays or unsettling projects for reform. From the start Addington's Ministry was close to the heart of the English country gentleman. It goes without saying that it was even more precious to the King who considered it as his own creation. "The King cannot find words," he wrote to Addington on 15th March when the arrangements were complete,[4] "sufficiently expressive of His Majesty's cordial approbation of the whole arrangements which his own Chancellor of the Exchequer has wisely, and his Majesty chooses to add, most correctly recommended."

"The Speaker," wrote Wilberforce[5] a few days after Addington's appointment had become public, "we know, is a man of talents and integrity, and of generous feelings, but not qualified for such rough and rude work as he may have to encounter, but if peace can be made, the Government may last." If a consensus had to be made from the opinions of those that were neither blind enemies nor partisans of the new régime, it would be close to this. The Government was frail and neither it nor its leader were likely to relish the abuse and ridicule which would be their lot. But they would be good enough for the run of the mill work of governing the country. Let them not be tested too high, above all let the strains of war be spared them, and there was no reason why they should not run on happily for many years.

*　●　*　*　*

While Addington was still toiling over his Ministry the King fell ill with a feverish cold. From this he quickly degenerated into long periods of torpor mingled with bouts of extravagant frenzy. It was clear that no constitutional decisions could be expected from him until he was much improved. Pitt and Addington were caught in the midst of their laboured transition, like unskilful players of grandmother's footsteps frozen in an ungainly posture and painfully trying not to lose their balance. One was *de jure* Prime Minister, the other *de facto*; their Ministers had no idea whether they were in or out of office; the Prince of Wales confounded confusion by sending first for one man and then the other and intriguing with the Whigs behind the backs of both. Only the closest co-operation between Pitt and Addington made any sort of administration possible: luckily this was forthcoming and England muddled through with little harm.

Pitt probably suffered most from the confusion. The King emerged from the darkness of his insanity into a frail but lucid state of mind. From his sick-bed he sent Pitt a message[1] to say that he was now quite recovered; "but what has *he* not to answer for who is the cause of my having been ill at all?" The idea that he had been to blame for the King's illness evidently disturbed Pitt deeply; his response was extravagantly generous. In a message to the King sent through the royal doctor he pledged himself never to raise the issue of Catholic Emancipation during the lifetime of George III, whether in or out of office. The King was naturally delighted. ". . . after saying the kindest things of you," reported Dr. Willis,[2] "he exclaimed 'now my mind will be at ease'."

It is difficult not to see some levity in Pitt's abandoning in March a principle which, in February, he had broken up the Government to preserve. His "unalterable sense of the line which

104

public duty requires of him" was now altered to suit the whim of an invalid who, at the best, was overwrought. However deep his sympathy for the King, it is hard to believe that he felt much real responsibility for this latest bout of madness.

Stanhope and others of Pitt's biographers find it natural and proper that he should so swiftly have dropped his principles so as "to soothe his old master's shattered mind."[1] They refute with indignation any suggestion that he could have had in mind the smoothing of his own path back to office. Probably they were right; Pitt was not the man to put his career ahead of his honour or the interests of his country. It is easier to see him acting as he did in a spirit of chivalrous pity than out of deliberate calculation. But one may still feel some sympathy with Lecky's acrid verdict, that Pitt "would have deserved more credit for his delicacy if it had not coincided so perfectly with his interest, and if it had not involved him in what may be not unfairly called a gross breach of faith with the Catholics."

As soon as the news of his renunciation got around Pitt's friends were quick to urge that this removed all bar to his return to office. Dundas, Pelham and Camden insisted that the needs of the country must come first; disingenuously Canning dismissed any idea that this would be unfair to Addington:[2]

Believing that he spoke the sentiments of his heart when he averred . . . that his first wish and object was that you should return to the situation which he held, as it were, in trust for you—it would be in the highest degree unjust and uncharitable if I were not to believe that he is the first man to hail the opportunity which he must . . . see is now presented for the accomplishment of a wish in which all mankind joins with him.

Pitt found these counsels tempting. Even his few weeks out of office had taught him how much he valued power. But he could not bring himself to suggest overtly that he should return. "He was anxious to come in," wrote Malmesbury,[3] "but his *pride* led him to wish that it should be by entreaty, not by any voluntary forward movement of his." Since Addington showed no signs of making a move, Pitt's friends could make little progress. Eventually Lord Camden was deputed to explain to Addington that he should now hand back to his friend the place which he had been privileged to keep warm for him over the last few weeks.

Camden's action did not have Pitt's specific authority but none of the devoted Pittites doubted that the master would approve.

For Addington the *démarche* was a singular embarrassment. He knew that, neither legally nor morally, was he under any obligation to vacate his place. He had besought Pitt to keep the position for himself. He had resisted his own substitution with a vigour which would have been shown by few. He had only yielded and given up his own secure and honourable place at the pressing request of Pitt. He did so because he had been convinced that the issue of Catholic Emancipation would stand between Pitt and office for the foreseeable future. This conviction Pitt had done all he could to foster. Now he was told that Pitt had changed his mind, that Catholic Emancipation was not after all of the first importance and that he should therefore vacate his position without being given any chance to prove himself and without any other situation being promised him.

But though Addington could convince himself that he would be justified in rejecting Camden's suggestion, he could not escape the belief that most of his own Ministers, let alone those who had resigned, would prefer to have Pitt back. Nor could he doubt that the country at large, if it knew all the facts, would agree that he had been hardly done by but would still recall its former leader. He knew that he himself had spoken loosely to many people about his wish to see Pitt restored to office. If Pitt or the King had suggested to him that he should now act accordingly there can be little doubt that he would have made the sacrifice. But, in the last resort, he did not see why he should volunteer to do so at the prompting of any secondary figure.

Addington therefore shuffled almost as much as Pitt; did not refuse to resign but feared what effect this further disturbance might have on the mind of the King; expressed his eagerness to return to family life but doubted whether Pitt's resumption of office would be considered altogether honourable. Camden reported to Pitt that Addington was showing unexpected reluctance. The news seems to have brought home to Pitt the enormity of what was being asked of his friend. He now firmly declared that[1] "he thought the project utterly improper, and that he would hold no intercourse with those who would not concur in a strenuous support of the New Administration; nor should he think those persons friends to himself who croaked about their instability." Discouraged, the intriguers temporarily reconciled themselves to an Addingtonian Government.

* * * * *

Such were the circumstances in which Addington replaced Pitt as Prime Minister. "The motives which I and my colleagues have assigned for our resignation, drawn from the Popery question, no historian will believe,"[1] remarked Dundas. Certainly his contemporaries found it hard to swallow. "A mystery," cried Lord Auckland,[2] "a notorious juggle," was Fox's view.[3] Some people held that Pitt's resignation had been a put-up job and that he planned to step back into office after a purely formal delay; as in the Arabian Nights when "a man puts himself in a rage with his wife and divorces her; then wants her again; but according to the Asiatic laws she must marry another man and be divorced from him before she can take her first husband. So England is the *Bride* and Addington the *Hullah*." "I trust he will play Pitt the same trick that one gentleman did in the book and refuse to give up the lady," concluded Lady Malmesbury.[4]

A variety of more or less discreditable explanations were dreamt up. Lord Guildford knew "from unquestionable authority" that Pitt had recently been mad.[5] Canning believed that Dundas had forced the issue "not that he cared three brass farthings about the Catholic question—but he had for a long time been weary of his situation . . ."[6] Pelham was quoted as saying that Pitt's resignation was the only way by which he could evict the intractable pro-war party from his Cabinet.[7] St. Vincent considered that Pitt's Cabinet was split and that its leader might anyway soon have been ousted.

There was little of substance in this welter of rumour. The evidence of all those most closely connected with the negotiations leaves little doubt that Catholic Emancipation was the substantial reason for, as well as the immediate cause of the withdrawal of Pitt from office. It was Addington himself who told Croker that "the Catholic question was the real, and he believed, sole cause of Pitt's resignation."[8] Addington was by then very old, anxious no doubt not to disinter forgotten scandals, but so categoric an assurance from a man who had little reason to shield Pitt's memory must carry much conviction.

But though accepting that it was the most substantial, one may still doubt whether the Catholic question was indeed "the sole cause" of the change of Ministers. Other factors which made acceptable a temporary retreat from office must have occurred to Pitt as the crisis took shape around him. For one thing, he was a sick and tired man. It is not necessary to believe the wilder stories of his insanity to accept that, after his recent illness, he was still overwrought and conscious that his judgment had lost its clarity. His always volatile nature now veered erratically between extremes of optimism and despair. Even the doting Tomline referred to "the declining state of his health. His mind had lost part of its natural strength and energy."[1] Pitt knew that he was unfit for the continuing drudgery and mental tensions of office, he suspected that if he did not now take a rest he would never regain his powers. This may not alone have impelled him to his resignation but it must certainly have made the sacrifice seem more supportable.

And then Pitt had convinced himself that peace with France was necessary. He would have liked to broach it himself but knew that it would be difficult if not impossible to find terms acceptable at once to the French and to the more belligerent members of his Government. There is no need to argue from this that Pelham was right in seeing Pitt's resignation as a device for ridding himself of certain Ministers. But Pitt was the more ready to break up a Ministry which carried within itself the makings of a future conflict on an issue of first importance to his country.

In sum, even though Pitt himself may hardly have known it, there must have been some truth in Malmesbury's judgment that "Pitt went out because he felt himself incapable either of carrying on the war, or of making peace."[2] Military disasters, errors of strategy and the defection of his allies had left his European policies as barren as they had ever been. Near starvation, mutinies and discontent at home completed the pattern of a war which it seemed could never be won and yet might well be lost. In the past his own efforts to make peace had failed dismally. Now he knew that he would not even have a united Government behind him in any fresh essay. He was beginning to despair.

Perhaps even, in the black moments of early 1801, it may have seemed that any peace which might be achieved would be one likely to bring discredit on its negotiator. What could be more tempting than to hand over the whole sorry mess to someone else and leave him to do what he could with it? At the best a new hand might be able to contrive a tolerable settlement, at the worst the blame for England's ruin would at least be shared with another.

If such ignoble defeatism had possessed Pitt's mind it would not have lasted long. Apart from anything else he was congenitally incapable of looking at the black side of a situation for more than a little while. Nor was he the sort of man to shuffle out of his own responsibilities and cynically load them on a successor. But the factors that might have justified such logic in a lesser man were ever present in his mind, they contributed to the dejection and malaise which were stamping all his activities. They built up within him a distaste for office and all its burdens so strong that when the question of Catholic Emancipation offered him an honourable means of retreat he accepted it with an alacrity which two years earlier would have seemed inconceivable and two years later was to seem ill-judged. He did not consciously seek to saddle Addington with all the country's troubles but it was with profound relief that he accepted the change of horses in the middle of one of the most turbulent and treacherous streams which he had ever had to cross.

5

Addington, as Prime Minister of Great Britain in 1801, suffered from three handicaps which were always to cripple and in the end to destroy him. He was not an aristocrat, he was not an orator and he was not William Pitt.

"The hostility he met with from the upper classes of society," admitted Lord Holland, "proceeded, I fear, more from his want of birth than his other manifold deficiencies."[1] Want of birth was certainly no total bar to office in the early nineteenth century. Lord Eldon was the son, if not, as picturesque legend has it, of a coal-heaver, at least of a coal merchant in a small way of business. Canning, who sneered more maliciously than anyone at Addington's origins, had a failed wine-merchant for a father and an occasional actress for a mother. George Rose came from a family of non-juring clergymen. There was a surprising fluidity in the ruling classes and talented and industrious young men, with luck and an influential patron, could rise from something close to the labouring classes to positions of great dignity and power.

But to become Prime Minister was still felt to call for rather different qualifications. It was one thing for a blue-blooded Minister to sit at the same table as a middle-class or even plebeian colleague, it was far more to expect him to act with deference towards someone so patently his social inferior. ". . . though they will not certainly enter into faction and opposition," Dundas warned Pitt,[2] "all the aristocracy of the country at present cordially connected with Government, and part of it under you, feel a degradation in the first Minister of the country being selected from a person of the description of Mr. Addington. . . ." Overwhelming talents could have overcome this fine distaste; if Addington had been on heroic scale his origins might have been forgiven or tactfully forgotten. But nothing less than the extraordinary could conquer the instinctive caste-sense of the early nineteenth-century aristocrat.

On top of this there was the freakish fact that for a Prime Minister to be a doctor's son was considered not only socially distressing but irrepressibly comical as well. Much of the fault, or perhaps credit for this lay with Addington himself. Instead of prudently concealing his origins he took pride in his father's prowess and aired his own smattering of medical knowledge whenever an opportunity arose. His greatest coup, which he was wont to recall in infinite detail, came during the King's illness in 1801. Willis, the royal doctor, emerged in despair from the sick-room. "All is over; sleep cannot be obtained." "Hops!" said Addington, and a pillow of hops was brought. The King slept for an hour and a half and from that moment continued to mend.[1]

The wits of the age found exquisitely ridiculous Addington's pride in this achievement. The nickname of "The Doctor" was now coined. It stuck to him for the rest of his life and the constant ridicule which the concept provoked did much to destroy his reputation as a serious statesman. Some politicians can survive ridicule, others even thrive on it, but Addington lacked either the wit to reply in kind or the stoicism to suffer in silence. So "The Doctor," with flowing coat-tails and clyster-pipe sticking from his pocket, became more and more the cartoonists' butt and so the sniggers of fashionable society gradually rippled out throughout the country until the idea that the Prime Minister was at least faintly ridiculous became common currency at every level of society.

Addington's second handicap, his lack of oratory, seemed at first as if it might almost prove an asset. The House of Commons had had a great deal of fine oratory over the previous ten years and was not sure that it was much the better for it. "At the close of every brilliant display," wrote Sydney Smith of Pitt, "an expedition failed or a kingdom fell. God send us a stammerer!" Now the stammerer had come. What the county Member asked was that the Prime Minister should get on with the job and leave the speeches to whoever liked to make them. "To the eloquence of his predecessor, the present Premier makes no pretensions, and he is liked the better for it,"[2] wrote Southey, one of Addington's few literate admirers. "The English say they have paid quite enough for fine speeches; he tells them a plain story and gains credit by fair dealing . . ."

But though the taste for fine oratory might be temporarily sated the charm of Addington's laboured and stumbling sentences was equally quick to pass. The image of a Prime Minister, embarrassed and stammering, at the best pompous, at the worst unintelligible, urged on by a claque of almost equally inarticulate supporters, became accepted as the true portrait of life in the House of Commons. Here, too, Addington found himself the butt of the wits:

> When the faltering periods lag,
> Cheer, oh cheer him, brother Bragge!
> When his speeches hobble vilely,
> Or the House receives them drily,
> Cheer, oh cheer him, brother Hiley!

The public image was, of course, exaggerated. When left to himself and on a subject which he had mastered, Addington was a competent and at times even impressive speaker. But let him be interrupted, angered or steered on to unfamiliar ground and he quickly lost the thread of argument and became discursive and incoherent. "He is wonderfully improved in speaking," reported Isaac Corry after Addington had been in office for a few months,[1] "and . . . accounts for it by the agitation which all the circumstances of the session then caused, and his being at this time less embarrassed . . ." But agitation and embarrassment were to be Addington's common lot as Prime Minister and the moments few when he could expound his ideas to an appreciative House at his own time and in his own way.

Addington's third and most considerable handicap lay in the continued and conspicuous existence of William Pitt: not the Pitt of reality but a larger-than-life, an infallible Pitt, a dream Pitt incapable of acting save with the noblest motives and absolute felicity. The redeeming feature about John Brown was that, though his soul might go marching on, the body at least was safely mouldering in the grave. The unfortunate Addington had to compete with a rival who enjoyed all the privileges of a sanctified spot in the obituary column and yet was evidently and embarrassingly alive. Many of Pitt's followers were not sorry to have a rest from him; jealousy, the dissatisfaction of those who had been passed over, the hostility of those who thought themselves despised, the urge for a change; all these combined to make his temporary retirement not wholly unacceptable. But nce he was out of office all grudges were forgotten. In a matter of days Pitt became a hallowed figure of legend, the saviour of his ation, "the pilot who weathered the storm."

Measured against such a standard few Prime Ministers would ot have seemed a little shoddy. Certainly the prosaic Addington vas ill-equipped to compete. So long as things went smoothly nd prosperously he knew he could get along. But he also new that if his Government ran into trouble then immediately clamour would arise for the return of the master. At such a noment the temptation to reappear would be more than flesh and lood could resist. And Pitt, in spite of his premature enshrine- nent, was still unquestionably mortal.

If the great mass of Members, indeed of Englishmen, felt that 'itt was essential for national survival, how much stronger was ne feeling of the little group of his devoted intimates. "Pitt is ne object of my political idolatry," wrote Granville Leveson- Gower to his mother, Lady Stafford,[1] "and it is impossible to ave any opinion of any Government of which he is not head . ." Inspired by this faith, he and his associates strove to make npossible the task of anyone who presumed to occupy their ero's place. No weapons were too cruel to use, no holds barred 1 this almost sacred quest. To her son, Lady Stafford wrote egretfully[2] to report rumours that ". . . of all the violent parties nere is nothing to equal that under the influence of Mr. Canning, onsisting of Mrs. Canning, Mr. and Mrs. Ellis, Lord Granville .eveson-Gower, Lord Boringdon, Mr. Sturges (and some of esser note) who are more vehement in their abuse of Mr. Adding- on than can be imagined but by a virulent temper." Lady tafford went on to hope that the rumours were false. Her son's ehaviour, if not his answer, must soon have disillusioned her: ne rumours were exact, not least in the significance which they ttached to the influence of George Canning.

Few men can have done more than Canning to earn the distrust nd dislike of their contemporaries. Passionately loyal to Pitt, he ssumed that anyone who did not share his affections was an nveterate foe and that anyone who did was trying treacherously ● usurp his own favoured position. Passionately ambitious, he enigrated and attacked anyone who seemed capable of rivalling is talents. Vain to the point of megalomania, he treated with ontempt all those whom he considered less intelligent, eloquent

or witty than himself. Arrogant, insensitive, spiteful, there seem
no end to the pejorative adjectives which can fairly be applied t
this tempestuous character. Such condemnation is, of course
only half the picture. He was probably the most far-sighted an
generous-minded statesman of his age. His courage, personal c
political, was unlimited. He loved not wisely but too well;
trait which, though often disastrous, commands respect an
sympathy. His wit, intelligence and learning were almost a
impressive as his own conceit would have had the world believe
Pitt was enraged by him, bored by him, distressed by him, bu
with it all cared for him as he cared for no other man.

From Addington's point of view the real trouble about Cannin
was that he had never grown up. Slowly the walls of his play-pe
had expanded to include first Eton, then Oxford, finally th
House of Commons. In each, Canning had pursued the sam
end and adopted the same tactics. Addington, in Etonian phrase
was just another beak to be mobbed up, a beak moreover wh
had supplanted a popular hero and therefore deserved treatmer
even more harsh than usual. Canning dedicated himself to th
sport with all the cruelty and unscrupulousness of the vindictiv
schoolboy.

Even in the vendetta-rich world of politics it is difficult 1
explain and impossible to excuse the venom of his attacks. Car
ning had no reason to hate Addington; the two men, indeed
were no more than acquaintances and though Canning may hav
had little respect for the Speaker's accomplishments he had neve
had cause to complain of his fairness or his courtesy. His con
viction that Addington was not worthy to occupy Pitt's plac
could not alone justify his malice. In part his jealous affectio
for Pitt must have contributed. To Canning it was intolerab
that anyone should be as close as him to Pitt, let alone this sob
and prosaic figure. To personal jealousy was added the resen
ment that youth and brilliance must always feel at seeing medio
rity installed in high places. And to these was added an instinctiv
antipathy so profound that every word or mannerism of Addin
ton's seemed to provoke the uncontrollable irritation of his enem
In such a spirit, Canning devoted the full force of his considerab
talents to making Addington's Government a failure and his li
a torment.

His first objective was to persuade people not to join Addin ton's administration: when the Government was formed in spite of his efforts he devoted himself to hardening the hearts of its enemies and suborning its friends. He had tried to convince Pitt, when he could get him to listen, or anybody else when he could not, that Addington had unscrupulously grasped at office and had betrayed his friend. When forced from this position he maintained that Addington clung to office in clear defiance of the wishes and interests of the country. He denounced Addington's meanness, his cunning, his obtuseness (for inconsistency was never a bar to Canning in his finer flights of vilification), his obstinacy, his feebleness, and reverted continually to the total inadequacy of the new Prime Minister and his wretched supporters to rule the country.

But in Canning's hands ridicule was a more dangerous weapon than abuse and it was by ridicule that he did most to undermine Addington's authority. Few weapons could have proved more destructive or more hurtful to the victim. His speciality was doggerel, a trivial art form in the mastery of which he took great pride. Addington, therefore, was repeatedly pilloried in rhyme. It is hard to believe that anyone found the weaker efforts very amusing but it was fashionable to know Mr. Canning's latest and the word was passed eagerly from drawing-room to drawing-room. His most successful effort was the celebrated analogy between Pitt, Addington, London and Paddington. This had the merit of brevity, which was more than could be said for a tedious mock eclogue which began:

> My name's the Doctor. On the Berkshire hills
> My father purged his patients—a wise man,
> Whose constant care was to increase his store,
> And keep his eldest son—myself—at home
> But I had heard of politics, and longed
> To sit within the Commons and to get
> A place; and luck gave what my sire denied

and continued almost interminably in the same strain. As Canning's generous-hearted biographer found himself forced to comment, "Truly a marvellous production to come from the pen of one who was himself the son of an actress."[1] Some of the satires were a good deal better than this, in particular the cream of those which appeared in 1803 and 1804 in *The Oracle*. But good or bad they were widely acclaimed and little by little gave common currency to the concept of Addington as a weakling, a blockhead and a figure of fun.

After a few weeks of embittered skirmishing Pitt called his acolyte to order. He even induced Canning to send Addington a letter of "apology or explanation . . . fulsome in expression, but manifestly written under constraint . . ."[1] This letter, with its protestations of "personal esteem and good will" and promises of unqualified support,[2] was accepted at its face value by Addington, who was always delighted to put an end to any quarrel. It was too late to offer Canning any post in the new Ministry, which anyhow the latter had declared he would never accept, but he made unequivocally clear his readiness to be friends. This was not enough for George Ellis, another member of the little gang, who wrote splenetically[3] of the vile lies which Addington and his friends were spreading about Canning and praised the latter's forbearance; "would not such meekness soften any heart but that hard heart of the son of a mad doctor become Prime Minister of a great country?"

The quarrel may not have been entirely one-sided. Even if Addington himself had given no provocation his brother Hiley and others of the entourage were certainly less innocent and did their best to answer Canning blow for blow. But no one studying the contemporary accounts can doubt that Addington was far more sinned against than sinning and that Canning's hostility was savage, unscrupulous and without reasonable grounds. Nor did Pitt's intervention mend matters for long. Within a few weeks Canning was professing his loathing and contempt of the Prime Minister as loquaciously as ever. For a while he checked the more public expression of his views but never did he relax the campaign of intrigue and slander by which he and his associates strove to undo the Government.

* * * * *

Addington was convinced that the most important service he could render his country was to make peace with France. In this view he was supported by the majority of thinking Englishmen. With the disappearance of Pitt's continental allies at the Treaty of Lunéville the war had degenerated into a miserable stalemate in which both sides suffered but neither could strike a lethal blow. Addington believed that England was coming worst out of the struggle. Certainly there was much in the state of the country to support his view. Subsidies to the continental powers had cost Britain dearly over the last few years and the gold reserves were low. Disastrous harvests had led to further expense for the import of grain and, even with this, bread was dear and hard to come by. The alliance of the Northern League with France threatened to make imports still more costly and difficult in future. The country was sick of war and national morale can rarely have been lower. From the west of England, where famine was a commonplace, General Simcoe reported that "the law of the country was totally overthrown,"[1] while Colonel Bastard bemoaned "the diabolical spirit of the times."[2] Ireland, too, was on the verge of another revolution. It seemed to Addington that, unless peace were made quickly, the alternative might have to be surrender.

In allowing his judgment to be formed by such gloomy images, Addington paid too little heed to Napoleon's own, very real difficulties. Conditions on the Continent were little if at all more comfortable than those in England and Napoleon, too, was under pressure to contrive a peace. If Addington had realised this it is possible that the negotiations might have been handled to greater advantage. But English intelligence was hardly good enough to provide an inkling of what was going on in Napoleon's empire, let alone in Napoleon's mind. From London the Continent presented an appearance of distressing solidity, certain to outlast this dispirited and undernourished island.

Addington further believed that a period of peace was essential if Britain's potential allies on the Continent were ever again to wage effective war against the French. It is often claimed against Addington that he wilfully abandoned Pitt's system of European coalitions and seemed positively to rejoice in the ensuing state of inglorious isolation. In fact he knew well that Napoleon could never be overcome except with the help of continental powers. But he also believed that it was useless to pour money into European countries without the will or means to use it and worse than useless to egg them on into a war which would inevitably lead to their own destruction. Austria, Russia, Prussia, must have a few years in which to rebuild their strength and their will to fight. The argument was open to counter, still more so two or three years later when the war had been resumed. But it was a tenable thesis; at least the basis of a policy rather than the futile drifting with which Addington is usually credited. Its success depended on the buying of time and for this time Addington believed that he could afford to pay dearly and still make a good bargain for England.

In his first speech as Prime Minister in the House of Commons[1] Addington stated categorically:

> that it was the determination of His Majesty's servants to take such steps as appeared to them best calculated for the restoration of peace; that no consideration, arising from the form of government in France would, on their part, obstruct negotiation; and that if there were a corresponding disposition on the part of the enemy, the grand object to which the efforts of government would be directed would, he trusted, be accomplished.

This statement was generally well received. Windham and the other irreconcilables smelt treason in the air, but the Whigs were delighted with such "becoming moderation"[2] and the county Members supported Addington to a man. *The Times* spoke for them all when it welcomed this "first open overture" and rejoiced that politeness and good manners had returned to the intercourse of statesmen.[3] Above all Pitt was whole-heartedly behind him. He did not urge Addington on, no urging was needed, but he made it known that he believed negotiations must take place and that he would support peace on any terms which did not imperil the vital interests of the country.

The knowledge that Pitt would underwrite his peace was of inestimable value to Addington. With the support of the great war-leader he could discount in advance the hostility of all those who would seek to decry him as a coward and a pacifist. He was left a free hand to make peace on terms which seemed to him just and reasonable; a far freer hand indeed than Pitt would have enjoyed without a violent refashioning of his Ministry.

Though their positions were now reversed the two men were as close friends as ever. In May Tierney criticised Pitt's administration and, in particular, reverted to the old canard that Pitt's resignation had been a put-up job; protesting, of course, that he could not bring himself to think so hardly of the former Ministers and attributing the rumours to certain unspecified "bad men."[4] Addington rose quickly to his friend's defence: "There were points upon which he differed from his right honourable friend [Mr. Pitt], for he gloried in calling him by that name, and he was sure he always should, but he was convinced it was owing to the measures adopted by that administration that the country was preserved from the imminent danger with which it was threatened: it was to them that the country was indebted for the security it now enjoyed." On Tierney's oblique accusation of some sort of connivance between Addington and Pitt, Addington commented in verse:

> Twixt Pitt and Addington *bad* men agree
> (So Tierney thinks) some juggle there must be.
> If this be so—Good Sir—pray tell me how
> This slanderous charge *you* chanced to disavow.

The rhyme is bad enough, though not much worse than some of Canning's. It gains a certain piquancy, however, from the fact that in only two years Tierney was to have become a staunch political ally and a member of Addington's Government.

*   *   *   *   *

Confident that Pitt and the country were behind him, Addington quickly followed up his conciliatory speech by rescinding Dundas's Order which had instructed the Royal Navy to arrest French fishermen on the grounds that they might otherwise be pressed into the French Navy. Few measures had more irritated the French and Addington's gesture in its turn led to the return to London of Monsieur Otto, a diplomat in theory charged with arranging for the exchange of prisoners but in practice given wide discretion by Napoleon to arrive at a peace settlement. Negotiations between Otto and Lord Hawkesbury were quickly begun and continued, behind a most successful screen of secrecy, through the summer and autumn of 1801.

Meanwhile, Addington's bargaining position was strengthened by events in Egypt and the Baltic: in March Abercromby destroyed the French army at Alexandria, in April Nelson did the same for the Danish fleet at Copenhagen. For the first of these operations Addington could claim little credit; Abercromby had sailed from Malta by the time that the new Government took office. With the second he had more to do. The plan was Pitt's and it may well be doubted whether Addington would ever have initiated anything so bold in design or ruthless in its indifference to international law. But he supported it to the full and did everything he could to help the force's preparation. Sir Hyde Parker, sixty-two years old and aged beyond his years, prudent to the point of timidity and dubious about the merits of the whole project, had already been given the command; otherwise, Addington said, he would have appointed Nelson. Addington's faith in Nelson was unexpected, indeed incongruous. It would be hard to find a sharper contrast than that between the two men; one staid, prudish, cautious in thought and deed, the other flamboyant, volatile and brilliantly daring. Distrust on the one hand, disdain on the other, would have seemed their most probable relationship. Affection and admiration were to be found instead. Addington believed without qualification in Nelson's talents as a sailor, Nelson equally in Addington's as a statesman. In neither case did their confidence weaken. When almost all England had turned on Addington, Nelson remained faithful, convinced that he was an excellent Prime Minister and that sooner or later he must return to power.

The object of the expedition, in a few words, was to break up the Northern League which was carrying its policy of malevolent neutrality almost to the verge of war. Addington was anxious to avoid an attack on Denmark unless no other recourse was left. He sent Vansittart to negotiate with the Danes and try to persuade them to quit the League. By the time Vansittart arrived, however, Prussian and French influence in Copenhagen was so strong that there was no hope of detaching Denmark from its allies. "Nothing remains but to strike a speedy and severe blow . . ."[1] he reported to Addington, and with Nelson there the blow was duly struck.

The latter's daring plan for a direct attack on the Russian fleet at Reval had been vetoed by the tentative Parker. This robbed the expedition of its main purpose. It is doubtful whether, without the coincidence of the death of the Emperor of Russia, the destruction of the Danish fleet alone would effectively have disrupted the Northern League. But whatever the merits or morality of the operation, its execution was impeccable. The story of Nelson clapping the telescope to his blind eye and ignoring the signal to retire is an essential feature in the education of every English schoolboy. Even though he may have been given some discretion to continue the battle if he wished, his decision to do so was still a most courageous one, putting his reputation and his career as well as his life at risk. After Nelson's return Addington congratulated him on his boldness in disregarding the orders of his superior. ". . . In the midst of it all," replied Nelson, "I depended upon you; for I knew that, happen what might, if I did my duty you would stand by me." Not surprisingly, this exchange was quickly added to Addington's repertoire of favourite anecdotes. In telling it he would always add that never in his life had he received a compliment which gave him greater pleasure.

A few weeks after the Copenhagen incident the question arose of what should be done with Danish ships taken during the period of embargo. Grenville wrote to express his strong view that they should not be given back to the Danes. Addington began his reply:[1] "I really cannot sufficiently express to your Lordship my sense of obligation for the unreserved manner in which you communicate to me opinions to which I attach the greatest value and importance . . ." He then proceeded to ignore Grenville's advice and to return the ships. Few letters could illustrate more vividly that an obsequious manner need not necessarily connote a servile mind. Addington would much rather have accepted Grenville's advice if he had felt able. If some compromise had been practicable he would certainly have sought it. Since there was none he was careful to wrap his decision around in swathes of flabby verbiage in the hope that it might pass unnoticed. But in the last resort he would stick to what he believed to be right and pay no heed to the protests of his opponents.

Napoleon's response to these reverses was to make ostentatious plans for the invasion of England. Probably his purpose was to frighten Addington into making peace but the danger was taken most seriously by the Government. "The country is prepared, and all upon the watch to receive his armies whenever they appear," wrote Huntingford[2] from the cathedral calm of Gloucester. His authority for the assurance was obscure. With the army scattered around the world, a mutinous Ireland and food shortages in almost every part of the country, England had rarely been worse placed to resist invasion.

As if Addington had not enough on his mind already, the Prince of Wales, as happened every so often, reverted to his grievance in having no high military command. Addington, because of "the kind and obliging interest I believe you so particularly take in whatever essentially relates to myself,"[1] was dragged in as intermediary. He does not seem to have taken his duty very seriously; it was nearly six weeks before he interceded with the King and, in reporting failure, he admitted:[2] "The conversation, from causes which it is unnecessary for me to state to Your Royal Highness, was unavoidably short, but on many accounts I should not have thought myself justified in attempting to protract it . . ." The Prince found Addington's handling of his affairs decidedly offhand. He made no secret of the fact that he was displeased and inclined to blame the Prime Minister almost as much as his own detested father. Fox had already imbued him with a low opinion of Addington, certainly this incident can have done nothing to repair it.

*   *   *   *   *

As the threat of invasion loomed and then dwindled the negotiations between Otto and Lord Hawkesbury went quietly on in London. Addington seems to have kept closely in touch with the day-to-day detail of the discussions. Canning indeed assumed that Addington was solely responsible and that Hawkesbury "merely . . . held the pen,"[3] but then Canning was convinced that the peace was a disastrous one and did not wish his favourite scapegoat to share the blame with anyone. Probably he was more right than wrong, however. For Addington, peace was the all-important object of his Ministry and it is not likely that he would have allowed domestic troubles to divert him far from the negotiations. Nor was Hawkesbury the man to resent his Prime Minister's interference in foreign affairs; on the contrary he argued well from a brief but liked that brief to be spelt out in detail, especially when the word of Addington was backed by the immense authority of Pitt.

At all events it was Addington who gave to the world the news that the preliminaries of peace had been signed. He did so in a series of letters to the more prominent figures in public life, praising the beauties of his peace and giving such details as the importance and probable reactions of the recipient seemed to justify. This burst of epistolary energy behind him he settled down to see what the country would have to say.

The terms of the peace were certainly not such as to delight the rabid patriot. A great deal had been given up. Of all Britain's war-time conquests only Trinidad and Ceylon were retained; rich enough prizes certainly, but small in comparison with Malta, Minorca, the Cape, Cochin, the Spice Islands and all our other acquisitions in India, Africa and the Caribbean. In exchange for this, all Britain gained were French promises to compensate the House of Orange for their expulsion from Holland and to evacuate southern and central Italy.

Hawkesbury told Holland that, as soon as Addington was certain of the best terms he could hope to get, he and Pitt passed a night in study of the country's finances. At the end of their work, Pitt concluded that the war could not be carried on and that the terms should be accepted.[1] But though in part he was bowing to economic *force majeure*, Addington was also satisfied that he had negotiated a peace on both honourable and reasonably advantageous terms.

The most uncertain element in any evaluation of the treaty was the future policy of the French. Addington himself was doubtful whether it would ever be possible to live at peace with a Europe dominated by Napoleon. But he believed so little was to be gained by war that even this small chance should not be neglected. To secure it he was prepared to give France as much, perhaps more, than she could reasonably demand. ". . . the best that can be said of them," wrote Mulgrave[2] of the terms, "is that their moderation is such, as not to be likely to create any feelings of regret or humiliation, which might provoke an early renewal of hostilities on the part of France." Experience was to show the folly of seeking to appease Napoleon but in 1801 he was still new in office, his character little known, the scale of his ambitions barely suspected. Addington felt that the experiment of trusting him had to be tried; only if it failed could the English fairly be asked to carry on the war.

Nor did Addington feel that he was risking very much in adopting such a policy. True, he was abandoning a number of colonial conquests but, in common with almost all statesmen of the age, he saw little attractive in such exotic kickshaws unless they produced immediate dividends of gold. If war started again then it would be relatively easy for the English, with their clear naval supremacy, to win the colonies back again as need and convenience dictated; the surrendered colonies would be, in a sense, hostages for French good behaviour. Besides, Cochin, the

Cape and the Spice Islands were to be restored not to France but to Holland, Minorca was given back to Spain. These might temporarily be aligned with France but Holland at least was more her victim than her ally. A display of generosity now might earn dividends later if one day war was renewed.

The weakest point in the settlement was undoubtedly Malta. Here Addington was much influenced by Nelson, who began a memorandum to him on the subject: "It must never belong to France. England do not want it [sic] . . ."[1] The need therefore was for a solution which would deny the island to both parties. To meet this requirement there was devised one of those ingenious but in practice unworkable solutions which are so often propounded by negotiators instructed to reconcile the irreconcilable. The essential elements of the plan were that British troops were to be evacuated within three months and full control then to be vested in the Knights of St. John under the international guarantee of one or more "disinterested" powers.

Quite apart from the inability of any disinterested and therefore, by definition, distant power to take effective action in support of their guarantee, their very lack of interest ensured that they would bear their responsibilities lightly. Pitt praised the decision to quit the island; "the sight of the Union Jack at Malta would have hurt French pride,"[2] but others had serious doubts and Addington himself was so little certain of the rightness of his decision that he was playing for time over the evacuation of the British troops within a few months of the preliminaries of peace being signed.

If Addington had held out for them he could probably have got better terms. Certainly he underestimated the desire of Napoleon for peace. But it would be wrong to suppose that he was bluffed by Napoleon's threats of invasion or by messages from Paris that peace must come quickly or not at all.[3] He discounted three-quarters of the French threats and was not particularly impressed by what remained. But, in the last analysis, the bluff was not one which he wished to call. For Addington peace, a breathing-space for England, was more important than Malta, Minorca or any number of desirable colonial properties. The sole other essential proviso in his mind was that the *status quo* in Europe should be preserved: this he believed had already been ensured by the terms of the Treaty of Lunéville and by the new French undertaking to evacuate central and southern Italy. Time was to show that the correlation in his own mind between the two treaties was by no means so evident to Napoleon but in 1801 the assumption did not seem unreasonable.

*   *   *   *   *

Reactions to the news of the armistice were much what might have been expected. Windham would have been against the peace whatever the terms. Almost before he had had time to study what was intended he wrote to thank Addington for his advance warning:[1] ". . . however dreadful the intelligence which it contains . . . I have no idea how the effect of this measure is ever to be recovered; chance may do much, but according to any conception I can form, the country has received its death blow." This critic, at least, wrote from sincere conviction. Canning did not share Windham's view of the war but for him the fact that it was Addington's peace was quite enough to condemn it. No one was surprised that he should find it ". . . most disgraceful and calamitous."[2]

But many others, less extreme than Windham and less biased than Canning, saw much to bemoan when the terms were published. To Spencer it seemed that we had given up everything and taken nothing, had shown weakness and timidity bound to damage our interests.[3] Villiers saw no defence for the peace except that, since the Government was incompetent to carry on the war, it was best to end it on any terms.[4] Dundas was dismayed at our abandoning both Malta and the Cape: "the only wise and friendly thing I can do is to impose upon myself silence."[5] Grenville bewailed "such an act of weakness and humiliation." "All confidence in the present Government is completely and irretrievably destroyed."[6] It is fair to say that these were all former Ministers or place-men, predisposed to dislike a peace which reaped such meagre fruits after their own painful and protracted efforts. But they were also men of weight and sense whose criticisms cannot be ignored.

Not all the men of weight and sense deplored the peace. The Whigs, of course, were delighted: "even those who are most dissatisfied," wrote Fox scathingly, "only say that *every gentleman* is against it and every blackguard for it."[7] The Whigs, perhaps, could be dismissed as pacifist Francophiles, yet nobody could say the same of St. Vincent, who described the peace as[1] "the very best this country ever made." Anyone could have guessed that Wilberforce would support the peace but the congratulations of Nelson were more remarkable.[2]

But in the long run the opinion of only one man was of prime importance. No one was better qualified than Pitt to gauge how much more the country could endure or what dangers the peace terms might contain. No one's courage and fortitude was less in doubt. No one so possessed the confidence of the country. As the news of the preliminaries ran through London it seemed that, for a moment, everyone turned towards their former leader to watch for his reaction. Few people were certain what it would be. Grenville poured out his angry disapproval,[3] and concluded: "If the impressions resulting from an intimacy of near to twenty years do not mislead me strangely as to your probable sentiments on this occasion, they will not differ from mine." He sent to Addington a letter containing the same criticisms. Addington passed it on to Pitt without comment,[4] "though I feel persuaded that it suggested the same, or nearly the same reflections to each of us." With the best will in the world Pitt could hardly have pleased both his correspondents. It was Addington whose confidence proved justified.

Pitt stated his opinion categorically the day that the signature of the preliminaries was announced.[5] "The terms are such as I am persuaded you will be well satisfied with, and though they are not in every point (particularly one material one) exactly all that I should have wished, I have no hesitation in saying that I think them on the whole highly honourable to the country and very advantageous." To this opinion he held unswervingly; not all the doubts of his former colleagues could shake his conviction that peace was essential and the terms as good as could be expected. The point on which he had some reservations seemed to have been the return of the Cape of Good Hope to Holland. Certainly he told Bathurst that he regretted in particular the surrender of this conquest.[6] Yet in the House of Commons he rated it as less important than Ceylon, as he was also to rate Malta below Trinidad. His emphatic support of Government so swayed opinion that, when the peace was debated in the Lords, only a handful voted in opposition.[7] In the Commons Windham did not even force a division. The debate was a triumph for Addington, who spoke with "much dignity, much firmness, sufficient fluency, great discretion and great urbanity."[1] Unfortunately for his reputation he had to speak twice, and his second effort was less happy. But he had still brought home the peace and no amount of oratorical floundering could blur the fact that the glory of the day was all his own.

But even if Pitt had roundly denounced the preliminary terms it is not sure that he could substantially have affected their popularity in the country at large. The British people were not disposed to give the mouth of this gift horse even the most cursory inspection. The three-per-cents rose by seven points in a day, the price of wheat fell by ten shillings a quarter, illuminations were everywhere, Otto and Napoleon's special emissary, General Lauriston, had the horses removed from their carriage and were towed in triumph from St. James's Square to Downing Street and all the cows, calves and asses of Falmouth were bedecked with ribbons. A few staunch belligerents like Cobbett considered the rejoicings as degrading, almost treasonable. "If the whole nation were not become advocates for soup shops and sunday-schools there would be some hope; but now there is none."[2] But such jeremiads could not prevent the multitude from cheerfully going its way. Addington's reputation was always higher in the country than in Westminster: in the first months of peace he was the most popular man in England.

* * * * *

The King's first reaction was not unlike that of Cobbett: to negotiate a peace at all was base; to give away more than you got, inconceivably so. He was said to be consulting with Windham and Lord Rosslyn and to have in mind a possible change of Government.[3] Yet in the end he stuck to the Prime Minister of his choice. "I did not think you right," he told Addington some months later,[4] "but I have now made up my mind to your peace and I'll support you like a man."

This change of heart in a man as obstinate as the King was remarkable proof of the esteem which Addington now enjoyed at court. There seemed no issue on which he could not count on George III's support. It did not follow from this that the King trusted blindly to Addington's judgment, though certainly he paid it more attention than was the case with most of his counsellors. Nor did it mean that Addington did no more than obsequiously follow the royal bidding; he was extremely reluctant to oppose the King but on certain issues, as on that of the peace with France, felt bound to go his own way. The harmony between King and Prime Minister rested far more simply on the fact that on virtually every important issue both men thought the same way and arrived at the same conclusions. Unanimity of view is an excellent basis for mutual admiration; the King and Addington admired each other exceedingly and neither saw any reason why this happy situation should ever end.

George III's esteem for his new Prime Minister may in part have stemmed from his relief at being rid of Pitt's sometimes arrogant and always assertive ways. He admired Pitt and sincerely liked him but it was not comfortable for a King, let alone a Hanoverian, to deal always with someone who was obviously the greater man. With Addington he could revert to the avuncular and slightly condescending affability which he found came most easily when dealing with his subjects. Yet his affection for Addington and respect for his wisdom and probity was of a depth and fervour which was rarely to be found in his relations with his Ministers and never in those with his family. "*His* Chancellor of the Exchequer," he would call him, ostentatiously underlining the possessive pronoun. "The King," he wrote,[1] "is highly gratified at the repeated marks of the sensibility of Mr. Addington's heart, which must greatly add to the comfort of having placed him with so much propriety at the head of the Treasury. He trusts their mutual affection can only cease with their lives."

He bestowed more than fair words on his favourite. Addington had no home nearer than Woodley so the King offered him Richmond Lodge, a royal house on the fringes of Richmond Park. The previous occupant had only just died and Addington was reluctant to evict the widow. The King then pulled out a still richer plum. Stone Lodge, soon to be rechristened White Lodge, had been built for George II by Lord Burlington. A large, handsome house deep in Richmond Park, it had been much sought after over the previous years. Now the King offered it to Addington. What was more, since the house was open to the Park, the King set out with a servant and himself staked out an area of sixty acres to be fenced as his Prime Minister's preserve. Addington's ideas were more modest. He besought the King to recast his ideas and in the end got away with a garden of five acres.[1] Before Addington took possession of the house, George III insisted on taking the Queen and Princesses in a family party to show the new occupants what had been done, at royal expense, to make the house comfortable. Addington was an hour late; the King waited placidly for him to arrive and then led him, room by room, round the house in which he was to pass much of his life and eventually to die. No other favour could have been more acceptable to Addington. Since leaving the Speaker's house he had been squatting at a villa which Dundas had lent him in Wimbledon. Now he could establish himself in a base of his own within easy reach of Westminster. With some reluctance he sold Woodley. Another estate so near to London was a luxury he could not afford. In time he hoped to settle farther afield; for he moment he decided to make do with his royal present.

* * * * *

There was much to be done to establish Addington's authority and to get the Government working smoothly. His close relations with George III enabled him to lay down the general rule that access to the King should only be through him. "This is the notion of a Prime Minister as known formerly sometimes under the French government," noted Glenbervie,[2] "but I question if the other Ministers will submit to such an inferiority, and whether Addington is equal to so uncommon a situation." With the exception of Eldon who, as Lord Chancellor, could hardly be denied a royal audience, and to a lesser extent the President of the Council, the new system seems in fact to have been quickly accepted as the norm. Certainly the change was an improvement; too many governments had been weakened by the intrigues of Ministers with the King behind the back of the Prime Minister. Certainly, too, the King approved the change, perhaps even inspired it. There were not many of Addington's Ministers whom he felt much wish to see in private conclave, complaining, for example, that Hawkesbury "always approached him with a vacant kind of grin, and had hardly anything businesslike to say . . ."[3]

In spite of the initial doubts, the Cabinet seemed on the whole to be a united and like-minded body. Addington himself recorded that only one member of the Cabinet had ever dissented seriously from the general view and that was Pelham on a point on which he was personally pledged.[1] Within the circle, Addington relied most heavily on Hawkesbury, Law and Eldon. St. Vincent he left a free hand with the Admiralty, to the other Cabinet Ministers he paid little attention, applauding them politely if they were acquiescent and ignoring them if they were not. His most influential adviser was William Pitt; when Pitt was not available he would be as likely to discuss any question relating to the war with Dundas as with a member of the Cabinet.

Thomas Pelham, the Home Secretary, was the chief irritant within the Cabinet. An amiable time-server of moderate but by no means extravagant talents, he considered that his readiness to serve under Addington had been the greatest favour that he could bestow and that the Prime Minister owed him everything as a *quid pro quo* for his condescension. When Addington removed the colonies from Pelham's bailiwick and gave them instead to the Minister of War—a more sensible though still far from satisfactory arrangement—Pelham sulked and threatened to resign. There was trouble, too, when he claimed the lead in the Lords as his right. Addington had made a vague promise that it should be his but since then Pelham had shilly-shallied for six months while Hobart did the work. Addington pleaded that Hobart should be allowed to keep the lead but Pelham insisted that the role was pledged to him.[2] Reluctantly Addington gave way and with even more reluctance Hobart, second only to Pelham when it came to exigent ambitions, accepted that the latter should take over his position.

Outside the Cabinet, Addington made frequent use of his brother Hiley as political fixer and contact-man. During the formation of the Government Hiley was everywhere, darting from one quarter to another like an agile, if sometimes misdirected Mercury, pouring poison into one ear and, less often, honey into another. His perpetual busyness led him into occasional mischief but, by and large, he was accepted as a convenient and reasonably reliable go-between.

Once the Government had settled in, Hiley's most important responsibility became the organisation of the Press. Rose, Secretary to the Treasury before Hiley, had exercised the same function and had done it extremely well; this made Hiley's work a great deal easier for, though Rose himself might deplore the move, the Pittite press swung loyally behind Addington. Without resorting to outright bribery there were still many ways in which Government could make itself helpful to friendly journals. Official and semi-official advertising was a valuable source of income. The Government could buy many copies for distribution to its servants. The post office could give preference to editors of whom it approved. Places and pensions abounded for obliging editors and journalists. Advance items of governmental intelligence could give the favoured papers a clear start over their rivals.[1] It was temptations such as these that Hiley dangled in front of the English editors; the surprise is not so much that many succumbed as that several of wide circulation, including the *Morning Herald* and the *Morning Chronicle*, stood out for opposition.

Hiley's greatest achievement was to win the whole-hearted support of *The Times*. Since 1799, when Pitt had cut off the official subsidy, *The Times* had been equivocal in its attitude; "a paper," wrote Grenville,[2] "which, under cover of a pretended support of Government, is in decided hostility to it." From Addington's succession to power, however, the policy switched to one of full-blooded support for Ministers. Not only did John Walter, proprietor of *The Times* and founder of a dynasty of the same name and situation, support the Government in all its actions, but he gave Hiley something close to *carte blanche* to fill the columns with articles of his own authorship.[3] "The Addingtons were for a long time our daily scribes," confessed John Walter II many years later.[4] "Every article of a personal nature was obtruded upon us by the Addingtons . . ." Hiley fancied himself as a journalist and, indeed, his pieces were always lively though too often spiteful. His name never appeared but it is certain that he contributed many articles and leaders, and probably also a string of letters signed "Valerius Constans," "An independent Man" and other disingenuous pseudonyms.[5] His brother's activities were in the end to involve Addington in serious embarrassment but in 1801 it seemed a harmless, indeed a useful pursuit.

But not all the benevolence of the Press could conceal the fact that this, at least in debating powers, was a weak administration. Pitt and his friends being inaccessible, Addington looked nervously for help towards the Whigs. "Sheep as he is," wrote

Canning peevishly, "he is calling in the wolves to his assistance . . ."[1] But the wolves hesitated to come into the fold. Tierney was eager to arrange an alliance, but Tierney had a middle-class background and was insufficiently convinced of the divinity of Charles James Fox: two crimes certain to discredit him in the eyes of the Whig aristocracy. With his usual optimism Tierney concluded that he had an excellent chance of disengaging some at least of the more moderate Whigs from their leader's thraldom. He wrote to Moira: "For a great variety of reasons I am satisfied that the sooner a junction is decidedly and formally brought about with Mr. Addington, the better, a matter of which he is as well convinced as myself."[2] With Moira he hoped to seduce Bute, Thurlow, Erskine, Bedford and perhaps Grey.

Addington had good cause to be nervous over such a bevy of recruits. Against Whigs as such he had no objection; the only subjects on which he might expect to disagree were parliamentary reform and Catholic Emancipation and no one seemed likely to revive these issues until the international future was more settled. But he was uneasy about Pitt's reactions. It seemed that Pitt was prepared to agree to the purchase of Tierney's support with some suitable office, preferably out of the country.[3] But such an influx from the Opposition was another matter. He could hardly have preserved his attitude of avuncular benevolence towards a Government including so many of his former enemies. The King, too, would not have been enthusiastic. Certainly it would have delighted his vengeful soul to see Fox deserted by all his friends, but he would have had good reason to fear that the injection of so potent a dose of Whiggery would have been a stronger stimulant than the frail constitution of Addington's Government could support.

In the end, however, it was the Whigs who balked. Moira first refused to serve in the same Government as Portland then, when this difficulty had been smoothed out, rejected the Board of Control which had been offered him. Grey stood out for[4] "real security for myself and a certain indication to the public that the Government is to be conducted on different principles from those which have prevailed of late years." If "different principles" meant no more than a relaxation of Pitt's repressive policy, then Addington would have been delighted to oblige. But the "certain indication to the public" presented greater problems since the one thing Addington could not contemplate was to annoy Pitt by boldly advertising that he was bent on correcting the errors of his predecessors.

Negotiations petered out: "my escape from the scheme of last year I think one of the happiest of my life," wrote Grey to Fox.[1] But Tierney, who disliked Fox, and Sheridan, whose relations with Grey had long been cool, maintained informal links with the new Government. They did not openly quit the Whigs but their speeches grew warmer in support of Ministers. By early 1802 Tierney at least could be counted as a *de facto* Addingtonian.

*   *   *   *   *

Under Addington as much as any other Prime Minister it was inevitable that Ireland should be a source of trouble. Conceivably Pitt, under no restraint from his allies and his King, might have found means to bring the Irish into harmonious union. Addington, without the knowledge or the imagination to understand the problem and inexorably limited in his choice of solution by personal prejudice and the circumstances of his rise to power, had not the remotest chance of success. The surprise indeed is that Ireland was not still more turbulent. The Catholics of Ireland had been seduced into Union by the unspoken promise that emancipation would follow. Cornwallis, who understood the problem as well as any Englishman, had stated categorically:[2] "until the Catholics are admitted into a general participation of rights . . . there will be no peace or safety in Ireland." Now all hope of such advance seemed passed, at least so long as George III retained his senses and the throne.

Addington's Irish policy was destined to failure before it was even enunciated; indeed, circumstances hardly left him room for any coherent policy at all. His first step was to prolong the state of martial law. That done, all that remained to him by way of new departure was to instil some efficiency and probity into the welter of ill-managed corruption in which the Irish Government traditionally wallowed and do a little to stimulate the economy of the unhappy island. The measures were worthy and desirable but had as much chance of curing Ireland's ills as the laborious application of iodine to the superficial scratches of a man in the death throes of a fatal sickness.

133

Abbot, the new Chief Secretary, was Addington's chosen instrument for the carrying out of his Irish policy. Under the benevolent direction of Hardwicke, the Lord Lieutenant, this gad-fly sent to clean the Augean stables conducted himself with a frenetic enthusiasm which drove the Irish to despairing rage. Within a few days of arrival he issued circular orders to all the Departments of Government calling in peremptory terms for details of their establishment, duties, salaries and every other aspect of their work. Lord Clare, the reactionary Lord Chancellor, exploded[1]: "surely a more unwise, unpolitic and insolent proceeding never has taken place on the part of a Chief Secretary. . . . Is there wisdom, justice or policy in suffering this upstart prig to disgust and offend the gentlemen to whose support we are indebted for carrying the Union . . . ?"

Abbot noticed with regret[2] that the replies to his circular were made "very reluctantly and sometimes evasively." However, he continued unperturbed in his efforts to impose order on the Irish finances. In September he sent a certain Colonel Littlehales to England to discuss policy with the Prime Minister. The Colonel's report[3] makes it clear that Addington, while as anxious as anyone to get affairs in Dublin running smoothly, saw the dangers of Abbot's excessive zeal:

Mr Addington concurred with me, that the character of the King's government would suffer materially if any abuses were to be overlooked in Ireland; but he was of opinion, that by probity, honour, and an impartial administration of justice, those evils would be gradually cured; whereas the immediate adoption of violent remedies would not only disgust many of those who had supported the Union, but the nation at large might be induced to feel that it was a manifestation of the intention of the cabinet to act towards them in a somewhat harsh and oppressive manner. . . .

Though Abbot may have enraged the more rigidified sections of the Irish establishment, his effect in the rest of the country seems to have been beneficial. Within a month of Littlehales's visit to London things had settled down sufficiently to allow the lifting of martial law. The country remained generally tranquil and the machinery of government was noticeably more effective. In early 1802 Abbot reported proudly:[4] ". . . you will find a large accession of revenue without any new taxes, from the mere regulation of these departments upon principles of assimilation to the British practice . . ."

In a letter to Auckland,[1] Hobart suggested that Addington regretted the appointment of Abbot and would have liked to get rid of him. There is no doubt that the general lines of Abbot's policy, if not its execution, were worked out in consultation with Addington and fully approved by him. But Abbot's tactlessness and consequent unpopularity undid much of the good which his reforms had yielded. An opportunity to start things again on a better footing arose with the death of Clare in January, 1802. Addington profited by this to bring Abbot back to London as Speaker of the House of Commons and to send Mitford to be Lord Chancellor of Ireland. Wickham, a connection of the Grenvilles and already well acquainted with Ireland through service with Castlereagh at the Home Office, was to be Chief Secretary. With Clare and Abbot out of the way, Addington could look forward with some optimism to a period of tranquillity in Ireland. He can hardly have hoped that such a period would cure Ireland's political and social ills but he believed that prosperity and security would make those ills seem less important. In the case of many countries this belief would not have been a foolish one; it was the misfortune of Addington, as of so many other British statesmen, that Ireland did not lend itself to solutions based on economic rationalism and sentiments of vague goodwill.

6

Addington's tenure of office as Prime Minister falls conveniently into four phases of more or less equal length. In the first, from his accession to the signing of the preliminaries of peace, he was feeling his way, uncertain of his supporters and heavily dependent on the backing of William Pitt. The second, from the preliminaries to the formal conclusion of peace, was Addington's golden age. His policies seemed triumphant, his support in the country was overwhelming and his confidence in his own powers swelled dramatically. The third phase, from the election to the renewal of war, saw the storm clouds gather. It became every day more evident that Addington's much admired peace was only an uneasy truce. As war became inevitable, so Englishmen nervously asked themselves whether Addington was the man to prepare for or to wage it. Last scene of all found Addington sans teeth, sans eyes, sans taste, sans everything, alone at the helm of the ship of state with the enemy boarding, the crew mutinying and every circumstance contributing to his discomfiture. Mere oblivion was denied him: it would have been a happier ending than his indecently protracted final agonies.

The pattern of Addington's period in office was shaped and dominated by his relationship with William Pitt. Addington had taken office in the conviction that nothing could shake their friendship, that Pitt's support and complete confidence would endure so long as he remained Prime Minister. If he had not believed this he would never have accepted the position. Throughout the first phase of his Government his faith had been justified. Now, with the preliminaries of peace behind him and the second phase under way, the two men seemed as firmly allied as ever.

Addington knew that several of Pitt's closest associates, Rose, Canning and Tomline in particular, were working sedulously to nurse Pitt first into neutrality and ultimately into opposition.

But he was also confident that they would not succeed. "They may do with him what they will," wrote Canning in early 1801,[1] "and they are right to break him in by degrees to bear all their caprices . . . With this discipline he is become as tame as a chaplain . . . I am perfectly satisfied that he begs pardon, gives up his instigations, and feels bona fide that every thought of resistance or self-assertion into which he has suffered himself to be betrayed or goaded has been an act of treachery and *Lèze-Médecine* which he cannot too much atone for by increased devotion, blind obedience and self-abasement. And yet this is the mind that governed the world." Addington would hardly have recognised this atrabilious contortion of his own deference and love of Pitt. But if he had read the letter his indignation would have been leavened by the thought that such bitterness could only stem from Canning's failure to persuade Pitt to modify his views.

Yet within a month of Canning's letter the possibility of a breach between Pitt and Addington became suddenly evident. The occasion was trivial but calls for some notice for the presage it gave of the future and the light it cast on the characters of the two men. The trouble began on 8th February in the House of Commons when Tierney praised the new Ministers and, with especial relish, contrasted their rectitude with the vicious and irresponsible folly of their predecessors, in particular William Pitt. Steele and Dundas both concentrated their speeches on refuting Tierney; Addington, who had already spoken at length, merely rose to dismiss in a few words Tierney's accusation that Pitt had deliberately kept back budgetary expenses so that they would have to be met by his successor. No one in the House seemed to have expected that he would say more and one member at least[2] reproached him with "identifying himself with the late Chancellor."

To Pitt, however, reposing himself at Walmer Castle, it seemed that he had been sadly misused. He claimed that his source of information was the newspapers;[3] in part it may have been but so distorted was his impression of the debate that it seems likely one of the Doctor-baiters had profited by the occasion to feed Pitt with slanted reports. He wrote to Addington:[4] "I think I have much to wonder at and to complain of . . . I hope I have never been captious, and I am sure I can never suffer my public opinions to be influenced by personal feelings; but there may be attacks under which, from the mode of their being received rather than of their being made, it may be impossible to acquiesce."

Addington's answer[1] was a cry of pain:

"Your letter is a severe addition to the trials which it has been my lot to undergo. I trust however that I shall not be found unequal to any accumulation of them which it may please God to permit—It will be to Steele only that I shall communicate your letter. I shall do so without comment; and shall only request that he will abstain from letting me know his sentiments on the occasion of it till he has stated them to you. I will not describe any of the feelings which possess me at this moment. It is however a support and consolation to me to know that I have ever been, and ever proved myself, affectionately and unalterably yours . . ."

Steele, to whom Addington turned as honest broker, was a man of little consequence save as being almost the only ardent Pittite who had shown himself happy to serve in the new Ministry. He hastened to write to Pitt[2] "in a state of agitation of mind such as I have never felt before at any period of my life." "No man," he assured his leader, "be he editor of a newspaper or otherwise, can be justified in reporting Addington's conduct in the unfavourable light in which it seems to have struck you . . ." Pitt was shaken but unconvinced, he announced portentously to Addington that final judgment would be suspended until he had returned to London and discussed the matter further with other witnesses.[3] His investigations were presumably satisfactory; a few days later he wrote again[4] to say: "I am led to believe, that your taking so little notice of the offensive parts of Tierney's speech . . . proceeded either from the difficulty of treating such a subject after you had once spoken in debate, or from your persuasion that whatever impression he had made had been sufficiently removed by others. I have now, therefore, only to hope that this unpleasant incident may lead to no public inconvenience, and no further uneasiness to yourself."

For Addington this reply had the sovereign virtue of showing that all was forgiven and that Pitt now held himself reconciled with Ministers. But he found it hard to forget how quickly his friend had been ready to think the worst of him. It was impossible not to draw from the incident disturbing deductions about the future.

Formally, all was as smooth as ever between Addington's Government and the former Ministers. Rose and Long, two of Pitt's most fanatical followers, were admitted to the Privy Council, a gesture of friendship on Addington's part and of reconciliation on theirs. Wickham's appointment to Ireland was a sop to soften the Grenvilles. But at the heart of the relationship between the two groups, the friendship between Addington and Pitt, a slight malaise lingered. The root of the trouble was that Addington thought he was doing rather well as Prime Minister. He had made peace, he was about to introduce a budget which he knew would be popular, King and country were whole-heartedly behind him. To support a hesitant and timid Addington would have been a role which Pitt would have continued to fill with grace, to advise a self-confident and self-satisfied Addington was altogether less attractive. There was no question yet of a split. Pitt accepted that Addington's Government was largely his creation and that he had certain responsibilities towards it which time alone could not expunge. But he was beginning to wonder whether he had wrought altogether wisely in bringing his friend to power and for the first time it must have crossed his mind that one day Addington might have to be dispossessed and the only man worthy to rule England reinstated in his place.

* * * * *

For Addington, one of the purest pleasures of office lay in the help that it enabled him to give his friends and relations. This is, in a sense, a criticism; an ideal Prime Minister would base all his appointments on the most sternly objective assessment of the candidates' talents. But to find such talents in those dear to one is an amiable weakness and certainly one shared by the majority of Addington's contemporaries.

Pellew, husband of Addington's daughter Frances as well as his biographer, has said that when Addington recommended Huntingford to the King as Bishop of Gloucester, it was "one of the happiest moments of his life."[1] Such happiness would not be out of character; Addington cherished profound if misplaced gratitude for this intolerable pedagogue and Huntingford's letters suggest that the Prime Minister still asked for and even listened to his old tutor's advice on many of the problems of the day. When, a month or two later, Addington was able to promote his former crammer, Dr. Goodenough, to the Deanery of Rochester, yet another debt to the past was amply requited.

His relations were not always so easy to satisfy as his former teachers. Hiley, in particular, was importunate in his demands and sparing in his thanks. He felt strongly that a mere Secretaryship at the Treasury did not fairly reflect either his talents or his kinship with the Prime Minister. Addington was sympathetic but had no other job to offer. Hiley went on protesting and, it seems, must finally have threatened to resign. Addington's incoherent dismay shows vividly how fond he was of his brother and how heavily he relied upon his comradeship:[1]

"Your letter has astonished and shocked me. It found me comfortable, and has taken away all the antidote which the last few days had furnished . . . Neither the state of my family, nor of public affairs can be opposed to the influence which this most unexpected communication *must* have on my mind, and exertions; and it comes in the midst, and not at the end of them; unless indeed it should occasion the end of them . . . I have said everything I could devise and devised everything of which my mind was capable, to induce you to persevere till the sacrifice became too great, and to look forward to the means of combining the enjoyment of health and domestic happiness, as much as possible, with the discharge of numerous and important public duties. The idea of seeing any person living in the situation you now hold, whilst I remain where I am, has always been revolting to me . . . You have most unfortunately and most unseasonably unhinged me; it would be kind in you to call and repair what has been done before I go to bed."

Hiley remained in office, but his recriminations became no less bitter. Eventually it proved possible to shift Lord Glenbervie from the Joint Paymastership to be Surveyor General of Woods and Forests. Hiley was appointed in his place. "They have been plotting to find a pretext to give my paymastership to Hiley Addington ever since their Government had any appearance of stability," wrote Glenbervie,[2] angrily aware that his new position, though equally honorific, was financially less alluring than the old. Hiley was by no means satisfied with his promotion but it did accord a little more closely with his own estimate of his merits. He made it clear that he expected more to follow but, for a time at least, ceased perpetually to pester his brother about his own ambitions.

The two brothers, however, nearly quarrelled again over the respective claims of their children. Harry, Addington's eldest son, had had a successful career at Winchester. "Did I not always prophesy," rhapsodised Dr. Goodenough,[1] "what glory would attend that serenity of mind and that soundness of understanding with which God had blessed him?" He was now nearly seventeen and it was time to give some thought to his future. Addington was aware that when he had given up the Chair without accepting the traditional pension he had done damage to his son's interests. This he was anxious to repair if he could and in July, 1802, an opportunity offered.

The Clerkship of the Pells was a sinecure worth some £3,000 a year. At the death of Colonel Barré, whom Pitt had presented with the post a few years before, Addington first offered the vacancy to Steele. This offer refused, he pressed it on Pitt who felt, however, that the equally lucrative Wardenship of the Cinque Ports already gave him as much as he could need.[2] Villiers and Glenbervie were then considered, but the King objected to the first and everyone to the second.[3] After such efforts to bestow the prize elsewhere Addington felt that no one could complain if he presented the sinecure to his son. "I rejoice most sincerely that you have found it practicable to dispose of the Pells as you have done," wrote Pitt.[4] "Under all the circumstances it is infinitely preferable to any other use you could make of it."

But Hiley was quick to see another use to which the vacancy could have been put. He protested that his own son would have been a more deserving recipient. As always, Addington was startled and pained by his brother's reproaches. He wrote to justify his decision:[5] "Affection, prudence and duty to my family all pointed one way . . . I should never cease to reproach myself if I had acted otherwise. Need I add that you and yours (with the exception of my own family) are more to me than all the rest of the world . . ." If Hiley replied, the letter has not survived. It would have been in keeping with his character if he had found Addington's solitary exception thoroughly unreasonable.

So much was it taken for granted at the period that a Prime Minister would distribute financial titbits to all his family that Addington's disposal of the Pells caused little comment. Viewed from the detached heights of posterity his action was clearly unjustifiable. If rich sinecures are to be given to anyone, then it should be to those who have deserved well of the State, not to intelligent children with every chance of making their own way in life. Addington did no more than act in the same way as most of his contemporaries but, though this may explain, it can hardly condone his action. It stands out the more because habitually he was modest in his financial demands. It was, indeed, only because he had rejected a pension to which he had a clear and unquestioned right that he now sought this more dubious way of mending his family's fortunes. For the sake of his reputation he would have done better to accept the pension and reject the sinecure.

*   *   *   *   *

As the negotiations to transform the preliminaries of peace into a permanent settlement dragged tediously on, Addington found himself ever more involved in the field of foreign affairs. His policies were by no means universally admired. "Addington and Lord Hawkesbury dread alliances," wrote Malmesbury,[1] "think commercial treaties useless, and seem to have filled their minds on foreign connexions with the silliest and most dangerous ideas." There was some truth in this. Addington saw little purpose at the moment in entanglements on the Continent and there was certainly a risk that what was then no more than discreet aloofness would harden in a few years into incurable isolation. But Malmesbury's remarks on commercial treaties read oddly, coming as they did only a few weeks after Addington had championed in the House of Commons a Bill for removing obstacles to our trade with the United States.

In the debate on this Bill Windham, "the first gentleman of his age, the ingenuous, the chivalrous, the high-souled Windham," had contributed some distinctly foolish remarks about the need for looking rather to our martial spirit than to our commercial prosperity to support our international standing. Addington struck in with a vigorous defence of the tradesmen and businessmen to whom he was so much closer than Windham could ever or would ever hope to be.

"It appears of late," he said,[2] "more fashionable than it should be to pronounce commercial pursuits incompatible with high sentiments of honour and national glory, and to assert that a nation can not excel in both. This is a sentiment which in principle is not just, in policy is not eligible, in experience is not true . . . Every branch of the public service repudiates the supposition that a commercial and wealthy country cannot preserve its advantages over other states by uniting military excellence with its superior wealth. This country is happily a splendid instance of both."

Unhappily the trumpet voice of the nation of shopkeepers struck a less certain note on other subjects. "Hare says he heard but one sentence in Mr. Addington's speech the other night," wrote Lady Bessborough.[1] "He woke from his sleep and heard 'For as this is that which was said to . . .' Hare was quite satisfied and turned to sleep out the rest." To hear Addington, especially when he spoke impromptu, was often to wonder what link there could be between his mind and the sounds which issued from his mouth; words they certainly were but their purport and their relationship to each other remained mysterious. "To doubt is to decide" was another of these obscure pronouncements which left his audience wondering if they had heard correctly. Canning seized on it and made it the theme of one of the more successful pieces in his cycle of anti-Addingtonian doggerel.

It took almost six months for the British and French negotiators to put the last touches to what was to become the Treaty of Amiens; six irritating, wearisome months of bickering over detail and constant re-negotiation of what had seemed satisfactorily settled the day before. Lord Cornwallis was the chief British negotiator, accompanied by the same Colonel Littlehales who had been Abbot's emissary to Addington and who now seemed specially charged with keeping the Prime Minister posted on what was going on. It is not clear whether Cornwallis realised that his Chief Secretary was conducting with the Prime Minister correspondence in parallel with his own reports to the Foreign Secretary. There was nothing in the content of Littlehales's letters to which he could have taken exception and Cornwallis may well have found it a relief to be saved the pain of duplicating his reporting. But the practice was a dangerous one and it is on the whole surprising that the terms were finally settled without serious misunderstandings on the British side.

Joseph Bonaparte, the chief French negotiator, was responsible for most of the delay. He appeared incapable of maintaining a line of any consistency and regularly disowned in public session the arrangements which he had himself put forward privately the day before. Eventually Cornwallis was instructed to present what was virtually an ultimatum stating the British position on all the outstanding points and announcing that he would leave Amiens in eight days unless a settlement was reached. Addington accompanied this gesture by ostentatiously putting in train a build up of naval power in the Channel ports. It is doubtful what Bonaparte had hoped to gain by spinning out negotiations; certainly he had no wish to risk a final breakdown. In the face of this threat his negotiators quickly came to terms. The Treaty of Amiens was concluded on 25th March, 1802.

The terms of peace were debated in Parliament in May. Addington's opponents, notably Windham and Canning in the House of Commons and Grenville in the House of Lords, concentrated on discrepancies between the preliminaries and the final terms and on events which had occurred since the previous October which made the peace now seem less desirable. In this latter category one item which particularly offended Windham was Bonaparte's dispatch of a fleet to suppress the rebels at San Domingo. This legitimate if ill-fated foray was interpreted by the more chauvinistic as a direct threat to British interests in the West Indies. Addington had, indeed, already taken alarm at the size of the expedition and had secured a promise that several of the ships would not be armed and that the bulk of the fleet would soon return to Europe. Prepared with these assurances and the knowledge that our own fleet in the Caribbean had already been reinforced, he had little difficulty in satisfying all save the most belligerent of the doubters.

Windham had much stronger grounds for concern when he pointed to Napoleon's virtual annexation of Northern Italy. Windham felt that this barely veiled expansionism, accompanied as it was by France's acquisition from Spain of Louisiana, Elba and the Duchy of Parma, was proof that Bonaparte did not intend to respect the precarious balance of power which the Treaty of Amiens was supposed to perpetuate. If this was so, he maintained, the fundamental justification for the Treaty was destroyed. Why sacrifice so many conquests for a settlement which was upset even before it was formally concluded?

To a great extent Addington shared Windham's doubts. He

saw little reason to hope that the French had abandoned their ambitions or that peace could endure for more than a year or two. But he had suspected this from the start and recent French activities had done no more than reinforce his scepticism. They had not weakened the arguments for a peace. The plight of our continental allies was no less miserable, the need for a breathing space in England no less pressing. Though Windham and Addington might have few doubts over French intentions most Englishmen were not going to be convinced until the peace had been tried and failed. There were, Addington freely conceded, grounds for the gravest fears. But nothing had happened which made it desirable to tear up the treaty and renew the war.

The sharpest criticism in the debate centred on the future of Malta. Here Addington was uneasily conscious that his ground was weak. The already complicated project for the management of the island had been still further refined in the course of negotiations. Great Britain, France, Russia, Austria, Prussia and Spain had now been named as the guaranteeing powers and it had been decided that there should be no French or English members in the Order of the Knights of St. John. But, as Windham pointed out, the real flaw in the plan was that "the attempt to revive the ancient splendour and the spirit of chivalry of the degraded order of Malta"[1] never had the remotest prospect of success. This decadent relic, economically unstable, under the control of a French-dominated garrison of Neapolitans and guaranteed by powers which were either under French influence or remote from the problems of the island, would inevitably enjoy no real independence. To leave Malta in its care would be to invite annexation by the French.

Addington stuck publicly to his line that the arrangement was an excellent one for Malta and for Europe. In private he made little attempt to hide his doubts. He was not prepared to denounce the agreement but was equally reluctant to carry it out. When the three months had elapsed after which all British troops ought to have been evacuated, there was still no sign of their going. Amid a mounting clamour of French reproaches it gradually became clear that our retreat from Malta was to be the last step in the performance of our obligations, a step which we had no intention of taking until satisfied that everything, in letter and in spirit, had been done on the other side.

Finally Windham complained that the House of Orange had been shabbily treated and that the Government had failed to revive all the ancient treaties between ourselves and France. The first accusation was undoubtedly well based; the honest answer would have been that it was not worth renewing the war to secure a more handsome indemnity for the Dutch royal house but, not surprisingly, Addington preferred to argue that the terms were satisfactory rather than to offer so brutal an exposition of the realities of power. On the second point there were excellent commercial reasons why the treaties should not have been renewed; our position in India in particular was the stronger for our not being bound by earlier commitments.

On the whole Addington came out of the debate with credit. His tremendous majorities in both houses, only twenty voting against in the Commons and sixteen in the Lords, exaggerated the solidity of opinion in Parliament. But doubters were still few. Canning was anxious not to force the question to a vote. "Do not help Addington out of the scrape into which he has blundered himself," he wrote to Windham.[1] "Leave Parliament unpledged—and let him never have to say, The Treaty was my work, to be sure, but you all of you approved it." When the vote was taken in spite of him he professed to be not at all disheartened by the small minority. "Perhaps after all," he consoled himself "it would not have been brave and gentlemanlike to have shirked a division."[2]

Among members of the Cabinet Pelham was the only one to dislike the peace. He had no wish to leave the Government however, finding that he agreed with all other points of policy and was no more ready to abandon his increments than he had been a few months before. He therefore contented himself with recording his dissent and keeping his doubts for his colleague and closest friends. Auckland, the Postmaster-General, had no such inhibitions. He said nothing to warn Addington or other Ministers, then spoke in the House of Lords against several important features of the definitive treaty. Addington reacted with uncharacteristic sharpness:

"It was with great surprise and concern," he wrote,[3] "that learnt . . . the sentiments expressed, in Wednesday's debate, by your Lordship . . . This information has necessarily led me to suppose that it cannot be the wish or intention of your Lordship to continue to hold an office connected with a government, of whose conduct you have publicly declared your disapprobation upon an occasion so important."

Auckland was taken aback by this retaliation from one whom he had thought too unassuming to take notice of his behaviour. He beat an undignified retreat, protesting his "marked respect for the King's government" and concluding "it seems superfluous to add, that it cannot have been 'my wish or intention' not to continue to hold my office."[1] Addington relented and Auckland remained in office, showing in future greater discretion in his public utterances.

Even Windham, the most indomitable opponent of the peace, seems finally to have been convinced that it was necessary. In July, 1809, according to Addington,[2] he was dining at White Lodge when he said: "Lord Sidmouth, I have for some time wished to tell you that I am thoroughly convinced, if it had not been for the Peace of Amiens this country could never have maintained the struggle to the present period." Dr. Beeke, who was also present, then intervened: "That is an important admission: am I at liberty to report it to my friends, or must I regard it as confidential?" Windham replied: "Not at all: it is my deliberate opinion, and I wish it to be known."

The anecdote is remarkable but it is inconceivable that Addington and Dr. Beeke invented it and, even if it had been embellished with the years, it shows that Windham at least came to accept that there was something to be said for the Government's actions. Pitt certainly felt no doubt. "This is a subject for exultation," he remarked to Addington on the day peace was signed. "No," replied Addington, "not for exultation but for satisfaction under all the circumstances."[3] Sheridan said the same thing more neatly in the House of Commons when he stole Philip Francis's epigram and referred to "a peace which all men are glad of but no man proud of." In fact, Addington did feel pride in his peace but only because he believed that war would be still more disastrous and because he felt that it had taken courage and resolution to accept that fact and to pursue it to its conclusion.

*　　*　　*　　*　　*

The official ending of the war came just in time for Addington to introduce his first budget in peace-time.[4] Normally, indeed, the budget would have been introduced in January or February but the uncertain outcome of the negotiations led to its postponement until April. Addington had not been left in any doubt that the English people expected a drastic reduction in taxation. He was quite clear that the income tax must be the first to go.

He had several reasons for this conclusion. Pitt's income tax was a primitive and singularly inefficient means of raising money. It depended for its efficacy on the individual tax-payer making a reliable calculation of his aggregate income, honestly deducting from it all the various allowances to which he felt himself entitled and paying over a minimum of ten per cent of the residue to the State. No distinction was made between earned and unearned or precarious and permanent income. Nor was there any mechanism to establish whether the right amount had been paid. If they thought that they were being cheated it was open for the Commissioners to call for a breakdown of the suspect's income but even if the breakdown were provided, it was almost impossible to establish its accuracy. It was small wonder that Pitt's originally estimated yield of £10 million a year had to be reduced to £7. million and finally turned out to be only £5.8 million. In the second year, despite attempts to refashion the tax, an estimated £7 million once again was in practice only £5.8 million, and in the third year, when Pitt in desperation reduced his estimate to £6 million, yield fell away to a mere £5.3 million.

Addington had decided that the tax would need drastic overhaul before it would be effective. He was clear on the broad lines of what he wanted to do but his ideas were not yet worked out. More important, he felt strongly that the income tax "should not be left to rest on the shoulders of the public in time of peace because it should be reserved for the important occasions, which he trusted, would not soon recur."[1] In other words, he wanted to keep the income tax free of commitments so that it could be devoted solely to the needs of war when such a need arose again.

But even if no such good causes had existed, Addington would have still found himself under great pressure to abolish the tax. Its unpopularity was deep and widespread. In the course of the budget debate it was variously described as "destructive," "unjust," "oppressive," "pernicious," "vexatious," "odious," "monstrous," "intolerable," "detestable," "inquisitional," "unconstitutional," "fraudulent" and "boldly tyrannical." To the

148

Court of Common Council of the City of London it was "destructive of the trading world . . . hostile to the liberties and morals of the people and incapable of being made equitable or efficient."[1] Addington believed nothing of these accusations; he stated firmly in his budget speech that only the income tax had enabled the country to surmount the recent crisis. Neither House of Commons nor public paid any heed. What counted was that he was announcing the abolition of income tax; beside this his own opinion mattered nothing.

Unfortunately Pitt's tax had already been mortgaged for £57 million. This meant that it would have had to be continued for another eleven years if it were to be entirely freed. To pay off this mortgage and to deal with the expenses of the war Addington raised a massive loan of some £98 million, the interest on which was to be defrayed by new permanent taxes worth £4 million, raised under the heads of Malt and Beer, Assessed Taxes and Exports and Imports. This left the income tax free of all encumbrance as an emergency arm to invoke if the war should be renewed.

The simple yet effective pattern of this budget was approved by almost everyone except the brewers. Even Canning was forced to admit[2] that the budget was "a very well conceived one (as it strikes me), but certainly a very popular one from the single circumstance of the repeal of the Income Tax." He regained some of the lost ground, however, by concluding: "That the materials of the Budget are in fact Pitt's, no one doubts—and you will not. But Addington worked them up himself—or rather Vansittart did." Even this was not true. Addington certainly discussed the lines of his budget with Pitt before presenting it but the manuscript notes among his papers prove conclusively that the broad principles were neither Pitt's nor Vansittart's but his own.

In this budget Addington introduced the practice, now a commonplace, of opening not with a bare announcement of taxes imposed or lifted, but with a broad exposition of the state of the British economy and the principles on which the country's affairs were to be managed. The presentation might to-day seem oversimplified but it was a first attempt to introduce order and coherence into what had too often been a ragbag of ill-assorted items, inspired by expediency and strung together in a spirit of surmise and anxious optimism. It brought a flavour of professionalism to what had for long been a field for amateurs.

The same flavour was to be found in almost all Addington's financial measures. It is remarkable how regularly his detractors, even when less ill-disposed towards him than Canning, ascribed to Pitt anything of merit in Addington's economic policy. Yet in fact finance was the one field in which Addington was unequivocally the more capable. Neither man had any profound understanding of the economic forces shaping their country but Addington at least was aware of the need to stimulate trade and build up nascent industry. He had studied the history and science of taxation with a thoroughness which Pitt found unnecessary. He had that elementary but still valuable gift, a quick comprehension of figures and statistics. His estimates of income and expenditure were far more accurate than anything Pitt had been able to achieve. He showed a striking readiness to experiment and conceive new techniques. As will be seen, the remodelled income tax which he was to introduce in 1803 is still the basis of our present system.

The budget once behind him, Addington set to work to remedy some of the other inefficient weapons in the armoury of the Exchequer. The Lottery was overhauled to such effect that it yielded twenty per cent more revenue and offered less opportunities for cheating. The two sinking funds were consolidated so that all parts fell to be liquidated at the same time. The various duties levied by the Revenue Departments were consolidated and revised, to the benefit of both Treasury and public. The Civil List was recast so that the different heads of expenditure were exposed and Parliament accepted unequivocal responsibility for public works, departmental salaries and the cost of the colonial, foreign and consular services. Finally, if with less benefit to the country, provision was made for the Prince of Wales's massive debts to be paid off over three years and arrears of the civil list were also settled.

On financial subjects Addington was at his best; on slavery, another major subject that session, he was less at ease. One of Otto's negotiating techniques had been to drop vague hints before anyone who might be of influence about the marginal benefits which they personally might gain from an early peace. To Wilberforce he had suggested that a settlement at Amiens might be accompanied by a general agreement on the abolition of the slave trade. Such an agreement, he pointed out, would defeat the argument of those who claimed that for Britain to abolish the trade would be to hand it over to her continental rivals. Wilberforce took no persuading. He wrote at once to Addington[1] urging him to take the lead at Amiens in a crusade that would finish slavery for ever.

"It is not (to a friend I may make the avowal) without emotion that I relinquish the idea of being myself the active and chief agent in terminating the greatest of all human evils . . . I hope I can truly assure you also, that it helps to reconcile me to *my* loss on this occasion, that it would be *your* gain; and I should look on with joy, if the Disposer of all human events, who has already rendered you the instrument of good to mankind in the termination of one of the most bloody wars that has raged in modern times, should further honour you, by making you His agent in dispensing to the world this greatest and most extended of all earthly benefits."

Addington was moved by Wilberforce's appeal and, at least in principle, anxious that slavery should end. But he could not bring himself to be more than cautiously sympathetic. His object at Amiens was to conclude the peace; no extraneous issues, however important, could be allowed to cloud the issues. But he promised that the following year he would raise once more the issue of gradual abolition and do his best to see it through. With this inadequate but still far from insignificant grain of comfort, Wilberforce had to rest content.

A more immediate issue now distracted his attention. The question was whether Crown lands in Trinidad should be sold without a specific proviso that no Negroes should be employed unless they had already been imported. Wilberforce wrote to Addington to urge him to prohibit any new importation of slaves. Pitt took up the question too and in February wrote:[2] "I have had a long conversation with Addington, and have great reason to hope from it that he has in no degree committed himself on any point that can lead to an increased importation of Negroes and that he is quite open and in many views favourable to all the powerful considerations which we have to urge . . ."

Meanwhile Canning seized on the issue as one by which he might contrive to separate Pitt and Addington. "Though I must not goad and pelt the Doctor, as I could wish," he wrote to Hookham Frere,[1] "I am enabled just to put a thistle under his tail, and Pitt must aid and abet me. This Slave Trade—Trinidad —Question is delightful. He writhes and kicks under it, every time that it is renewed by a little hint or enquiry, in the most amusing and preposterous manner. . . ." To Pitt, Canning wrote to suggest a day in the country to discuss the slave trade:[2] "I promise not to allude, in the most distant manner, to treaties, nor to motions of thanks—whether personal or to all mankind generally —nor to public dinners—nor any other anti-Doctorial matters— or 'machinations'. "

Probably Addington was never as embarrassed as Canning had imagined, certainly he escaped from the debate with little trouble. He explained that he was opposed to legislation affecting one island alone since this would merely lead to a traffic in slaves between the islands; then blandly informed the House that the question did not arise since there was no intention of selling Crown lands in Trinidad. He followed this with a promise to set up a commission the following year whose terms of reference would be to carry out the gradual abolition of the slave trade. Canning wrote with indignation[3] that Addington had "veered round and pledged himself body and soul" to all that had been asked of him "and a great deal more"; a deplorable failure to persist in his ways which had confounded Canning's amiable expectation of exposing him to the anger of Pitt and Wilberforce.

*　　*　　*　　*　　*

It is traditional to present Addington as a devotee of harsh authoritarian rule. The description is not wholly false. He had an exaggerated respect for law and order and valued the safety of society far above the independence of the individual. But he was also scrupulously careful not to intrude on the rights of the individual when the State was not in peril. One of his first decisions, even before peace had finally been made, was to cut to a third the funds at the disposal of the Secret Service.[4] When the time came to renew the suspension of Habeas Corpus he allowed it quietly to lapse. It would have been difficult to justify any other course in time of peace. But when war came again he still allowed this pet recourse of the would-be autocrat to remain in abeyance. While he remained Prime Minister, the impression spread throughout England that repression was at an end. It was indeed an impression, a question more of atmosphere than precise enactment, but there can be little doubt that Addington's moderation and reluctance to coerce did much to lessen the tensions and ease the fears which the previous government had bequeathed the country. Lord Holland spoke for Whig opinion when, in a thoroughly disparaging survey of Addington's career,[1] he admitted that his domestic policy "had a very beneficial effect on the country, and assuaged, if it did not heal the wounds which the anti-revolutionary and jealous spirit of Mr. Pitt's government had inflicted." And Southey had not yet deserted radicalism when he wrote:[2]

"They call him the Doctor . . . .—a minister of healing he has truly been; he has poured balm and oil into the wounds of the country, and the country is blessing him. The peace with France is regarded by the wiser persons with whom I have conversed as a trifling good, compared to the internal pacification which Mr. Addington has effected. He immediately put a stop to the system of irritation; there was an end of suspicion, and alarm, and plots; conspiracies were no longer to be heard of, when spies were no longer paid for forming them. . . ."

Nor was Addington incapable of a generous or enlightened attitude when the plight of the poor and overworked was in question. Certainly he was no distinguished innovator of social legislation; his record indeed places him unequivocally with those who felt that the State had little part to play in redressing the misfortunes of its citizens. But at this stage of his life at least he did not wholly reject the responsibility of Government. It was during his time in office that the first attempt was made to remedy the appalling conditions then endured by industrial labour. Sir Robert Peel's first Factory Act, "The Health and Morals of Apprentices Act" to describe it more formally, was hardly electrifying in its proposals. It was a severely watered-down edition of ideas originally put forward by Robert Owen. But though modest and difficult to enforce, it was at least a start, laying down a maximum working-day of twelve hours and rules for the proper feeding, clothing and teaching of apprentices. Addington was not among Peel's most clamorous champions but he made it clear that Government looked kindly on the measure. No more was needed to ensure that it passed.

Though he would sometimes drive reformers to rage by his slowness and prudence, Addington was never mean. One of the few things which made him really indignant was an attempt to defeat a Bill which allowed relief to be given to the poor even though they were not wearing the beggar's badge required by statute. "He was astonished," he said,[1] "that any gentleman should advocate delay on such a subject. The question was, whether those whose poverty made relief not an act of bounty but of justice should be compelled to wear a badge of servitude. Reflecting upon the exemplary conduct of the poor, he was sure he would not be told that without a badge they must go without relief."

It would be farcical to argue from straws such as these that Addington was at heart a radical. On the contrary, his innate conservatism and reverence for the rights of property made it certain that he would usually prove an obstacle to reform. But within these limitations he was anxious that everyone should be treated fairly and that unnecessary suffering should be avoided. He was hesitant when it came to checking the industrialist in maltreatment of his labourers. The industrialist had the right to do as he liked within the walls of his home or of his factory. But the labourer, too, must have the right to profess his views. Repression was to be used only in the case of violence, when imminent revolution threatened. A political doctrine which maintains that the ant has as much right to trample on the elephant as the elephant on the ant may reasonably be felt to be limited in its justice. But the ant had grown unused even to such small mercies; in 1802 he was grateful that harsh constraint was no more in fashion and that the Prime Minister, even if slow in deed, seemed to have some sympathy for his sufferings.

Though the war was at an end and the need for economy obvious, Addington did not feel able to cut down the armed forces as far as he would have liked. Only a fortnight after the final treaty had been signed Malmesbury found "his exultation . . . with respect to the advantages of peace less than before; and the whole bent of his language went to the necessity of a strong and powerful peace establishment."[2] So long as Napoleon remained in power in France, Addington knew that it would be dangerous to relax. The strength of the army was settled at 95,000; more than twice the size of the pre-war force, with 48,000 militia and a further 24,000 reserves. Organisation was on a skeleton basis so that numbers could quickly be increased in emergency. Some cuts were possible but the burden still seemed unfairly heavy to a country of eleven million inhabitants, all of them totally unused and most of them deeply opposed to the concept of a peace-time army.

The navy fared worse. St. Vincent flung himself into a crusade for economy. By June, 1802, manpower had been cut from 130,000 to 70,000; within a short time it was hoped to bring it down to a mere 30,000. Line-of-battle ships in commission were reduced from over a hundred to less than forty. The Royal Navy's reserve, the Sea Fencibles, was abolished. The staff at the dockyards was cut to the point where work became impossible, contracts with private yards were withdrawn and surplus stores were sold off.

Addington looked on with some disquiet. In principle he must approve but he could not avoid a fear that St. Vincent was moving too fast in thus destroying an asset of which England would soon have need. The country as a whole, however, was delighted with anything which seemed likely to reduce its taxes. To interfere with a popular hero, pursuing a popular course, in a field in which he was supposed to be the ultimate authority, was more than the Prime Minister could contemplate. He deserves some sympathy; St. Vincent was not an easy man to cross. A threat of resignation was his habitual weapon and one which Addington did not feel strong enough to combat. He never liked St. Vincent, believing him "an ungenerous minded man and a very unsafe one to be connected with in politics,"[1] but the Admiral was one of the few people in the Government with popular appeal and to let him go would have been too great a risk.

Wellesley was another servant of the Crown who gave his Prime Minister a lot of trouble. Though he approved the Peace of Amiens he doubted the wisdom of returning to the French their possessions in India. On Pondicherry he refused to act without further instructions from London. This caused Addington little concern; indeed, by the time that London was ready to reconsider the question it was so evident that war must come again that the Governor-General's truculence was a cause for relief rather than censure. But Wellesley's quarrels with the Court of

155

Directors, mainly over questions of patronage, were more difficult to ignore. A man of arrogance and conviction of his own infallibility, it seemed to the Governor-General intolerable that a gang of bureaucrats in London should meddle with his arrangements in what he considered to be his private empire. To the Directors it seemed equally intolerable that this vainglorious grandee should ignore their instructions and insult their emissaries.

Early in 1802 Wellesley announced that he was going to resign. Addington both liked and admired him; he believed that Wellesley was doing an excellent job in India and felt that he should be kept in office, even at the price of upsetting the Directors in London. He sent private messages to the Governor-General urging him to change his mind. Wellesley replied,[1] referring with superb inaccuracy to the "respectful tone" of his despatches to the Directors and agreeing to remain on condition "that the Court of Directors should themselves ask him to stay on and that the Government should promise him their protection against any possible interference on the part of his employers."

Addington responded with characteristic mildness to this aggressive overture. He persuaded the Court of Directors that the Governor-General's resignation would be a disaster for British rule in India, procured from them a letter dulcet enough to satisfy even the exigent Wellesley and himself wrote:[2] "Let me now thank you for the confidence and kindness which pervades all your letters as far as I am personally concerned. Be assured that I shall be invariably attached by reciprocal sentiments, and that I shall connect your honour and happiness with my own."

Appeased, the great proconsul agreed to stay in office for another year; congratulating the Prime Minister on "the zeal, assiduity, and firmness which have distinguished your support of my character and public services."[3] He spoke of the pain which he felt at hearing that Addington and the Grenvilles had fallen out over the peace, regretting that there should be differences between "some of those persons who must ever be the primary objects of my esteem and regard, as well as of my respectful attachment." Whimsically describing himself as "having no personal objects to pursue," he protested his desire to act as an intermediary between his friends so as to restore to them the unity which they should never have abandoned.

In 1802 Addington's quarrels with the Grenvilles still caused him little concern. Pitt was loyal to the Government and, so long as Pitt stood firm, his cantankerous cousins could do no harm to Ministers. Addington's administration had been strengthened in the middle of 1802 by the addition of Lord Castlereagh. The appointment came as no surprise, for Castlereagh had given the Government consistent and conscientious support from its inception. His attitude may in part have been based on a debt of gratitude. According to Hobhouse[1] he had, during the negotiations for the Union in Ireland, become involved in various semi-official financial engagements. The sum of these was formidably large and Castlereagh, who was not a rich man, was so disturbed over his difficulties that he was "affected by a brain-fever." He only recovered when Addington, on behalf of his Government, accepted responsibility for £18,000 worth of such debts. The story is not improbable. He was undoubtedly very ill about this time and certainly he showed his goodwill to the Government by piloting its Irish legislation—in particular the Suppression of Rebellion Act—through the House of Commons.

Although he was still a champion of Catholic emancipation, Castlereagh approved of Addington's Irish policy, writing to him in July, 1802:[2] "I . . . feel excessively grateful for your kind intentions towards our Union friends; indeed I am truly sensible of the cordiality and zeal with which you have fulfilled not only every engagement, but even every fair expectation which the supporters of that measure were entitled to entertain. . . ." About the Treaty of Amiens he was less happy, submitting a memorandum to the Cabinet in which he argued that it was essential to take a stronger line with France. But in spite of this difference it did not need much pressure from Addington and Pitt to persuade him to join the Government. In July, 1802, he took office as President of the Board of Control with a seat in the Cabinet; his predecessor Dartmouth being removed to an honorific backwater in the royal household.

Addington told Glenbervie[3] that he meant Castlereagh to be his right-hand man in the House of Commons. Certainly Hawkesbury was not much of a hand at extempore debate and, with his father Lord Liverpool seriously ill, was anyway poised for a retreat to the Lords. But Castlereagh also was prosy and inarticulate, his presence made the front bench little better equipped for the sort of political in-fighting which Canning and his assistant assassins were shortly to begin. From every other point of view his accession was of great benefit to the Government. His courage, his pertinacity, his vast capacity for work, his common sense would have made him a useful member of any Cabinet: to Addington's light-weight band he lent a stability and distinction which otherwise was little apparent.

*   *   *   *   *

By the summer of 1802, therefore, Addington's Government was in good trim. He had every right to feel confident about the elections which were due. "It was the fashion at first to say *that it would not do* etc," Wilberforce had written to Wellesley a few months earlier. ". . . I always maintained the contrary, and the event has justified my expectations."[1] Among the less fashionable Britons there had, indeed, been many who from the start had said that it would do very well. But even among the doubters a fair proportion had now rallied to the Government.

Addington's chief difficulty was in Scotland. Dundas, "Harry the Ninth," the uncrowned King of Scotland, was ready to keep his docile cohort loyal to Addington but on his own terms. He alone must decide who should stand for the various seats, must organise their support and control their voting. In January, 1802, for instance, Addington let it be known that he would support the Duke of Montrose's candidates in Stirling and Fife. Dundas, not sorry to show that he took little account either of dukes or of Addington, promptly put up rival candidates. When Addington protested at this uncivil treatment, Dundas wrote in dudgeon to Pitt:[2] "If they let me alone . . . they need not be afraid that I have any disposition to stand between them and the full exercise of their ministerial authority, but it must be done with decency." His power in Scotland was not to be "dissolved by the breath of any Minister." Prudently Addington let Dundas have his head in most of the Scottish constituencies, though in some half-dozen it seemed that a conflict could not be avoided.

Elsewhere all seemed promising. A month or so before the election Addington wrote to Lord Hardwicke[3] to report that, his side of the Channel at least, things were likely to be quiet and the results extremely satisfactory. He was more doubtful about

Ireland but in the event few elections there were contested and Castlereagh was able to report[1] that "the individuals chosen were perfectly proper persons, both in principles and property." In Scotland, Dundas had the chagrin of seeing Montrose's protégés successful, but he claimed to have returned the compliment in Galloway where his candidate defeated a Government man. In England also there were few contests and the results of most of these were certain from the outset. One of the few exceptions, as so often, was at Middlesex, where the Radical candidate Burdett comfortably beat the official man. Addington gained an effective if hardly noble revenge when the Government reserves were later withdrawn from Coutts, the bank of Burdett's father-in-law.[2] General Simcoe was beaten in the West Country but otherwise almost all the Prime Minister's more faithful supporters were successful. Out of ninety-five members elected through the East India Company interest, thirty-seven were declared Addingtonians.[3]

"The election had little or no effect as far as party strength was concerned."[4] Addington's sober assessment was numerically correct. But he did himself less than justice, for Government in fact achieved a far better result than had seemed possible a year or so before. He had succeeded in retaining Pitt's massive majority while attacked by the Whigs on one side and the war-party on the other and without the priceless asset of Pitt himself. In the process several of Addington's most inveterate enemies had been removed; Windham, in particular, losing at Norwich, though admittedly to a Foxite opponent. True, Pitt was still strong in the cause of Ministers and the King had used all his vast influence in the same direction. But the elections were a striking victory for Addington and his own immediate followers. A less popular man could not have done as much.

The most remarkable feature about the election was that there was little interference or effort on the part of Government. In part this was because of the massive cost of buying parliamentary boroughs; Ministers wrote off in advance all those seats in which only a heavy investment could have secured victory and were pleasantly surprised by the small loss which they incurred. But the Government's attitude was also decided by Addington's aversion to the electoral methods which had sullied the politics of the eighteenth century. He was not prepared to wallow in the morass of bribery and abuse, blackmail and threats which made up the traditional pattern of a British general election. To some his attitude seemed like feebleness, to some lassitude, to some exaggerated squeamishness. From none of these frailties was he free. But there was also a certain pride, even nobility. If the country did not want him then let them say so; he would not seek to alter their decision in any undignified or unscrupulous scramble for their votes. It was not the standpoint of a man likely to succeed in politics—an unwillingness to fight with whatever weapons might be to hand is usually disastrous as a disability—but it spoke of a man who believed whole-heartedly in the rectitude of most at least of those who were going to vote. The attitude may have been naïve; in 1802 at least it was remarkably successful.

7

In the late summer of 1802 Addington's reputation stood higher in the country than at any other moment. As the first flock of tourists, renewing the pleasures of their acquaintanceship with Paris, began to send back cheerful reports of their reception, it seemed for a fleeting period as if peace might have come to stay. A reasonable harvest and reduced taxation at home offered relief from the strains of the last few years. At the polls such parts of the population as had the privilege of voting had shown unequivocally their approval of the Prime Minister and his policies. In the smart drawing-rooms jibes were still heard at Addington's middle-class absurdity while the more robust patriot continued to denounce the degrading terms of the national surrender. But in most of Britain criticism was still. Calm, confident and comfortably bland, Addington faced the future with the reasonable expectation that it would continue to unroll in a way gratifying both to the country and to himself.

But it was his very prosperity which was to contribute to his undoing. Pitt had now been out of office for nearly eighteen months and it seemed that he was as far from the Cabinet chamber as at any moment since his resignation. It would be unfair to say that this was more than he had reckoned with since, even in his private thoughts, there is no reason to believe that he had set a term to his retirement. But though his body was still debilitated by alcohol and overwork his mind was as keen as ever. The life of a retired statesman, precluded even from active opposition, was becoming intolerable to him. He viewed the activities of his pupil swollen to master with an ever more apparent lack of enthusiasm, sharpened at times by a tincture of jealous distaste. After so long in office it was inevitable that Addington should find less need of a mentor; he still consulted Pitt on every major issue but the advice was listened to with noticeably slighter deference. Tomline records that, in July, 1802, Pitt referred to Addington as "without exception the vainest man he ever met with."[1] A year later the remark would have caused no surprise. Even in 1802 it is easy to see how such a mood could have arisen.

Pitt was too big and too honest a man to turn against Addington simply because he felt an itch for office. He continued to keep most of his rancour to himself and to encourage his friends to stay loyal to the Government. But it became more and more certain that he would look with suspicion at any act of the present Ministers, would no longer let it be known that he whole-heartedly supported them and would listen with greater complaisance to criticism of their incapacity and assurances that he alone was fit to rule the nation.

It is impossible to establish any exact chronology. Did Pitt wish to supplant Addington because he believed him incompetent to conduct the coming war or did he believe him incompetent to conduct the war because he wished to supplant him? Did Addington seek the help of the Whigs because Pitt had deserted him or did Pitt desert him because he sought the help of the Whigs? Both men would have believed the presentation of the case most favourable to them and both would have had some justice on their side. Moments of coldness were followed by moments of reconciliation; to one observer it would seem that the breach was widening, to another that Addington and Pitt had never been more closely united. All that can be said for certain is that, by the autumn of 1802, Pitt was ill-satisfied with his lot and ready to admit, not only to himself but to his intimates, that the present Prime Minister had many defects. It was no longer inconceivable that it might prove necessary to replace him.

Canning was the impresario who presided over the swelling discord. One successful operation was contrived in the summer of 1802 at a banquet in honour of Pitt's birthday. For this occasion Canning was called on to indulge his talent for versification and produced one of his more accomplished efforts. The first verse set the pattern of the rest:

> If hushed the loud whirlwind that ruffled the deep,
> The sky if no longer dark tempests deform,
> When our perils are past, shall our gratitude sleep?
> No—here's to the pilot that weathered the storm.

As a reference to Pitt this might reasonably have been felt to be misplaced. Even on the most benevolent analysis of his actions, Pitt as pilot had committed the considerable offence of abandoning his ship when the storm was at its height. But in the sentimental euphoria which prevailed at the banquet any such reflection on the achievements of the master would have seemed sadly out of place.

The sting, however, was in the tail. To the last verse Canning attached particular significance:

> And O! if again the rude whirlwind should rise,
> The dawning of peace should fresh darkness deform,
> The regrets of the good and the fears of the wise
> Shall turn to the pilot that weathered the storm.

This clear declaration that only Pitt was fit to govern the country in time of war can hardly have been pleasant hearing to the Government of the day. Addington was present at the banquet and Glenbervie noted with amusement that he did not seem "much delighted with this song."[1] Pitt was absent. But few men in his position could have failed to find to their taste the flattery and the genuine enthusiasm of their friends. He began indeed to see himself as the indispensable pilot and to look ahead to a time when it might be necessary to thrust aside the frail hands that clasped the wheel.

Pitt now viewed every act of Addington with the distaste of one who feared that it would prove fatuous and suspected that it might be malevolent as well. In August, Dundas was given a peerage and renewed life as Lord Melville. He had, on the whole, behaved well since Addington had been in office, and the Prime Minister wished both to reward him and to ensure his future benevolence. When the honour was announced in December, the King remarked,[2] without much confidence, that "he hoped it would keep that gentleman quiet, and that he would not enter into that captious opposition that did no credit to some members of the House of Lords." But to Pitt the manœuvre was a matter for the gravest doubts. Was there a conspiracy? Did Addington plan to bribe all the former Pittites into subjection? He told Rose[3] that he was "beyond measure surprised" at the news and, the same day, settled down to an analysis of Addington's current budget in a spirit of animosity and pique. Wellesley Pole reported that[4], "Pitt is as firmly with Addington as possible;

they must go hand in hand." But those who knew Pitt better were confident that the breach was already made.

* * * * *

It was not long after the Pitt fan-club had bawled their approval of their patron around the banqueting table of the Merchant Taylors' Hall that early presages of the rude whirlwind began to disturb Europe's fleeting peace. They were first made manifest in Napoleon's grumblings at the shelter offered by England to the royalist emigrés and the offensive publicity given him by the British press. On the first count Talleyrand complained bitterly of the "disgust and inconvenience" caused to the French diplomatists in London at meeting relics of the *ancien régime*, decorated with all their pre-revolutionary orders, around the court of George III.[1] To this the Government returned a firm reply:[2] "His Majesty would feel it inconsistent with his dignity, with his honour, and with the common law of hospitality, to deprive them of that protection which individuals resident in his dominions can only forfeit by their own misconduct."

Napoleon now turned to the excesses of the British press. Here he had rather more to complain about. There had been some particularly vicious articles by Cobbett and one or two other British journalists but also, still more offensive, a series of personal attacks on the First Consul by a French emigré called Jean Peltier which set Napoleon storming as they were read to him in his bath. Glenbervie did his best to persuade M. Otto that British politicians and even crowned heads took the same sort of abuse for granted and had long accepted that nothing could be done to protect them. Otto was not impressed. He knew too well that Napoleon's susceptibilities were sharper than those of any mere Briton and argued, with irrefutable if limited logic, that, since Parliament was said to be all-powerful, it could certainly keep in check a few recalcitrant journalists.[3] He got no satisfaction. When fresh and formal complaints were made in August Hawkesbury commented:[4] "Our Government neither has nor wants any other protection than what the laws of the country afford: and . . . never can consent to new-model their laws, or to change their constitution, to gratify the wishes of any foreign power."

But in spite of this uncompromising reply, Addington did what he could behind the scenes to meet Napoleon's complaints. The law officers were instructed to consider a prosecution in the case of Peltier. No action proved possible and Addington can never have felt it likely that there would be but at least the fact that such an instruction had been given might have done something to placate the First Consul. Rather more to the point, he also let it be known informally among the editors whom Government could influence that attacks on Napoleon would be looked on with displeasure. In the case of one "abominable paragraph" in the *True Briton*, Vansittart was instructed to reprimand the editor and threaten him with the withdrawal of government protection if the offence was repeated. Heriot, the editor, admitted that the paragraph should never have been printed, but responded sharply to Addington[1]. ". . . I am satisfied, Sir, that it must be as far from your ideas that I, or any man, should be *threatened* into a support of Government as it is inconsistent with my feelings to receive such a threat with apathy and submission." In a conciliatory reply,[2] Addington protested that he had had no wish to wound Heriot's feelings and referred to the damaging "consequences produced by opprobrious observations, in papers of such established reputation as yours, on the proceedings of foreign governments, and on the characters of those who are at the head of them." Heriot was appeased, an example was made of the man responsible for the offensive passage, and the *True Briton* was more careful in the future. But there were not many papers over which Addington could enjoy even this measure of control and Cobbett, in particular, thundered abuse at the wretched foreigners across the Channel in any paper that would take his work.

Before the end of the year cause for quarrel had arisen between England and France more serious than mere newspaper abuse; "reciprocal Billingsgate" as Fox described it. In October, 1802, Napoleon organised an insurrection in Switzerland, detected amidst the growing tumult an appeal, inaudible to all but himself, to preside over the regulation of the differences and instructed Ney to march his forces into the Republic. Addington was outraged but impotent. The Treaty of Amiens contained no provision relating to Switzerland. He sent a special emissary with instructions not to encourage the Swiss to resist but, if they seemed determined to fight for their liberty, to promise them money and moral support. The bearer of this not very tempting offer perhaps fortunately arrived only just in time to witness the surrender of the Diet. Addington's solemn remonstrance to the French succeeded only in annoying Napoleon without diverting him from his course. It seemed to Addington possible that the affair might end in war: ". . . for such a result," he wrote to Hardwicke,[1] "much as we should lament it, we are preparing with as little bustle as is consistent with a degree of activity and exertion." British forces were ordered to delay their evacuation of the former French and Dutch colonies and steps were taken to mobilise the fleet. But with Switzerland surrendered and Napoleon showing no signs of renewing the war, Addington found himself frozen in a posture of defiance which at the best never looked particularly heroic and, as time wore on, began to appear decidedly grotesque.

England had no wish to go to war for the sake of Switzerland and Napoleon knew it, nor was any other European country more ready to leap to the help of those admirable yet somehow unappealing cantons. The Russians, though sympathetic, were in no mood for war. Austria appeared "neither to have the disposition nor the means for any vigorous exertion." Hiley was dispatched to visit Pitt at Bath and to seek his views. Pitt was in little doubt that we could not plunge alone into a continental war and advised Addington[2] to content himself "with a state of very increased and constant preparation, both naval and military; and by endeavouring, in the meantime, to lay the foundation of a defensive system in Europe . . ." This was near enough to what Addington had worked out for himself. "The question is not one of justice, but of discretion," he wrote to Pitt,[3] with disconcerting honesty. To desert the Swiss might not be noble but the policy made sense; the Swiss had anyway settled the question when they had refused to undertake a hopeless war. Addington had been made to look foolish. But he could hardly have allowed French aggression to go altogether unchallenged. In retrospect it seems that he would have done better to bluster less and concentrate instead on building up his strength. But at the time, with the intentions of the Swiss uncertain, even a more skilled diplomatist would have found it hard to achieve a satisfactory result.

Though he had failed to deter Napoleon, Addington had still

given an ugly fright to the Whigs. Fox was shortly to return to England much disillusioned over the virtues of the First Consul but official Whig policy remained that the French were more sinned against than sinning and that peace must at all costs be preserved. Addington's belligerent response to Napoleon's Swiss adventure filled them with dismay. "I am afraid of this damned Addington being bullied out of his pacific disposition," wrote Creevey.[1] "He will be most cursedly run at, and he has neither talents to command open coadjutors, nor sufficient skill in intriguing to acquire private ones." Though this particular escapade had not led to war, the Whigs did not delude themselves that the danger was over. Sooner or later, they knew too well, some fresh incident would arise on ground which the Government would feel both able and morally bound to defend.

*   *   *   *   *

The imminence of war was certainly real enough to prevent Addington introducing the sort of budget for 1803 which would best have pleased both the public and himself. He found he was in the uncomfortable position of having to maintain England on something close to a war footing while deprived of the income tax, the chief source of funds for such an effort. He did not regret having abolished the tax, still being convinced that it must be held in reserve for the intenser strain of actual warfare. But the twilight period through which England was passing left him embarrassingly short of money.

Fortunately for Addington, the new "permanent taxes" which he had imposed in his last Budget had proved so successful that he still had enough in hand to meet the interest on a new loan of £10 million without fresh taxation. To such a loan he had recourse. He stated the likely produce of the revenue with some optimism, not taking into account the sharp downturn which occurred in the last quarter of the year when the threat of war was beginning to hamper trade. With exemplary caution, however, he took credit only for £4 million, £2.5 million less than his original estimate and £1.1 million less than the actual surplus for the year. It was a characteristically sound Budget, introducing no dramatic new feature but adequate to meet the needs of the times.

It was initially well received. The funds rose by nearly five per cent in a day, a sure sign that the financial policy of the Government was deemed satisfactory by the monied classes. As usual there was a tendency to ascribe its virtues to the hand of Pitt. "The Doctor's Budget is very much admired here," wrote Lady Bessborough from Paris,[1] "but my new acquaintances say '*C'est trop bon pour sortir de cette boutique-là, l'on y reconnait la main du Maître*'." But Pitt would not have been flattered by the attribution. Worked on by Rose and Canning—"there is not a part of the Budget that is not too stupidly wrong even for the Doctor's dullness and ignorance . . ." wrote Rose[2]—Pitt had been convinced that Addington's proposals were, at the best, ill-founded, at the worst deliberately contrived to mislead the country. He made his point of view patent by remaining in Bath and taking no part in the debate.

Pitt objected that the estimate of revenue was grossly optimistic. There was indeed some over-estimation though, on the facts as known at the time of the Budget, Addington's figures were reasonable, indeed conservative. But Pitt's more important objection was to the raising of a loan for the cost of defence when the country was not at war. "I have repeatedly stated to him," he told Rose,[3] "the indispensable necessity of providing at once for any extraordinary expenses which might occur in years of peace. Addington always admitted the principle . . ." But the question posed itself, how peaceful do "years of peace" have to be before they can be treated as such for budgetary purposes? To Addington it seemed that the extraordinary requirements of the international situation called for extraordinary means to meet them. He saw his loan as a stop-gap measure to keep the forces going until the inevitable war should come. Only when war did come would it be prudent or legitimate to have recourse to greatly increased taxation.

It is rarely possible to say that anyone is unequivocally right or wrong in the world of economics. By the classical principles of sound budgeting Pitt had some justice on his side. In terms of expediency Addington's measures were reasonably effective. Given the unexpected bonus from the taxes of the previous year and the exceptional international circumstances, Addington could certainly put up a good case to justify his departure from financial purity.

But it was the Budget speech as much as the Budget which

irritated Pitt. In spite of the sycophantic friend who referred to Addington's "animating and impressive speech" and its "electrical effect upon the public mind,"[1] the speech introducing the Budget for 1803 seems to have been one of the Prime Minister's shabbiest efforts. Almost incoherent with embarrassment, he stumbled and blundered his way through figures of which his mastery was, in fact, complete and only found anything approaching confidence in the diffuse and tedious passages of self-congratulation on the state of the country and the wisdom of the Ministers.[2] It was these last which particularly offended Pitt. Every reference to the prosperity of England at the end of 1802 seemed to him a direct attack on the conduct of affairs by the previous Government; every compliment to a Minister a slur upon his predecessor.

The record shows that Pitt was being over-sensitive. There was little in the speech which he could reasonably construe even as implicit criticism of his own administration. Certainly there was nothing which did so explicitly. The nearest approach was a reference to the "economical administration of the navy under St. Vincent". This left Melville, St. Vincent's predecessor, calm but was seized on by Pitt as a direct attack on the extravagance of the war Cabinet. Isolated at Bath, Pitt depended for his parliamentary commentaries on Rose, Canning and Tomline. Through such a medium mildly injudicious, or even perfectly innocent remarks were transformed into the darkest slanders. It would have been astonishing if Pitt had found nothing to offend him in any speech of Addington's.

St. Vincent's "economical administration" was to do still more to damage relations between Pitt and Addington. In December, 1802, the Admiral demanded that a Commission be set up to inquire into the affairs of the Navy Board, responsible only to Parliament and able to call for documents and examine witnesses on oath. He had good reason to suspect extravagance and even financial malpractices but the proposal, questioning as it did the efficiency and perhaps the honesty of Melville's administration of the Admiralty, was well calculated to cause extreme political embarrassment. The Cabinet was reluctant to touch it; the former members of Pitt's Government in particular having no wish to see their dirty linen washed in public. "Excepting my Lord Chancellor, the whole Cabinet has mutinied today!" stormed St. Vincent, after a turbulent meeting.[3] "My commission is rejected!—but we'll read them a lesson out of the Articles of War, tomorrow, Sir!"

Once more the bigoted and indomitable Admiral had his way; the mutiny was quelled and the Commission accepted. Addington on the whole was on St. Vincent's side. He attached great importance to financial probity and felt that an inquiry was indeed needed. But he was as nervous as any of his colleagues about the effect the Cabinet's action might have on Pitt and his associates. He had good reason. "A flagrant Admiralty job," Canning described it,[1] "job not in the sense of *interest*, but of trumpery spite, originating in Lord St. Vincent's violence, and forced upon Addington's imbecility . . ." Addington could have endured Canning's bad opinion with equanimity but, in the circumstances of 1803, what Canning said to-day was too likely to be what Pitt would think to-morrow.

Meanwhile the Whigs continued the policy elegantly described by Creevey as the "judicious dandling of the Doctor."[2] Officially no overtures were being made on either side. Fox, indeed, found that Addington was more cautious than usual in his relations with the Opposition, he presumed from fear of offending Pitt.[3] But things were still smooth between the two groups. So long as the peace continued Fox had no intention of weakening the only man who could keep Pitt out of office and, so long as the Whigs did not openly assail his Government, Addington was ready to pay them every courtesy at his disposal.

Fox seems to have felt nothing but contempt for Addington; indeed it would have been surprising if the latter's slow and bourgeois prudence had won much sympathy from this brilliant and raffish aristocrat. Sheridan, on the other hand, though he shared most of his leader's prejudices, genuinely liked and even admired Addington. He seems never to have had any particular hope of deriving profit from their friendship and claimed on one occasion to have rejected a peerage which Addington had offered him. "My visits to you may possibly be misconstrued by my friends," he remarked while dining at White Lodge,[4] "but I hope you know, Mr. Addington, that I have an unpurchaseable mind." The support of Sheridan meant that the Government had at least one tolerable orator to speak for them in the House of Commons. By the end of 1802 drink and financial worries had worn him down so that he was no longer the brilliant figure of his youth. But his assistance and the demonstration it gave that it was possible for a man of talent and, still rarer, fashion to think well of Addington, must have done something to raise the stock of the Government.

Sheridan's support inevitably had to be paid for in Pitt's increasing coldness. In his speech on the Army Estimates[1] Sheridan defended the record of Addington's Government, accusing all who were against him of resembling those people who disliked that other Doctor, Dr. Fell:

> The reason why I cannot tell;
> But this I'm sure I know full well,
> I do not like thee, Dr. Fell."

Then he turned his attention to Pitt, reminding the House of all the kind things which the former Prime Minister had said about the new administration and challenging him either now to withdraw them or to continue public support of Ministers. With especial bitterness he attacked those who spoke of Pitt as indispensable to the country's salvation. "Mr. Pitt the only man to save the country!" he cried. "If a nation depends only upon one man, it cannot, and I will add, it does not deserve to be saved; it can be saved only by the Parliament and people."

In a letter to Malmesbury[2] Canning recorded a conversation which he had recently held with Pitt. Though he may have twisted the words into a form more suitable to his taste, the gist of the discussion is convincing and gives what must be something close to a fair picture of Pitt's frame of mind at the end of 1802. Pitt stressed that he considered himself pledged to support Addington and that this pledge was "not redeemable by any lapse of time, nor ever to be cancelled without the *express consent* of Mr. Addington."

"I will not affect a childish modesty," he went on, "but recollect what I have just said—I stand pledged; I make no scruple of owning that I am ambitious—but my ambition is *character*, not office. I may have engaged myself inconsiderately but I am irrevocably engaged."

"You nevertheless admit," asked Canning, "that at this moment it is a duty for you to resume office?"

"I do."

"And that you are withheld from performing it, solely from the solemn engagements you say you have contracted?"

"Yes."

"But you said these engagements could be dissolved, if Mr Addington chose it?"

"Most certainly."

"Does it not then follow that it is also a duty in you to apply to Mr. Addington to release you from them? He has all along declared he looked upon himself as your *locum tenens*, and ready to resign his office back to you, whenever the country or you require it at his hands?"

"Not distinctly this, in any conversation with me, but something, I own, very similar to it."

"I repeat, therefore, is it not your duty, after the sentiment you have avowed, and the dangers you admit the country to be in, to require this release from him?"

"I cannot bring myself to do it. It is impossible to prevent it wearing the aspect of caballing and intriguing for power . . ."

Canning was not prepared to wait until Pitt had overcome his scruples. With Lord Granville Leveson-Gower, Lord Morpeth and Mr. Sturges-Bourne, and some rather half-hearted assistance from Lord Malmesbury he worked out a devious scheme by which a memorandum signed by "several persons of great political weight" would be submitted to Addington. The memorandum would call upon the Prime Minister to take account of the perils facing the country and at once resign the Government to Mr. Pitt. Unfortunately, except for Mr. Canning, Lord Granville Leveson-Gower, Lord Morpeth and Mr. Sturges-Bourne no person of great political weight or indeed any weight at all showed enthusiasm for the memorandum. Undeterred, Canning now proposed that it should be sent to Addington anonymously. A polite preface would explain that it had been felt more respectful to suppress the signatures, though of course those responsible were perfectly ready to sign if called upon to do so.

It is hard to imagine that Canning thought this vague denunciation would frighten or shame Addington into resignation. But in fact the Prime Minister's nerves were not to be subjected even to so slight a strain. Pitt discovered about the plot and quickly put a stop to it. "If my coming into office is as generally desired as you suppose it," he wrote dryly to Lord Malmesbury,[1] "it is much better for me and for the thing itself to leave that opinion to work out its own way: and this must happen if the opinion is a prevailing one in the public mind; and if it is not, my coming into office at all is useless and improper."

It seemed that everything that winter was destined to make a deeper breach between Addington and Pitt. On 2nd December *The Times* published a leader praising the present Ministry and criticising Pitt for skulking in retirement at a time when all good men ought to be coming to the aid of the party. Rose seized on the article with relish. "On talking to Pitt this evening . . . he grew to feel the utmost resentment and indignation at it,"[1] he reported in an ingenuous phrase which showed how much he had done himself to ensure that Pitt looked on the matter in a proper light. It was Rose's claim that Hiley Addington was responsible for the leading article. Probably he was right; Hiley's relationship with *The Times* was such that any article intended to smoke Pitt out from his cover was likely to have been inspired if not actually written by this energetic and malevolent amateur journalist.[2]

What is more interesting and important is the degree to which Addington knew and approved of such activities. Nothing which survives among his papers throws light on this problem. He can hardly have failed to realise that Hiley had at least a hand in this and a series of similar if less offensive articles which were appearing almost daily in *The Times*. Yet his main preoccupation at this period was undoubtedly to placate Pitt and he was already making overtures intended to end in a coalition government. It seems most probable that he approved the line if not the style of Hiley's journalism, believing that it might spur Pitt into activity and never reckoning that, in Pitt's present frame of mind, such activity would probably be directed against rather than in support of Government. The idea that Pitt might emerge as an open enemy seems, indeed, hardly to have occurred to Addington. The activities of Pitt's false friends might keep him for a while aloof from politics but further than this he would never go and soon he would be won back to full support of the Government and his old, devoted friends. In December, 1802, *The Times* hopefully predicted[3] that Mr. Pitt would "take his seat in the House after the recess" and that his first words would "crush the base and selfish hopes of a faction the most bare-faced and profligate that ever disgraced the country . . ." The hand may have been the hand of Hiley but the thought was undoubtedly the thought of Henry Addington.

The moment of disillusionment was near. The Grenvilles, after caballing at Stowe and exchanging shocked letters about the ignorance and imbecility of the Cabinet,[1] had told Pitt that they were not prepared to enter into any coalition which left Addington with a place in the Government.[2] *A fortiori*, the same was true of Windham. Pitt for his part had already made attempts to withdraw from the advisory role in which Ministers were so eager to retain him; indeed, as early as November, Rose had reported triumphantly[3] that Pitt was determined to accept "no responsibility whatever" for what was done in future by the Government in foreign politics. It seemed that Addington's enemies needed only to coax Pitt a little further to provoke a public and final breach. But Pitt was still not ready. He promised Rose that he would make his position unequivocally clear to Ministers yet instead contrived to give them the impression that only lack of full information about the current problems prevented him giving them his advice. Inevitably Addington responded by asking him to leave his retreat at Bath and come to London, where all the facts he wanted would be at his disposal.

After long reflection, Pitt consented to take up the invitation. In a chilly note,[4] written ominously from Lord Grenville's home at Dropmore, he agreed to call on Addington in a week or so. "Whatever may be your sentiments on public affairs, and of the conduct which ought to be pursued," concluded Addington's reply,[5] "I cannot doubt your wish to concur with me, and I have a firm reliance on your justice and friendship."

Like assiduous seconds at the start of a boxing match the Grenvilles, with Canning and his clique in close attendance, bustled around Pitt, advising him to keep up his guard and to distrust everything his adversary might say or do. They would far rather have kept Addington and Pitt apart but, if they had to meet, then at least no measure was going to be neglected which might serve to poison the atmosphere in advance.

The two men met three times in January. Addington described their conversation as "extremely comfortable and satisfactory," and Hawkesbury reported to his father that "Pitt professed himself friendly to Government and determined to continue his support of them."[7] But in fact the meetings do not seem to have produced any real rapprochement. Pitt expounded his dislike of Addington's financial policy and Addington failed to con vince him that his measures were sound. Pitt then insisted that Addington should publicly admit his errors and withdraw his Budget; if Ministers did so, he graciously assured Rose,[1] he would wish to "add as little as possible . . . to the pain and discredit of such a retraction." But if they did not, then Pitt would have to undertake the task of exposing Addington's blunders, "both for the sake of my own character and the deep public interests involved."

In spite of this somewhat exigent demand, Addington seems to have kept his temper and the two men parted affably. At some stage Addington put out a feeler to test Pitt's reactions to the idea of a coalition government. Equally tentatively, Pitt parried it with a vague comment that it would first be necessary to establish the wishes of the King.[2] If the futility of the meetings needed any demonstration it lay in the fact that Pitt believed he had made it clear that he would never agree to come into office unless he himself were to be Prime Minister. Addington, in equal good faith, was convinced that Pitt had declared himself ready to serve in the government of some congenial third party. The misunderstanding did little harm in itself but sharpened the bitterness which both men were to feel over their final rupture. The meeting did not weaken Pitt's resolve to have no more to do with the policy-making of the Government; a few weeks later Mulgrave[3] wrote to express his relief at Pitt's "full and final conviction" that there was to be no more "private advice or public palliation" so long as the Government was composed of the present Ministers.

Abandoned once more in London, Addington continued to brood on means of bringing Pitt back to office. Personally he had no doubts about his own capacity to continue as Prime Minister. He knew that the King would back him and was reasonably confident that most Englishmen, above all the country gentlemen, would be ready to do the same. But he could not view with complacency the prospect of remaining in office in the face of Pitt's sulky neutrality, let alone opposition. He knew too that, whatever they might feel in the shires, in Westminster, even in the Cabinet itself, many of his titular followers looked to Pitt as the leader of their choice. The feeling would be redoubled once war was renewed. Pitt therefore must be persuaded back. After their recent meetings Addington had been left with no

illusion that Pitt might be ready to serve under him. On th
other hand he was reluctant to accept a reversal of the roles an
to hand back to Pitt the office which the latter had almost force
him to take some two years before. As a compromise he decide
to develop the theme which he believed Pitt had already en
visaged, that both men should serve under a third party whor
each could trust and like. Pitt's elder brother, Lord Chatham
seemed the obvious choice.

Lord Melville was selected as Addington's emissary to broac
this proposal with Pitt; a choice that would once have bee
excellent but was less wise now that Pitt suspected his old col
league might have sold himself to Addington for a paltry title. I
March Melville made an expedition to Walmer Castle. From th
first words he uttered it was clear that his mission had no hop
of success. But he ploughed gallantly on and was able to repor
that he had passed on his message. There was little else for con
fort. Pitt reiterated that he had no wish to return to office bu
that the "fatal errors" of the present Government were drivin
him towards open opposition. For the moment he would remai
cloistered at Walmer but he could not predict for how muc
longer his duty to his country would allow him thus to cloa
his views. As to Addington's proposal of a Government und
Chatham, he dismissed it without hesitation, emphasising th
absolute necessity that:

> in the conduct of the affairs of this country . . . there should
> be an avowed and real minister possessing the chief weight
> in council and the principal place in the confidence of the
> King. In that respect there can be no rivalry or division of
> power. That power must rest in the person generally called
> the First Minister; and that minister ought . . . to be the
> person at the head of the finances.

Obviously Pitt was right in his reply. A Government under
puppet Chatham would have satisfied no one and would hav
slowed and made less efficient the processes of government. Bu
Pitt can still be criticised for the manner of his refusal. Whe
Melville explained the outline of Addington's plan Pitt cut hi
short without waiting for details. "Really," he commente
arrogantly to Wilberforce. "I had not the curiosity to ask wha
I was to be." It seems never to have occurred to him tha
Addington, in offering to give up the office of Prime Minist

when under no possible compulsion to do so, was acting with self-sacrifice. Misguided though Addington's proposal might have been, it deserved better than a blunt refusal and an injunction to mind his ways.

Addington was prepared to make still further concessions in the interests of re-enlisting Pitt. A week later Long, a close friend of both Pitt and Addington, posted down to Walmer with an offer that Pitt should himself become Prime Minister. Addington's only condition was that the Government should be reshaped but not wholly dissolved, in other words that the Ministers who had stood by him should not suddenly be dispossessed of office. Not even this proviso was made too exigent. Addington was ready to accept that some of his closest associates, brother-in-law Bragge among them, would have to lose their offices.[1] The only recompense for which he asked was that the Grenvilles and their followers should not be admitted to office straight away. Their opposition to him and his policies had been so violent that he would have found their inclusion altogether too ignominious. But he made it clear that he had no wish or intention to bind Pitt's choice of Minister for longer than the period of the change of Government and perhaps a month or two beyond. After that if Grenville had to come in there would be no difficulty. As to Canning and Rose, Addington gave Long to understand that he would accept even them in office. It was agreed that Pitt and Addington should meet in ten days to discuss a settlement upon these lines.

Long left Walmer satisfied that the way was open to an agreement. But even as he clambered into his chaise, Lord Grenville's carriage arrived at the door. Grenville saw few attractions in a compromise which did not involve his own immediate return to office. He strongly urged that Pitt should insist on a free hand in forming a Government and refuse even to discuss the details with the present Prime Minister. Pitt must hold out for unconditional surrender; nothing else would satisfy the dictates of honour and England's need. One small concession Grenville was prepared to make, though even that heavily qualified:[2]

... although we might consent (under the present circumstances of public difficulty) to act in a government where Mr. Addington and Lord Hawkesbury continued to hold Cabinet situations, yet I saw very little probability of our agreeing to extend that acquiescence so far as to their holding any efficient offices of real business.

It was casually suggested that an office of Speaker of th House of Lords might be invented in which honorific grav Addington could inter any shreds of ambition and pride tha were still left him.

When Pitt and Addington met at Long's house Pitt dul presented this surprising ultimatum. Even then Addington di not rebel. He said that the Speakership in the Lords was quit unacceptable to him but that his own claims to office should n be allowed to stand in the way of an agreement. If he cou recommend such a settlement on public grounds, he wrote t Pitt,[1] ". . . the only honourable course I could pursue would b to concur in the sacrifices it would require, and to put myse entirely out of the question; and this I should do with the utmo readiness and the most perfect satisfaction." But he was sti unhappy at Pitt's insistence that the present Ministry should b dissolved and Grenville brought in immediately. He undertoo to consult the Cabinet. In the meantime he offered to visit Pi once more to discuss the matter further, hoping "that you ma not find it necessary to adhere, in its full extent, to the propositio which you have made." To this Pitt merely replied that he ha already set out his final terms and that, if Addington could n accept them, he had better not waste his time on a further visit

When the Cabinet met they concluded that,[3] agreeable thoug it might be to all of them to have Pitt at their head, they cou not:

think it proper or justifiable, under the present circumstances, to promote a course of proceedings which had for its object, to new-model, reconstruct and in part to change the government, instead of strengthening it, as has been suggested, by the union of those, who had concurred in opinion respecting its leading measures; and that, considering what had been the declared opinions, and the conduct in parliament, of some of those whom it was proposed to comprehend in the intended plan of arrangement, they could not, consistently with what appeared to them to be due to the interests of the public, and to their own characters, give their advice, that steps should be taken to carry it into effect.

With this sentence, of characteristically Addingtonian turgidit the negotiations came to an end. In a correspondence of increasing chilliness, degenerating from "affectionately yours," by way of "sincerely yours" to "I am, my dear Sir, your faithful and obedient servant," the two protagonists restated their cases for the sake of posterity and their own consciences. Pitt asked that all the letters should be laid before the King. Addington agreed to do so but found that though one may take letters to a King one cannot make him read them. "It is a foolish business from one end to the other," grumbled George III to Pelham.[1] "It was begun ill, conducted ill, and terminated ill." Pettishly, he refused even to break the seals; conduct which Canning, in a letter to Pitt of twenty-three pages,[2] ascribed to the timidity of Addington and probably his active malevolence as well.

A foolish business perhaps it had been: foolish of Addington to think that Pitt would serve under Lord Chatham as Prime Minister but surely still more foolish of Pitt, when so much was offered him, to strain for the last slice of the cake. Loyalty to Grenville may explain his actions, but even on the most generous analysis the loyalty seems misplaced. All Addington asked was that the policy of his Government should not be overtly condemned by the immediate appointment of its harshest critics. If this were given him he was prepared to sacrifice his dignity, his office and even the future of his closest friends. To reject the sacrifice so as to bring Grenville a few months earlier into office betrays a pathetic misjudgment of essentials. Reflecting that almost exactly twelve months later Grenville was to refuse to serve under Pitt himself, it may be felt that tragic would be a better word.

Melville was no admirer of Grenville but he was still a convinced Pittite. Though friendly with Addington he often criticised him harshly. His judgment on the issue should therefore be reasonably impartial. ". . . no step could be more injudicious on your part," he wrote to Pitt,[3] "than an attempt to form an administration mixing in it Lord Grenville with the leading parts of His Majesty's present Government. None of them, in my opinion, could sit down in council with him without depreciating their character in the eye of the public. . . . You must therefore decide between Lord Grenville and those in the present administration of whose attachment to you there can not exist a doubt." He argued that Lord Grenville had consistently taken a different line to Pitt, while in the case of Ministers "from the moment you retired from office, your wishes have been paramount with them in the regulation of their conduct." He ended with a solemn warning. "I am now going to Scotland, where you have much support. . . . If they were to conceive that your not being at the head of the Government proceeded from any sentiment on the part of Mr. Addington adverse to such arrangements, I have no words to express the dissatisfaction the belief of such an exclusion would create, but the dissatisfaction towards you would not be less, if it was conceived that you would not lend yourself to the public service unless you could bring Lord Grenville along with you."

One thing at least was shown conclusively by these negotiations. At his own initiative Addington had offered to hand over the leadership to Pitt and to accept the humiliation of seeing many of his closest associates and possibly even himself excluded from office. This he did in spite of a commanding majority in Parliament, the whole-hearted support of the King and the country gentlemen and his own conviction that the record of his Government could withstand the most hostile criticism. His motive was simply that he believed Pitt to be the leader preferred by many of his colleagues and that the thought of continuing in office in the face of Pitt's hostility was almost intolerable to him. On these grounds he may be accused of feebleness, of lacking the will to fight, even of a tacit admission of his own inferiority, but the more common accusation that he clung to office against the wishes of the country is patently unfair. On the contrary, his readiness to divest himself of office was one of the most remarkable features of his career as Prime Minister. Only when it became evident to him that his great renunciation would not be enough and that Pitt would only be satisfied with abject and unconditional surrender did he finally revolt. Even then he did not make his stand until he had established that his colleagues as well as he felt that they were being driven too far and that it was their will as well as his that he should turn and fight.

* * * * *

Once the breach with Pitt had become complete, Addington could feel less inhibited in his dealings with the Whigs. The Grenvilles reported that Addington had been passing his time at

Devonshire House;[1] he may have gone there on occasion but certainly he must have felt himself sadly out of place in the rarefied air of that aristocratic Shangri-La. More to the point the protracted flirtation between Tierney and the Addingtonians was consummated in May when Tierney was appointed Treasurer of the Navy. The job was more or less a sinecure; an hour and a half's work a day, said the new incumbent.[2] But the appointment meant that Tierney could speak officially for the Government in the Commons; a valuable gain, for though he lacked some of the power of Pitt and Fox and the wit of Sheridan, he was still one of the most lucid and effective debaters of his day. The appointment to his Government of the man who had fought a duel with Pitt only a few years before may also have given Addington a little malicious pleasure. "This seems to be an indication of Pitt's never taking office any more,"[3] was Malmesbury's comment when he heard the news.

With the rest of the Whigs, Addington's relations remained amiable but distant. Fox saw clearly that the only viable alternative to the present Government must be the return of Pitt. "I do not think you will suspect me of being partial to the Doctor," he wrote to Grey,[4] but in the circumstances support of Ministers seemed the lesser evil. This, however, was to be the limit of it. If the Whigs were to come in it was to be with a majority in the Cabinet; nothing else could justify them in allying themselves with what they suspected to be a dying administration.[5]

Tierney's appointment made it possible for Addington to strengthen the woefully feeble team which the Ministry could field in the House of Lords. He did this by bestowing a barony on Lord Hawkesbury. The decrepitude of Lord Liverpool was now such that it seemed Addington was doing no more than anticipate by a few months the promotion which nature would shortly have granted of its own. Hawkesbury, however, who considered himself indispensable in the Commons, was decidedly offended. In the end he accepted grudgingly on the grounds that otherwise there would be nobody in the Lords but Eldon to argue with Grenville on foreign policy.[6]

St. Vincent, on the other hand, was clamouring to be released from office altogether. His health, he claimed, was rapidly declining, he could no longer meet all the claims which office made on his fading energies.[7] The excuse was probably genuine;

he seems to have had no particular grudge against the other
Ministers and certainly his spiritual leader Fox had no wish to
weaken the Government further. But to Addington, whose hopes
of bringing back Melville had been dashed by the breach with
Pitt, even St. Vincent's death would have been an inadequate
excuse for releasing him from office. Insufferable though the
arrogance and narrow-mindedness of this arch busy-body might
sometimes be, his fame was still great among the public and
only someone of his stature could have hoped to see the Royal
Navy through the welter of reforms and economy cuts in which
he had embroiled it.

* * * * *

Meanwhile relations with France had been growing rapidly
worse. At the end of January Napoleon caused to be published
in the *Moniteur* a report on the state of Egypt by a certain Colonel
Sebastiani. This report, officially dealing with trade prospects, in
fact turned out to be an explosive political tract which urged the
reconquest of Egypt and the overthrow of the Ottoman Empire.
A fortnight later Napoleon summoned the British Ambassador.
In a two-hour tirade which, even by his own standards, was
monumental in its insolence and crudity, he insisted on the
immediate evacuation of Malta. With rich hyperbole he assured
Lord Whitworth that, if he had to choose between the two, he
would rather see the British occupy the Faubourg St. Antoine
than remain in Malta. When Whitworth counter-attacked with
references to Switzerland and Piedmont, Napoleon dismissed
these as mere bagatelles which were not mentioned in the treaty
and had obviously been foreseen during the negotiations and
dismissed as irrelevant.

"His purpose was evidently to convince me that on Malta must
depend peace or war . . ." reported Whitworth.[1] Addington had
reluctantly made up his mind that, if the choice was to be presented in those terms, he must opt for war. The proof that
Napoleon had given of his insatiable ambition, his new conquests
in Europe and now a clear threat to Egypt and the East, could
not be answered by the evacuation of this essential stepping-stone.
Talleyrand cheerfully admitted that "the acquisition of Egypt
was a favourite object of the First Consul" but claimed that he
would not pursue it to the point of war.[2] Whitworth was instructed

to reply that the deeds of the French, not their words, would be what would decide our future policy. We would not evacuate Malta until Sebastiani's escapade had been explained and the *status quo* restored in Europe.

Expounding his policy,[1] Addington declared that:

his maxim from the moment he took office was first to make peace, and then to preserve it, under certain reservations in his own mind, if France chose, and as long as France chose; but to resist all clamour and invective at home, till such time as France (and he ever foresaw it must happen) had filled the measure of her folly, and had put herself completely in the wrong . . . he had waited till insolence was coupled with hostility, or (which was the same) hostile declarations, before he moved . . .

He felt that this point had at last been reached. A stand must be made and here, unlike in Piedmont or in Switzerland, could be made effectively. At least, as Addington proudly claimed,[2] no one was going to be able to say that he was the species of Minister who, "to preserve peace, would timidly submit to any ignominy or disgrace, and . . . let the country be trampled on with impunity!"

But for every sturdy patriot who accused Addington of feebleness in the defence of Britain's vital interests, there was a peace-loving Whig to tax him with provocation of the innocent French. Fox believed that the country could have been saved from war.[3] The fault was that of Ministers and not of the French. He attributed Addington's belligerence to the King's influence: "the moment the Doctor found that the King's madness took the turn of wishing war against Bonaparte, he was determined to humour that on which his sole existence depended, viz., the King's madness."[4] Sebastiani's report was dismissed by the Whigs as an empty pretext, a device to suit the needs of a warmongering and blood-thirsty administration.

As is usually the case with Ministers whose policy is assailed by extremists on either flank, Addington's policy was substantially right. But in strictly legal terms the Whigs had a certain amount of justice on their side. By the Treaty of Amiens the British should have evacuated Malta months before; nothing had been provided to indicate that this should be conditional on French good behaviour elsewhere nor was there anything in the treaty to preclude the French activities in Italy, Holland and Switzerland. When Whitworth demanded that the *status quo* be first restored, Napoleon turned to the text of the treaty. "I cannot find it, 'tis not in the bond," he could justifiably retort. "Il faut donc respecter les traités, malheur á ceux qui ne respectent pas les traités."[1]

The English had been out-manœuvred. The Treaty of Amiens had taken too much for granted. Belatedly Addington had discovered that the underlying assumptions which had dictated his signature of the treaty had never been present in the minds of the French. But though juridically the French position might be strong, they did not gain as much by it as they must have expected. A handful of noisy Whigs might shout that Britain was in the wrong but on this issue at least Addington had no reason to fear the Whigs. The British people, in so far as the term had any meaning in the early nineteenth century, had been convinced that war with Napoleon could not be avoided and that their Ministers had done all that they reasonably could by way of concession and conciliation. Thereby one of Addington's main objects in seeking peace had been achieved; a united country, revived if not fully restored by the truce, was ready to continue fighting until the end. Nor were the Russians and other potential allies on the Continent particularly interested in the legal niceties; they knew too well that Napoleon's appetite was insatiable and awaited with apprehension but little disappointment the renewal of a war which they had never considered to be more than temporarily adjourned.

Addington decided it would be poor tactics to allow Napoleon to develop the situation in his own time. He called out the militia and made provision for adding 10,000 men to the navy—"Whenever it is necessary, I am *your* Admiral," wrote Nelson[2] with characteristic bravura—then sent fresh and drastic instructions to Whitworth. The Ambassador was told to ask for perpetual possession of Malta and the retreat of the French from Holland and Switzerland. In return Britain would accept affairs as they stood in Italy and indemnify the Knights of St. John. If the French would not accept these terms or propose others equally satisfactory for British security then Whitworth was to ask for his passports.

Napoleon was taken aback; he was not yet ready for war and

had assumed that, even if the British could not be frightened out of Malta, negotiations would drift on for some time more at least. Talleyrand was told to play for time, a tactic in which no statesman was more proficient. But not all his counter-proposals, private assurances and hints of compensation elsewhere could win more than a few weeks' grace. As the ostentatious and carefully protracted process of packing the Ambassador's goods and papers went on it seemed on several occasions as if the French might still come forward with acceptable proposals. But the important concessions were always just out of reach; Napoleon *might* agree to them the following day but for the moment it would be indiscreet to press him. Hints that more might be possible pursued Whitworth to the coast and across the Channel but Addington and his Ministers had made up their mind. Even a last-minute proposal that Malta should be leased to the United Kingdom for ten years in exchange for French control of the Otranto peninsula was rejected out of hand on the grounds that the peninsula did not belong to the British and therefore was not theirs to dispose of.

It would be difficult to exaggerate the reluctance with which Addington took the final steps. The Peace of Amiens, even though he had never believed that it could last, had been his own achievement. It had been his hand which had spared the lives of many unfortunates and brought rest to a shattered Europe. Now he was called on to undo his work. "I used to think all the sufferings of war lost in its glory"; he remarked long afterwards "now I consider all its glory lost in its sufferings. So one's feelings change."[1] By 1803 his belief in the glory of war was already tarnished. He saw before him only death, destruction and all-pervasive misery. He had satisfied himself that, in conscience, no other course was open to him but it was a course which he followed with loathing and in the knowledge that to do so must mean that he had failed.

On 23rd and 24th May the renewal of war was debated in the House of Commons. Of all the occasions of drama which may arise in the life of a Prime Minister none can be more high-wrought than the moment at which he leads his country into war. Then if ever he will find an attentive and sympathetic House, ready to respond to any impulse of grandeur and asking only to be lifted above the humdrum level of their normal business. Never was

Addington's inability to provide even a modicum of inspiration more harmful to his reputation and his future. Not even the habitual chorus of sycophants pretended that he had achieved anything very remarkable; by more objective commentators his effort was either ignored or scornfully dismissed.

Instead Pitt seized the occasion. Returning to the House after a long absence, he enthralled and inflamed them for more than two hours. "If Demosthenes had been present" said Fox,[1] who disagreed with almost every word that Pitt had uttered "he must have admired, and might have envied." Only on the capacity of Ministers to meet the needs of the crisis was Pitt conspicuously silent; it was not only Lord Malmesbury who felt that his reticence must be "construed into negative censure."[2]

It is not essential to be an orator in order to be a good Prime Minister. Administrative efficiency, good judgment, integrity, calm, assiduity: all these are as, if not more, important. But there must be occasions, above all in war, when they are not enough. At such moments men demand to be led, to be excited, to be inspired, to be convinced in dramatic terms of the rightness of their cause and the certainty of their victory. The fact that Pitt could supply this need while Addington could not did not in itself prove that Pitt was the more effective leader of the two. No one in the House of Commons would have claimed it did. If asked to explain why he believed Addington to be inadequate as Prime Minister it is doubtful whether a single Member would have listed a lack of oratory among his most dangerous failings. But it still went far to create that lack of confidence which was ultimately to nullify all Addington's efforts and to lead to the classification of his Government as a hopeless failure. If, for once in his life, Addington had been able to give the House of Commons what it wanted, it would have made no iota of difference to his command of strategy or his understanding of economic forces. But he would have won the House to his side, have created an atmosphere in which his successes might have been fairly appreciated and his failures indulgently received. He would have had a chance of succeeding as Prime Minister in time of war. As it was, he began his weary course with a Parliament convinced that he was a *pis aller* to be discarded as soon as the mighty Pitt was ready to step back into the pilot's place.

Addington regained a little stature a fortnight later. On 3r

June, Colonel Patten moved a resolution of censure on the Government for their conduct of the negotiations with France. Addington believed that Pitt had at one time agreed to support the resolution[1] but later regretted his decision; at all events Pitt sent Melville to him with a proposal that the resolution should not be pressed to a vote but shelved by Pitt moving the orders of the day and thus cutting off discussion. To Addington this suggestion was intolerable; he made it plain to Melville that, in his eyes, to evade such a challenge would be to admit that the censure was merited. Melville suggested that, in that case, the Government might be in danger. "I do not know how that might be" replied Addington[2] "but I will never consent to be placed in a situation in which a drawn sword is to be kept suspended over my head and be indebted to the forbearance of the adverse party for its not being allowed to drop."

When the day came, Patten duly launched his onslaught. Addington insisted that the competence of the Government be put to the vote while Pitt, in a shuffling speech, refused either to support or condemn the Government. The result was a triumph for Addington. Only the most ardent Pittites voted to shelve the issue—58 against 335—while on Patten's motion, on which all the Pittites except Canning abstained, only 36 Grenvillites or kindred spirits were found unequivocally to condemn the Government. Fox and his followers, numbered by Fox at sixty-nine but by most other authorities at considerably less, also abstained on Patten's resolution.

The King was delighted at the result which "His Chancellor of the Exchequer" had achieved.[3] Addington, too, found nothing to complain of in the voting figures. For him, however, the debate had possessed peculiar bitterness as publishing to all the world that the breach with Pitt was now complete. Though he did not realise it the very scale of his victory had made that future still more hazardous. Fox had been appalled at the vastness of Addington's majority.[4] A weak Addingtonian Government dependent on the tolerance of the Whigs could be accepted. An Addingtonian Government with a majority of hundreds, dedicated to the continuance of the war to victory, would be insufferable. For the first time Fox thought seriously of joining with Grenville to defeat the Ministry.

There were signs, too, that Addington's majority might not be as solid as it appeared. The *True Briton*, a paper traditionally pledged to support of Ministers, now swung away into opposition. Cobbett ascribed their action to "the same motives that sagacious vermin desert a house that has long been their favourite haunt."[1] It would have been a wise rat which studied the results of the recent debate and still deduced that the Government was near its end. But even among the ranks of those who voted so solidly for Addington there was little feeling that their action was in any way a commitment for the future. For the moment they were loyal but let some reasonable alternative offer itself and the rats would swiftly be on the way.

8

From the moment war was declared the only question was how long Addington's administration would be able to survive. It is easy to chart the course of the illness, the gradual ebbing away of strength, the phases of fitful recovery, the inevitable relapses and the sudden, catastrophic deterioration which heralded the end. But diagnosis is another matter, for though it was perfectly simple to observe that Addington's Government was dying it was a great deal more difficult to understand exactly why.

The most unexpected feature about Addington's career as a war-time Prime Minister is that he did a certain amount that was conspicuously right and very little that was disastrously wrong. It is certainly impossible to hail his Government as more than a qualified success. But equally it is impossible to find it guilty of the sort of incompetence and slothfulness, almost of treachery, which alone could explain the wave of disgusted execration amidst which it was washed to its defeat. The contrast between the deeds of Addington's war-time administration and its reputation, between its reality and its public image, is the most perplexing problem in the months which followed the renewal of the war. So far as Addington is concerned it is also the most revealing passage in his career.

*   *   *   *   *

Addington's first task was to put the country's economy back on a war footing. He based his measures on the supposition that the war would be a long one, in a moment of prescience even predicting that it might last for another twelve years.[1] Any new tax, therefore, must be built to last, able to yield constant or increasing revenue over a long period without doing damage to the national economy. After much consideration and research into the history of English and continental systems of taxation he had concluded that this could only be done by the reimposition and complete remodelling of Pitt's old income tax. This measure he introduced in his Budget speech of 13th June, 1803.

"Addington does better than was expected; rated our establishment at 26 millions; his taxes heavy but not bad; no opposition to him, nor any speech but his." Lord Malmesbury's staccato comments[1] show how few people realised from Addington's speech that the Property Tax, as the income tax was now styled introduced fundamentally new principles which were to transform the whole structure of British taxation. Such a transformation was badly needed; Pitt's tax had failed and its revival without radical revision would have served little purpose. Its weakness had lain in its dependence on the thoroughness and integrity of the individual tax-payers. This Addington proposed to remedy by the resurrection, refurbishing and vast extension of the principle known as "Taxation at the Source."[2]

It is now so much taken for granted that the individual should receive his income, whether earned or unearned, with the basic tax already deducted, that it is hard to conceive of a time when such a system seemed a daring, indeed improper, innovation. Yet to many of the financial experts of the age, above all to Pitt, it seemed that there was much to cavil at in the new proposal and that the optimism of Ministers as to their results was absurdly misplaced. As far as the income derived from property was concerned Addington could claim for his idea the respectable ancestry of the Land Tax Act of 1692 which provided for tenants deducting from their rents the rates which the landlord ought to bear and being responsible for this amount to the tax collector. But when it came to extending the principle to the income derived from the Funds and Corporation Stocks as well as from personal property, trade pensions and offices there was indeed a most radical departure from existing practice.

Addington saw three main advantages in his procedure. If tax was deducted at the source there would no longer be need for individuals to make a full declaration of their fortune. The levying of tax on money borrowed on mortgage would be simplified since the debtor would become responsible for the whole of the tax and nineteen shillings in the pound become legal tender to the mortgagor. Finally, and most important, "the execution was infinitely more easy and simple to the Commissioners than it was before, as persons now will not be in a situation in which the will have to decide between their interest and their duty."[1] This last advantage seemed to Addington so real that he boldly predicted that a tax of one shilling in the pound would produce about £4.5 million. Yet Pitt's tax at double the rate had produced only a little more than this, some £5.3 million. Addington's pride in this prophecy was particularly irritating to Pitt. It stung him into opposing the Budget on a variety of counts which otherwise might hardly have occurred to him.

At first, indeed, Pitt offered no opposition. He let it be known that he had doubts about some aspects of the income tax but reserved his position until the debate a month later in July. Then he indulged himself in a whole-hearted attack on what he considered to be the weaknesses of Addington's measure and vaunted the beauties of his own income tax under which "the spirit of the country grew up with rapidity and vigour; its triumph extended, its good fortune as it were revived."[2]

First he condemned Addington for trying to distinguish between the various forms of income. In a spirit of unexpected social progressiveness Addington had proposed that exemption should be given to the first £150 of earned income but not to that derived from other sources. This outraged Pitt. "It was a fallacy," he claimed, "to suppose that there ought to be a distinction between income derived from industry and that from capital without industry . . . This was nothing more than a premium or a bounty held out to people to enter into trade." Relief should be given either to all incomes or none. Addington defended his proposals in the House and won through by 150 votes to 50, then next day surrendered and extended the exemption to all classes of income. "See here," wrote Pitt's biographer,[3] "the inborn ascendancy of genius. Addington, although he had conquered in the division, felt himself beat in the debate . . ." It is quite certain that Addington felt himself nothing of the sort: he remained convinced that his own proposal was the better both from the point of view of social justice and of revenue. His withdrawal was a tactical one, induced by a sense of the weakness of his position in the House of Commons and doubts as to the loyalty of his supporters in the face of Pitt's onslaught.

If Addington calculated that Pitt would be softened by this show of subservience and treat the rest of the Budget more gently as a result, he misjudged entirely the mood of his former friend. Pitt now attacked what was one of the essential elements of Addington's new system, that the individual components of every man's income should be taxed rather than a tax levied on the general total. He directed his attack on the separate assessment of income from the funds but couched it in such terms that, if his criticism had been accepted, all the five schedules of the new tax would have had to be abandoned and the principle of taxation at the source become unworkable.

This attack Addington was bound to resist if his ideas were not to be totally abandoned. But he still found something almost indecently daring in venturing to oppose the will of Pitt. He felt bound to make a compensatory withdrawal on another important though less fundamental point. Pitt maintained that the proposal that the Bank of England should deduct tax on income from the funds before paying it to the fund-holder was the most objectionable part of the Bill, a "violation of the public compact entered into between the Government and the holders of stock"[1] and "a first blow at the credit of the country." In his Budget speech Addington had referred to the difficulties of taxing this source of income but had continued: "It cannot be contended that at a time like the present, when every possible exertion must from necessity be adopted, that even that species of property should alone stand exempted." This Pitt did not dispute, but he perceived a profound difference in principle between the payment of interest in full and the subsequent reclaiming of tax and the payment of the interest with the tax already deducted. Backed by the conservative experts of the Bank of England he had his way; Addington accepted that income from the funds should be exempt from taxation at the source. Pitt's scrupulousness proved expensive. When Lord Henry Petty scrapped the restriction two years later the revenue derived from this source was almost doubled overnight.

On all these grounds history has proved Addington right and Pitt wrong. Yet though the net effect of the amendments forced on the Government by Pitt was sharply to reduce the revenue, it still did as well as its inventor had hoped and far better than its detractors had believed possible. Addington's original estimate for the first year of the income tax had been £4.5 million. The final figure was £4.76 million, a remarkable contrast to the consistent shortfalls of the tax in its previous form. On four of the five schedules of taxation into which Addington divided the national income the final figure was slightly greater than his estimate; only in the case of Government stocks where taxation at the source had been abandoned did his figures prove too optimistic. For a first essay into a new and vastly complicated field his techniques had proved almost miraculously accurate and successful.

Nor was this a lucky chance. For the year 1804-5, Addington estimated that the tax would yield £4.8 million. In fact the final figure was £4.9 million. That even Pitt was convinced by these successes was shown when it was again his turn to introduce a Budget in 1805. He adopted Addington's tax with only the most minor changes to some details of its administration and an increase from 1s. to 1s. 3d. in the pound. As a result, for the first time his estimate of the yield of the tax proved justified; indeed he gathered far more through Addington's income tax at 1s. 3d. in the pound than he had ever secured through his own at 2s.

In his skilful monograph on Addington's taxation policy Dr. Farnsworth[1] has demonstrated how Addington's income tax became the basis of the present law. What the Royal Commission on the Income Tax described in 1919[2] as "a principle which has been of incalculable benefit to the revenue of this country and which in spite of some modern encroachments remains the great buttress of Income Tax stability and efficiency" had its origin in Addington's Budget of 1803. In 1948 the Nineteenth Report of the Commissioners of Inland Revenue,[3] describing deduction at the source as the keystone of our national income tax, went on to outline the principle in words drawn almost exactly from the official exposition of Addington's income tax. That Pitt was the first to impose a tax on income is indisputable, but it is equally sure that it was Addington who introduced the vital element which made it work.

The point would hardly be worth reiterating if it were not for the fiction, constantly repeated, that it was Pitt's income tax—the income tax of 1805—which has carried through without fundamental change to the present day. The fact that Pitt's tax of 1805 is an exact copy of Addington's of 1803 and 1804 is rarely mentioned. Still more unjust is the complementary assumption that it was Addington's incompetence as Chancellor which in great part contributed to the downfall of his Government. During his years as Prime Minister Addington laid the economic foundations of the system which was to carry Britain to victory. All that can be said for Pitt in these closing years of his career is that he had the sense not to let his resentment at Addington's success lead him into dismantling Addington's principal achievement.

* * * * *

For some time after the declaration of war the struggle between Pitt and Addington was of far greater interest to the politicians at Westminster than the war between Britain and France. Certainly it reached a pitch of bitterness to which the international conflict did not yet attain. After the debate on the budget Pitt retreated to his fastness at Walmer whence occasional critical rumbles served to remind the Government of his presence. He expounded his policy freely to anyone who inquired: he did not feel himself able to go into systematic opposition, on the other hand he would not help Ministers in any way or abstain from criticising them when their bungling became too disastrous. This satisfied nobody. To Canning, Grenville and others of Addington's more truculent enemies Pitt's retirement seemed feeble and futile, sacrificing the interests of the country to a mistaken sense of loyalty. Pitt himself it left in frustrating inactivity which it seemed need never end; convinced that his talents were essential to the country he found himself debarred from taking the one step which would have made them useful. For Addington, who had accepted office only with Pitt's blessing, the withdrawal of the light of Pitt's countenance seemed almost treasonable, a denial of the rights of friendship as harsh as the most direct attack upon the Government. Finally to the British people it meant that their leaders dissipated their time and energies in sterile bickering instead of concentrating on the only issue of real importance, the winning of the war.

Even before war had been declared certain members of Addington's Government had begun to test out the possibility of engineering the return of Pitt. In May of 1803 the Duke of Portland intrigued with the Duke of York to find a way by which Addington might be put to one side "upon a bed of roses, in a dignified and official station."[1] Portland was an honourable man and his intentions were certainly excellent; he believed that Pitt

194

must eventually return to power and dreaded the effects on the King's mind and the morale of the country of a prolonged and bitter struggle for power. But even then things had gone too far for such a palliative, by the late summer it was certain that a direct confrontation would be necessary before Addington would yield or Pitt return to office.

Addington still made tentative gestures of goodwill in the direction of Walmer Castle but in September any possibility of reconciliation became still more remote. A pamphlet appeared written by "A Near Observer" and titled "A few Cursory Remarks upon the State of Parties during the Administration of the Rt. Hon. Henry Addington." It praised lavishly all the personalities and policies of the present Government and, with some skill, abused all those who did not whole-heartedly support them. Pitt came in for particularly harsh treatment; indeed the only failing which the anonymous author could find in Addington was his "attachment and deference . . . for Mr. Pitt."

The pamphlet caused much indignation among its victims. "The most atrocious instance of private ingratitude and personal injustice that ever was published," wrote Canning.[1] ". . . as stupid as it is impudent and false," was Fox's comment.[2] Pitt himself was as offended as anyone and told Rose that it was one of the most "malignant, false and artful statements he ever saw."[3] Rose seized the opportunity to insist that it was Bragge who must have given the material to the author—anonymous but since identified as a Mr. T. R. Bentley. The combination of malice with inside information suggests that Hiley Addington also played a part. At all events, Government showed that it approved even if it did not sponsor the publication when Vansittart instructed the Post Office to circulate copies to a list of chosen friends.

Addington himself always denied that he knew anything of the pamphlet before it was published. The denial is reasonably convincing. Nothing in the text reminds one either of his prose style or his way of thinking; the jibes at Pitt were altogether alien to his feelings and, if he had been consulted, his invariable reluctance to make enemies would certainly have led to the curbing of some of the sharper passages. It is possible that he knew vaguely what his partisans were planning but even this is not certain. Hiley had already shown his readiness to take his own course without awaiting prior instructions and, in a matter of this kind where he knew his brother would be unduly pacific, he could well have decided to go ahead without risking a veto.

Pitt was not interested in the possibility of Addington's innocence; he demanded a full and unqualified denunciation of the pamphlet. But even if he had got it he did not pretend that this would have been enough to appease his wounded feelings. For a time he played with the idea of instructing Canning to write a counter-blast, then decided that the style would be too well known and the antipathy to Addington too obvious. In the end a Mr. Courtenay from the Stationery Office was selected as Pitt's standard-bearer and in due course a "More Accurate Observer" presented to the public his "Plain Answer to the Misrepresentations and Calumnies contained in the Cursory Remarks of a Near Observer." The Addingtonian salvo hurtled back in the guise of "A Plain Reply to a plain Answer," and from the side-lines the battlefield was disturbed by stray shells such as "The View of the relative situations of Mr. Pitt and Mr. Addington" by Robert Ward and the riposte "A Letter to Robert Ward, Esq., M.P. occasioned by his pamphlet."

This paper warfare shed no blood but was little less mischievous for that. The pamphlets, wrote Malmesbury,[1] "produced no other effect than creating a degree of personal enmity between them [Pitt and Addington] they till now never had, nor ever would have entertained, if these officious scribblers had not come forward." Malmesbury underestimated the degree to which the two men were already estranged. But though the pamphlet war may have been no more than a late phase of an already protracted conflict it was typical of all the rest in that neither Pitt nor Addington were its instigators or even the principal participants. If ever men had cause to curse their friends they were Pitt and Addington. The two men had once been deeply attached to each other. With a minimum of good-will on either side the same could have been true again. Left to themselves they would quickly have reached an amicable settlement; Pitt would have taken over the Government and Addington been settled in a place of honour where his qualities could have been used to best advantage. Instead, rabidly hostile groups on either side goaded them into enmity, every attempt at reconciliation was poisoned in advance, the lines of communication gradually worn away. In the case of the pamphlet war it was Addington's friends who began the trouble, more often it was Pitt's who proved the more malevolent. But put the blame where one will, the fact remained that the dogs were at each other's throats while their masters hovered ineffectually in the background, disapproving of the carnage yet unable or unwilling to bring it to an end.

*   *   *   *   *

Addington therefore was left to conduct the war as best he could. His activities have normally been portrayed as ineffective, sporadic and misdirected. Certainly there was much in them which fell short of the ideal. But in deciding whether Addington failed or succeeded it is reasonable first to inquire what he was trying to do. His critics at the time assumed that he was trying to wage a Pittite war with bold adventures in every direction and an endless, costly struggle to destroy the French upon the Continent. When nothing happened to support their thesis they assumed that Addington was incompetent to manage the weapons of his great predecessor. They saw Addington's inactivity as spineless and criminal inertia and condemned it at the top of their voices. Few if any stopped to wonder whether Addington might not have evolved his own philosophy of war and now, however inadequately, be seeking to put it into practice.

Addington believed that in 1801 the war had reached a deadlock. Napoleon controlled the Continent, Britain the seas and all that lay beyond them. So long as this broad division of power was accepted then, though each side might inflict painful wounds upon the other, no death blow could be struck. This situation had now been reproduced in 1803. The only way that Britain could break the deadlock was by stirring up some continental power to join in the war against France. But Addington did not believe that any such power, psychologically or militarily, was ready to do so. To press them into action would merely allow Napoleon to win glory through cheap victories and reduce the chances of effective opposition to the French when the would-be allies had recovered their strength. Count Stahremberg, the Austrian Ambassador, told Addington that Austria would be ready to come forward if Britain wished but that the longer the delay the better it would be. "We are a giant," he said, "but a giant exhausted; and we require time to regain our strength."[1]

197

As for the French, the only way that they could win the war would be by the invasion of Britain. So long as the British Navy held the Channel and Nelson guided the British Navy, then Addington was confident that such an attempt must fail. It was indeed his earnest hope that the French would try. His belief that, if left long enough, they would eventually do so was one of the main considerations which led him to evolve his strategy. Then, and only then, with the flower of the French Army drowned or cut to pieces on our beaches, it might be the moment to recreate one of Pitt's beloved coalitions and take the war back to the Continent.

In other words, victory would go to the side which could remain inactive the longest. Addington had no doubt that his patience would outlast Napoleon's. It was inconceivable that the latter would not threaten to invade and, having done so, mass his army along the Channel coast. If it took to the water it would be destroyed. If it stayed where it was morale would sink and it would suffer in health and discipline. Meanwhile the English could mop up the enemy colonies—an agreeable diversion which Addington at once set in train in the West Indies where St. Lucia, Tobago and the other French islands were in British hands a few months after war was renewed.

The strategy was hardly a noble one. Nor was it immune to criticism. Discouraged by the inertia of the British, the continental powers might lose all interest in opposition to Napoleon. Inactivity might suit our army no better than the French. The Navy might blunder and an enemy army reach British shores. Ireland was a tempting target for a French diversion. The policy, in short, had its dangers. Certainly it offered no recipe for quick or brilliant victory. But it was still reasonable, coherent and consistent with the view of Europe which had led Addington to conclude the Peace of Amiens. It is easy to see why it appealed to someone of Addington's unadventurous and prudent spirit and there are good grounds for contending that the occasion was one when prudence was to be welcomed and adventure to be deplored. Certainly subsequent history did nothing to prove that Addington was wrong. When Pitt's new continental coalition gave Napoleon a chance of extricating his Grand Army from its futile posture on the Channel coast it had already suffered from its long and frustrating confinement. Another year staring out to sea might

prising that the ills of Ireland continued unabated. Given the condition of the island and its inhabitants it would have been astonishing if Napoleon had not tried to make trouble there. The only surprise is that he did it so ineffectively. Vague promises of help from Paris were taken far more seriously in London than in Ireland. Certainly Robert Emmet, whose futile conspiracy and rising caused such alarm, seems to have approached his task in a mood of fatalistic pessimism unrelieved by any hope that the French might come to his aid. This talented yet wholly ineffectual revolutionary in August, 1803, led a few fanatics in an operetta rising which rose to tragedy only in the messy murder of the Chief Justice, Lord Kilwarden, and the eventual execution of most of the protagonists. The rebels never had a chance of success and were eventually quelled by a handful of regular troops. But in England, where the spectre of a French invasion in the name of Irish independence seemed very real, news of the disorder caused consternation and much criticism of the Government. It was considered that the military had been taken by surprise, and the vague belief that the Government should have acted in advance added to the miasma of disenchantment which was beginning to envelop all the activities of Addington's ministers.

A Cabinet reshuffle in the early autumn did little to win back popularity. The aged Lord Liverpool, now unable even to stand, grudgingly agreed to abandon the Duchy of Lancaster. Addington who wished to promote Yorke to the Home Office, took advantage of the vacancy to ease Pelham into the vacant sinecure. Importunate as ever, Pelham stood out for a life-tenancy of the lucrative office but hurriedly changed his tune when Addington treated, or affected to treat, his proposal as rejecting the original offer altogether.[1]

It was something to have moved this vain and exigent toady a little further from effective power and, though Charles Yorke had not been a conspicuous success as Secretary at War, his new post gave some hope that Government would in future run more smoothly. But there unhappily the process ended. Pelham's partial removal did little to strengthen the Ministry. Instead of introducing new blood Addington gave Yorke's job to his brother-in-law Bragge. The appointment was respectable enough but was hardly likely to inspire the country. By the autumn of 1803 it might well have proved difficult to persuade any promising young man to risk his career by accepting office in a decaying Government. But Addington should at least have tried. Instead, he once again allowed his loyalty to his friends and relations to transcend both the interests of the country and the needs of his own administration.

Superficially, the Government still seemed strong at the start of the recess. Addington wrote with approval to Hiley[1] that "the latter few weeks of the session went off as satisfactorily as any part of it"; "smiling, complacent and confident," Elliot described him,[2] and he did not seem to be without grounds for his attitude. His majority was massive, his support in the country strong if no longer unquestioning, the King was still whole-heartedly behind him. Addington's favour indeed seemed to know no bounds in the royal mind. When Addington refused the Garter, the King asked if he had yet begun farming. Addington replied that he had, whereupon, next morning, seven fine cows arrived as a present from the royal farm.[3] It is probably true to say that each of those cows was worth twenty votes in the House of Commons.

But it is only necessary to study the correspondence between the Yorke brothers, Yorke, the new Home Secretary in London and his half-brother Hardwicke, the Lord Lieutenant in Ireland, to see how far his seeming strength was a façade. Even by August Yorke was predicting that the Government would find itself destroyed "by weight of superior artillery."[4] He described the Cabinet—Hobart, Hawkesbury and Castlereagh aside—as "absolutely detestable,"[5] and bemoaned the need of a "governing mind of real energy and resources."[6] Hardwicke advised his brother to sound out the King and Pitt about forming a broad-bottomed administration. With scrupulousness unusual in a member of Addington's Government, Yorke first mentioned to his Prime Minister what was contemplated. Addington, he reported to Hardwicke,[7] was convinced of the need to bring Pitt in and ready to sacrifice his "personal feelings of ill-treatment and injustice." But the insurmountable difficulties which remained were Addington's loyalty "to those who embarked with him" and the "delicacy of his position with respect to the King."

When a Minister of the Crown wrote to a Lord Lieutenant in such terms it was clear that all could not be well. There is nothing

the least unconvincing in Yorke's report of his talk with Adding-
on. The Prime Minister was notoriously ready to agree with
ny of his colleagues that his tenure of office was uncertain and
ie need to bring back Pitt of paramount importance. Secretly
e may have considered himself as good a man as Pitt but such
as his state of mind that he would by now not have dared whisper
o blasphemous a suggestion even to the closest of his intimates.
Ministers, above all the Prime Minister, had lost faith, not so
uch in their ability to rule, as in the readiness of others to be
led by them. All government rests fundamentally on an act
f faith; the belief of Ministers that they have a right to command
id of the people that they have a duty to obey. From Addington's
dministration the faith had seeped away. The Government was
ck, a sickness not based on real weakness but psychosomatic,
most imaginary. It would not be too much to say that if the
overnment had not clearly been about to die, no one would
ave suspected that they were ill at all.

Certainly there was nothing in the progress of the war to make
ddington despair. On the contrary, it was developing much as
e had expected. While British troops cleaned up the relics of the
rench colonial empire, Napoleon massed his troops on the
hannel coast and busily constructed barges with which to ferry
iem to England and to victory. The fighting ships which alone
uld gain control of the Channel and make invasion practicable
mained cooped up in isolated pockets all along the Atlantic sea-
oard, their crews decaying steadily in morale, discipline and
amanship while the boats themselves rotted from inactivity.
et, egged on by his contempt for his adversary, Napoleon com-
itted himself ever more deeply to the folly of a maritime adven-
re. Sooner or later it seemed he must try to strike and this
oment could only be fatal for French hegemony in Europe.

Tom Grenville reported in November[1] that Addington was
determined to take the lowest possible tone, and at all events,
patch up peace with France on any terms." The story had
out as much truth as the other rumour, incompatible but quite
sedulously circulated by the Grenvilles, that Addington was
onfident that France must give way in this struggle in the course
the next six months, from absolute want of money and means."[2]
fact Addington was convinced that no settlement with Napoleon
is possible and was resigned to the prospect of a long war. But

he believed that he had found the way to win it at least cost
England; to that policy he would stick in spite of all the jeers
his critics and the reproaches of his more swashbuckling friend

By December it seemed that invasion would come at ar
moment. Napoleon had left Paris, Addington told Abbot,[1] ar
the army of Reserve was marching to the coast. The French we
slaughtering oxen at Bordeaux for the immediate victualling
their fleet. In England all plans were made. If the attack can
in Essex, Addington and the King were to move to Chelmsfor
if in Kent, to Dartford. The Queen and the royal treasure we
to be packed off to Worcester, the Press censored and the bool
of the Bank of England incarcerated in the Tower. Only th
French were lacking, and the constant expectation of the
arrival—or at least departure—kept Addington from getting ev
as far as Richmond until well on into February. Not until Ap
or May did Napoleon abandon hope that the kindness of th
weather and the negligence of the Royal Navy might sudden
combine to open the way in front of him. Even then he did n
renounce his pledge to destroy the English on their own grour
but merely made the ambition subject to the prior requireme
to destroy them on their chosen element, the sea.

In this moment of emergency it seemed that opposition w
temporarily stilled. "We are not likely, I think, to experien
much opposition in Parliament before Christmas," wrote Addin
ton early in November,[2] and, though his handling of recruitme
was criticised, his optimistic forecast proved correct. "Addingt
has, apparently, the whole game in his hands," wrote Aucklan
But the lack of votes against Ministers concealed many doub
and a certain loathing. Creevey voiced the latter when l
splenetically surveyed the behaviour of the Government duri
the first part of the session:[4]

They are, upon my soul, the feeblest—lowest almost—of
men, still more so of Ministers. When there is anything like
a general attack upon them, they look as if they felt it all;
they blush and look at one another in despair; they make
no fight; or, if they offer to defend themselves, no one
listens but to laugh at them. When the House is empty and
their enemies are scattered, they rally and fall in a body upon
Windham, call him all kinds of names, and adopt all kinds of
the most unfounded misrepresentations of his sentiments.

Upon these occasions they are quite altered men; they talk loud and long, and cheer one another enough to pull the house down . . . These creatures of imbecility have no such thing as a plan; they live by temporary expedients from hand to mouth—by the contrary views and characters of their opponents—by that very feebleness which in itself cannot rouse up personal animosity in nobler minds—by low cunning —by appropriate adoption of humility and innocence.

Little though there might have been in common between Addington's various opponents, the spirit of Creevey—the "personal animosity" which could not be roused by Ministers in nobler minds"—burnt strongly within them all. Grenville, Windham, Fox: all were reaching a point at which they would have welcomed the rule of Satan himself rather than that Addington should continue as Prime Minister. Disdain for his talents and his birth, resentment at being kept from office, pain at the wounds inflicted on them by his less scrupulous relations, a genuine conviction that he was leading the country to disaster: the sum was a determination to evict him at all costs which diluted every other political animosity and drew together Addington's disparate opponents in a formidable cohort against him.

To Wellesley, returning to England after his long sojourn in India, it seemed that all his friends were scattered "in innumerable parties almost without a single point of agreement."[1] He found that the only place where any "harmony or union" was to be met with was in the Cabinet and he outraged Grenville by telling him that nothing had happened to lessen his respect and esteem for Addington.[2] But Wellesley's was a lone and belated voice. From the other flank, Grenville besought Pitt to join him in out-and-out opposition and, incidentally, to save him from a disagreeable alliance with Fox. ". . . it will be necessary for me pretty soon to make up my mind on the line to pursue . . ." wrote Pitt,[3] but he found that he had almost lost the habit. He had been sitting on the fence for so long that it seemed as if all that was left to him now was to stick to it for ever.

On the 9th of January Grenville paid Pitt what was announced to be a final visit. Affably, Pitt agreed with almost everything his cousin said but, at the end of the day, an agreement to act in outright opposition seemed as remote as ever. "Middle lines, and managements, and delicacies *où l'on se perd*,"[4] summed up Grenville angrily. He could bear Pitt's equivocations no longer, the time had come to turn to Fox. A convenient intermediary was to hand. Grenville's brother Thomas had contrived to remain on tolerable terms with the Foxites when most of the Portland Whigs had quarrelled ferociously with their former colleagues. Now he was employed as go-between to engineer an alliance for the destruction of Ministers.

"Stowe and all its appendages, Lord Spencer and Windham," reported Fox to Grey,[1] were anxious to league with him and his friends in solemn union against the Doctor. As for Pitt, "the same proposal was made to him," but though he agreed that the present Government was weak and inadequate, was ready to lead an alternative Ministry if the King desired it and would join with the new Opposition in many points of their attack, he could not commit himself whole-heartedly to any alliance. "In short he could not be what is called *in Opposition*."[2] Fox had a nervous suspicion that the result of his labours might be to substitute Pitt for Addington but the urge to hunt down the Doctor was too strong. The alliance was on.

So Grenville and Windham, Fox and Grey, the extremist champions of the war and its most bitter enemies, joined together in an unseemly union with no object in mind save to destroy the Government. When he wrote to Pitt[3] to apprise him of what was in the wind, Grenville emphasised that there was to be no communication or agreement between the two parties save in the co-ordination of parliamentary tactics and a vague resolve to work for an administration "comprehending as large a proportion as possible of the weight, talents and character to be found in public men of all descriptions . . ." "Co-operation" was the word used to describe this alliance; a co-operation with sternly limited objectives and a readiness on both sides to terminate it as soon as it had served its purpose.

The already complicated political situation was now further tangled by the illness of the King. As if in anticipation of the mental anguish which the departure of his favourite was likely to cause him, the King's gout had suddenly grown worse and all the familiar symptoms of royal insanity were appearing. As befitted Dr. Addington's son, the Prime Minister took a keen and critical interest in all the activities of the doctors; ". . . even you would not have treated (the gout) more improperly," he wrote o Hiley[1] and, sure enough, by the middle of February the King was back in his strait-jacket, gibbering nothings at all the world. The derangement bore every sign of lasting for many weeks, perhaps, indeed, for ever.

Once again the King confounded everyone. All the old papers about the Regency were dusted off and preparations made for a protracted constitutional battle, when it suddenly became clear that, after all, he was on the way to recovery. By the end of the month Addington was able to announce the happy news to the House of Commons. But the King's state was still so frail that Addington felt bound to warn the House: "It would be prudent for some time to spare him all unnecessary exertion of mind."[2] Thoughts of a Regency were set aside but instead, it was rumoured, the Government planned to take advantage of the royal weakness so as to consolidate their fast crumbling position. According to the Lord Advocate,[3] "ministers, or rather Mr. Addington, are following a most extraordinary game." The idea, it was alleged, was to smuggle the King down to Kew and there induce him to set up a limited Council of Regency which would refer to him only matters of outstanding importance and otherwise enjoy full powers. The Prince of Wales, reported the Lord Advocate, was to be a member of the council but Addington and his friends would make up the rest of it.

The Prince would hear nothing of such a plan. He was convinced that his father's illness would last for several months at least—"Thy wish was father, Harry, to that thought," as Pitt observed[4]—and gleefully made plans for a Government designed to his taste. Moira would have been his preferred Prime Minister but it was hinted to Melville that, under pressure, he might agree to Pitt. "With respect to the Prince's intentions," cautioned Pitt,[5] ". . . I fear no very certain dependence is to be placed on any language which he holds."

But the Prince's good faith was not to be put to the test. Though he clung hopefully to his vision of a prolonged bout of royal lunacy it became steadily more evident that Addington's prognosis had been the better. By the beginning of April George III was himself again. His recovery saved Ministers and, indeed, opposition from the monstrous task of contriving a solution to the country's difficulties which would satisfy all the whims and prejudices of the Prince of Wales.

Over the previous few weeks Pitt had gradually been persuading himself into the policy of outright onslaught on Ministers which Grenville had failed to press upon him. He expounded his position on 29th March:[1]

> ... I am strongly confirmed in my opinion that the present Government cannot last for any length of time, and still more so in the full conviction that every week for which its existence may be protracted will be attended with increased danger to the country. I have therefore satisfied myself that the time is near at hand at which if a change does not originate from the Ministers themselves, or from the King, I can no longer be justified in not publicly declaring my opinion, and endeavouring by parliamentary measures to give it effect.

It is pardonable to wonder what had happened to make him change his mind since he had refused so decisively three months before to enter into "systematic opposition." The risk of invasion had diminished so that the immediate danger to the country could hardly have increased. The King's illness provided, on the whole, more of an argument for avoiding a crisis than for inciting one. There had been no major activity on the part of Ministers to which Pitt had found it necessary to object. The truth seems to be that the "increased danger" to which Pitt referred related not so much to the country as to himself. The alliance between Grenville and Fox was going ahead in spite of his abstention. There was a serious risk that, if he continued to stand aloof, enough of his own supporters would be won away for the dissidents to bring down the Government without his help. In such circumstances he could have been forgiven for feeling all the pique of a prima donna seeing an opera brought to a triumphant end while she was still sulking in the wings.

It would be unfair to Pitt to suggest that this was the only, or even the principal reason for his change of heart. It is indeed remarkable that his long maturing resentment against Addington and his wish to take back power himself had not long ago produced the same result. What to an Addingtonian was a treacherous hanging back from the support of Ministers, to Canning or Rose must have seemed like superhuman restraint. A factor which may well have helped to break this restraint and bring matters to a head was Pitt's discovery of how much opposition there was to Addington within Parliament and within the Government itself.

He told Melville[1] that Portland, Eldon, Chatham, Castlereagh, Yorke, Hobart and even Hawkesbury had made it known that they were ready to retire but that their loyalty to Addington would lead them to support him so long as he was determined to cling to office. The sense of impending calamity made it almost impossible to reinforce the Government; Lord Redesdale cautiously refused to become the Lord Chief Justice and Yorke complained to Hardwicke that for one reason or another two-thirds of the House of Commons were not available for appointment to office.[2] Tierney worked busily to bring over some recruits from the Foxite Whigs but his success was confined to Colonel Porter and Mr. Brogden; "two cursed rum touches," in Creevey's phrase.[3]

But the decisive spur to Pitt's resolution was probably provided by Lord Chancellor Eldon. With a lofty indifference to the interests of the Government of which he was a member or the feelings of colleagues to whom he was supposed to be a friend, Eldon on 20th March opened private communications with Pitt. He seems to have announced himself as the—self-appointed— representative of the disaffected Ministers and to have offered to act as intermediary between Pitt and the King. When the keeper of the royal conscience cast himself in such a role it can hardly be surprising that Pitt assumed the Government was doomed. Whether Pitt thought that Addington approved of the Lord Chancellor's *démarche* is uncertain but he can hardly have credited what was in fact the truth, that Eldon did not even mention the interview to his Prime Minister until more than a month later when events had already moved far towards their climax.

Yet even before Eldon's approach Pitt had made his first foray in the company of Fox and Grenville; "Pigging it, three in a truckle bed," in Sheridan's malicious phrase. On 15th March he introduced a motion on the state of the Navy. The ground was well chosen, for the fleet was weaker than it should have been, but Pitt had little to contribute except recriminations for the past and splendid phrases about "this grand and proud bulwark of our fame." Almost the only positive suggestion in his speech, in fact, lost him some credit since he urged the building of a fleet of flat-bottomed gunboats to attack invading craft in shoal water. "A mosquito fleet—the most contemptible force that could be employed," retorted Admiral Pellew, arguing that any such building programme would withdraw essential resources from far more important work. This staunch Addingtonian was recalled from active service specially to take part in the debate. His performance more than justified the journey. "I see nothing," he asserted, "in the arrangement of our naval defence to excite the apprehension even of the most timid amongst us; but, on the contrary, everything to inspire us with confidence . . . I can assert with confidence that our navy was never better found, that it was never better supplied, and that our men were never better fed nor better clothed."

It is said that twenty members who came to vote for Pitt switched their support to Ministers after they had heard Pellew speak.[1] The combined forces of Whigs, Pittites and Grenvillites were defeated by seventy-one votes. But though the result was not discreditable it confirmed many of Addington's fears. Under pressure from Pitt the Government's majority had already begun to melt away. Many of their traditional supporters abstained and a handful voted with the Opposition. Even in this victory, the shape of future defeat was to be seen.

That Pitt was not yet dedicated to out-and-out opposition was proved a few days later when the Volunteer Consolidation Bill was brought before the House of Commons. Fox inveighed against the "weakness, the incapacity, and the imbecility of the present Ministers!"[2] and Windham and Thomas Grenville supported his efforts. Pitt, however, who had always approved Addington's policy over the volunteers, chose to support the Government. The Opposition could muster only fifty-six votes. For Pitt this was most satisfactory. It sharply reminded Fox and Grenville that his were the big battalions and that the Government could be overthrown only at his pleasure. At the same time, so he hoped, he had demonstrated that his hostility to Addington was not invariable but aroused only when the actions, or inactivity, of Ministers made it essential.

But this was the last occasion on which Pitt made even a parade of neutrality. By the beginning of April he was committed to unrelenting opposition. In the first fortnight of the month Pitt circularised his friends or those who might wish to be considered so, announcing his new-found resolution and urging them to help him give it effect.[3] On the Government side Yorke wrote to Hardwicke in Ireland asking him to send over all dependable friends as soon as possible. "Our ground I conceive to be impregnable," he wrote, "but whether our artillery and ammunition is to be depended on is another question."[1]

His words betray the artificiality of the whole conflict. While Addington prepared for battle, mustered his troops and mouthed the appropriate clichés about his confidence in victory, neither he nor any of his followers had the slightest doubt that the Government was doomed. The appeal of Pitt was such that, even if Addington's Ministry had been an unqualified success, he would hardly have been able to hold his followers together. Now, with his reputation already gravely shaken, the only question was how long he would survive and with what credit, if any, his Government could retreat from office. The hard core of the Addingtonians, a few of the King's friends and, with luck, most of the Irish and some of the Scottish Tories would stay loyal; as for the rest Addington could only speculate at which vote they would desert.

The Easter recess gave him his last breathing-space. Then, on 16th April, in a vote on the Irish Militia Bill, the Government majority fell to twenty-one. This result was something of a freak since the Addingtonians did not vote their full strength, but it shook still further what confidence was left to Ministers. It was tacitly accepted by both sides that the vote on 23rd April on Fox's motion about the defence of the country would prove the real trial of strength. Hiley reported on the debate to his sister.[2] "Fox's first speech wretchedly bad. My brother's reply admirable and the best speech he ever made. Pitt bitter to an uncommon degree, egotistical and disgusting. Yorke well. Perceval and Tierney very well—particularly the latter. Windham smart. Fox capital in reply. Many rats about." The majority fell to fifty-two: nearly twenty less than the comparable vote of little more than a month before. Within two days Hiley had the chagrin of seeing that the rats were still on the move; in the vote on the Army of Reserve Act on 25th April, Addington's majority fell yet again to thirty-seven. Prospects seemed still worse for the forthcoming debate on Lord Stafford's motion of censure in the House of Lords.

In part at least this loss of strength was due to the influence of the Prince of Wales. After much wavering the Prince had finally dedicated himself to winning all the votes he could for opposition.[1] It was on his instructions that Erskine refused the post of Attorney-General which Addington had offered him early in the year. Sheridan, too, had been forced to reject the honours and financial rewards of office.[2] Now these Addingtonians at heart had been prevailed on to vote against the Government, even Tierney found time for some smooth words about Pitt's transcendent talents in the debate of 25th April.

But the Prince could make no more than a marginal difference. The deciding factor was the defection of the run-of-the-mill Tory, the honest if not over-intelligent Member who thought well enough of Addington but wished to win favour with the future Government and was anyway unable to resist their superior glamour and debating power. Rats in a sense they were, but it is no more than justice to say that Addington and his Ministers were doing little to preserve their loyalty or to convince them that a viable alternative existed to the restoration of William Pitt.

It is difficult to guess whether Addington's support would in fact have melted away so as to leave him in a minority or whether something near rock-bottom had already been reached. Certainly the current view was that Addington's majority would shortly vanish; definitely in the Lords and probably also in the Commons.[3] Addington himself told his friends that, by the next vote, he expected his majority to fall to ten in the House of Lords and to a maximum of twenty-two in the House of Commons. But the test was never to be made. Already, after the vote of 16th April, Addington had sent a message to Pitt[4] to ask "what his opinions were as to the present state of things, and the steps to be taken for carrying on the King's affairs." Perhaps he still hoped that there might be a last-minute change of heart and some kind of reconciliation. But Pitt was implacable. He retorted that he would tell the King's emissary alone his views; with Addington he could have no further dealings.

Then, on 22nd April, Pitt put matters in the hands of his solicitor. He sent Lord Eldon an open letter and requested him, if he thought proper, to pass it on to the King. In this letter[5] Pitt defended his conduct during Addington's Administration and explained that he was at last convinced that "while the administration remains in its present shape, and particularly under the direction of the person now holding the chief place in it, every attempt to provide adequately and effectually for the public defence . . . will be fruitless." Lord Eldon had no hesitation in passing on this letter, though he admitted that, in so doing "much may be, properly or improperly, observed upon my conduct."[1] This time he did at least feel that it would be reasonable to let the Prime Minister know what he had done, though he still did not do so till two or three days after the letter had been received.

Even before the King read the letter Addington had decided that he could no longer carry on. He seems to have reached this decision when his majority fell first to fifty-two and then, within forty-eight hours, by a third to only thirty-seven. To Addington this calamitous loss of support was tantamount to his rejection by the House of Commons. He must have told the King some time on the day after the fatal vote. He expected distress, he encountered blank despair. For George III Addington's resignation was not just the loss of a favourite Minister, it had become fused in his mind with the threat to establish a Regency and the accession to power of the abhorred Charles James Fox. Reason asserted that Addington would be replaced by Pitt, a known and trusted servant, but the King's grasp of reason was at the moment more than usually frail. Pitt and Fox were together assailing the royal favourite; Pitt therefore, if not as bad as Fox, was the latter's ally and likely to be used as his path to power. "Why are we to part?" the King asked his Prime Minister. "Can I do nothing to reconcile you and Mr. Pitt?" Addington knew well what the answer was. It was too late to turn back. On 29th April he told the Cabinet of his decision and early the following day that ubiquitous messenger-boy, the Lord Chancellor, informed Pitt that Addington considered his administration at an end.

It remained only for Addington to bring forward the Budget for the following year—an action oddly similar to Pitt's in 1801 when he too brought forward the Budget after he had fallen from office. Of necessity it was uncontroversial. Addington set to one side certain improvements which he had planned to his income tax and contented himself with increasing the other war tax, the Special Customs and Excise Duties, and raising a loan of £10 million. Pitt had approved the general lines and no discussion followed Addington's speech. Lord Hawkesbury had already postponed all business in the Lords, for "reasons of the highest and most weighty importance."[2] When Fox rose to inquire whether the same reasons applied to business in the Commons, Addington replied briefly that they did. The House then broke up, without, Abbot noticed, ". . . any clamour or apparent exultation." "Fox and his friends seemed to be gloomy, and the Grenville party as entirely silent." The probability that it would be Pitt and not they who would benefit from Addington's defeat must every moment have been more painful to them.

It was the King who seemed least able to bring himself to accept the change in Government. When Pitt outlined his ideas for a broad-based Ministry including both Grenville and Fox among its Members, George III replied lamenting Pitt's rooted dislike: "to a gentleman who has the greatest claim to approbation from his King and country for his most diligent and able discharge of the duties of Speaker of the House of Commons for twelve years; and of his still more handsomely coming forward when Mr. Pitt and some of his colleagues resigned their employments to support his King and country when the most ill-digested and dangerous proposition was brought forward by the enemies of the Established church." This hardly conciliatory reply continued with an outraged protest that the inclusion of Fox in the Government should even be considered. If Pitt refused to come into office except with Fox then the King, he threatened vaguely, would have to look elsewhere for his Prime Minister.[1]

What the King wanted was to keep Addington as his Prime Minister or, if that was impossible, at least to contrive that he should remain in the Government. His only other objective of comparable importance was to keep Fox out. It was a most felicitous coincidence that by making Pitt leave Fox out the King could create the circumstances in which, sooner or later, it would prove necessary to bring Addington in.

*   *   *   *   *

Given such intemperate royal support and a still workable majority in the two Houses it is obvious that Addington could have put up a sterner fight. Even if doubts among his fellow-ministers and defections among his parliamentary followers had made it impossible for him to hold his own in Parliament, it would still have been open to him to go to the country. Certainly he would have found there more support than was evident in Westminster. "Believe me, Sir," wrote Warren Hastings,[2] "the voice of the House of Commons is not the voice of the people. This is very generally in your favour, and every day increases the number of your adherents." Hastings, perhaps, had no very obvious claim to speak for England but he was reasonably objective and a shrewd observer. Nor was his a solitary voice. Indeed Lord Holland later told Addington that even Fox had admitted that the administration was still popular in the country. "From that point of view," Fox remarked,[1] "the resignation was premature."

Addington himself claimed to believe that, if he had dissolved Parliament, he could have won a large majority at the elections. The King, he told Malmesbury,[2] had urged him to do so but he could not "bring himself to consent to a measure which would, at a moment like this, throw the country into confusion." "*Quaere*," was Malmesbury's only comment. Certainly Addington's was one of those predictions which are the less convincing because the prophet takes good care that they should never be put to the test. But it was not *prima facie* ridiculous. There was still much goodwill for Ministers in the country; a feeling that they had been hardly done by and that the Government was, by and large, as likely to be competent and reliable as any other. Addington himself was still widely liked and respected; an honourable, safe man who could be trusted always to do his best. Probably Pitt's attraction would have proved too strong at the polls but Addington, with the King behind him, had at least a chance.

But however real Addington's chance, it is not surprising that he failed to grasp it. No conviction of remote popularity could arm him against the chill winds which blew at Westminster. The treachery of Eldon, the desertion of his Whig supporters, the depressed pessimism of his Cabinet colleagues, the tacit assumption of most Tory Members that Pitt was the Prime Minister the country needed: all these bore crushingly upon him so that he had no will to carry on. Even nearer at home there seem to have been doubts. Glenbervie claimed to have been told by the King[3] that Hiley Addington "disapproved of his brother's conduct" and, when asked by an Opposition Member to pair in a vital debate replied that "he would not pair off with him as he was of the same opinion with himself and was going out of town that he might not witness or contribute to his brother's discredit."

Neither Glenbervie nor the King rank high as reliable witnesses but it is not unlikely that the volatile Hiley might have swung from defiance to a mood of black defeatism. The belief that even his brother felt that he should resign could well have been one of the deciding factors in Addington's sudden and abject collapse.

Addington himself claimed that, paradoxically, it was only his respect and love for the King which led him to defy the royal wishes and retreat from office. "To keep his health safe is the cause of the country," he told Abbot.[1] "At present, if necessary he may still change his Ministry without being driven to it by a junction of the three oppositions. Mr. Pitt is not now pledged to any man . . ." In other words, if he resigned at once, Pitt could still form a Government more or less acceptable to the King; if he delayed, the coalition would become irrefrangibly welded in opposition against him and Pitt be left with no option but to insist that Fox be included among his Ministers. Nothing would have been better calculated than this to break the old King's fragile grasp on sanity.

The argument was valid and Addington, whose gratitude to and affection for George III can be in no doubt, must certainly have allowed it to bulk prominently in his mind. But it cannot have been predominant. Addington would have resigned with almost as great alacrity if the King's health had never been in question. The chief reason for his surrender lay in his own character and experiences. The world-weary statesman who retires from office with indifference or even deep satisfaction is a stock figure of political history. Almost always the image is palpably false. Resentment, chagrin and a keen regret for vanished power and consequence are the authentic traits of the defeated minister. All these Addington felt, but he felt also a sweet and almost overwhelming relief. The office of Prime Minister, above all of a Prime Minister in war-time, assailed by an energetic and pitiless Opposition discouraged by the defection of his friends, above all opposed by the man whose support he had long deemed indispensable, had proved altogether too much for his health and his equanimity. He was close to being a broken man. To Pole Carew he confessed[2] that, physically, he had suffered much and that his mind had been "thrown too much, perhaps, off its bias by the nature of the opposition he had experienced, and the quarter, especially, whence it came."

One observer described him, well before the end, as already bearing far too heavy a load. "He wants spirits and courage for his situation and though a temperate man, now drinks perhaps 20 glasses of wine at his dinner before he goes into the House of Commons to invigorate himself."[1] By 1804 the affable and complacent figure who had presided so urbanely in the Speaker's Chair had been reduced to a haggard neurotic, sleeping badly, short-tempered, scenting insults and hostility even where there were none, doubting his own capacities and pathetically uncertain even of his closest friends. Where others would have revelled in the parliamentary battles, traded insult for insult and greeted each new enemy with the satisfaction of a big-game hunter spotting a further target for his gun, Addington asked only to be left alone. The last few months in office had come close to destroying his spirit. It is hard to conceive any circumstances in which he would have consented to become Prime Minister again; certainly in April, 1804, he was absolutely resolved that he had left the post for ever. If the circumstances of his resignation had not arisen then he would have contrived them. It is indeed less surprising that he resigned when he did than that he sought to remain in office even for a while once Pitt had turned irrevocably against him.

* * * * *

Addington should never have been a war-time Prime Minister. So much is obvious. He was a Prufrock figure:

> Deferential, glad to be of use,
> Politic, cautious and meticulous;
> Full of high sentence, but a bit obtuse;
> At times, indeed, almost ridiculous—
> Almost, at times, the Fool . . .

Yet, conceded that he was the wrong man for the job, one is still far from having formed any balanced or worth-while judgment of his administration. To say that Addington was not a great man is a platitude, of some, but strictly limited importance. To argue from thence that his administration must have been a failure is not necessarily a sound or even reasonable deduction.

Certainly his Government was not the abject disaster which, in popular fantasy, it is so often held to be. Addington was an honest and competent administrator. His conduct of the nation's finances was always capable and sometimes masterly, in his new modelled income tax he made a contribution of importance and daring novelty which has served Britain well to the present day. His recruitment campaign was a failure, but not noticeably worse than the comparable campaigns of Pitt. His foreign policy and direction of the war were never put to the test of time; at least, however, his approach was far more reasoned and coherent than is generally allowed him. If his policies yielded no outstanding successes they also produced no great disasters; no more can be expected if one elects to play a waiting game.

Yet a Government which is swept from power despite the support of the King and which forfeits the support even of half its own Cabinet cannot deserve the title of success. Few Governments have been subjected to more intense or far-reaching criticism, few Governments have more completely lost the confidence of the leading statesmen of the country. This unique contrast between performance and reputation is the most intriguing element of Addington's Administration. It was suggested earlier that, when Addington took office, he laboured under three crippling disabilities: that he was not an aristocrat, was not an orator and was not William Pitt. All these remained to hamper him throughout his tenure of office; together they added up to a catastrophic failure in public relations. His failure was a failure of communication, a failure to put himself across so that his authentic talents could stand as much chance of being noticed as his equally authentic though on the whole less serious defects.

In spite of the ponderous solemnity with which his time in the Chair had invested him, Addington seemed to exude an aura of pettiness; "The indefinable air of a village apothecary inspecting the tongue of the State," was Rosebery's vivid phrase.[1] It was this impression that he was somehow too small for his post which drove his peers to an often blind and irrational opposition. Something in the public presentation of his case, unctuous yet incoherent, impelled people to criticise and resist. If Addington blundered, then the blunder was automatically outrageous, humiliating, the sort of thing to be expected from this "damned eternal fool," this "pitiful, squirting politician," this "mean, shuffling, interested mortal . . . not fit for anything but a shop . . ." If Addington had a good idea then it was just an idea; if it actually succeeded it was usually attributed to William Pitt.

Addington's failure, therefore, was not so much one of achievement as of personality and of will. He was not a bad Prime Minister but he was bad at behaving like a Prime Minister and at convincing others that he was an effective Prime Minister. In the end, he could not even convince himself. He fell primarily because the House of Commons, the Lords, the aristocratic drawing-rooms judged him on his manner and judged him harshly. If he had been judged objectively on his performance then he would certainly not have been free from criticism, but the crushing ignominy of his defeat at least would have been spared him.

9

The King's obvious consternation at his favourite's downfall must have done something to relieve the pain. George III's first reaction, once he had accepted that he must part from his Prime Minister, was to load him with every kind of honour.

"The King's friendship for Mr. Addington is too deeply graven on his heart," he wrote on 9th May,[1] "to be in the least diminished by any change of situation: His Majesty will order the warrant to be prepared for the creating Mr. Addington Earl of Banbury, Viscount Wallingford, and Baron Reading; and will order the message to be carried by Mr. Yorke to the House of Commons for the usual annuity, having most honourably and ably filled the station of Speaker of the House of Commons. The King will settle such a pension on Mrs. Addington, whose virtue and modesty he admires, as Mr. Addington may choose to propose . . ."

Addington was touched but horrified by the King's well-meant efforts to comfort him. He had no wish for a title, be it of Banbury, Wallingford, Reading or all stations west, and would have found it degrading to be awarded an annuity by that same House of Commons which had so recently rejected him. As to Mrs Addington; Addington was second to no one in his admiration for her virtue and modesty but he could not feel that it would be a happy precedent to grant a pension to the wife of a retired but still vigorously alive Prime Minister. He assured the King that to accept such favours would utterly destroy his peace of mind and begged that he should be suffered to depart without more ado.[2]

The King was moved, intrigued and slightly offended. "Am I to be the only man in England," he exclaimed, "who cannot lay his head on his pillow without the painful consciousness of having rather injured than benefited the fortunes of the best friend he has in the world? Why is Mr. Addington too proud to accept a proof of friendship from the King? I am a proud man too, and is *that* the situation in which the King of England ought to be placed?"[1] But Addington stuck to his point with unwonted obstinacy and succeeded in frustrating a royal ploy by which some members of the House of Commons would "spontaneously" put forward similar proposals. The only satisfaction the King could get was Addington's grateful acceptance of an offer to leave him undisturbed in White Lodge, a house which it would have pained him much to leave. To cap this favour, George III sent to White Lodge a copy of his full-length portrait by Beechey as a token of his esteem for "his truly beloved friend Mr. Addington, whose honour, truth and personal attachment will ever be a source of the greatest pleasure and comfort his Majesty can enjoy . . ."[2]

But it was not enough for the King to proclaim his regret at Addington's passing; he made it his first preoccupation to ensure that Addington should soon return to office. He realised that, to achieve this, there must first be a reconciliation between Addington and Pitt. His preliminary soundings showed him that he should not move fast, Addington being still "perplexed between returning affection for Mr. Pitt and great soreness at the contemptuous treatment he met with . . ."[3] Pitt, he believed, was "truly ready to take Mr. Addington in his arms"[4] but he must wait until the King judged that injured pride had healed and both men would feel themselves "not humbled but exalted by giving the strongest *testimony*, of having warm and good hearts." The King saw his erring children through a rosy glow of misconceived benevolence, convinced that only a touch of the royal magic was needed to make all right again. When he assumed that the division between the two men was by no means as final as it appeared, he judged the position better than did most of his subjects. But he miscalculated sadly when he concluded that the trust and affection which had once reigned between Pitt and Addington could easily be restored.

Yet with all this parade of affection and, indeed, his sincere desire to help his friend, George III was still incapable of sustained loyalty or gratitude. An egocentric dotard, he judged others solely as they affected his own standing and his own power. His affections, though intense to the verge of insanity, were fleeting and could give place in an instant to an equally irrational dislike. Addington, perhaps, was the Minister on whom he doted above all others. His grief at their parting was genuine and his efforts to restore him to office showed a consistent energy usually only inspired by the interests of the established church or the pleasure of thwarting the Prince of Wales. But he is still said to have told Glenbervie that it was high time Addington had gone and that he had been forced to explain to his ex-Prime Minister "that there was one thing wanting in him . . . to be plain, it was talents."[1] To Lord Melville, he complained about the same time of the "insipid milk-and-water style" of speech which he had been compelled to read from the throne when Addington was the author.[2]

Such remarks were probably exaggerated by malicious reporters and, anyhow, indicate little more than the desire to startle and impress which was one of the hall-marks of that intellectually decrepit monarch. But George III's volatile and shallow nature had proved itself in too many betrayals and desertions of old supporters to encourage anyone to take at face value his protestations of eternal affection. The King did indeed love Addington well but if Addington had ceased to be of use or had given real or imagined grounds for offence then the years of devoted service would quickly have been forgotten. He would have remained only as an irritating encumbrance, to be got rid of at the first occasion.

* * * * *

For Addington, the nightmare was now over and though in retrospect its horrors might not seem so stark and its moments of pleasure more frequent, he never found cause to regret that it had ended. Indeed he was quite content at the prospect of a time in opposition. His family was of great importance to him, but for the last three years he had been compelled to neglect them. Now he would be able to give his wife the attention she deserved. Though a series of disastrous childbirths had done much to weaken her, her spirit was unimpaired and her love for and loyalty towards her husband as proudly intemperate as ever.

His son, too, had become almost a stranger to him. In October of 1803 Harry Addington had gone up to Oxford. For some reason his father was so disloyal to his old college as to prefer Christ Church to Brasenose. Possibly he thought that Christ Church would offer more chances for a wider social life. Harry, he knew, could be trusted to work but was as yet a shy and stumbling figure in fashionable circles. He took time off from the conduct of the war to urge his son:[1] "Let your intercourse with the worthy and most cultivated members of your college and of the university be easy and unreserved; but avoid exclusive connexions, and never allow yourself to prefer the society of Wykehamists to that of persons, equally deserving, who were bred at Eton or Westminster." Though thus authorised to mix with all sorts of men, Harry unfortunately proved ill-equipped for a convivial life. His father's preoccupations with greater things had led to his education being resigned to the willing hands of Bishop Huntingford. With hideously well-intentioned zeal, Huntingford had instilled in his pupil the conviction that, if he did not achieve outstanding academic success, he would be betraying his father's trust. Harry was a clever boy but, in spite of what sycophantic tutors might tell his father, by no means brilliant. Trying to achieve what was beyond him, he was quickly out of his intellectual depth. He plunged, admitted his father later "prematurely into studies which strain the mind by producing abstraction and laborious reflection and meditation."[2] By the time that he was sent to Oxford he was a nervous, over-worked and sickly child; a friend unlikely to be chosen even by a Wykehamist, let alone those, equally deserving, who were bred at Eton or Westminster.

Addington's pleasure at his escape from office was not clouded by any serious financial difficulties. His own £2,000 a year, his wife's £1,000 and the £3,000 drawn on Harry's behalf from the Clerkship of the Pells made up a provision which, even after his own income tax had been deducted, allowed him to live in considerable comfort and to refuse the offer of a pension with an easy mind. The position of other members of the inner group was less happy. Hiley was hard put to it to keep up life in the style to which he had grown accustomed while Bragge, with nine children and only £1,000 a year, was in a still worse plight. Luckily for the latter, an aged relation died just in time and left him the Lydney estate, then worth some £2,500 a year.[3] As a concomitant of the bequest Bragge now became Bragge-Bathurst; as is not uncommon in this kind of evolution, the "Bragge" slipped away over the years, leaving only the Rt. Hon. Charles Bathurst in its stead.

Amidst the inevitable chorus of lamentation from the faithful one letter gave Addington peculiar pleasure. It came from that lone romantic among the otherwise humdrum Addingtonians, Lord Nelson, who wrote from *Victory*, "almost worn out and blind," to express his sorrow:[1]

Friend I may call thee now, without the suspicion of adulation to a minister; but believe me that my opinion of your honourable abilities as a minister, and your constant friendship for me as a man, have ever held the same place in my heart.

I feel pride in avowing it, now you are a private gentleman. I will not say too much; because when a change takes place, if honourable men are to take the helm, I am sure among the foremost will be placed one Henry Addington . . .

Addington, "the private gentleman," was now discovered by many people to possess qualities which had been lost sight of in Addington the Prime Minister. Castlereagh spoke for the great body of moderate Pittite opinion when he remarked[2] how painful he found it to see "Mr. Addington and several valuable men withdrawn from the King's service." In an unusually perceptive passage, Lord Liverpool referred to Addington's rise in favour since his resignation and commented:[3] "in truth, men of his character will always recover the good opinion of the public when they are out of office though they are neither praised nor sufficiently respected as long as they retain their power. He is calm, sensible, cautious, and has shown himself to be very disinterested . . . and he will give no offence by the conduct he will hold while he may be said to be in Opposition."

But Addington was still a party leader and his party, though it might be short in glamour, was a coherent, respectable and reasonably substantial body. Rose, who was as astute a judge as any of parliamentary strength and no friend of Addington, calculated that some sixty-eight members of the House of Commons would follow his lead;[4] relatively, in the House of Lords his strength was less. Fox gave him slightly fewer but no one doubted that he could muster one of the largest blocs of sure votes among the medley of splinter groups which dotted the parliamentary scene. "You will find a much smaller number of adherents to Mr. A than you have imagined and Pitt will retain as many of you as he can," predicted Dr. Beeke.[5] But when it came to the point the Addingtonians stayed more loyal to their leader than Beeke had believed possible. Vansittart was one of the few whom Pitt deemed it worth his while to woo away and the firm refusal which he met with must have convinced him that, if there was to be any reconciliation, it would have to be with Addington himself.

Indeed, Pitt's final Government was so weak that it was inevitable Addington's stock would rise in contrast. It had never seemed probable that the King would let Pitt include Fox in his Government but it could at least be hoped that Grenville, Windham and the rest of the war party would rally behind their former leader. Fox generously gave such a union his approval even though he resented the fact that he himself must be excluded. Yet Grenville made it his business to weaken his cousin's Government and set himself up as leader of an inveterate opposition. So successful were his efforts that Pitt was forced to rely on Castlereagh, Hawkesbury, Eldon and Chatham from the previous Government; Melville, Harrowby, Canning and Rose from the traditional Pittites and a froth of more or less ornamental light-weights such as Camden, Mulgrave and the Duke of Montrose. It was as feeble a team as Addington's and its frail and dejected leader could not be expected to rule it with much greater distinction. "I saw Pitt in the House of Lords," wrote Grey to his wife,[1] "and I think he looked miserable . . . I would rather be any man in England than him."

It would have been astonishing if Addington had not felt some satisfaction at his former friend's predicament. But on the whole he kept his opinions to himself. He refused to oppose Government outright but was still more reluctant to support it. With an ingenuity reminiscent of Pitt over the previous years, he stated and restated his position; each time with a fresh inflection or variation. In a letter to Hiley he set out what was probably the nearest he got to a definitive outline of his policy:[2]

My determination is to keep clear of all parties, to avoid the reality, and, as far as possible, even the appearance of cabal, to attend the house not constantly but upon such occasions as seem to me to require it, either from a sense of duty to the public or myself: but I will not be the stalking-horse or cat's paw of Opposition nor will I be extinguished by Mr. Pitt. My course seems clear before me . . .

Needless to say, it was clear to nobody except himself or, rather, every observer interpreted Addington's policy in his own light. Too much of Addington's resentment lingered at Pitt's "ungovernable passion for power and pre-eminence"[1] to allow him to be truly objective. Canning was not being unreasonable when he taxed Addington in the House of Commons with systematic hostility to the Government and mockingly commented how glad he was to see "inefficient administration atoned for by a vigorous opposition."[2] Yet Addington, too, was justified in resisting the slur; for certainly Fox and Grenville found him quite as uncertain an ally as Canning himself had found Pitt in the old days when he had been busy trying to upset the Doctor's Government.

The first test of Pitt's strength came in June when he introduced his Additional Force Bill. The Bill was intended to strengthen the regular army at the expense of the militia, a worthy end which it unfortunately came no nearer to achieving than any other with the same object in the past. "A bad measure, both weak and mischievous,"[3] Addington described it, and on this subject at least he spoke with the same voice as Fox and Grenville. The measure was eventually passed by only forty-two votes and Canning, in the course of the debate, was stung into so violent an attack on the record of the last administration that Addington hopefully predicted Hawkesbury would find it impossible to remain in office.[4]

A freakish by-product of the debate came when the King reproached Addington for not giving his support to Pitt. "So are the tables turned," commented Buckingham with some amusement[5] and, indeed, the reversal of the two roles was so complete that statements by the one could easily be put forward or backward by a year or two and attributed to the other. But though the King chided Addington he remained as attached to him as ever; indeed he saw in Addington's attitude fresh reason to engineer a reconciliation before new political habits hardened and Addington found himself bound in alliance to Grenville or, worse still, to the unholy Fox.

A week or two later Addington was placed in greater embarrassment. Wilberforce introduced another Bill for the abolition of the slave trade. As usual Addington professed himself an ardent supporter of abolition in principle but, in practice, a champion of the gradual approach. He told Wilberforce that his Bill would be better called "A Bill for increasing the Atrocities of the African Slave Trade, and perpetuating its Duration,"[1] and argued in the House that premature abolition would merely damage our trade by handing over the traffic in Africans to our less scrupulous rivals. "Addington most vexatious," recorded Wilberforce crossly in his diary.[2] He attacked Addington in the House, accusing him of hypocrisy and indifference to human suffering. Typically he repented afterwards of his anger and was glad that his remarks had not been recorded in the newspapers.[3] In spite of all discouragement, Wilberforce still had faith in his friend's sincerity and believed that he would eventually see the light. Yet sadly he had to note that the doubts which possessed Addington's mind appeared to gain in force rather than to weaken. The abolition of slavery remained a distant goal and every year the distance seemed to grow and the goal became more inaccessible.

Though Fox opposed Addington whole-heartedly on this question and felt little liking or respect for him as a man, he was still quite ready to partner him in opposition to Pitt in the same spirit of restrained dislike as he had shown when voting with Pitt to defeat Addington. The Prince of Wales was said to have been seeking to organise a coalition and every move of Addington's was studied for clues to his intentions. "There has been a private flirtation between the Prince and the Doctor," reported Buckingham,[4] "who rode over several times from Worthing and met H.R.H. on the Downs." The concept of such a tryst has a certain romantic charm but it seems unlikely that it was either made or kept. Overtures to Addington were, however, made in plenty. In spite of the temptation to score off Pitt by aligning himself with his enemies, he refused them all. He was constant in his resolve not to be made the cat's-paw of opposition; partly from dislike of the Whigs, partly from respect for the King but most of all because the forces working for a reconciliation between himself and Pitt were now gathering strength and the prospect of his return to office becoming more than a distant mirage.

*   *   *   *   *

Once Grenville and his followers had ranged themselves with the traditional Whigs, there was no direction in which Pitt could look for support, save towards the Doctor and the Addingtonian hard core of the last Government. The only factor holding the groups apart was the animosity between the two leaders; once this could be removed or forgotten coalition would follow almost automatically.

Within a few months of the fall of his Government, Addington's bitterness against Pitt was fading and memories of their boyhood friendship and their long, so comfortable alliance were recapturing his benign and accommodating mind. To make it up and be friends again was his dearest ambition, if scarcely admitted even to himself. But pride stood in the way: ". . . considering himself as the party injured," he told the Speaker,[1] "he could not in honour or with any utility, make any approaches to a reconciliation with Mr. Pitt; but . . . a single expression of genuine kindness and sense of justice towards him would be fully sufficient to renew with him the sentiments of early and long friendship . . ."

With such a spirit on Addington's side, the only question was when Pitt's parliamentary weakness, the residue of his affection for his old friend and the pressure of the King would induce the Prime Minister to make an overture. By the winter the first and last of these at least were becoming urgent and Hawkesbury, who had always wanted to bring his former leader back to office, was authorised to feel out the ground. At first things went badly. "Everything is more embrouillé than ever," Addington reported.[2] "Van tells me that Canning is now talked of to succeed Lord Harrowby at the F.O.: this I don't believe will take place as it must be known that it would be received with general disgust."

Then, on 12th December, Hawkesbury tried again, this time armed with a firm offer from Pitt and the formal blessing of the King. Cautiously, Addington inquired whether the proposal "originated in a sense of the difficulties of the Government, or in a corrected and altered feeling towards him."[3] Hawkesbury assured him that his mission was actuated only by "the most thorough cordiality and good feeling." For Addington this was enough; his surviving rancour mollified he sought only to consummate what seemed to him so proper and desirable a union. The principle was accepted; all that remained was to work out the details.

Mainly these related to the provision of places for Addington's relations and closest supporters. Pitt offered to find suitable situations for Bragge-Bathurst, Bond, Vansittart and Hiley Addington; Addington held out as well for St. Vincent and the Earl of Buckinghamshire as Hobart had just become.[1] He defended this haggling on the grounds that, if the union were to be useful, ". . . it must be efficient, there must be a practical influence and share in the councils of the King, and this cannot be accomplished unless there is associated with me in office a due proportion of my friends."[2] The argument was not entirely specious; isolated in Pitt's Cabinet, Addington would have felt bound to make himself obstreperous if only to assert his individual existence. But Addington's determination to take his coterie into office with him as the price of his support still lent to the reconciliation an air of commercial haggling which had little in common with the idealistic drawing together of two high-minded statesmen. It was natural, even proper, that Addington as a party leader should do his best for his supporters. But it was equally natural that Pitt, having been made to pay a high price for Addington's services, should show signs of resentfulness as soon as the Addingtonians began to steer an even slightly independent course.

As it turned out St. Vincent had no wish for office. Buckinghamshire was accommodated with the Duchy of Lancaster and Vansittart sent as Secretary to Ireland. Minor jobs were found for Bragge-Bathurst, Bond and Hiley Addington with a promise of better things to come. Addington much regretted that he had not been able to carry Bragge-Bathurst at least with him into the Cabinet: ". . . I found it impossible to propose any third person," he apologised to his brother-in-law,[3] "though you would have been that person."

Addington's own position gave more trouble. When negotiations began he stated firmly that he was happy for his friends to join but had no wish to serve in the Government himself. Benevolent support from the background was to be his role. It is likely that he meant what he said; it would have suited him well to linger gracefully on the side-lines for at least a year or two. But whatever his real views, his proposal was rapidly dismissed. The King would not hear of it and Hawkesbury made it his business to draw Addington into the Ministry.[4] ". . . I am convinced," he wrote, "that it is not possible to reap all the public advantage that is to be desired from a return of intimacy between

231

you and Pitt, unless we are all fairly embarked together in the Government. Believe me, the Devil will be at work to separate you, as he was before: nine times he will fail, but the tenth he will succeed."

Addington allowed himself to be convinced. But he was far less ready to be overruled when Pitt insisted that he must first accept a peerage. It is hard to see why Pitt was so bent on forcing Addington into the House of Lords. There was some feeling that a former Speaker should not sit in the House of Commons save in such wholly exceptional circumstances as had arisen in 1801[1] but it does not seem that any of the main protagonists took this view seriously into account. Addington's friends alleged that Pitt was afraid of being outshone in the House of Commons but Addington's parliamentary record hardly makes this tenable. Probably Pitt felt that the burden of the last twelve months of conflict would be too much for the frail coalition to bear if every day its memories were to be rekindled. Certainly it would have been an uncomfortable situation but the House of Commons had witnessed odder partnerships. It showed exaggerated sensitivity on the part of Pitt to seek to avoid it at the price of sullying the bourgeois purity of his friend.

But it is also hard to be sure why Addington viewed the prospect with such repugnance. His years as Speaker had certainly given him an affection for the Lower House but his experience as Prime Minister had just as thoroughly dispelled it. Temperamentally, it might have been thought that the House of Lords would suit him better. But he seems to have had high ideas of the status which he would need to maintain as a peer and to feel that he could not aspire to it unless his fortune were handsomely augmented. Nor could he accept that this unwanted elevation was as necessary as Pitt maintained. "My earnest wish is to be completely and cordially embarked with *you*, for the purpose of affording all possible ease and satisfaction to the mind of the King . . . but I cannot satisfy myself that, from these objects, it can be material that I should take office, and much less that I should quit the House of Commons."[2] Surely a seat in the Cabinet without office would do as well?

Pitt was obdurate and the King now made it plain that he agreed. Hawkesbury, too, did his best to persuade him though the real grounds for his opinion were unfortunately unsuitable for Addington's ear. "He never would be able to keep up his credit as second in the House of Commons, attacked as he would be by the Opposition," he wrote to his father.[1] ". . . no man can be of any consequence in the second situation in such a body as the House of Commons who is not an able debater in detail and has not, above all, the talent of quick reply." Eventually Addington gave way. He refused an Earldom, however, on the grounds that the consequential rank would be a nuisance to his daughters. For his Viscountcy he deserted the lands around Oxford in which the King had tried to settle him some months before and chose the unpretentious village of Sidmouth in Devonshire. He was on the point of accepting a barony as Raleigh of Combe Raleigh when he discovered that it would cost him an extra £300 and was quite unnecessary. With relief he settled for the single title and, as Viscount Sidmouth, was sworn Lord President of the Council on 14th January, 1805.

". . . the son of Lord Chatham's family physician," wrote Windham to Mrs. Crewe,[2] "will submit to take the blue riband and a peerage. I give him this description," he continued magnanimously, "not as considering it to be any reproach to him, but as a further proof of what the peerage has become of late years." As to the view taken by others of the new alliance: "I can speak with more certainty as to impressions," continued Windham. "That of the public seems, I think, almost universally to be disapprobation." But Windham's fine disdain was as nothing to the outrage felt by Canning, Tomline, Leveson-Gower, Rose and all the others who had led the campaign against the Doctor with such gusto. Rose inveighed against this junction with a man "whose imbecility and falsehood" had already weakened the country. "What next will happen, God only knows," probably that the Government would "drag on a wretched existence and expire not creditably."[3] In a letter to Lady Hester Stanhope,[4] so restrained as to suggest that it was intended for Pitt's eye, Canning poured out his disappointment. He threatened resignation but without much conviction and, sure enough, quickly allowed Pitt to persuade him out of his resolution. His relationship with Canning was, indeed, almost the only point on which Addington made any reservation. He had no wish to interfere with Canning's private friendships or prospects of success and therefore accepted that he should serve in the same Government, but he stated

233

plainly that he was not prepared to have dealings with the man who had baited him so remorselessly over the preceding years.

The Whigs and the Grenvillites might scoff and all those who put their dislike of Addington before their loyalty to Pitt or the country might deplore the Government's seeking reinforcement from such a quarter. But to the Englishman at large the reunion between Pitt and Addington seemed eminently proper and only surprising in that it had been so long delayed. Whatever Windham might say about the views of the public—something on which he had almost uniquely small authority to speak—they in fact coincided with those of the King. "Mr. Addington has the entire confidence of the King," reported Lord Hutchinson.[1] "He [the King] cannot bear Mr. Pitt who finds him very difficult to manage." George III indeed felt, not without reason, that he was the true architect of the reunion. He proclaimed his delight at Addington's return to his counsels by calling without notice at White Lodge and staying there for two hours. Next morning he made Addington visit him at Kew, kept him in conversation for an hour and a half and then sat him down at table to share his dinner of mutton chops and pudding. "It is hardly possible," wrote Addington,[2] "to convey . . . a just idea of the satisfaction he manifested."

But gratifying though it was to be thus fêted by the King, to Addington the all-important feature of his return to office was the renewal of his friendship with William Pitt. The first meeting took place at Hawkesbury's house at Coombe Wood on 24th December. The two men talked for three and a half hours and Addington reported that "there is the fairest prospect of the renewal of old habits of intercourse and friendship."[3] "I must say," he wrote to Ellenborough,[4] "that every part of Mr. Pitt's conduct, and every sentiment he uttered, convinced me that it is his ardent wish, as God knows it is mine, that past differences should be forgotten and that our public conduct and private intercourse may manifest perfect coincidence of opinion, and the establishment of former friendship."

It would be wrong to deduce from these well-rounded phrases that Addington felt little real excitement at what had happened. To be reconciled with Pitt, to see "yours affectionately" replace once more the chilly and mendacious "I am, Sir, your obedient servant," had been his earnest wish since they had first fallen out.

Now, every kind word, every mark of confidence was carefully recorded, as if he was striving desperately to convince himself that their reconciliation was more than just a political expedient, that they were intimate friends again.

Pitt certainly gave him cause to believe it. It would be wrong to exaggerate the animosity which he had felt for Addington over the previous two years. Pitt could not endure to be second to anyone, let alone to a former protégé whom he felt to be palpably his inferior. But once this impediment was removed then his respect for Addington's honesty, industry and good sense was able to reassert itself. He made up his mind to court Addington for the votes he brought with him but he welcomed him into his Cabinet as a well-tried friend and adviser. "I am sure that you are glad to hear that Addington and I are one again," he said to Wilberforce.[1] "I think they are a little hard upon us in finding fault with our making it up again, when we have been friends from our childhood, and our fathers were so before us."

Yet even though both men were sincere in their protestations, there must still have been some element of the factitious in their reconciliation. The new alliance was so patently expedient that, even though it were also based on the most profound goodwill, each man was bound to suspect the sincerity of the other. The assumption of almost everyone in politics that this was just a neat political manœuvre inevitably eroded whatever there was of real friendship in the minds of Pitt and Addington. Pitt could not banish altogether the contempt which he had learnt to feel for Addington, nor Addington his suspicion and injured pride. Each action by the one was scrutinised by the other in search of malign intent. Each was surrounded by a circle of embittered friends whose consistent aim it was to poison their principal's mind against the other. The new year began with Addington lapped in the euphoria induced by healed wounds and assuaged irritations. Yet even at this high point of reconciliation he can never fully have convinced himself that things were what they had used to be or that Pitt and he were irrevocably at one.

*   *   *   *   *

The extreme frailty of the new coalition was quickly evident to everyone who wished it ill; a group which included most of the parliamentarians not included in the Government and a certain number of those who were. Sheridan was particularly active and efficient in making mischief. A debate on the state of the armed forces since Pitt's Additional Force Act afforded him an admirable chance. He compared the failure of the new measure with the comparative success enjoyed by Addington, then, when Pitt was rash enough to refer slightingly to his "insidious and hollow support" of Addington's administration, mounted an attack on the record of Pitt's relations with the former Prime Minister.[1] Certainly he had supported Addington's Government, he said, principally as being the best way to avoid the national disaster of Pitt's return to office. But he deserved no criticism for this. If, on the other hand, he had originally recommended Addington for office and "seduced him into that situation," if he had tapered off his support when he saw Addington grow too popular, and if:

> when I saw an opening to my own return to power, I had entered into a combination with others, whom I meant also to betray, from the sole lust of power and office, in order to remove him,—and if, under the dominion of these base appetites, I had then treated with ridicule and contempt the very man whom I had before held up to the choice of my Sovereign, and the approbation of this House and the public,—then indeed, I should have merited the contempt of all good men . . .

There was enough truth in Sheridan's venom to ensure that Pitt would be hurt and angered. But even if there had not been, such an attack was bound to foster Sidmouth's latent sense of grievance. There was no shortage of partisans to assure Sidmouth that Sheridan's words were justified, if anything too moderate, and to suggest to Pitt that it was Sidmouth himself who had inspired the onslaught. Nor was there such perfect trust between the two men that they could treat the malevolent murmurings of their friends with the indifference which they deserved.

But pin-pricks of this kind were as nothing to the hammer blow which was now to strike the unfledged partnership. In February, 1805, the Tenth Report of St. Vincent's Committee of Naval Inquiry was presented to the House. It dealt with the office of the Treasurer of the Navy and, beneath its guarded language, made it alarmingly clear that Melville had been guilty at the best, of gross negligence and possibly also of malversation of official funds. It was uncontested that large sums of money had been withdrawn from the Bank of England and mingled with the personal accounts of an official, uncontested too that Melville had been aware of this and had taken no steps to check it. What was uncertain was whether Melville or any other official had gained financially by the transactions or whether they were simply a misguided attempt to achieve greater efficiency at the expense of approved procedures.

Pitt's inclination was to play the whole thing down; he did not believe that anything very serious had happened and felt for Melville the loyalty due to an old colleague who, once at least, had been among his closest friends. Besides, Melville's misdemeanours, if misdemeanours they were, had been committed when Pitt was last Prime Minister. For him to fall now on such a charge could not fail to damage the reputation of the present Government. But Sidmouth could not agree to inter the scandal in hugger-mugger. He was less sanguine than Pitt about the probity of Admiralty officials and, as the Prime Minister originally responsible for the setting up of the Committee, felt that its report could not be ignored. Rancour against Melville may also have made it easier for him to decide his course. ". . . if there is one man more than another who ought to feel conscious that he had acted a most false and scandalous part towards you, it is that very man . . ." Steele had written to him,[1] and certainly Sidmouth was disposed to believe that Melville had shown little gratitude for favours received under the Addingtonian Government.

Whatever Sidmouth's line, however, the House of Commons would never have suffered Pitt to hush up the affair. Whitbread and the Radicals were determined that it should be publicly investigated and even many staunch Pittites felt an inquiry was called for. Sidmouth urged Pitt not to become involved in Melville's defence; a defence which was almost sure to fail, would damage Pitt's standing in the country and would make it difficult for the Addingtonian contingent to remain in the Government. He argued that the question should be remitted to a Select Comittee; a proposal to which Pitt reluctantly concurred.[2]

As the day of Whitbread's motion in the House of Commons drew near it became clear that many Members were not disposed to be so moderate. "As you are a spiteful, factious Ivy," wrote Lord Dudley triumphantly to Mrs. Stewart,[3] "you will be glad to know that everything is looking as ill as possible for Melville. It is generally supposed that the Doctor means to desert him." The Doctor did not and most of his followers voted with Ministers. But Pitt's promise of a Select Committee was not enough and, by the Speaker's casting vote, the House adopted what amounted to a vote of censure on Melville. He resigned the following day, in the uncomfortable certainty that a demand for his impeachment was sure to follow. "Is that all," commented the King when told what had happened. "I wonder how he slept after it. Bring my horse."

So far it had proved possible for Pitt and Sidmouth to work out a compromise which, though unsuccessful and satisfactory to neither, had at least preserved a parade of ministerial unity. The next phase in this unhappy drama proved more damaging. A successor had to be found for Melville and Sidmouth made up his mind that by this appointment he would judge the sincerity of Pitt's goodwill. He found Pitt reluctant even to discuss the matter. "Observing as I do," he wrote darkly,[1] "that the intercourse with a certain person, who is more imprudent and obnoxious than ever, is growing more and more frequent, and that he is allowed to appear in the House of Commons more and more as the *prochain ami*, I look with uneasiness and distrust to the relation in which I stand to the Government." Canning in fact seems to have had no hand in Pitt's Cabinet appointments but Sidmouth was right to think that he missed no chance of arguing that Government would run more smoothly without the Doctor's half-hearted co-operation.

To Sidmouth it seemed obvious that Buckinghamshire should take Melville's place, making room for Bragge-Bathurst as Chancellor of the Duchy. This would, he felt, both be a proper appointment and the performance of Pitt's promise to give Bragge-Bathurst cabinet rank as soon as possible. Failing this, he suggested Hood, Castlereagh, Yorke or Hawkesbury and, if all these were ruled out, promised Pitt that he would acquiesce in any appointment "which did not appear to me to be injurious to the public interest and disgraceful to myself."[2] Pitt, however, was bent upon appointing Sir Charles Middleton: a sailor of unquestioned professional ability but almost eighty years old. "a superannuated Methodist," wrote Creevey in disgust.[3] ". . . to catch the votes of Wilberforce and Co. now and then." For Sidmouth he possessed the more important defect of being a close friend of Melville's and a known enemy of the Committee of Enquiry;[1] a man, therefore, whose appointment seemed to proclaim the Government's defiance of the recent vote of the House of Commons.

It was undoubtedly this feature of Middleton's appointment which caused him most distress. But he was also sadly disappointed by Pitt's attitude and the apparently gratuitous unfriendliness with which a chance to oblige the Addingtonians had been ignored. On 25th April, after some cogitation, he and Buckinghamshire tendered their resignation. At Cabinet next day Pitt blandly ignored their action and made no report to the King of what had happened. He seems to have felt confident that he could talk Sidmouth out of his decision, nor did he overestimate his power. In a series of conversations he convinced Sidmouth that his friendship for him was as strong as ever and Middleton's appointment only a temporary affair. But the reconciliation carried with it the seeds of the next disruption for Sidmouth emerged from his talk convinced "that every allowance would be made for the peculiar situation of my friends on many questions that might arise, and every consideration shown to their just and admitted pretensions."[2] To Sidmouth this could only mean that he and his friends could take whatever line they chose over the Melville affair without reproach from Pitt or prejudice to their promotion.

Such a patching up of differences could not indefinitely be repeated. Few observers doubted that Sidmouth must shortly leave the Government, only the time and the occasion seemed in doubt. As it fell out, the next phase of Melville's protracted saga was to provide the breaking point. If further action had to be taken against Melville Pitt wished that this should be by way of impeachment. Sidmouth, however, argued in favour of criminal proceedings. His followers took the same line in the House of Commons. There was an unpleasant flavour of vengeance about their attitude, more than a flavour in the speeches of Bond and Hiley Addington who attacked Melville with savage and quite unnecessary bitterness. Gillray portrayed two jackals prowling around a wounded lion. "Very highly indebted to the lion, brother Hiley," said the one. "Then kick him again, brother Bragge!" came the answer. The efforts of the Addingtonians were enough to defeat Pitt's appeal for an impeachment. Only an astute if somewhat unscrupulous parliamentary manœuvre a fortnight later reversed the verdict and saved Melville from a prosecution which would have exposed him to the greatest danger. "The universal idea," wrote Buckingham after the second vote,[1] "is that Pitt was more actuated by the desire of overthrowing Addington's measure than by the wish of saving Melville . . ." Inevitably Sidmouth and his friends interpreted Pitt's action as fresh evidence of his hostility.

Pitt could forgive the Addingtonians their vote but not the rancorous speeches which accompanied it. He told Sidmouth that, in present circumstances, he was not prepared to do anything for Bond or Hiley Addington. Sidmouth in his turn was prepared to forgive the silent deferment of his brother's promotion but not that it should be proclaimed as punishment for behaviour which, though intemperate, he believed had previously been sanctioned by Pitt himself. On this insubstantial difference the alliance foundered. At the instigation of the King the two men met to try to reconcile their differences. But there was no longer any trust between them. "It is evident to me," wrote Sidmouth sadly after the meeting,[2] "that he has a connection with opposition in his view, and that he is desirous of maintaining that sort of relation with me and my friends, which without hampering him in any way, may be very convenient for the purpose of negotiation."

The King still did not despair of holding together the coalition. The Duke of Cumberland was sent hurrying from one man to the other;[3] the choice of emissary was eccentric but even a more congenial go-between would have had no chance of success. Sidmouth was resolved not to remain in office and Pitt no longer seriously anxious to retain him. The occasion was of no real significance; even if Hiley Addington and Bond had never made their unfortunate speeches some other *casus belli* would have arisen. Left to themselves Pitt and Sidmouth might still have managed well enough. But the extremists on both sides had now established so firm a grasp over the thinking of their principals that each saw the other through a miasma of malevolent suspicion. Only mutual tolerance and trust could have made the partnership work; not only were these lacking but a readiness, almost a determination to think the worst of each other was in its place.

William Pitt, by Hoppner

Addington addressing the House as Prime Minister, by Gillray

White Lodge, Richmond Park

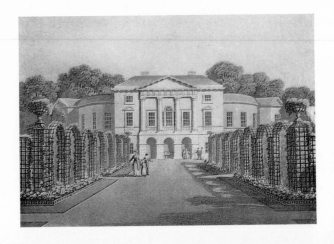

On 5th July, six months after the ill-fated alliance had been renewed, Sidmouth tendered his resignation to the King.

> The Doctor is out again
> So things may come about again

was Canning's laconic epitaph on a coalition which he had disliked from the start and to whose decomposition he had made so marked a contribution.

Sidmouth felt little regret at his withdrawal from a Cabinet in which he had had only a trivial role to play. Yet Pitt's "injustice" and "arrogance" as he saw it[1] caused him much distress. In his last interview with Pitt he records that he asked whether there had been anything in his conduct which Pitt felt improper.[2] "The latter holding out his hand, replied, with tears in his eyes, 'Never: I have nothing to acknowledge from you but the most generous and honourable conduct, and I grieve that we are to part!' 'Then forgive me if I say that I cannot reconcile the *Causes* of this separation with any notion I entertain of honour, generosity or justice '." Whether or not the words were recorded exactly, the spirit of the exchange shows that for Sidmouth the tragedy was not political but lay rather in the seeming betrayal of a friendship which after so many vicissitudes had at last been restored.

*　　　*　　　*　　　*　　　*

To resign office because you do not trust your fellow-ministers and feel that your views are being ignored is a respectable procedure. Anything else, indeed, would suggest humiliating weakness. This, in effect, Sidmouth had done. But with that disastrous bungling of public relations which was so invariable a feature of his career, he had contrived his resignation so as to make it appear to almost everyone as inspired by petty and selfish motives. It was natural that he should feel indignant if his brother and closest friends were not receiving the promotion which he felt to be their due. But to make this the apparent grounds for weakening an already precarious Government in the middle of a war was to expose himself to damaging accusations of irresponsibility and indifference to the interests of the country. His enemies were quick to press such charges.

To one friend at least his conduct seemed hard to justify. As early as May the King was said to be "more reconciled" with

Pitt and "considerably alienated" from Sidmouth.[1] Now he was hurt and angered by what he regarded as Sidmouth's desertion. To him it smacked of disloyalty and a defective sense of what was owing to a royal benefactor. But Sidmouth made things far worse by the manner of his going. Shortly before his resignation he told Sheridan what was in the air and rashly authorised him to pass the news on to the Prince of Wales. He may have hoped that such a display of confidence would raise his stock at Carlton House; if so he miscalculated sadly for the Prince's only comment was: "What does the damned insignificant puppy mean by troubling me?"[2] News of Sidmouth's overture got back to the King who was outraged that his detested son should hear of his Minister's intentions before he did so himself.

When Sidmouth finally sought an interview with the King a few days later George III seriously considered refusing the request. It might have been better if he had for the meeting was a dismal failure, the King remarking that he had never been so fatigued with any audience since the days of Grenville.[3] Sidmouth attempted to thrust the key of the Council-box upon the King. That rigidly protocolaire monarch refused it in dismay and said that it must be surrendered to Lord Hawkesbury. "Sir," said Sidmouth, "I am not on speaking terms with Lord Hawkesbury." "That is nothing to me," replied the King crossly and tried to end the audience, but Sidmouth retained him for a further hour and a half of self-justification.[4] "Everything passed as I wished . . ." reported Sidmouth hopefully after the interview.[5] He might have been less complacent if he had known the King's comment when he returned to his family: "that—has been plaguing me to death!"[6]

The worst of the King's anger quickly passed. By September he was telling Bond that Sidmouth must accept a reward for his services as Speaker and that he planned to reconcile Sidmouth and Pitt again in the near future.[7] But George III could never quite forgive anyone who had crossed him. Politically the estrangement was bound to weaken Sidmouth's position, emotionally it distressed him that anything should tarnish the relationship that had been so precious to him.

Three years as Prime Minister, in constant proximity to his King, had done nothing to abate Sidmouth's royalism. The arcane mysteries of a crown blended with the bluff good nature of a worthy *père-de-famille* were even more irresistible to him than to the rest of George III's faithful subjects. Himself credulous, warm-hearted and inclined to servility, he never for an instant questioned the authenticity of the public image. He looked through the obstinacy, the ingratitude, the selfishness, the warped and partial judgment, to a monarch infinitely benevolent, infinitely wise. He did not credit the King with complete omniscience, was even, on occasion, prepared to admit that he might err. But such lapses, he would have contended, were rare indeed; the exceptions which proved the rule of royal sapience. Sidmouth knew that he owed the King much and would not have presumed to calculate that the debt might have been requited through faithful service. To have lost the royal favour altogether would have been a calamity so great as to have driven him from public life; the knowledge that his standing at Court was impaired was a constant pain and an incentive to win back his place in the sun by diligent and unquestioning service.

In part at least it was devotion to the King which made Sidmouth hold back from whole-hearted opposition to Pitt's Ministry. As after his fall in 1804 he stationed himself resolutely on the fence between Government and Opposition and, from this vantage point, paraded his distaste for the party warfare which he observed raging beneath his feet. ". . . I will enter into no concert or co-operation . . . to subvert or distress the King's Government," he enunciated nobly.[1] "My determination however is unalterably taken: with that Government, constructed as it is, I will *never* again be connected." To Tierney he said less grandiloquently that he wanted only to be left in peace.[2] The wish was probably a sincere one but, in view of the sixty votes or so which he controlled in the House of Commons, hardly likely to be gratified.

The Whigs had felt confident that Sidmouth's resignation would soon be followed by an alliance with them in out-and-out hostility to Pitt:

"The Doctor's resignation," wrote Fox expectantly,[3] "may do great good, as furnishing evidence of the impossibility of Pitt's going on with any set of Ministers who are not his own mere creatures and tools. If the Doctor will fall in with these views, I am sure I have no objection to coalescing with him; on the contrary I should like whatever would tend most to show that the contest was between Pitt on one side, and *all* the men of influence on the other. I mention *influence*, because I think that it is the only circumstance in which the Doctor is considerable, and I am sadly afraid lest, by mismanagement, he should lose what he has of that kind in the House of Commons."

But even though the Prince of Wales himself was deployed to woo Sidmouth into opposition, Fox was disconcerted and annoyed to find that his putative ally showed little eagerness to accept his overtures. "The Doctor, Lord help him, is a great fool, and one whom experience cannot make wise," he wrote crossly.[1] But Sidmouth continued placidly on his way. His resignation at the very end of a session had given him a few months' breathing space before he need decide what tactics to follow; in the meanwhile the Addingtonians took refuge in their constituencies while their leader parried all approaches with bland and non-committal platitudes. It was a game at which Sidmouth had grown skilful and he played it with diligence and a certain amount of relish.

*   *   *   *   *

But a flirtation with opposition, however judiciously managed, was small consolation for the estrangement from Pitt and the coldness of the King. He felt too the pains of loss of office, not so much as far as he was concerned as for his needy relations and retainers. In the winter of 1805 all seemed to grow together to make the period among the bleakest and most distressing of his life.

In October came Trafalgar and the death of Nelson. Just before he sailed on his last voyage, Nelson had called at White Lodge. During the visit he pressed Sidmouth to hold his proxy in the House of Lords. Sidmouth refused, on the grounds that it would not be proper to cast the vote of a serving officer against the Government. If Lord Sidmouth would not take it, replied Nelson, then he would give it to nobody else.[2] On a table in Sidmouth's study he then sketched out the plan by which he proposed to defeat the combined fleets of Spain and France if he should be fortunate enough to meet them. Five weeks later, the plan was carried into practice.

Sidmouth did not know whether to rejoice or mourn at the news of Trafalgar. "I begin, now the feelings excited by the victory have somewhat subsided," he wrote to Hiley,[3] "to reflect with bitter sorrow on the loss of Nelson, to shudder at the chasm he has left . . ." For Sidmouth, as for England, the loss was indeed irreparable. It would be wrong to claim that Nelson had much influence over his friend but the mere fact that Sidmouth considered him with affection and deep admiration ensured that a small part of his mind was kept alive; a curiosity, a tolerance, a hankering after heroic grandeur. His friendship with Nelson would always have been extraneous to the humdrum course of Sidmouth's life but his life was the poorer for its disappearance.

With the death of Nelson, Sidmouth not only lost a friend, he gained a constant suppliant for his favours. As early as 1803 Lady Hamilton had been writing to him to extol her role in keeping the Queen of Naples well disposed towards the British.[1] Now, with Nelson gone, she found herself left by his will as a legacy to the nation. Since the nation showed a distressing reluctance to accept the charge, she made an effort to transfer the responsibility to the equally reluctant Sidmouth. "Lord Nelson told me on parting that I might rely on him . . ." she wrote to Sir William Scott,[2] and she would have found it disrespectful to Lord Nelson's memory not to have done so. For the moment her extravagance had not overwhelmed her with debt and her demands were relatively modest. But in the future this embarrassing memento of his former friendship was to cause Sidmouth much worry and vexation.

By the time that the news of Nelson's death reached England Sidmouth himself was dangerously ill. From early August he had been suffering from what his doctors tentatively described as congestion of the liver. Through September and October he grew weaker and his pain increased. Characteristically he brooded over every feature of his symptoms, discussed them with his doctors and reported them in excruciating detail to his friends. For a few days at least he seems to have believed that he would not survive, for weeks "the pains in my back were very acute, and the sense of languor . . . almost intolerable."[3] To make matters worse his wife, to whose nursing he attached great value, was herself racked with rheumatism and kept often in bed.

But these misfortunes were as nothing to those which overtook his son. Harry Addington was an intelligent and willing boy but strained beyond his talents. The heavy spiritual and intellectual burden which Huntingford had seen fit to lay upon him proved

245

disasters, had been too much for Pitt. A fortnight at Bath did nothing to restore his health and on 9th January, 1806, he dragged his emaciated and pain-torn body back to London for the opening of the Session. At his villa at Putney he seemed for a few days to rally but soon the doctors lost all hope. George Tomline, now Bishop of Lincoln, was at the bedside and in a series of ever more gloomy reports kept his old enemy Sidmouth posted on the state of the man who had been so dear to both of them. The last message came on 22nd January. "The symptoms are growing gradually worse, and indicate approaching, though perhaps not immediate, dissolution."[1] Next day Pitt died.

* * * * *

"May everlasting happiness await him!" wrote Sidmouth.[2] "To me it is a comfort not to be expressed, that I have been enabled at this crisis to show, not merely attention, but the affection that has never been extinguished . . ." The tradition that all grievances are forgotten with the death of their creator is as comfortable in theory as it is rarely realised in practice. Sidmouth never forgave Pitt for what he considered the shameful treatment meted out to him as Prime Minister and later in the Coalition Government. But in spite of this abiding sense of injury Pitt could always have won back his loyalty with a few kind words and a protestation of continued friendship. Sidmouth's most ardent desire, even at the moments of their worst enmity, was to be admired by Pitt, approved by Pitt, admitted to the innermost conclave of Pitt's intimates. When he left the coalition in 1805, the most deeply rooted if also the least proclaimed of his motives, was jealous resentment that Pitt preferred the company and counsel of people like Canning to himself. Sidmouth was content to play second fiddle for ever, provided only that Pitt would treat him with affection and place him among the most valued of his advisers. When Pitt died, it was the realisation that now he could never win back his cherished position which caused him the sharpest pain.

But Pitt's death did more than put an end to the complex of political and emotional stresses which had composed their relationship. Sidmouth had come up to great position in the wake of Pitt. By Pitt's influence and at his instigation he had become first Speaker, then Prime Minister. His term at the head of Government had wilted and failed in the shade of Pitt's great prestige. Every public attitude he had adopted, every important speech he had delivered, had been to some extent shaped by the existence of Pitt; designed to win his applause, to soften his criticism or to provide a defence against his attacks. He remained a Pittite even in opposition; however independent his line might seem it was devised with one eye glancing over his shoulder to observe the reactions of the master; however strongly he might criticise Pitt's policy it was always with a mental reservation that Pitt was still a being with powers beyond the normal lot of man.

When Pitt died, the chief force that had shaped Sidmouth's career vanished with him. It was as if a compass had suddenly been cut off from magnetic north so that the needle was left to spin helplessly without an external force to guide its energies. In this case the needle quickly came to rest, pointing in the direction where it believed that north had used to be. From this rigid and inefficacious posture it was never to stir again. Sidmouth's reaction to Pitt's disappearance was a tenacious adherence to everything that already existed, a profound, almost pathological resistance to the erosion of time or the insidious inroads of progress. In the end for Sidmouth immobility was to be raised to the level of a political philosophy, in 1805 it was no more than a straw to which he clung in the faint hope that by it might be found at least a measure of stability. The cloak of complacency with which he had enveloped his public personality sufficed to preserve the image of a statesman who knew with confidence where he wished to go and how he proposed to get there. Under the cloak was only emptiness, doubt, irresolution, a paralysing reluctance to go anywhere in any way at all. In later life Sidmouth was, with reason, to be described as a reactionary. Immediately after the death of Pitt it was inaction and not reaction which shaped his existence. He had reached a dead-point in his career and there seemed no good reason to believe that he would ever move beyond it.

manence for his new alliance but he was a sufficiently experienced politician to know that failure to participate could not fail to lead to an early rupture. "It seems to me indispensable, at the present moment," he wrote,[1] "that we should have a strong Government and a weak Opposition; and I have thought it incumbent on me to lend my assistance to the attainment of that object in the only way which circumstances could admit of."

The deciding factor was probably Sidmouth's loyalty to the King and his belief that the new Ministry would be less likely to make mischief if he were inside it. This was certainly how his friends interpreted his decision. Yorke marvelled at his joining up with people who had treated him with so much insolence but still rejoiced that his membership would "bar the introduction of many party, whimsical or new-fangled notions," while Lord Rous[2] compared him to a "faithful old steward . . . watching new servants lest they should have some evil designs against the old family mansion." Sidmouth therefore joined the Talents not only in spite of his doubts about its membership and policies, but almost because of them. He warned Grenville plainly that on certain issues—in particular Catholic emancipation—he might find it necessary to oppose him.[3] In such circumstances neither he nor anyone else was very sanguine that the upshot was likely to be that "strong Government and weak Opposition" which he believed to be so necessary for the country.

His sense of public duty was not so great as to induce Sidmouth to join the Government without some part at least of his retinue. "I was . . . as moderate as I could be without unbecoming concession or sacrifice,"[4] Sidmouth reported to Bragge-Bathurst. The traditional appendages, Bond, Buckinghamshire, Vansittart and Hiley Addington, were accommodated in suitable niches and a strong claim was laid for Bragge-Bathurst himself to have a suitable job whenever there was a vacancy. Hiley's pretensions to take the lead in the House of Commons went near to disrupting the negotiations but Buckinghamshire proved in the long run still more troublesome. The latter was not at all pleased when fobbed off with the joint postmastership and no seat in the Cabinet. He made Sidmouth promise to try to do better for him in the future. A few months later he renewed his lamentations. Sidmouth did his best with Grenville but got nowhere in "one of the most trying and irksome conversations

I ever had." He could only bring further pressure by threatening resignation or ill-will; "neither of which would, I think, have been fair to Lord Grenville or honourable to myself."[1]

But though prepared to leave Buckinghamshire in the ante-room, Sidmouth did not intend to venture into this hazardous and ill-disposed Cabinet without a single friend. Grenville equally had no wish to carry a passenger merely to save Sidmouth from feeling lonely. A solution was found when Ellenborough, who had already refused the Chancellorship, was admitted to the Cabinet as Lord Chief Justice. The idea seems to have originated with Grenville but it was eagerly taken up by Sidmouth: "as to the purity of whose views and conduct in the formation of the present arrangement I can bear the fullest testimony," wrote Ellenborough,[2] "and whose earnest request overcame my reluctance . . ."

The impropriety of placing in a Cabinet, which might decide upon the prosecution of an individual, the man who would probably be called on to act as judge in the resultant trial, seems never to have occurred to Sidmouth. The Government relied on the legal argument that, since the Cabinet had no constitutional standing, there could be nothing unconstitutional in including in it any adviser whom the Prime Minister might find of use. "The question was hunted down, and the objections to your cabinet situation are dead and buried," wrote Sidmouth in triumph[3] after the matter had been debated in both Commons and Lords. But the appointment was unpopular in the country and caused pangs of conscience even among Sidmouth's closest friends. Whatever the legal strength of the Government's case the precedent was never repeated and the appointment tacitly recognised as an error.

Sidmouth's own position also gave difficulty. Grenville had no intention of offering him a serious departmental post, nor did Sidmouth desire one. At first it was proposed that he should take back the position of Lord President of the Council. This Sidmouth declined, partly on grounds of health, partly because he thought it would be embarrassing both for himself and for his colleagues if he were placed in a post which involved frequent meetings with the King. Eventually it was decided that he should be Lord Privy Seal, a position which gave him no departmental responsibility nor chance of exercising influence on his colleagues.

Sidmouth, indeed, had no wish to play a large part in the work of the Cabinet. He saw his role as a defensive one and, if all went peacefully, would be perfectly content to take a back seat and rarely if ever interfere in the running of affairs.

"Though in the arrangements there are subjects of regret, those which are strictly political are upon the whole satisfactory," wrote Sidmouth[1] in a moment of optimism. "I see efficiency, zeal and good humour; not however more than sufficient for the difficulties of all governments which we have to encounter . . . There is . . . a prevalent disposition to support Government and if they act, as I trust they will, with unison and discretion, they will go on very well."

Sidmouth's good opinion of the new Government was not widely shared and among the features most harshly criticised was his own part in it. Canning and the rest of his coven were, of course, stirred by the coalition to fresh heights of rage and scorn. "What a scene of rapacity, self interest, discontent, envy and heart burnings, this change of administration has occasioned," wrote Lady Bessborough.[2] "What a torrent of low, degrading, selfish petty passions . . . !" Canning himself expressed his contempt more economically if no more sympathetically when he commented that "Mr. Fox has got the Doctor, as people must have the measles once in their life."[3]

But even among the more temperate Pittites there was indignation. It was believed that Sidmouth had first, by his refusal to collaborate, made it impossible for Hawkesbury to carry on the Government and had then worked zealously to ensure that not a single Pittite found employment in the Talents. "A standard is raised under the firm of Castlereagh, Hawkesbury and Canning," wrote Sidmouth.[4] Add Eldon and Perceval and there was the makings of a serious Opposition, numerically still weak but a nucleus for a new Conservative Party able to flourish in a world deprived of William Pitt. The animosity which Sidmouth had inspired among these people, still more among their rank-and-file, was to linger on long after the original cause had been forgotten.

To the English at large, Sidmouth's new associations were little more appealing. In the public memory Sidmouth and Grenville were inveterate enemies; the first the victim of the second's constant and unrelenting criticism. Intellectually the English were prepared to concede that there might be excellent reasons for the two men to suppress their differences and join in temporary alliance. But emotionally they could only perceive that this gathering of enemies was shabby politics, the fruit of expediency and lust for office, in its own way as improper as the ill-famed North-Fox coalition of 1783. Fox was still there; for North read Sidmouth and the parallel seemed superficially exact. Sidmouth had still not lost his hold on the affection and trust of the country gentlemen but the discovery that he, too, could play politics and make pacts with his enemies disturbed their simple faith. It was to be several years before he would regain his reputation as the champion of all that was straightforward and honourable; never again were the knights of the shire quite to recapture their perfect confidence that Sidmouth was one of them, ranged on their side against the rapacious and unprincipled London politicians.

*　　*　　*　　*　　*

To Sidmouth one of the main features of his watch-dog role was to ensure that the war was unremittingly carried on. As the architect of the Treaty of Amiens he felt that he had established beyond doubt that peace with Napoleon could never be more than a temporary truce. But he was not satisfied that Fox had learnt the same lesson. He had no doubt that, if he tried his hand at negotiation, Fox too would be swiftly disillusioned. In the meantime, however, there was much to be done. Sidmouth feared lest Britain might neglect the winning of the war while Fox was experimenting with the making of a peace.

In a Cabinet Minute which Sidmouth circulated to his colleagues he argued that:[1] "The present state of the Continent and the movements of the French armies make it important that the first measures of the new Administration should be marked by vigour and decision." He urged that France should be deprived of the naval resources of Spain by landings at Ferrol and Cadiz during which the Arsenals should be bombarded and the ships captured or destroyed. "If it should be determined to withdraw our troops from Hanover," concluded Sidmouth, "they might be employed for such an operation, with peculiar advantages of preparation and secrecy." Such belligerence is not altogether easy to reconcile with Sidmouth's cautious holding back when he was himself Prime Minister. He seems to have argued that the destruction of the Spanish fleet would make it safe to pursue the waiting policy which still suited England best. But even more important, he believed that only some such act of aggression would commit the more pacific members of the Cabinet to continuing the war. By it he sought to involve them and their reputations irrevocably in the pursuit of final victory.

The minute was allowed to settle among Windham's papers and it is unlikely that Sidmouth's ideas had much effect on the evolution of Britain's strategy. But the presence in the Cabinet of a man who had devoted so much effort to negotiations with Napoleon and was now as convinced a belligerent as any must certainly have strengthened the hand of those, like Windham, who felt that the war must be carried on. "You see on what friendly terms Lord Sidmouth and I now are," remarked Windham to his private secretary in another context.[1] The alliance of the architect of the Peace of 1802 and of its foremost critic might seem at first incongruous but Sidmouth saw nothing illogical in his position. In 1801 peace had been necessary because of the physical and psychological state of the nation; in 1806 the same was no longer true. If he and Windham could induce Fox to show caution in his approaches to Napoleon and make it more difficult for him to conclude a peace which was dishonourable or incompatible with England's safety, then Sidmouth would feel that his decision to join the Talents had been amply justified.

Sidmouth's first serious disagreement with his colleagues came over that hardy perennial, the abolition of the slave trade. On this issue, while public and still more parliamentary opinion had evolved, Sidmouth had stayed obstinately still. Grenville wrote hopefully to enlist his support:[2] "If I understand your sentiments rightly . . . you agree with me in the strong disapprobation of the nature of this trade, in the earnest desire to see it put an end to, but you think that the steps for that purpose should, on political considerations of the colonial and commercial interests of the country, be more gradual than I can bring myself to think they ought to be." He pleaded against "the disgraceful methods of delay which have so much hurt the character of the House of Lords" and urged that, at least, Sidmouth should support a resolution agreeing in principle to the ending of the trade.

But Grenville underestimated the force of Sidmouth's doubts.

Ursula Maria, Addington's first
wife: portrait by Downman

Mary Anne, his second wife, in
silhouette

Viscount Sidmouth in 1823, by Richmond

under Buckinghamshire but in general Sidmouth's parliamentary following remained absolutely loyal. Most of Sidmouth's followers were mediocrities but few of them were fools and they could hold their own with any other group for reliability, integrity and honour. It is possible to disagree with the policy of the group on almost every issue and yet still to admire their unselfish and dignified self-discipline.

If Sidmouth had any claim to be classed as a successful politician it lay in his ability, with no apparent advantages, to retain the loyalty of so many diverse individuals. They had every inducement to desert him and yet they would not leave their unfashionable leader. Sidmouth had no magnetic personality, no Pitt-like capacity to win and hold the blind loyalty of his followers, none of the brilliant charm by which Fox had commanded not only obedience but love. And yet this quiet, inoffensive, undistinguished man exercised power over his followers in its own way as absolute as that of any of his great contemporaries. It is a curious paradox of history that Sidmouth should be remembered as a pattern of all that is least noble and least inspiring—least, in short, like a leader—and yet that the record shows him as a party chief whose command of men's loyalties for many years and through the least propitious circumstances was as unquestioned as it was extraordinary.

I I

... I have said, and said most truly, that if the country was well governed, and its affairs ably conducted, I cared little in whose hands the Administration was placed. To a *very few* I have been more explicit, by declaring my strong and increasing repugnance to office, arising from various causes, (amongst the rest from the present state of my family) and my fixed determination never to return to it, except under the positive obligation of public duty; and that, after the experience of the last four years, I could not admit the existence of such an obligation, unless I was to be placed in a situation of perfect and unqualified responsibility: in other words, to use a recent expression of the Speaker, that I would not be a Noun adjective to any Government.[1]

Such protestations on the part of Ministers out of office rare deserve to be taken at face value. Sidmouth's later history show that he was to prove as ready as the next man to move back in Government when acceptable terms were offered him. But in t period directly following the downfall of the Talents there can little doubt that he genuinely looked forward to a period seclusion. His experiences as Prime Minister had convinced h that the tribulations of this office were far greater than t rewards. His next two essays as a Minister had proved that could be even more difficult to work with other people than try to make them work with him. Now he found himself reject even by those whom he felt to be his friends. He was out sympathy both with Government and with Opposition and v uncertain whether he could hold his own party together in th unpromising straits. His enemies proclaimed triumphantly t his political career was closed; sanguine though his nature mi usually be, Sidmouth found it hard to convince himself that t were wrong or even to feel much regret at the thought that t might be right.

". . . the present state of my family . . ." indeed offered him little encouragement to continue active in public life. The unhappy Harry still lingered in a twilight between infantilism and complete unconsciousness. Sidmouth continued hopefully to note every encouraging symptom: "He had the appearance of perfect health and is *very stout*"; "You will be surprised and rejoiced to hear that today I prevailed upon Harry to mount Pearse's horse. He took my stick, and held the reins quite perfectly . . ." But every flicker of animation was followed by relapse into apathy: "Nothing was said nor even the eyes opened"; "Poor Harry is very much reduced . . . the attack is wholly unaccounted for."[1] The fitful course of the disease could hardly have been better contrived to put the utmost strain on all those who loved the victim. To Sidmouth it seemed that the burden was one which he could hardly bear.

His wife Ursula, by her unfailing courage and light-heartedness, helped him through the bleakest hours. "We dined today at two o'clock," reported Sidmouth to his brother,[2] "and have since all been to Hampton Court by water, where we had the delight of seeing the cartoons and a few other good pictures. Tomorrow a detachment consisting of Ursula, Mary Anne and myself mean to go to town to see the pictures at Lord Stafford's. These are gay proceedings, of which Lady S. is the chief promoter." Whatever gaiety there was in Sidmouth's household—and it was rare enough—was promoted by his wife. Even as a child he had had little gift for spontaneous enjoyment. The depressing though benevolent regimen of Huntingford and his father had helped what there was to waste away. Now ill-health, increasing age and his innumerable worries had almost finished the process. Sidmouth was never a melancholy or morbid figure; his habitual mood, indeed, was one of placid optimism and he derived much pleasure in a minor key from his family, his friends, his wine, his reading and hazardous gallops through Richmond Park. But above this level only the keenest of stimuli could raise him and of all those around him it was only from his wife that such a stimulus could come. Yet Ursula was herself enfeebled and often in pain. At least she was now spared the tribulation of a succession of miscarriages but her body had been debilitated by the early disasters and not even her fine spirit could enable her always to rise above her weakness.

As his sense of political isolation grew, so Sidmouth depended more and more upon the support of his intimates. His son, his wife, his brother Hiley; these were the three people for whom Sidmouth cared the most. "The full persuasion that we can never differ materially upon any important point is one of the greatest comforts I have in this world," he wrote to Hiley[1] in 1807. Yet Hiley himself was often ill during this period, proclaimed himself indeed upon the point of death and won from Sidmouth letters worthy of their father extolling the virtues of soda-water poured upon a teaspoonful of brandy; "Nothing is so effectual in cleansing the kidney and in bringing off nebulous matter from the bladder."[2] Hiley was prone to hypochondria but, whether his maladies were imaginary or real, they were yet one more cause of distress to his overburdened brother.

Sidmouth himself fitted well into this sombre portrait of a sickly family. His principal malady was St. Anthony's fire, more pompously erysipelas, a fever which had ravaged Europe in the great pestilence of 1089 but by the nineteenth century had dwindled to a disagreeable but not particularly dangerous complaint. To this were added certain minor afflictions stemming from too liberal a recourse to wine and the injuries which usually plague the intrepid but unskilful horseman. Towards the end of 1807 his health broke down altogether. He was confined to White Lodge, in bed for the most part, with pains in his side and back and occasional fevers. In November he was "never free from sensation in the head, at times extreme pain, rigour, drowsiness." It was not till early 1808 that he was able to take any vigorous part in public life and not until the end of 1809 that Sir Lucas Pepys prescribed a "bracing mode of treatment" and removed the "scorching hand of my persecutor, St. Anthony," for the rest of Sidmouth's life.

In 1807 Sidmouth was fifty years old. Increasing age had brought him not only disillusionment and ill-health but absolute inflexibility of mind. His old beliefs had been refined and finally fused into a blind faith in the transcendent virtues of the British Constitution. To this concept he clung with tenacious, almost despairing energy. The Constitution, with its twin pillars the monarchy and the established church, possessed for Sidmouth an almost sacred significance; wisely designed, benevolently administered and, with God's grace, eternally immutable. He would not claim that it was perfect, but it was as near perfection as the work of man could ever be. At times indeed he found himself wondering whether it could be the work of man or whether some obscure and medieval Moses might not have received and filtered into the body politic divine instructions for the future of the British people. He believed with absolute conviction that any attempt to tamper with the Constitution would disturb the inspired balance of its construction and lead to its disintegration. The belief coloured his reaction to almost every problem. It provided a philosophical justification for implacable resistance to any kind of reform. Whether the proposal be to amend the rating powers of the Justices of the Peace or to abolish the House of Lords and proclaim a Republic, it seemed to Sidmouth in essence almost equally reprehensible. The first, certainly, was less outrageous but both aimed towards the subversion of the Constitution and both must therefore be condemned.

The only man who might have been able to prevent these dogmas rigidifying in Sidmouth's mind was William Pitt. But Pitt was dead, and the side of him which Sidmouth chose to remember was the authoritarian war-leader who had found it necessary to clamp down on all radical movements and to abandon his own schemes for the improvement of the Constitution. The mantle of Pitt the reformer had fallen to George Canning. Its adoption by that statesman would alone have been almost enough to convince Sidmouth that reform was a noxious growth which, left to itself, must infallibly corrupt the whole of the body politic. He saw the rising tide of radicalism not as an indication that change was needed but as proof that too much had already changed. If, to check the process, it must first be ruthlessly repressed, then let there be ruthless repression. The need for such a recourse was one which Sidmouth honestly deplored but he could see no alternative compatible with the safety of the State.

It is incontestable that this rigidity of mind made him a doubtful asset to any government. His enemies claimed that it rendered him unemployable; this was untrue but it did mean that his usefulness was limited and that he could only be employed in special circumstances and in pursuit of a carefully defined and circumscribed objective. The time was to come when the Tory Ministry would have a need for his talents but in 1807, except among the most inflexible reactionaries, the extra votes which his participation would have gained them were sacrificed with little regret. Most members of the Government indeed felt some relief that they had been spared the trammels of his obsessive inactivity.

*   *   *   *   *

Almost the first act of the new Government was to dissolve Parliament and go to the country. The Tory platform was the papist menace; a choice of electoral gambit which in others might have seemed cynical but in Perceval indicated only an evangelical background and a somewhat warped view of the facts of life in Britain. Success in such a cause was bound to work to the advantage of Sidmouth as well as Ministers and in fact the Addingtonians recouped some of the losses which they had suffered in Grenville's election the previous year. Their maximum voting strength remained at about fifty but within this total the fully committed Addingtonians were now by far the majority. It was a larger personal following than that of any other man who could not dispose of the patronage of Prime Minister or the backing of the King.

Buckinghamshire, as usual, threatened to be an embarrassment. When Portland formed his Government Sidmouth urged his former colleague to accept any office that might be offered him on the grounds that, since he had not been in the Cabinet under the Talents, he was not bound, like Sidmouth and Ellenborough, to stand to one side.[1] The logic was obscure but greedy Buckinghamshire took little convincing. Portland, however, either thought him as scrupulous as the other Addingtonians or had no place in his Government to give him; at all events no offer came. Buckinghamshire was therefore thrust willy-nilly into opposition. But Sidmouth's failure to secure him a seat in the Cabinet under Grenville still rankled. He assuaged his vanity by ostentatiously taking his own line; so much so that Sidmouth was on one occasion forced to ask him to instruct his friends to show their solidarity with the Addingtonians by "occasionally at least" sitting with them in the House of Commons.[2]

"Whatever may be my opinion of his Majesty's present servants," wrote Sidmouth,[3] "I cannot join in harassing them by a leagued and systematic opposition; and on the other hand, whatever may be thought of the late ministry, **it** is utterly inconsistent with any notions I have of constitutional principle or public duty to attempt to force them back upon the King." He pledged himself, in short, to an attitude of benevolent neutrality. But this by itself would not be enough to safeguard the interests of his group. A subservient acquiescence in all their doings would never induce Government to consider his views or remind the public of his continued independence. On any question of principle, therefore, he reserved the right to criticise and, if necessary, to vote against Ministers. It was evident to almost everyone that, if such questions of principle did not arise, then, in the interest of the Addingtonians, they would have to be invented.

Sidmouth's first demonstration of his independence came with Castlereagh's Militia Transfer Bill. This Bill was designed to draw some 28,000 men away from the militia to the woefully undermanned regular army; a useful stop-gap device which could never be a substitute for an efficient system of recruiting. To Sidmouth, however, the proposal infringed the very basis of his military philosophy; that the object of the British Army was to defend the British Isles and only in exceptional circumstances to intervene on the Continent. For the defence of Britain the militia seemed an efficient and economic instrument, the object of Government ought to be to reinforce and not to weaken it. The argument had had some validity in 1801; in 1807, with the Peninsular campaign just around the corner, it was already beginning to seem less reasonable. Fortunately the Government was not to be moved from its purpose and the regular army received its reinforcement in spite of Sidmouth's objurgations.

But it took the unsavoury incident of Copenhagen to prove that the Addingtonians were on occasion ready to work closely with the Whigs in opposition. The facts of what happened are beyond dispute, the interpretation less so. The British Government was convinced that Napoleon was on the point of seizing Denmark and with it the Danish fleet. They believed that the addition of this fleet to the ships which the French already possessed would put our naval supremacy in jeopardy. The survival of Britain, therefore, might well depend on the Danish fleet being removed before Napoleon could seize it. A British fleet was sent to Zealand and the Danes asked to hand over their ships on the understanding that they would be returned at the end of the war.

When the Prince Regent of Denmark refused this somewhat brusque invitation Copenhagen was bombarded for three nights. Only then did the defenders surrender so as to check the slaughter of civilians and save their city from total destruction. The Danish fleet was removed in triumph and such parts of it as proved still seaworthy incorporated in the British Navy.

The operation could be presented according to taste as a harsh but necessary operation, brilliantly conceived and boldly executed, justifiable on the strongest grounds of national interest, or as a wantonly savage, pointless and ill-managed attack upon an innocent and largely defenceless friend. To Canning, who had excellent if partly unpublishable grounds for his belief that the action had been vital to forestall Napoleon, it was pre-eminently the first. To Sidmouth, who had no such information and anyhow considered Canning's championship of the operation conclusive proof of its iniquity, it was the second. Both, in a sense, were right.

Sidmouth was genuinely shocked by this apparently unprovoked attack on a harmless bystander. He vied with Howick and Grenville in condemning the immorality of Government. Britain, he wrote,[1] was imitating "the treachery, rapacity and injustice of our adversary. When this system is sanctioned by parliament, England will be a rotten carcass, which had once been animated by a great and virtuous soul." "When I die," he fulminated in another letter,[2] "Copenhagen will be found at the bottom of my heart in conjunction with two or three associates whom I hesitate to name."

Sidmouth's stand for morality did him little good in the country. The British were hungry for glory and only a Gladstone could have persuaded them that this rather sordid incident was other than a noble victory. The Government's majority was unimpaired and Sidmouth himself came in for much ridicule as the Prime Minister in office when the first battle of Copenhagen had been fought six years before. Were our soldiers and sailors, it was asked, to be like Dryden's apothecaries:

> . . . who must but kill
> When Doctors first have signed the bloody bill?

The analogy, though far from exact, was still effective as a debating point. Yet in spite of his failure to convince the Government or the people that wrong had been done, Sidmouth's resolute defence of what he believed to be a first principle of international morality did much to rebuild the morale of his followers. It restored to the Addingtonians some of the philosophical justification for their continued existence as a group which they had largely lost in the preceding years. In this crisis they were more than just a clique held together by family relationships and reasons of expediency; they stood out firmly as champions of a code of decency and responsibility to be applied as much to their own country as to any other. The attack on Copenhagen may have been justified but England would have been a poorer place if there had not been a Sidmouth to cry aloud[1] that: "Might now constitutes right: we have given the death-blow to all that remained of the law of nations. Our magnanimity and our honour have surrendered to our convenience and our fears, and Bonaparte has swelled his triumphs by a victory over the good faith and moral character of Great Britain."

Over Copenhagen Sidmouth had demonstrated that, if need arose, he could unite with the rest of opposition against Ministers; shortly afterwards an occasion arose for showing that, if his conscience made it possible, he was still more ready to unite with Ministers against the rest of opposition. In May, 1808, Lord Grenville put down a motion for extending the franchise to certain classes of the Irish Catholics. Here Sidmouth could feel himself at one with all the more right-minded members of the Cabinet— Eldon, Hawkesbury and Perceval in particular—and, better still, at variance with the well known, if temporarily muted, views of Canning. His notes for the peroration of his speech survive among the Sidmouth papers and epitomise the strange blend of fear, prejudice and awestruck affection for the established church which underlay his attitude towards the Catholics.

Disclaim bigotry. . . . More mature consideration. The time may arrive but that depends on Catholics themselves. Not a question of theory. These laws have arisen like the British Constitution. Character purely defensive. Remedies gradually applied to existing evils. Security against the recurrence of evils inflicted by the R.C.s. Preserved tranquillity for more than a century . . . Latterly mask thrown off; what was once requested is now claim. Now demand a Revolution. Total subversion of constitution of this country. What is that constitution? That established at most splendid period of our history. What was its object? To secure Protestant establishment . . .

The rest of his speech was not so entirely negative as is suggested by these notes, though the positive measures which he recommended hardly seemed calculated to succeed. He pinned his hopes on "a well-digested system of education, and the increased residence of the Protestant clergy."[1] With this he was daring enough to suggest combining "a moderate provision at the charge of the State, for the deserving part of the Roman Catholic clergy." The object of policy must be "correcting the ignorance, promoting the industry, and improving the condition of the great mass of the people; by these means a feeling of confidence and security could be created, which, by encouraging the residence of the landlord, and bringing him into friendly communications with his dependents, must necessarily establish those links of mutual relation between the higher and lower classes so essential to a well conditioned state of society." The vague benevolence of this prescription may not have inspired much confidence in the Irish peasantry but it was hardly less relevant to their troubles than Grenville's remedies of giving votes to a handful of Catholic gentry and allowing them to rise to the higher military ranks.

Given the state of public opinion and the known views of the King, Grenville's measure never had a prospect of success. It was defeated in the House of Lords by 161 votes to 74 and gave Sidmouth an opportunity to demonstrate his value to the right wing of the Tories. "The Catholic question, on Friday," he reported to his brother,[2] "was met coldly and tamely by all the ministers except Lord Hawkesbury, who made a firm and able speech. I spoke for about an hour, and, I find, satisfied some of my friends better than myself. . . . I shall always have some pleasure in reflecting that I have, during the present session, used my best endeavours, although without success, to stem the new policy of surrendering principles, which have heretofore been held sacred to our fears of France . . ."

So Sidmouth continued on his course, to others devious, to himself eminently consistent, of bestowing his favours on Government or Opposition according to the principles which he felt each time to be in question. The Whigs never despaired entirely of winning him to out-and-out opposition. In June he dined unsus pectingly with the Duke of Gloucester, to find assembled there the Duke of Bedford, the Marquis of Buckingham, Lord Fitzwilliam and other big guns of the Opposition. "This was hardly fair . . ." he commented wistfully.[1] In July he took refuge in Devon: "You will smile to hear that my reading for some weeks past has been chiefly confined to Machiavel."[2] He flattered himself if he imagined that the Whig leaders ascribed to him great guile in his tactics. "Damn him!" exclaimed Lord Grey when told that a certain Addingtonian Member was too ill to come up to London. "I don't believe he would vote for me if he came. The Doctor can't make up his mind!"

Certainly Sidmouth seemed to be at pains not to commit himself for long to either party. On the issue of the Orders in Council, however, he was wholly with the Whigs. Napoleon's Berlin Decree, the retaliatory Orders in Council issued in London and Napoleon's final Milan Decree created a situation where a neutral who traded with the Continent except through Britain might have his ships confiscated by the British while, if he did have dealings with Britain, he might have his ships confiscated by the French. The only neutral with any trade of consequence was the United States. The Americans had no doubt how to allocate the blame between London and Paris. Jefferson was tempted to join in the war, instead he decided to bide his time and meanwhile cut off trade of any kind with the other side of the Atlantic. The result in America was much privation and bitterness against England. In England it led to the collapse of the cotton trade and near revolution in Lancashire.

From the first, Sidmouth doubted the wisdom of the Orders in Council. "It is at best a dreadful, even if a necessary expedient," he wrote[3] at the end of 1807. "It is kill or cure: if the Continent, under the influence of Bonaparte's authority and detestation of us, should acquiesce in the demise of British manufactures and colonial produce, what is to become of the commerce and revenue of Great Britain? And is there not a danger that, by such an exercise of our maritime power, we shall so exasperate and madden the whole civilised world as to unite it in one combined effort to accomplish our destruction? Bonaparte is now fighting us with two most formidable instruments; hatred of us and dread of himself."

These were arguments of expediency but, by the time the

Orders in Council were debated in the House of Lords, Sidmouth had taken up the same position of champion of the neutrals as he had adopted over the attack on Copenhagen. He stated three principles which should, in any circumstances, be observed[1]: "first: that neutrals have a right to carry on, during war, their accustomed trade, without any molestation or hindrance than such as arises from search or blockade; second: that this right of neutrals is sacred and cannot be forfeited but by their own wrong; and third: that neutrals have not a right to carry on, during war, a trade which they have never possessed."

In August, 1808, Pinckney, the American Minister, suggested that the United States should be exempted from the Orders in Council on condition that they lifted the embargo on trade with Britain. Sidmouth had a low opinion of the United States, describing it in the House of Lords as "a country in which there is little authority in the rulers, and as little public spirit and virtue in the people." The Orders in Council, however, had offended both his conscience and his common sense. He argued urgently that the American offer should be accepted. The Government did not give way but the force of opposition worried and disconcerted them and Sidmouth was not being more than usually sanguine when he reported that he thought that Ministers were changing tune.[2]

But just as it seemed that Sidmouth was allowing himself to become committed to the Whig alliance the start of the Peninsular campaign swung him again behind Government. From the moment that the King of Portugal sailed with his fleet for Brazil rather than submit to Napoleon, Sidmouth believed that in Portugal and Spain a battlefield had been found in which the British could take on Napoleon with some chance of success. When Wellesley landed successfully at Mondego Bay he wrote exultantly[3]: "You must, I am sure, be in a state of ecstasy . . . The importance of this event and its probable consequences is not to be calculated . . . We may expect every day to hear of the complete deliverance of Portugal and ere long of the re-establishment of lawful authority at Madrid." "Sir A. Wellesley is the Nelson of the army," he wrote in September, 1808, "and of course a tower of strength to the country."[4]

By the Convention of Cintra the French were allowed to escape the consequences of Wellesley's victory at Vimiero and to return to France with all arms and equipment; "an occasion," commented Sidmouth, "at which every British heart must sicken and which has broken down the honour of the country."[1] Though the Government could not escape all responsibility, the futile Sir Hew Dalrymple was mainly to blame for the debacle. Wellesley's part was at first obscure. "Sir Arthur Wellesley's friends say confidently that he is out of the scrape," wrote Sidmouth.[2] "I earnestly wish it may prove so, but I cannot conceive it to be possible. It is perhaps one of the greatest misfortunes that ever befel us." Wellesley was exculpated and Sidmouth reverted with relief to enthusiastic support of his new hero. When Wellesley landed in Portugal for the second time in April, 1809, Sidmouth announced himself convinced that he was the right man in the right place and that no sacrifice would be too great to keep him there. To this belief he clung even when it seemed that the campaign must end in disaster. When Wellesley fell back to the lines of Torres Vedras and despair was the fashionable mood in London, Lord Grey met Sidmouth in the street. "I am convinced," said the former, "that in six weeks' time there will not remain a single British soldier in the Peninsula except as a prisoner." "Though that should be the case I still should prefer it to our retiring from Portugal without making any further efforts." "Then," concluded Grey coldly, "we cannot talk on the subject."[3]

Sidmouth's claim to any understanding of military strategy has habitually been dismissed with derision. It has already been argued that his conduct of the war as Prime Minister, though neither noble in its conception nor exemplary in its efficiency, was nevertheless sensible, coherent and reasonably well geared to the needs of the day. His unfailing support of what was to prove one of the decisive campaigns of the Napoleonic wars must also be remembered to his credit. He held to his opinion against the views of opposition and even sometimes of Ministers themselves. His championship of Wellesley, like that of Nelson before him, showed his judgment of men could at least sometimes be sound. Writing to Lord Wellesley in 1837,[4] Lord Brougham thanked him for having drawn his attention to Sidmouth's "general character of boldness, which I am sure he had beyond most political men." Rarely was that boldness shown to better advantage than in Sidmouth's determined championship of the

Peninsular campaign at a time when many considered it a futile diversion and most believed that it must end in ignominious defeat.

In April, 1809, Sidmouth was happy to join with Grey and Grenville in criticising the Government's conduct of the war in Portugal. But it was clear that upon the fundamental issues of whether the campaign ought to have been started and should now be suffered to continue, the courses of the Whigs and the Addingtonians must part. Once more there was an end to the speculations of those who believed that the team which made up the Talents must be reconstituted and once more observers began to wonder how much longer Sidmouth would be kept out of a Government with which he had so much in common.

*   *   *   *   *

Meanwhile the Government seemed to be disintegrating without the need of any external stimulus. The root of the trouble lay in Canning's restless inability to put up with what he regarded— often with good reason—as the sloth and inefficiency of his colleagues. Castlereagh, the War Minister, for personal reasons as well as political, was his especial bugbear. He persuaded Portland and the King that Castlereagh must be moved to another post, then reluctantly accepted a delay in carrying out the sentence. For five disastrous months a senile, befuddled King and a Prime Minister reduced by illness to a shadow of his former inconsiderable self, sat upon their explosive secret. Inevitably it leaked out until it seemed that almost all members of the Government knew what was planned for Castlereagh except the victim himself. In August, 1809, Portland had a fit in his carriage and was reduced from inadequacy to inanimation. In the ensuing crisis Castlereagh at last discovered what had been going on. He blamed it all on Canning and poured out his indignation over three folio sheets concluding in a challenge. "I'd rather fight than read it, by God!" said Canning, and the two men met on Putney Heath; a duel which cost Canning a wounded thigh and both men any immediate prospect of retaining office.

"The intrigue and perfidy of which Lord Castlereagh was to be the victim and which led to the correspondence," commented Sidmouth, "if practised by Cesar Borgia, would have held a distinguished place in the Prince of Machiavel."[1] His previous summer's reading had perhaps disturbed his judgment. Canning had certainly been ruthless and not over-scrupulous. But he had no responsibility for concealing what was planned from Castlereagh; the point on which the latter had real reason to complain. Far more blame attaches to the futile dithering of Portland and, on grounds of honour alone, Castlereagh could as well have fought his duel with almost any other member of the Cabinet. Unfortunately for Canning, however, his record was such that Sidmouth's distrust and readiness to condemn him was shared by most of the country. Castlereagh gained much sympathy while Canning was labelled as, at the best, turbulent and malevolent, at the worst, outrageously dishonourable.

Portland's resignation could not be long delayed. It was rapidly followed by his death and the Government was thus deprived within a few weeks of two of its most considerable members and a leader who, with all his deficiencies, had still possessed the overriding virtue of being acceptable to all his followers. The Addingtonians pricked up their ears and began to speculate about office. Buckinghamshire predicted "a political hurricane never exceeded in the memory of man."[1] In his reply Sidmouth dolefully concurred; the only way out he saw was for the remaining members of the Government to try to reunite "all the friends of Mr Pitt."[2] There can be little doubt that, for this purpose at least, the category was taken to include himself.

Perceval, the Prime Minister chosen by the King and the rump of Portland's Cabinet, chose, however, to look to Grey and Grenville as props for the failing Ministry. It was a strange choice for this competent, courageous but narrow-minded man, fanatically anti-Papist and suspicious of all things radical or Whiggish. Probably it was forced on him by his colleagues who believed that the only way of disarming opposition was to incorporate it in the Ministry. But the Whigs were not interested in stepping into what they reasonably considered to be a sinking ship. Grenville came up to London for an interview, refused the invitation brusquely and sent the exchange of letters to Sidmouth for his entertainment. Grey did not even condescend to leave Northumberland. Willy-nilly, Perceval was forced to look to the Addingtonians.

With Canning out of the way there seemed no obvious obstacle to Sidmouth himself joining the Government. Perceval, however, was still obsessed by the difficulties. In a Cabinet minute of 18th September, 1809,[1] he concluded "that Lord Sidmouth's political conduct during the last years of Mr. Pitt's life had so alienated many of Mr. Pitt's friends, that it was to be feared more strength would be lost by their secession than could be gained by Lord Sidmouth's admission . . . His immediately attached friends, though highly respectable, were numerically so few, as not to counter-balance the loss which any such secession would occasion." It is hard to believe that this hard core of devoted Pittites still existed except in Perceval's imagination. Camden and Mulgrave would perhaps have protested mildly at sitting in Cabinet with Lord Sidmouth but they were not the sort of men to resign for such a reason, while Chatham, who should have felt more than anyone the responsibility for defending his brother's honour, did not see the slightest objection to co-operation with Sidmouth then or at any time. The only name which occurred to Sidmouth was that of Lord Lonsdale; even if he had chosen to leave, Sidmouth held that he could not have taken with him more than a handful of "the sourest, shabbiest and silliest" of the late Government's supporters.[2] But however unreal Perceval's fears—and it would have been unlike him to have completely misjudged the situation—his mind was made up. Sidmouth waited in vain his summons to a place in the Cabinet.

His chagrin was turned to indignation when he discovered that Perceval planned to take in his followers without him. First through Chatham as an emissary, then by personal letter, Perceval regretted that "the prejudices of some of the members of the old Pitt connexion"[3] made it impossible "at the moment" to find a place for Sidmouth in the Cabinet, but blandly hoped that the latter would nevertheless persuade Bragge-Bathurst and Vansittart to join the Government. The letter, remarked Sidmouth,[4] amounted "in substance only to this—if you will persuade *your* friends to support me, I will endeavour to persuade *mine* to permit you to come into office sometime or other. Mr Perceval ought to feel, for he must know, that these prejudices of his friends have not been excited by my conduct, but by a consciousness of their own. Mr Perceval is a *very* little man."

Eldon had warned Perceval that he was underestimating the capacity of the Addingtonians to cling together.[5] He proved right. For Bragge-Bathurst Sidmouth replied out of hand that, under no possible circumstances, would his brother-in-law be ready to agree; as to Vansittart, "I can only say that I wish to leave it to his own decision."[1] He had little doubt about the reply. Vansittart, though flattered at being offered the Exchequer, rejected the offer as being accompanied by the "systematic exclusion" of Lord Sidmouth "for the gratification of I know not what and I know not whose unexplained prejudices."[2] "Van cuts with a smooth, well-set razor," wrote Sidmouth approvingly.[3]

Buckinghamshire was one of the few Addingtonians whom Perceval might have been able to woo away. He claimed, of course, that he would always have remained loyal to his friends but was noticeably more noisy in his protestations after Perceval had failed to give him a chance to prove his loyalty. The omission was surprising, Buckinghamshire would not have added much to the administration but his little block of votes might have been very valuable. As it was he became a furious enemy; writing to Sidmouth to protest against the activities of this "cunning lawyer" who ought "to expand his mind beyond the narrow limits of the Inns of Court."[4]

Frustrated both by Addingtonians and Whigs, Perceval now plucked an unexpected trump from the pack when he persuaded Marquis Wellesley to join the Cabinet as Foreign Secretary. Arrogant, sex-surfeited and insufferably vain, Wellesley had nevertheless more pretensions to greatness than any other member of the Government. Canning, who had recently been building up a close alliance with the Wellesley family, was deeply offended at this unkind readiness to put the needs of the country before the calls of friendship; his chagrin to some extent consoled Sidmouth for seeing such an addition of strength to what Ellenborough had trenchantly dismissed as "a Baby-house and make-believe children's work of a nursery."[5]

It was inevitable that Sidmouth should turn his mind once more to an alliance with the Whigs. But before he could reconcile it with his conscience he felt bound first to satisfy himself that Grenville was, if not sound, at least resigned to inactivity on the Catholic question. First by letter, then by personal intercession at Dropmore, he tried to extract some promise that the matter would not be pressed if the Whigs returned to office. If Grenville had wished, it would probably not have been difficult to have found some formula compatible with Sidmouth's scruples yet leaving him a free hand. Instead he elected to take refuge in evasive answers. When Sidmouth referred obliquely to "setting the King's mind at ease," Grenville replied blandly[1] that he found it hard to say what would achieve this most desirable result. "Whenever the King may be pleased to signify to any persons whom he may be disposed to call to his service under what restrictions he may be disposed to place them with respect to that or to any other question of public policy, it will then be their duty to answer with equal precision whether on such grounds they can accept office . . ." "He took my answer *ad considerandum*" Grenville reported to Grey. "I do not believe that *this* ship will ever be launched."

Doggedly Sidmouth soldiered on behind the will-o'-the-wisp evasions of his elliptic friend. He wrote asking for a written résumé of what had passed between them—surely on paper he would be able to extract the truth. Grenville's reply—"it is impossible that anything could be more judicious," remarked Lord Grey[2]—merely restated that he felt the King's demand for a written pledge to have been unconstitutional but gave no clue as to his future intentions.[3] Lord Grenville's response, wrote Sidmouth, was "quite as open as I could have hoped and perhaps as it ought to have been."[4] But hard though he might try to look on the brighter side, he was in fact sadly disappointed. With a pretty faith in the latter's inquisitorial powers he now set Huntingford to the task of extracting a straight answer from the reluctant Whigs. Grenville's rejoinder[5] was still cautious but more nearly negative than anything he had so far offered. "With respect to any engagement to be now taken as to my future possible conduct in this respect, the Bishop of Gloucester has, I am sure, too just and honourable a mind not to see that a pledge which I declined giving to the highest authority, and for purposes for which no man could be more anxious than myself, cannot now be given for personal objects."

Reluctantly Sidmouth accepted that Grenville would never commit himself not to raise the rights of Catholics if once more returned to power. An effective alliance therefore became impossible. He complained of the impossible position in which he found himself.[6] Either he must support a Government "unfit for its status or its duties," or else co-operate in the agitation of measures which he believed to be "of all others the most dangerous to the country." His conclusion was inevitably that the present Government, distasteful though it might be, was still less mischievous than any probable successor. Wellesley's accession had given it a certain weight and, with the addition of the Addingtonians, it could probably settle down into a decent and efficient team. This was far more than could be said for the Whigs whom the Addingtonians had failed to control in the past and who now showed themselves completely unregenerate. "I am accordingly convinced," he wrote in December, 1809[1] "that our bias should be to support the measures of the present administration, which cannot now be considered so weak as to justify our concurring on that ground only, and before they are tried, in any parliamentary proceeding for their removal. The language I should recommend would be, that we were not hostile to government, and that our conduct would depend upon their measures, which we hoped would be such as to enable us to support them."

*   *   *   *   *

The policy was, indeed, little different from that which Sidmouth had pursued towards the Portland Government over the past few years. The general bias was a little more explicitly in favour of Ministers. Its first application came in the debate on the Address in January, 1810. Lord Grenville tabled an intemperate amendment which denounced the Government's conduct of the war and sought to condemn Wellington's achievements in the Peninsula in the same terms as the grotesquely mismanaged expedition to Walcheren off the mouth of the Scheldt. Sidmouth was prepared to demand an inquiry into the debacle at Walcheren but not to agree to out-and-out condemnation in advance, let alone to denounce the Peninsular campaign. When Grenville refused to modify his amendment, Sidmouth took his party into the lobby with Ministers, leaving the latter with a comfortable majority of fifty-two in the Lords and ninety-six in the Commons. "The most material defection was that of the Sidmouth party," wrote Lord Moira.[2] "The Doctor imagines that this administration must split, and he flatters himself that the King will then send for him and desire him to form a ministry out of the fragments." Such carefully planned intrigue was not in Sidmouth's nature. His tactics were dictated by two considerations; that he should show the Government that they could not continue without his support and that he should do nothing to alienate them irrevocably or to annoy the King. Two days later the Addingtonians voted in the House of Commons in favour of an inquiry into the Walcheren expedition. Government were beaten by 195 votes to 186. "The division," wrote Sidmouth cheerfully,[1] "it is thought must lead to consequences affecting the existence, or at least the present composition, of the government. Of its insufficiency, the opinion is universal."

When the campaign in Portugal was debated a month later, his line was strongly favourable to Government. Grenville wrote to urge Sidmouth to join in a common effort to prevent the waste of further men and money in Portugal. Sidmouth replied firmly:[2] "I continue to think that our honour and our own immediate interests impose upon us the obligation of affording to Portugal all the assistance in our power for the purpose of delaying its final subjugation." When the campaign was debated, Sidmouth criticised some aspects of the Government's policy but spoke in favour of continuing the fight. "That half faced concurrence of Lord Sidmouth is *temper* and not coquetry with Windsor," commented Lord Auckland.[3] "He cannot bear the idea of measures being apparently not communicated to him *before* they are finally adopted." Sidmouth was as subject as anyone to the onslaughts of injured vanity but in this case his championship of the Portuguese campaign was consistent and sincere; in refusing to collaborate with Grenville he had nothing in mind except to defend something which he believed to be right and necessary.

The favourable flavour which Sidmouth had given to his parliamentary tactics had not passed unnoticed by Ministers and the disposition to forget the Pittite past and draw all the true Tories together was steadily gaining ground. In the euphoric haze induced by their parliamentary successes, the Government played with the idea of a grand alliance which would bring back to the fold not only Sidmouth but Castlereagh and Canning as well. This unpromising project fared no better than might have been expected. Perceval knew there was no chance of securing Castlereagh's participation unless Sidmouth had agreed to the coalition.[4] As a first step, Yorke was sent to see what could be done. He had, he reported to Perceval, a ". . . most satisfactory conversation. I am persuaded that (supposing the *only obstacle* removed) you will find every possible disposition to conciliation, confidence and business." Unfortunately, "the only obstacle" turned out to be Sidmouth's flat refusal to sit in the same Cabinet as Canning. To include Sidmouth and exclude Canning would infallibly turn the latter to savage opposition, to do the contrary could only enrage the Addingtonians. Nervously Ministers decided to let things drift for a little while in the hope that some-how, somewhere, a change of heart would supervene.

Wellesley, who knew Sidmouth's character better than most of his colleagues, was by no means despondent. He believed that it would not take long for Sidmouth's animosity to Canning to settle down into a temperate dislike which would leave open the way at least to more or less polite co-operation. Time was to prove him right. Lord Sidmouth was to sit in the same Cabinet as Canning and deal with him in terms of cordial respect. But Wellesley still overestimated the speed at which Sidmouth could forget and forgive. His bitterness against Canning was too strong and too recently reinvigorated to make peaceful coexistence possible for a while at least. In June Wellesley called on Sid-mouth and tried to persuade him to swallow his pride. Sidmouth would have none of it. Perceval wrote to Castlereagh to give the news. "His objection to Canning was not a personal one," he explained,[1] "not upon any grounds of private or personal dislike; but upon the public ground that he did not think that, if Canning were to make one in a Government formed of himself, of you and of us, that the public would believe that there was that confidence and cordiality amongst ourselves which could alone give us the confidence of the country . . ." If only Canning could be kept out, then Sidmouth professed his readiness to accept Perceval as Prime Minister and to make this his "permanent and ultimate political connection."[2]

Wellesley disagreed with Sidmouth's point of view but wrote to Perceval that he thought "the judgment of so respectable a person" could not be lightly ignored. Certainly it seemed im-mutable. In July Perceval spent two hours at White Lodge and failed to make Sidmouth change his mind. Since by this time Wellesley had decided that he could not agree to any overhaul of the Government unless the inclusion of Canning was part of it, Perceval began to despair of achieving anything. A last futile effort was made to bring in Castlereagh and Canning without Sidmouth; this foundered on Castlereagh's refusal to co-operate and the whole chain of negotiations spluttered ignominiously out.

Sidmouth can fairly be accused of having shown pride, obstinacy and a certain amount of rancour in the face of assiduous efforts to placate him. In his defence it can be said that he had excellent reason to dislike the idea of serving with Canning and, anyway, had been given no assurance that Canning would be ready to serve with him. He had, indeed, quite good grounds to believe the opposite.[1] It was asking a lot to expect him to volunteer for this distasteful wedding when still unsure whether the other party might not then publicly humiliate him by refusing to let the banns be read. Nor were his overt arguments against such a union wholly frivolous. Sidmouth's experiences in the Talents had taught him the difficulties of working with uncongenial colleagues; given the discordant elements that would have to be amalgamated in this coalition it is not surprising that he doubted whether it would command the confidence of the public.

Canning's stock was anyway near its nadir in the summer of 1810. "You will not believe that all which has happened has been from Canning's monkey-tricks to make himself premier," wrote a Pittite junior Minister after the events of 1809.[2] The judgment was uncharitable but it reflected the deep distrust and even dislike of Canning felt by many Tories. Canning himself reciprocated the sentiments, describing Perceval a little later as "treacherous, hypocritical, mean and jealous."[3] Given such feelings on both sides it is not surprising, if still regrettable, that Sidmouth declined to make the necessary sacrifice. To serve with Canning, if all the Ministers had desired it, would have been unpleasant; to do so when clearly they did not, in Sidmouth's eyes, would have smacked of insanity.

A year after its accession to power Perceval's Government was still lingering on unfortified with a persistence and courage with which few had credited it. There seemed no reason why it should not remain in office. But in October, 1810, the King, flushed and ceaselessly chattering, made what was to prove his final plunge into insanity. With the Prince of Wales demanding his rights as Regent and Grenville and Grey already dividing up the offices, it seemed that Perceval's time as Prime Minister was almost over.

He hurriedly summoned Sidmouth to visit him at Ealing and together the two men worked out their tactics for the coming storm.[1] They were both decided that there must be a Regency but also that, for the first year at least, it must be subject to the restrictions which Pitt, and incidentally Grenville, had decided to impose on the Prince of Wales when the question had first been debated in 1788.

Sidmouth's decision to stick by the Ministers rather than to throw in his lot with the Prince and the Whigs, though consistent with his policy over the preceding years, was by no means inevitable.   Even though the King might yet once more recover— a prospect which seemed increasingly remote—he was now seventy-two years old. It could not be long before his son succeeded him in all but name if not in name as well. The future, therefore, lay with the Prince of Wales and it was believed by almost every political observer that his first act in power would be to dismiss his Ministers and bring in Grenville and Grey in their stead. It might have seemed common prudence for Sidmouth now to shift his loyalties. He had no commitments to Government nor any reason to owe them gratitude. The majority in favour of restrictions was small in both Houses of Parliament. If he had thrown in his weight with the Whigs he might well have secured the Prince the full powers for which he pined. The Prince was no more punctilious in the repayment of a debt than any other member of his family but such a service on Sidmouth's part must surely have earned him a place in the new administration. If, on the other hand, he sided with Perceval, the animosity which the Prince and the Whigs already felt towards him would be redoubled. It must have seemed to Sidmouth that he was likely thus to exclude himself and his followers from office until not only George III but George IV as well had vanished from the scene. It was true that if he had taken the Whig line and argued against restrictions he would have been inconsistent with his conduct in 1788. This, however, was a consideration which Lord Grenville had not allowed to discompose him and Grenville had played a far more prominent part in the earlier debates.

An explanation might have been that Sidmouth believed the Prince of Wales's hostility to be so immutable as to put reconciliation out of the question. Yet not even this was so. On the contrary, Sidmouth clung to the the pathetic illusion that the Prince viewed him with respect and even affection. He believed that he was sacrificing the Prince's esteem, not adding one more drop to an ocean of dislike. On this hypothesis he had everything to lose by supporting Perceval and nothing to gain except his peace of mind. He took the course which he considered proper and, if he stopped at all to calculate his own advantage, did not allow the result to deflect him from his purpose.

With a justice rare in life and almost unique in politics, his decision paid off handsomely. What neither Perceval, Sidmouth, nor indeed Grenville and Grey themselves had realised was the extent to which the Prince of Wales had sickened of the Whig leaders over the last few years. Himself vain and incurably frivolous, he found insufferable Grenville's arrogance and prosy lectures. Grey, it is often alleged, had years before been his rival in love, and a sense of injury still lingered. He knew that neither of the Whig Lords would be sympathetic to the claims of his own especial favourite, Sheridan. Above all, as Roger Fulford has so brilliantly demonstrated,[1] he was far from being as irresponsible and disloyal to his father as popular taste has usually portrayed him. After much hesitation and uncertainty he told Perceval that "the irresistible impulse of filial duty" made it necessary for him to keep the present Ministers in office. To the Whigs he broke it as gently as possible that they would have to wait at least another year in Opposition.

The Whigs were outraged at this failure of loyalty on the part of a man whom they had regarded as their creature. Before this debacle there had been much uneasiness between the Grenvillite wing, which hankered after alliance with Canning, and the pure, or Foxite Whigs under Lord Grey. The Marquis of Buckingham had written in horror to his brother at a proposal that Whitbread should be given the lead in the Commons and Grey, Ponsonby and Holland the three Seals:[2] "I know not why the idea of Mr. Canning, or of Mr. Perceval, or even of that contemptible animal Lord Sidmouth is to be abandoned as hopeless; *anything* is better than such an attempt on principles wholly undefensible. It is no disgrace to fail in forming a Government, and I should prefer infinitely that you should fail, rather than so attempt to man your boats." But when it became clear that the question of forming a Government was not to arise at all the different factions drew together in common abuse of the Prince

Their patent and vociferous indignation in its turn did much to increase the disenchantment which the newly created Regent already felt for his traditional friends and allies.

Strangely enough the Whigs attributed to "that contemptible animal Lord Sidmouth" much of the responsibility for the change in the Regent's policy. Sheridan had recently been often at White Lodge and Buckingham was quick to imagine him imbibing Tory principles and selling them subtly to his master. If Sidmouth did have any such influence it must certainly have been obliquely wielded since the Prince would have been quick to reject advice which he knew to have come from such a quarter. But the leading role which he played in the Regency debate was enough in itself to end all pretence of co-operation between him and the Whigs. Effectively from now onwards Sidmouth commanded not a section of opposition but a splinter group of the governmental party.

So far as Perceval was concerned, the past was now forgotten and the splinter should, as swiftly as possible, be reintegrated with the whole. But Perceval knew that the Prince Regent detested Sidmouth and he had no wish to annoy him unnecessarily in the uneasy interim period while the restrictions were still in force. No move was therefore made to put Sidmouth back into the Cabinet but equally no pains were spared to make him feel that was where he belonged and where he would shortly be. The days were almost past when the only talisman for membership of the Tory Party was former loyalty to William Pitt and the day almost come when Sidmouth could lead back his flock into the inner fold of Conservative orthodoxy. Spiritually indeed he felt that he had never left it.

* * * * *

Sidmouth occupied himself during his last months of independence in hectic pursuit of one of his favourite hobby-horses, the licensing of Dissenting Ministers. Under the terms of the Toleration Act any man or even minor—illiterate, lunatic or revolutionary—could obtain a licence to preach on the proffering of sixpence to the magistrates. The results of this provision were at times bizarre but do not seem to have caused much distress except to the tidy mind of Lord Sidmouth. The latter believed the very fabric of the State to be endangered by the outpourings of the various cranks and oddities who claimed the title of a licensed Minister. While vigorously paying tribute on every occasion to the spirit of the Toleration Act, "the Palladium of our Religious Liberties," he worked with equal vigour to amend the letter by imposing a bevy of conditions to be met before a licence would be granted. In May, 1811, he tabled a Bill to this effect in the House of Lords.

Sidmouth knew that he could never carry through his Bill unless Methodist opinion were ready to accept it. To this end he had long confabulations with Dr. Coke, the head of the Wesleyan Methodists, and in April reported triumphantly[1] that Coke was now completely satisfied: "His apprehensions are converted into zealous approbation." Certainly Coke's letters seem to show that he was ready to accept the plan but the Bill was no sooner tabled than the Methodists took fright, began to murmur darkly about persecution and addressed themselves to whipping up opposition to the measure.

Little whipping-up was needed. A great wave of indignation rose throughout the country; a wave as disproportionately violent to the trivial import of Sidmouth's Bill as Sidmouth's original fears had been to the mischief done by a few moonstruck Ministers. It found its most urbane expression in the measured denunciation of Sydney Smith:[1] "We are convinced Lord Sidmouth is a very amiable and well-intentioned man: his error is not the error of his heart, but of his time *above which few men ever rise*. It is the error of some four or five hundred thousand English gentlemen, of decent education and worthy character who conscientiously believe that they are punishing and continuing [*sic*] incapacities, for the good of the State; while they are, in fact, (though without knowing it), only gratifying that insolence, hatred and revenge which all human beings are unfortunately so ready to feel against those who will not conform to their sentiments."

The Government had never been enthusiastic about the Bill but, to humour its sponsor, had been ready to lend it their support. Now they recoiled in horror from the hornets' nest which Sidmouth had disturbed and begged him to withdraw gracefully rather than face certain and humiliating defeat. But for Sidmouth humiliation could only lie in retreat. This was a matter of right or wrong and nothing could induce him to give up. Grandly, he urged the Government not to be influenced by "a partial clamour, excited by misrepresentation, which I am satisfied has for its object a manifestation of influence and power, rather than the prevention of the measure from any serious dread of its consequences."[1]

The dawn of the debate found Sidmouth[2] ". . . still in the land of the living, though continually harassed with letters, pelted at by resolutions and annoyed by deputations." But he knew by then that his chances were non-existent. Lord Holland, who stage-managed the opposition for the Whigs, proudly recorded: "For some days no places were to be had on the stage coaches and diligences of the Kingdom; all were occupied with petitions to parliament against the measure. . . . The peers could hardly get to the doors, the avenues were so crowded with men of grave deportment and puritanical aspect; when there, they had almost equal difficulty in gaining their seats, for loads of parchment encumbered and obstructed their way to them . . ."[3] Against such opposition not even the most sublime orator could have made much impression; the unfortunate Sidmouth, followed as he was by the Archbishop of Canterbury, who argued that the measure was unwise, had no chance of swaying more than a handful of his fellow-peers. The motion was negatived without a division.

Sidmouth had set his heart upon the success of this measure. But even more than by his defeat he was distressed by the way in which his views seemed to him to have been misrepresented in the country and by the failure of his friends in the Government to stand by him. He wrote to Hiley[4] that: "Fear, faction and fanaticism have co-operated and Ministers, Opposition and Dissenters have contributed to produce the result of which you have been apprized." The debate did not alienate him from Government but it removed any feelings of loyalty which might have grown up in the previous months. He emerged from his ordeal with the conviction that he should only enter Perceval's Government on his own terms and that he would be showing quite unnecessary complaisance if he were to pitch those terms too low.

But Sidmouth's bitterness at his defeat was quickly to be swallowed up in a greater sorrow. Throughout the closing stages of the battle over the Dissenters' Bill Sidmouth had been distracted by the health of his wife. On 14th April he had written in some alarm that she was suffering from "languor, want of appetite, pain in the region of the liver and great liability to sickness." In the following weeks she got better, then there was a disastrous relapse. By 22nd June hope was vanishing and the following day: "My dear Hiley will be indeed grieved . . . to hear that our suspense has been fatally terminated. It pleased God to close the scene, and with the infliction of no severe suffering at last, at half past five this morning."

On the memorial which once stood in Mortlake Church the following lines appeared.[1] Their triteness of expression and depressing absence of life or imagination suggest strongly that Sidmouth himself was the author:

> Not that to mortal eyes thy spotless life,
> Shew'd the best form of parent, child and wife;
> Not that thy vital current seem'd to glide
> Clear and unmix'd through the world's troublous tide,
> That grace and beauty form'd each heart to win,
> Seem'd but the casket to the gem within;
> Not hence the fond presumption of our love,
> Which lifts thy spirit to the Saints above;
> But that pure Piety's consoling power,
> Thy life illumn'd, and cheered thy parting hour;
> That each best gift of charity was thine,
> The liberal feeling, and the grace divine;
> And e'en thy virtues humbled in the dust,
> In Heaven's sure promise was thine only trust;
> Sooth'd by that Hope, Affection checks the sigh,
> And hails the day-spring of eternity.

These lines, which echo all the flat and conventional phrases in which Sidmouth wrote of his loss to his friends and relations, are worth quotation as another illustration of his inability to communicate to others emotions which he himself felt passionately and profoundly. The death of his wife was the greatest tragedy of Sidmouth's life. He had depended on her implicitly from the day of their marriage. Never had his trust proved unjustified. She had given him companionship, she had given him support, she had given him constant and unhesitating love. She had fought on his side ferociously and unquestioningly, she had consoled him in his failures and had been ever first to applaud his triumphs.

Through all her own illnesses and suffering she had kept a home for him where he could find peace, seclusion and encouragement. She alone had found the touch to lighten his solemnity. Only from her could he accept ridicule without wincing, only in her company did he feel no need to exhibit the vain self-assertion which sprang so much from his own sense of inadequacy. She was his sense of humour and his sense of proportion. Her loss was irremediable.

He found no one able fully to share his sorrow. Harry, his eldest son, could not even understand the loss that he had suffered. William, a sickly child, was living a cloistered existence with a clergyman near Steyning in the hope that he might be equipped to grapple with the intellectual problems of life at the university. For companionship he relied upon his daughter Mary Anne. She "has been and will continue to be a treasure of support to us all," wrote Sidmouth to Bragge-Bathurst,[1] but though she was a faithful follower and a diligent secretary, Mary Anne could never replace her mother.

"He is in deep affliction and feeble health," wrote Vansittart three months after Lady Sidmouth's death,[2] "and anxious only for retirement." It was inevitable that Sidmouth's first reaction should be to retreat from public life and nurse his pain in solitude. But it was also inevitable that the mood would pass. In the same letter Vansittart announced the political event which was to open Sidmouth's way back into the Government; the permanent Regency, he reported, was now a certainty. Writing early in 1812[3] to one of his closest friends, Sidmouth referred to ". . . the most trying of afflictions which has rendered performance of my public duties more irksome to me than at any period of my life. Still however they shall continue to be discharged with zeal." He would not have been capable of making such a claim directly after the death of his wife.

But even though his interest in public affairs might have revived after a few months, it does not follow that his grief was therefore superficial or fleeting. His public duties were indeed the more irksome because he did not have his wife to help him bear the tribulations or to rejoice with him in the rewards. He still relished pomp and power but the flavour was largely lost. The responsibilities were more apparent, the fruits less tempting. His political life carried on because he was as deeply involved as any other public figure in the web of hopes and ambitions, vendettas and loyalties, duties and responsibilities, which together can constitute an almost inescapable commitment. But the role of private citizen, which would have seemed of little attraction to him in 1810, after the death of his wife bulked ever larger as a desirable if distant goal at which, with God's grace, he would some not too distant day arrive.

*   *   *   *   *

By the end of the year it was clear even to his most ardent champion that George III would never rule again. February, 1812, would therefore see all restrictions on the Regency removed; it would also—so most people believed—see the belated return of the Whigs to office. Perceval and Sidmouth continued to confer together and to make their dispositions for a spell in opposition. But the Prince Regent could not make up his mind. He had gained some respect for Perceval, had lost still more of his regard for Grey and Grenville. Yet the pull of old loyalties was strong. He cast about him for some formula which would satisfy everyone; admit his friends to office yet not drive his present Ministers into exile. It was a hopeless quest, made more hopeless by the Prince's ineptitude in pursuing it. Without any previous warning or consultation he wrote to Grey expressing his wish for a Government constructed "on a most liberal basis." It was his hope, he obligingly explained, that it would contain "some of those persons with whom the early habits of my public life were formed . . ."

The reaction of the Whig Lords was an explosion of arrogant disdain. The letter, wrote Grenville,[1] "contains, in substance, a panegyric on himself and his present Ministers; and in the last paragraph it expresses a wish that *some* of the opposition would unite with the Government. The whole form and terms of this paper are so offensive, that it would well have justified a much rougher answer than we shall this day return to it. The answer will, however, of course be a direct negative . . ." However dulcet Lord Grenville may have considered his reply, it was quite curt enough in tone to infuriate the Prince and end any possibility of a coalition. Once again the excessive exigence of the Whigs had led to their gaining no reward at all.

It is hard to be sure what the Prince Regent had in mind by his ill-managed overture. He can hardly have imagined that

Grenville or Grey would have served under Perceval or, indeed, Perceval under the Whigs. He may have sickened finally of the Whigs but have wished to make the breach seem of their making. More probably, however, he intended his letter as a devious approach towards a coalition government under some independent like Wellesley who would be accepted, or at least tolerated, by all parties. If this was really his plan he was woefully ill-advised. The Whigs stampeded into the extremes of sulky opposition and Ministers, finally exhausted by Wellesley's disloyalty and passion for intrigue, let him drop with relief and installed Castlereagh in his place at the Foreign Office.

"Lord Sidmouth," wrote the Bishop of Lichfield in January, 1812,[1] "who does not give up politics, though politics seem to have given him up, is come up to town." The Bishop was perhaps right in the first part of his observation, the scent of incipient office had indeed done something to overcome Sidmouth's longing for seclusion. But he was wrong on the second. On the contrary, Perceval was convinced that his Government would not be strong enough to stand without the support of the Addingtonians and did not intend a second time to make the mistake of trying to recruit the rank and file without first offering a job to the general.

Sidmouth's terms were high.[2] Buckinghamshire and Bathurst must have seats in the Cabinet. Hiley and some of the lesser fry were to have jobs, if not at once then soon at least. Negotiations also seem to have taken place on the Orders in Council and Sidmouth imposed certain conditions about their future.[3] The details are uncertain and Perceval died before it could be shown whether he had agreed that the Orders should be revoked or merely accepted that Sidmouth, although a member of the Government, should remain free to oppose them. To some Tories at least, Lord Lonsdale in particular, it seemed that Perceval was being asked to pay too high a price for the pleasure of Sidmouth's company.[4] Perceval, however, knew better than any of them the weakness of his position. He accepted the inevitable with grace. All that remained was to persuade the Prince Regent to accept it too.

Even before Lords Grenville and Grey had refused to enter Government save on their own terms, the Prince Regent had considered and rejected the idea of Sidmouth as a reinforcement to his Government. His objections were "some personal, others public; of the latter principally was Lord Sidmouth's known opinion of the Roman Catholic question."[1] When Perceval insisted he burst out angrily:[2] "Is it possible, Mr Perceval, that you are ignorant of my feelings and sentiments towards that person? I now tell you, I never will have confidence in him, or in any person who forces him upon me; if, after this, you choose to employ him, be it so; but I warn you that you must take all the responsibility of the measure upon yourself."

But with the prospect of a Whig government ended and Wellesley and Canning in the wilderness, it was clear that all the more serious Ministers were anyway of the same mind on the Catholic question as Sidmouth himself. Nothing the Prince Regent might do could alter it. There remained his "feelings and sentiments towards that person." In part these were coloured by the Prince's ancient grievance against Sidmouth for not having done more as Prime Minister to secure him high military rank, in part by his invariable dislike of anyone who had been a favourite of his father. But most of all the relationship was poisoned by the natural antipathy of the debauchee towards the prig, of the wastrel towards the solemn and conscientious labourer. It was a clash of characters, apparently fundamental. Events were to show that the two men could get on perfectly well with little pain to either but at the time it seemed as if the Prince Regent's dislike might prove an insuperable objection. Perceval, however, as usual stuck to his point and the Prince Regent, equally true to character, surrendered his. Grumbling balefully that the consequences could only be damaging for all concerned the Prince agreed to accept Sidmouth as a Minister. This completed the chagrin of the Whigs. "A history of low and dirty intrigue," protested Buckingham,[3] "in which there is not in any of the contending parties the slightest grain of public principle or correct object."

On 8th April, Sidmouth took his seat in the Cabinet as Lord President of the Council. The title carried with it no more intrinsic authority than it had when he had held it under Pitt and in the Ministry of All the Talents, but, as he explained with some naïvety,[4] ". . . he did not need to be so much on guard with this administration as with the other. He would be associated with those who had acted under him when Prime Minister. He must therefore have weight with them. . . ." Sidmouth, indeed, felt thoroughly at home in Perceval's Ministry. His influence might even have been as great as he had hoped and expected. But he was only to enjoy it for a few weeks. On 11th May a lunatic with a vague grievance against authority shot down Perceval in the lobby of the House of Commons. His bullet plunged Westminster back into the maelstrom of government-making from which it had so recently escaped.

The Prince's first idea was that Ministers should carry on more or less as they were. He had never had a particularly high opinion of Perceval and saw no reason why Liverpool should not keep Government running in the same effectively humdrum way. Ministers were therefore asked whether the Government could carry on without reinforcement. "No," said Mulgrave and Harrowby; "Doubtful," said Sidmouth and Buckinghamshire; "Doubtful, not desperate," was Liverpool's own contribution, while Eldon confined himself to a cautious "It might."[1] Liverpool wisely decided that, as a vote of confidence, this was too lukewarm to be satisfactory; he set out to recruit Wellesley and Canning and only when they refused to serve in subordinate positions, resigned himself to cobbling together the materials at his disposal.

Doctrinaire Whigs, Grenvillites, acolytes of Canning, could agree on little, but at least they were at one in their dislike and disapproval of such a Government. On 21st May they rallied behind Stuart-Wortley, the Member for Yorkshire, when he moved an address praying the Regent "to take measures for forming a strong and efficient administration." The Government was defeated by four votes and resigned with some relief, leaving the Opposition to discover that it was one thing to move and pass an address but quite another to form an alternative administration.

The crisis that followed, even for the early nineteenth century, was almost uniquely complex and bedevilled by personal vanities and dislikes. The gossip Creevey named at various times as the probable Prime Minister; Whitbread, Moira, Wellesley, Grenville, Grey, Canning and Liverpool. None was impossible, and it can have come as no surprise to Sidmouth when his band of faithfuls assured him not only that he should be added to the list but that he was the only rational choice for the salvation of the country. Rumours that he might be invited to form a Government were indeed widely heard outside the circle of the Addingtonians.[1] No one paid less attention than Sidmouth himself, being perfectly satisfied that he would not be asked and also knowing that, if he were, he would certainly refuse. He himself believed that Wellesley was most likely to succeed though he wrote despondently:[2] "It will be long before the country finds a resting place. Either of the chief parties in parliament, with the aid of the guerillas, in which it abounds, is strong enough to destroy but not to constitute, or at least uphold, a government. It must I think, fall ere long into the hands of Lords Grenville and Grey."

He viewed the prospect of his own eviction from office with equanimity and was indeed in notably good spirits through all the period that it seemed the Government must fall. At a levee one day in May Lords Hertford and Cholmondeley were leaning on a writing-table which broke under their weight. Lord Sidmouth caught at it to break their fall and smeared himself with ink. "Well," he said, looking ruefully at the mess, "I did hope to have gone out of office with clean hands."[3]

Yet though neither he nor anyone else suspected it, the country was on the point of finding a solution to its political troubles which was to last it for the best part of twenty years. At the beginning of June, 1812, the Regent's weary pilgrimage in search of Ministers led him back to his starting point. Every other combination seemed ruled out by the ambitions, arrogance or animosities of its members. In despair he turned again to Liverpool, less brilliant and eloquent than many of his rivals, a stumbling, ungraceful man, yet honest, solid, imperturbable and mercifully free from the vanity and vacillations which poisoned so much of parliamentary life. What was more, he had the substance of a Ministry at his command and even the most irresponsible of parliaments would hesitate to defeat the King's Government when experience had shown that there was no alternative to hand. The Prince Regent may reasonably have doubted whether this patched-up affair would do much more than stop the gap until Wellesley or some other leader had rallied a workable team behind him. In the meantime, however, he could trust his country to Lord Liverpool in the confidence that, though nothing very inspiring or dramatic might get done, Government would continue to run on with fair efficiency.

On 8th June Liverpool returned from his audience with the Prince Regent, his appointment as First Commissioner of the Treasury in his pocket. An expectant if slightly apprehensive Cabinet was awaiting him. "*You* must take the Home Department, Lord Sidmouth——" were his first words to his colleagues. "It will be everything to me!"[1]

12

Great Britain in the spring of 1812 was as near to violent class-warfare and revolution as at any moment of its history. To say that the time was one of sharp transition may seem so much of a truism as to be barely worth repeating. And yet the fact lay at the root of the country's difficulties. It was the inadequate understanding of this transition and the total absence of any attempt on the part of authority to control or direct it which was responsible for most of the social and economic ills which beset the British people about this time.

The closing decades of the eighteenth century witnessed the disintegration of the pattern of life that had ruled in England for several centuries. In 1750 the population was some seven million. Factories existed and the concepts of capitalism were by no means unknown but, over most of the country, the basic unit of society was still the village. By 1812 the population had almost doubled. Of these new six million the great majority lived in or around the growing industrial complexes. Britain was still in the main an agricultural society but the lines of the future were plain to see. Even in the country the spread of enclosures and the swelling power of the new upper-middle-class—the banker, the manufacturer, the Indian nabob—were breaking the traditions of centuries. "There is in the men calling themselves 'English country gentlemen'," wrote Cobbett, "something superlatively base. They are, I sincerely believe, the most cruel, the most unfeeling, the most brutally insolent; but I know, I can prove I can safely take my oath, that they are the most base of all creatures that God ever suffered to disgrace the human shape." The intensely conservative Cobbett would never have launched this diatribe against the traditional—perhaps even the fictional—squire whom he loved and almost revered; his targets were Pitt's *nouveaux-riches*, the men who had made the country a con venience instead of a way of life and treated with incomprehension or indifference the rules of the society into which they had worked so hard to rise.

In the cities the process was far more dangerously advanced. Here the old nexus of rights and responsibilities based on status had been forgotten altogether. The only bond that remained between employer and employed was that of money; the determination of the employer to extract from his worker all the labour that he could for a minimum of pay, the more modest pretension of the employed to stay alive and forget his misery in occasional doses of gin. Inevitably the worker, disorganised, inarticulate, groping uncertainly in a world which he did not understand, came off the worse in this conflict of interests. Wages were clamped down just above starvation level, employment was cut off without notice if demand should chance to slacken, working conditions reached a level of degradation almost inconceivable a hundred years later or a hundred years before.

The results were catastrophic both for the appearance of Britain and for the spirit of its working classes. The new towns which mushroomed all over the industrial areas were slums before they were even lived in. Shoddily constructed, hideously congested, growing rather than built in squalid anarchy, with facilities that would have disgraced a medieval village; these sores upon the face of the country had no purpose behind their existence save the provision of a fat rent roll for their usually absentee landlords. They were not towns in any proper sense of the word, rather dense acervations of shoddy tenement houses, destitute of drains and water, without charters or even rudimentary local government, dark, cramped and foetid, offering their inhabitants no pleasures in the present or hope for the future.

In such surroundings disease was not the exception but the rule. Almost half the children born in London died before they reached the age of five. Typhus ravaged those who survived. Smallpox and consumption were a commonplace, to escape them an exceptional dispensation. Even the churches were not there to teach the people to bear their woes with resignation, for few of the new industrial towns at first enjoyed anything so unproductive. Education, too, was a rarity; even if the facilities had existed the child could rarely escape from the factory for long enough to absorb the rudiments of learning. There were many and honourable exceptions; generous and enlightened employers, responsible landlords; but to any dispassionate visitor from another age it must have seemed that the vast majority of Britain's industrial working-class had nothing to lose in life.

The advance of industry in Britain was accelerated by the long course of the Napoleonic Wars. Quite apart from the demands of a war-time economy British exports boomed, both to a Europe too preoccupied by war to be able to manufacture for itself and to the rapidly expanding market of the United States. Yet simultaneously the urgent needs of the war distracted the attention of employer and government from the stresses which the new industries were creating. The groundwork of social dissension and discontent was laid behind a smoke-screen of patriotic phrases. When to the greater part of the population it seemed treasonable to be concerned with anything except the winning of the war, was it likely that what was still a minority, if a rapidly growing one, would secure attention for its incoherent pleas? Britain went in to the Napoleonic Wars as an agricultural nation; when the dust settled and it was too late to control what was going on she discovered that the basis of her economy had become industrial.

Sooner or later there was bound to be trouble. Circumstances dictated that it should be in 1812. Napoleon's closure of the continental markets to British goods, the collapse of our trade with South America and the decision by the United States to sever all her commercial links with the old world together proved disastrous for our exports. Between 1810 and 1811 they fell by a third. The cotton trade was worst hit of all. Wages fell by as much as a half, unemployment spread, by 1812 one-fifth of the population of Lancashire needed charitable relief. To add to the distress, a series of disastrous harvests forced up the price of corn. When, in 1811 and 1812, the crops on the Continent failed as well, the price of the quartern loaf rose to 1s. 8d. Even in the starvation years at the turn of the century it had never been more than 1s. 3½d.

With famine and unemployment widespread, neither King nor Government commanding the respect or the affection of the people, and the greater part of the regular army overseas, it seemed that Britain, as never before, was ripe for general revolution. Instead came a series of spasmodic incidents designed to serve limited and strictly economic ends. The workers in the most seriously affected industries, by sporadic acts of sabotage, sought to induce the less popular and scrupulous employers to grant them a minimum of security. In his majestic study of the British working classes,[1] Thompson has convincingly demonstrated that the Luddites were more rational, more widely organised and by far more formidable than historians have generally allowed. But though he has shown that the movement had much substance he does not disturb the judgment that, by and large, it lacked a common purpose and a central control. The Luddite riots were violent, feckless, occasionally indiscriminate. When they spread over the Midlands and the North, authority had good reason to take fright. But never did the forays of these desperately ill-treated labourers bear any serious resemblance to organised revolution or their mythical headquarters in Sherwood Forest emerge from the pages of schoolboy fiction. Well might they take as their patron-hero, Ned Ludd, an ignorant and ineffective village boy. Byron might sing:

As the Liberty lads over sea,
  Bought their freedom, and cheaply, with blood,
So we, boys we
Will die fighting or live free
And down with all Kings but King Ludd.

But when it came to the point there were few Luddites indeed required or willing to die fighting. As for republican principles, no one would pretend that the Luddites loved the King but what they wanted was fair treatment and a living wage. Political objectives ran a bad second in their minds.

The Luddite movement was partly concerned with the menace of new machinery, but this was by no means its only interest. In an age when the strike had hardly been developed as a means of bringing pressure on employers, machine-breaking—or preferably the threat of it—offered the only chance of obtaining better pay, shorter hours or a promise of regular employment. In Yorkshire the new shearing frames were the most immediate cause of discontent, but in the Midlands it was far more often sharp practice by the employers over wage rates which stung the workers into violent protest. At no time was there a coherent plan of national action, merely a large number of isolated incidents with certain common features such as oath-taking and blackened faces to convince the alarmist that some master criminal was stage-managing the whole campaign.[1]

The Government was reasonably alive to the need to check these symptoms of discontent but showed themselves both unable and unwilling to redress the wrongs which gave it rise. It did not even occur to them that there was anything for them to do. The doctrine of *laissez-faire* was not just an article of faith for the statesmen and administrators of the early nineteenth century, it was the very bed-rock of their political philosophy. Halévy, who viewed with wonder the "imperturbable apathy of the Establishment,"[2] concluded that only the self-discipline instilled by the Protestant churches preserved the stability of the English institutions. "Thus England was revealed as in very truth the country of self-government, the country which in the deepest sense—the moral and religious sense—of the phrase 'governs itself' instead of being governed by an external authority."

If, therefore, the British workmen were brutally oppressed by their employers the Government regretted it. If they starved, the Government deplored it. But it was not the function of the Government to mend the morals of the manufacturers or to ensure regular work for the unemployed. A modest distribution of charity was the maximum commitment which Westminster could contemplate. Yet if, on the other hand, misguided workmen, driven to desperation by poverty or ill-treatment, should steal a potato or smash a cotton frame, then the law was broken and the Government not only might but must act with speed and harshness. The Government might, it is true, have acted as swiftly and firmly if the law-breaker had been employer rather than employed. But the laws of the early nineteenth century had been devised for protection of property, not of the downtrodden workmen, and those whose task it was to enforce them were rarely given a chance to display what might otherwise have proved their impressive impartiality.

Lord Sidmouth was a convinced disciple of the doctrine of *laissez-faire*; not its apologist, since it never occurred to him that justification was needed, but a dogmatic adherent to its principles. In November, 1812, he wrote to deplore the rise in the price of grain at Leicester.[3] "The foreign demand for some branches of our manufacture," he went on, "is also likely, I fear, to remain very limited; and, under these circumstances, there must unhappily be a considerable degree of suffering, and, consequently, of irritation amongst the people. Those are their real and wisest friends who adopt the most effectual means to prevent or suppress tumults, whilst they manifest a sincere sympathy in their distress, and use their best endeavours to relieve it. But man cannot create abundance where Providence has inflicted scarcity." The Government's policy towards the depressed areas could hardly have been expressed more lucidly.

This defeatist approach to economic problems and rigidly limited interpretation of the Government's functions was not confined to the diehards of the Tory Party. It was the spirit of the age; sanctioned by Tom Paine himself; shared by Canning as well as Sidmouth; Wellesley as well as Eldon; Whigs as well as Tories. Lord Sidmouth, perhaps, was extreme in his disinclination to question the current dogmas but the difference between him and his fellows was one of degree and not of nature. The philosophy permeated every level of society; the coal-miner no more expected Government to protect him against his employer than the employer expected that a national fire brigade would prevent his house from burning down or a national police force guard him from burglary. It was every man for himself and if the weak went to the wall then—sad though it might be—such was the immutable law of nature.

Widely held though such a philosophy might be, the Government still occasionally found itself dragging behind public opinion. The case of the Lancashire weavers was an example. Their wages were so notoriously low that the Magistrates suggested reviving an ancient statute which gave them, on application, the right to fix wages.[1] Sidmouth was not only dismayed at the suggestion that such powers should be invoked, but astonished to find that the statute could even exist. When the Bill to repeal it was read for a second time in the House of Lords, it was Sidmouth who commented: "It did not require minds so enlightened as those of their Lordships to be aware how pernicious such a state of things must be both to the employer and the servant, but especially the latter . . ."

The weavers returned to the charge and a petition signed by twenty thousand of them was presented to Sidmouth by Thomas Ainsworth.[2] Sidmouth seems to have been vaguely sympathetic but to have done little or nothing to relieve their difficulties.

"I hope Your Lordship will pardon my being plain," wrote Ainsworth tartly. "I did feel most intensely the slight and cursory manner in which Your Lordship overlooked the paper, and the few minutes you took to give a decisive answer to what concerned near a million souls. Seeing their weekly earnings, you said, 'poor things! but can nothing be done for them?' I replied (feeling as I did, rather too warmly, for which I was afterwards very sorry), 'It is as easy for your Lordship to wind up your watch.' After a very few words, laying your hands upon the Weavers' Petition, you said, 'You may tell the Petitioners, I will present their Petition to the Prince Regent at the levée on Monday next!' Then obeying your Lordship's motion, I bowed and left the room. . . . Week after week I was enquired of, if any answer was received? No, No, No, was as often repeated."

Sidmouth, it must be said again, was a kindly and generous man, paying his own servants well and always ready to listen to any reasonable complaint. He viewed the misfortune of the weavers with the remote benevolence of a British Trade Union leader apprised of a disastrous famine in Northern China. The news, of course, was sad and a contribution to charity might be in order. But there the matter ended. The poverty of the weavers or of any group in society was not his fault nor its correction his responsibility. He would not refuse to put forward their petition, but he would obstinately resist any attempt to meet their needs by legislation.

Circumstances therefore had created a situation of great danger in Britain, with large parts of the country disaffected, poverty and unemployment rife, the threat of disastrous famine round the corner. This situation the Government had neither the will nor the machinery to correct. All it could do was hope that something would turn up; a good harvest, an end to the war, the renewal of trade with the United States. Until such happy events transpired there was nothing for it but to control the disaffection by the application of ruthless penal laws. There was no domestic policy properly so-called, merely a gigantic holding operation to be maintained until the situation at home should right itself. To-day's multifarious involvement of the State in every aspect of the life of the individual, in 1812 resolved itself into one lone but vastly significant function: the maintenance of law and order. It was his task which was the almost exclusive responsibility of the Home Secretary.

* * * * *

The Home Department was defined in 1812[1] as being responsible for ". . . all Grants, Pardons and Regulations in all Civil Matters . . ; Preferments in the Church, Matters of Police, the regular Army, Militia and Volunteers, Dispensations, Licences to Trade, Alien Regulations and all Correspondence regarding Ireland, Jersey, Guernsey etc." This hotch-potch covered almost the full range of internal happenings but for Sidmouth it was "Matters of Police" which were certain to prove the most important. Where the discipline and good order of the country was at stake it was the Home Office which acted as nerve centre for all operations. Considering the immensity of the task and its overriding importance, Sidmouth might be forgiven for thinking that the machinery given him was remarkably inadequate. Into the Home Office poured information from every part of the country to be sifted and collated as a basis for future action. Here this raw material should have been analysed and deductions for action drawn in the light of overall governmental policy; black spots should have been isolated, resources allocated, clear and precise instructions issued to the Lord Lieutenants and Justices of the Peace. Here, at any given moment, it should have been possible to chart the state of public opinion and to foresee and forestall the likely sources of future trouble. The Home Office should have been a kind of Scotland Yard without the telephones and with a few other Whitehall departments thrown in for good measure. A strong executive, a regiment of experts well informed about every part of England, an army of clerks and minor officials, would not have been too much to enable it to carry out its proper functions.

What Sidmouth actually inherited was very different. *The Times* commented sharply at the time of his appointment:[2]

There is, too, we believe, less of talent and energy in that office by which our Home concerns are chiefly directed than in all the rest put together. We say nothing of the Head of it, his is a recent appointment, but his subordinate officers are men who, through a long series of years, whatever might

315

be their competence to more arduous stations, have been at least thought sufficiently qualified for a department wherein no difficulty has ever till now occurred, so that it is evident to common reason that the Home Office must have become the sink of all the imbecility attached to every Ministry for the last thirty years . . .

This vision of the Home Office as the waste-paper basket for every other government department was harsh but not wholly unjust. The Permanent Under-Secretary, John Beckett,[1] was respectable, industrious and a good administrator. He was no more likely than his chief to formulate daring schemes or evolve fresh solutions for old problems yet, within these limitations, was a competent civil servant. But the burden of work on him and the Home Secretary was overwhelming. The personnel of the Home Office, in quality as well as numbers, was quite inadequate to help them bear it. Sidmouth employed two Under-Secretaries, a Chief Clerk, four Senior and eight Junior Clerks, joint Chamber Keepers and an individual beguilingly described as "the necessary woman."[2] To nine years of protests about the inadequacy of his establishment the Treasury responded by asking the Home Secretary to reduce his personnel to its pre-war level.[3] At this Sidmouth drew the line. He quite agreed, he said, that "the number employed should not be greater than absolutely necessary to carry out the current duties." But he was not prepared to accept that the state of the Office in 1797 should be taken as the magic standard by which all questions of establishment were to be decided. To do so would be to ignore the recent increase in the cost of living and the "very burdensome addition" of every kind of work. His protests were strong enough to prevent any reduction to his staff but not to win him reinforcements. For all his term of office Sidmouth had to make do with an effective staff of less than twenty people though he at least had the satisfaction of appointing connections of his closest friends to three of the Junior Clerkships.[4] Even this exiguous body found their quarters so cramped that health and efficiency were impaired. Sidmouth was compelled to do much of his work at home or in the houses of friends.

As Parliamentary Under-Secretary in charge of Home Office affairs in the House of Commons, Sidmouth chose his brother Hiley. The choice was not completely disastrous; when the work

316

was congenial Hiley could work with application and efficiency. But such occasions were not common and Hiley's real ill-health as well as his hypochondria and frivolity prevented him maturing into an effective departmental Minister. More and more he would be on holiday in Devon or nursing some half imaginary ailment in bed when he should have been grappling with a vast back-log of papers in his office. The result was that much work was not done at all and the rest of it increased the already insufferable burden on Sidmouth and the patient Beckett. Rarely indeed was Sidmouth stung to protest by his brother's slackness and, when he was, the tone was apologetic rather than accusing. "I am compelled, for the first time, to acknowledge that I want assistance . . ." His private secretary was ill, the Cabinet in constant session, the Prince Regent demanding his presence at Brighton. "I am grieved to tell you that I anxiously wait for your return; not that I desire it before Monday next: but, if you were aware of the state of things, I know you would not wish to defer it longer. I work morning and evening and can hardly prevent very inconvenient and unpleasant arrears."[1]

If the Home Office were inadequate to the needs of 1812, the instruments at its disposal were farcically more so. Nominally the Lords Lieutenant represented the Crown in the counties and were responsible for carrying out the Home Secretary's instructions. In practice they tended to find their country palaces boring in time of peace and dangerous in time of disorder. Except for a few favoured months of the year, they preferred to live in London and keep in closer touch with Court and Parliament. There were exceptions—Fitzwilliam in the West Riding of Yorkshire was notably industrious and efficient—but even in such cases it did not necessarily follow that their talents would be employed in ways of which the Government could approve. Normally the grandest of all the local grandees, the Lord Lieutenant was not invariably disposed to heed the dictates of the Minister in London. When, like Fitzwilliam, he was a staunch Whig as well, a clash between official policy and its execution by the Lord Lieutenant became not only possible but virtually inevitable.

But to maintain order in the country the Home Secretary depended above all on the energy, efficiency and courage of the five thousand or so Justices of the Peace. There were few limits to the powers which the ambitious magistrates could draw into their hands in time of trouble. They were almost entirely responsible for local defence; the militia and yeomanry could only be called out at their behest; they could proclaim states of riot, enrol constables and, if the worst came to the worst, invoke the help of regular troops. They were virtually irremovable once appointed and often ran their areas with autocratic disdain for the instructions of the foreigners from London. A good Justice could do a vast amount to keep his area contented; a weak one could quickly allow a situation, inherently not dangerous, to get out of hand. Still more mischievous, a Justice of bad judgment and misplaced energy could conjure up a crisis where none existed and then stampede the Home Office into unnecessary action by the urgency of his panic signals. The fact that England survived this period without civil war was thanks largely to the activities of the Justices; the fact that the Home Office almost invariably overestimated the seriousness of the danger was due in large part to the isolation and inadequate reporting of these same men. Seeing only the disorder around them they blew up every burnt hay-stack into the prelude to revolution and every poaching incident into a move in a centrally controlled and nefarious crime-wave.

It must be granted the Justices that they had some reason to feel apprehensive. The weapons available to enforce the law were pitifully weak. A professional, centrally organised police force was a concept distasteful to the vast majority of Englishmen. The objections to it were various and forcible. To Sidmouth such a force would have represented a gratuitous attempt on the part of Government to thrust themselves into the private sphere; an exercise which, for that reason alone, must be ill-judged and mischievous. To others it would have been the first step towards authoritarian rule, a potential death blow to the cherished liberties of old England. "We have heard much in praise of the admirable effects of the Police in Paris," wrote the *Morning Chronicle*.[1] "Certainly the Police in Paris is most dexterously contrived for the purposes of tyranny . . ."

The result was that the only regular police force was in London and that this consisted of no more than a handful of Bow Street Runners attached to the offices of the metropolitan police magistrates. For the rest of the country amateur, unpaid constables, drawn usually from the middle-classes, provided the normal support to the magistrate in his enforcement of the peace. If there were no volunteers then a compulsory levy could be instituted. Over and above this ramshackle force the magistrate might have recourse to the voluntary defence association if it so happened that one was operative at the moment in the troubled area or, more usefully, to the militia or yeomanry. Only if all these proved inadequate could he appeal to the Home Office for help from the regular army.

So effectively has the Whig historian done his work that the prevailing pictorial image of England between 1812 and Peterloo would most commonly be that of a pastoral frieze; dark, Satanic mills in the middle-distance; across which dragoons, with sabres drawn, perpetually pursued a band of hapless peasants. It is in fact remarkable with how much reluctance the regular army was used to quell civil disorder; reluctance at least on the part of the generals and of the Home Office. "I have been particularly charged by those members of the Government who attended the Cabinet yesterday," wrote Sidmouth to Peel,[1] "to express their earnest hope that the measure of dividing the army, or a large portion of it, into small detachments for the purposes of police work will never be resorted to, except under the pressures of an indisputable and urgent necessity; as it has the effect, not only of injuring most materially the discipline of the troops, but of teaching the magistrates to trust entirely to military aid, instead of placing their chief reliance on the vigilance and activity of the magistrates and on their own prudence and exertions for protection and security."

Unfortunately for the Cabinet's hopes, Justices of the Peace seemed to find "indisputable and urgent necessity" to call in the troops on embarrassingly frequent occasions. The Home Office checked them when it could but often saw nothing for it but to yield. Even in those cases, however, there was rarely any question of proclaiming martial law. Whenever possible the soldiers conscientiously took a Justice of the Peace along with them to read the Riot Act and only briefly did General Maitland find it necessary to suspend the civil power. The main criticism in fact, at any rate from the alarmed gentry of England, was that the army was too unobtrusive and too reluctant to intervene. Certainly such bloodshed as there was in the repression of riots arose more

319

frequently when the regular army was not there to impose order than from any excess of militarist ferocity.

With such frail resources, confined with a handful of clerks in his antiquated office, almost bereft of reliable information and constantly bombarded by a barrage of inflated and alarmist rumour, the unfortunate Sidmouth confronted the Revolution. He felt himself painfully alone. Traditionally the Home Secretary was left a free hand in the running of the interior; conversely the other members of the Cabinet took little interest in his doing and showed no wish to share his heavy and usually unpopular responsibility. Nor did Sidmouth make one of Liverpool's inner conclave where policy was worked out in the ponderous cosiness of Coombe Wood. Lord Bathurst, and later Wellington and Canning, were all far closer to the Prime Minister. With Sidmouth Liverpool's relations were friendly but never intimate; they trusted each other and should have had much in common but somehow, when it came to a stock-taking of their respective beliefs and affections, found themselves significantly far apart.

Solitary, the Home Secretary peered myopically into the night which lapped around the murky windows of his Department. He could hear, if not see, that the storm was blowing strongly, but whether it was likely to blow his house down he hardly ventured to predict. He might have felt panic, he might have felt a sense of helplessness at the immensity of the forces of disorder and the frailty of his own resources. It is a tribute to his temperament that he surveyed such small parts of the scene as lay within his vision with the placid equanimity of the man who knows that God and all right-minded citizens are on his side. His faults of judgment were many and he failed entirely to look below the surface froth of disorder into the real misery and discontent that was its cause. But such defects were shared by all his colleagues. The value of Lord Sidmouth lay in the fact that, in spite of all the troubles provoked by the ills of the country and the inability of Ministers to correct them, he never lost his head. His calm prudence, dislike of the dramatic or the unusual, all now served to curb the excessive panic of the country Justices. It may be argued with justice that greater dynamism at the Home Office could have led to an improvement in the forces of law and order but it is also true that less stability, less caution, less patience

320

might have precipitated a crisis in the country far worse than any which it actually experienced.

*   *   *   *   *

By the time that Sidmouth took over the Home Office, the worst of the Luddite troubles were already past. The siege of Cartwright's mill and the murder of William Horsfall represented the high-water mark of violence. By June there were more than 12,000 regular troops spread over the troubled areas. The new legislation against machine breaking together with the sharp sentences handed out at Nottingham Assizes to the Luddite prisoners had curbed the enthusiasm of all except the most intrepid agitators. To the authorities in London, however, there seemed little reason to believe that the tide had turned. Every post brought, if not news of fresh outrages, at least reports of plots and secret meetings. General Maitland himself was temperate in all his judgments and showed the greatest reluctance to use his power. Many of his subordinates, however, were less dispassionate. They gratified their sense of self-importance by detecting bloody revolt in every murmur of dissatisfaction and making sure that their alarm was heard in London.

Sidmouth's first step was to lay before Parliament the evidence which was causing such consternation in the Home Department. Secret Committees were set up by both Houses to pore over the blood-curdling messages from the provinces. The key document was probably the report from Major Seale at Sheffield[1] which contained the text of the "secret oath" and the claim, based on anonymous but allegedly respectable authority, that it had been administered ". . . to a vast number of people; that they act in concert, by the means of delegates all the way from Glasgow to London; that these delegates are supported by a salary; that they alone meet in committees and concert plans; . . . that their intention at present is, when the scheme is sufficiently ripe, to raise a few partial disturbances in this part of the country, to draw off as many troops as possible from the metropolis, and that then the great rising will take place there . . ."

To Members of Parliament, remote in distance and still more in temperament from the working-classes in the Midlands and the North and haunted by the recollection of events across the Channel little more than twenty years before, the reports seemed hideously plausible. As for Sidmouth, subjected as he was to the full bombardment of alarmist reporting and feeling himself solely responsible for the safety of the country, it was small wonder that he proved credulous. "On the fifth day of November next," wrote one imaginative correspondent,[1] "the Luddites mean to rid themselves of all their Enemys. They reckon 50,000 French prisoners as helpers, as out of all that are sworn among the French, not one did refuse. On that morning, several, a many heads in London are to be lain low, to cause a confusion, all the Mails are to be stopt'd. Castererleah, Liverpool, Gibbs, and several are to fall. . . . Though they appear quiet now, you are very rong, if you trust to that." Dutifully Sidmouth reported to the Committees that the mood of the country was very bad and the danger of revolution real. Dutifully the Secret Committee reported to the two Houses that an extensive secret organisation existed, consecrated to the subversion and overthrow of Government. Dutifully the two Houses hastened through a Bill to grant further powers to the Justices in the troubled areas.

Yet though Sidmouth undoubtedly believed that a nation-wide plot existed, his speech in the debate on the new Bill[2] was surprisingly calm in tone. He had tried conscientiously not to let himself be stampeded by alarmist stories. The economic as well as the political undercurrents were given some attention: "Although the conduct of the rioters may be, in some degree, traced to the high price of provisions and the reduction of work; still there is no doubt that these outrages were fomented by persons who had views and objects which it was the duty of government to counteract." The emphasis may still have been misplaced but as a summary it was neither so extremist nor so unbalanced as those of several of his colleagues. He showed little sympathy too with those Justices who clamoured for the use of emergency measures. When special powers were asked for to search for arms, Sidmouth commented tartly:[3] "The magistrates and inhabitants seem to be panic-struck, and Government is reproached for not resorting to measures the most rash and, under present circumstances, unwarrantable, because those who are on the spot will not employ the means which the law has placed in their hands."

In July, 1812, Sidmouth wrote to General Maitland to recommend an amnesty to all those that had taken illegal oaths but were now prepared to come forward and admit it. His charity, however, did not extend to the ringleaders. At the York Assizes in January, 1813, seventeen Luddites were condemned to death for their part in the murder of Horsfall and the attack on Cartwright's mill. Their legal guilt was certain and any hopes for mercy were dashed when there was a sharp recrudescence of Luddite attacks just before the trial. The men were hung and Sidmouth wrote to Maitland to congratulate him: "Everything indeed appeared to have been done with great judgement, and I confidently anticipate the happiest effects in various parts of the country."[1]

Even if the country had been entirely calm and there had been no potential revolutionaries to discourage, it is unlikely that Sidmouth would have seen a case for mercy. The most intolerable provocation could not possibly excuse recourse to violence; or rather, though it might palliate the offence in the eyes of God— a subject on which Sidmouth, with quite genuine humility, was disinclined to speculate—it could not relieve the criminals from responsibility for their acts on earth. As his biographer and son-in-law Pellew expressed it:[2] "It was of little moment, indeed, to Lord Sidmouth, in the fulfilment of his executive functions, from what cause this treasonable spirit originated, since in every case it was equally his duty, if possible, to put it down." The limits of a Home Secretary's function, as conceived by Sidmouth, could hardly have been more clearly stated. Violence must be stamped out; investigation of the causes, if a function of Government at all, must await the restoration of law and order. Unfortunately, by the time peace had been restored, the always faltering urge to inquire into the origins of the discontent had been suffered to die away, only to revive at the time of the next disorder. But though sometimes inexorable, Sidmouth was never promiscuous in his repression. The sentencing of the seventeen Luddites at York was made the signal for dropping all the other prosecutions and the Home Secretary wrote immediately to Maitland to propose the withdrawal of the regular troops and the suspension of 'all military interference."[3]

By the end of 1812 England seemed at peace. The wave of industrial violence had subsided, the great tide that was to bring in parliamentary reform had hardly yet begun to flow. To Sidmouth it was a proof that firmness and a refusal to truckle on principles was the only way to run the country. But he had not failed to notice how large a part economic causes had played in the transition from turbulence to tranquillity. The Luddites, in many cases, had won important concessions from their masters. More important, a decent harvest had given them food to buy and, more important still, the relaxation of the economic war between Britain and Europe was beginning to draw industry out of its depression and to put some money back into the pockets of the working classes.

* * * * *

Though the Home Secretary's main task was internal order, he also possessed a certain ill-defined responsibility for the work of the Chief Secretary in Ireland. The relationship between the two varied from man to man; in this case neither party was likely to wish that the supervision should be more than nominal. Sidmouth, easy-going and with his hands full in England, had no desire to offer his counsel where none was needed; young Robert Peel, forceful, opinionated and determined to make a name for himself, was equally reluctant to see an outsider trespass on his preserves.

Sidmouth admired Peel and treated him as something of a favoured protégé. "As an old statesman to a young coadjutor," he said, when Peel's appointment was announced,[1] "permit me to say, Mr. Peel, that if you persevere in the straightforward course you have hitherto pursued, nothing, according to all human probability, can hinder you from attaining the highest offices in this country." Peel may not altogether have relished the avuncular note of these commendations but he recognised the sincerity of Lord Sidmouth's goodwill and had the grace to respond to it warmly. He always looked to Liverpool as his main support within the Cabinet but his association with Sidmouth was close and friendly. "Thank you for your letter," Sidmouth wrote to him[2] in September, 1812, "which I regard as a proof of your confidence. Believe me, I value it from personal, as well as official considerations, and shall be most happy to cultivate it."

From time to time Peel found Sidmouth a useful ally in persuading the Cabinet to accept his views. Whether it was a question of stopping the Duke of York withdraw troops from Ireland without first consulting the Government in Dublin, meeting an urgent request for military reinforcements[4] or arguing in Cabinet for the revival of the Insurrection Act.[5] Sidmouth's support of his junior was prompt and wholehearted. He must, indeed, have been the ideal chief for Peel; detached, loath to interfere, content to leave the formation of policy to a man he trusted, yet always ready to take the side of his subordinate if so requested.

He was not able to take so detached an interest in others of his duties and his papers show that these were miscellaneous and peculiar. He was required to pronounce on the plans for a patent fire-escape, submitted by the Philanthropes. He was consulted about a new-modelled bear-pit for a London Zoo. He recommended appointments as postmasters, Charterhouse scholars and Poor Knights of Windsor. He was required by Wilberforce to come to the rescue of a young and respectable body-snatcher and defend him from the "present prejudices that prevail among the lower orders." The Prince Regent made him personally responsible for seeing that none of the trees in the Royal Parks were lopped, trimmed or mutilated except by express permission of the palace.

As Home Secretary, he found that he shared with the Lord Chancellor the role of guardian to the nation's morals. Lord Auckland wrote in consternation to report that, on the convict ships to Botany Bay, female convicts were parcelled out, one to each sailor. The system, he felt, was to some extent redeemed by the properly monogamous provision that there could be no chopping or changing on the voyage; once the original division of the spoils had been made each man must stick to his portion. But even allowing for this he felt that the practice was to be deplored. Lord Sidmouth agreed but was happy to assure his friend on the best authority that such things never happened.[1] The Rev. Mr. Young wrote to urge the tightening of the law relating to Sabbath-breaking, "that first stage of every enormity." Clergy in striking numbers asked dispensation from living in their parish.

Like every other Home Secretary he found most painful his responsibility for confirming the death-sentence. He seems never to have wondered whether capital punishment as such might be undesirable or even too promiscuously applied; his work was difficult enough without indulging in such fruitless theoretical speculations. It was made no easier by the Prince Regent who judged every appeal on grounds of maudlin sentimentality and proposed reprieves in the least deserving cases because there was an old mother who would grieve for the accused. The Prince Regent's judgment as to what if anything deserved the death penalty was, however, closer to contemporary morality than that of his Home Secretary. On one occasion the Prince argued for hours that certain criminals should be transported rather than executed. Sidmouth insisted that the crimes were too heinous for so light a sentence; to reprieve the criminals would be an encouragement to evil-doers and a grave blow to public morale. In the end, and after recourse to laudanum to soothe his nerves, the Regent gave way. The crimes for which these men were to die were uttering forged notes, robbing their masters, horse-stealing and cattle-stealing respectively.[1]

For one who never himself originated a plan of reform or felt that Government could properly participate in such adventures, Sidmouth was surprisingly ready to study and even support the schemes of private enterprise. Within a few days of his taking office, Jeremy Bentham was demanding the Home Secretary's attention[2]: "Being more in the habit of declining than seeking interviews with Ministers, and not at all in the habit of wasting words, I dare venture to mention ten minutes by the watch as the utmost quantity I should attempt to consume of an article so precious to the public as your Lordship's time." Sidmouth duly fixed an interview for the following day but it seems that even Bentham could not encapsulate the work of several years into a ten-minute lecture for he found it necessary to spell out his ideas a few days later[3]: "What I would propose to your Lordship to call into existence, for the use of the Department over which your Lordship now presides, is nothing more than a Penal Code— a proposed Penal Code in terminis, with a perpetual commentary of measures . . . and observations bringing to view all along, and under each head, the imperfections, or supposed imperfections of the existing rule of action in its present state."

Bentham asked, not for reward, but for encouragement and a promise of attention. These, it seems, Sidmouth gave, but possibly with insufficient enthusiasm for there is no record that he was ever sent an elaborated form of Bentham's ideas. The polite boredom of the Home Office, however, did nothing to abate Bentham's energies. That indefatigable utilitarian had either discussed or was shortly to discuss his cherished plan for codification with Bolivar, Quincy Adams and the Emperor Alexander. With correspondents such as these, Sidmouth's muted enthusiasm was quickly dismissed with the consoling reflection that this was the treatment habitually meted out to prophets.

Robert Owen was another reformer who appealed to the Home Secretary for encouragement and assistance. To him Sidmouth gave rather more effective support. Owen's model cotton-mills at New Lanark were the proof that profit need not always be extracted from human misery. This sort of practical accomplishment, achieved by private enterprise and asking for nothing from the Government except overt approval, was exactly of a nature to appeal to Sidmouth. So also were Owen's ideas themselves; paternalistic in spirit though radical in certain details and making no concessions to an unbecoming spirit of revolution. He wholeheartedly supported almost all of Owen's projects and circulated his pamphlet "A New View of Society" to the leading Governments of Europe and America. When the comments came in, the two men went through them together and were delighted to find them substantially approving. Encouraged, Sidmouth then circulated the pamphlet to all the English bishops.[1]

Sidmouth stayed loyal to Owen even when his growing radicalism and atheistic views put him out of favour with most sober members of the establishment. In 1816 a group of hostile manufacturers put up the Rev. Mr. Menzies, Minister of Old Lanark, to go to London and protest to Lord Sidmouth about a speech which Owen had recently made. He had not heard it himself, Menzies naïvely explained, but his wife had told him that it was "of a most treasonable character against Church and State." Sidmouth had already been sent a copy of the speech by its author; he curtly told the clerical busy-body that he approved it thoroughly and sent him about his business.[2]

It would be futile to deduce from this that Sidmouth was in any way converted to a policy of reform. But his readiness to listen to men like Owen does show that his inexorable opposition to reform was compatible with a belief that all was not well with society in England. He would have sincerely welcomed any move to regulate it from within. The cautious, benevolent, paternalistic attitude of the early Owen seemed to him to strike exactly the note that was required. Under his influence he was prepared to accept that Government might play a part in persuading industry into the path of reform; only when it became clear that little could be achieved by persuasion and that a measure of coercion would be necessary did the ways of the two men part and Sidmouth shrink back repelled into his shell of *laissez-faire* inertia.

A final responsibility arose not from his place as Home Secretary but as an embarrassing postscript to his friendship with Lord Nelson. Lady Hamilton had by now reduced herself to blowsy penury. This "unprotected, unsuspicious widow not tinctured with parsimony," as she euphemistically described herself to Lord Sidmouth,[1] had already caused him some tribulation in the past. He had been anxious to please her but had found it difficult to discover the proper means. In conversation with him she had referred to her liaison with Nelson and added ". . . as far as regards that matter, I don't know whether Nelson is a *man* or a *woman*." When Sidmouth politely replied that he had never imagined the contrary, she took offence at his suggesting that Nelson should have had no such passion.[2] Sidmouth found her disturbing and altogether beyond his ken. Now, to his dismay, she decided to put his loyalty to his dead friend to purpose and reverted to the ancient theme of her claims to a pension.

In February, 1813, she wrote to Sidmouth[3] to plead her case: "Lord Nelson was not more brave than he was honourable and noble-minded: would it have been either to have a criminal intercourse with the adored wife of his best his bosom friend. . . .

"Yet, my Lord it is the force of this unfounded aspersion that makes Ministers fearful of bringing forward the consideration of my memorial.

"Then my Lord I pray you to believe that it would afford me more pride and pleasure than any remuneration, that could be offered, to have this base aspersion thoroughly canvassed, as I would then be enabled to develop facts that would undeceive those who are ignorant, and to confound the malignant: above all to rescue the memory of my beloved husband and my brave lamented friend from the odium thus cast upon their fame and honour as well as upon my Lord."

Lord Sidmouth wisely avoided expressing any further views upon Lady Hamilton's relations with his old friend. The question of the pension he referred to Lord Liverpool. "It is very painful to me to acquaint your Ladyship," he replied a little later,[4] "that, after a full communication with Lord Liverpool . . . I am unable to encourage your hopes that the object of it may be accomplished." The funds, it seemed, were not available. When Lady Hamilton wrote again he ducked out of the correspondence and passed the letter to the Prime Minister. He may have had some qualms of conscience as he wondered what Nelson would have said at such lack of gallantry but it is hard to blame him for seeking to evade entanglement with this debauched and importunate harpy.

Lady Hamilton's final years were not without pathos. Deeply in debt, driven into exile, sadly conscious that her charms no longer held their ancient force, she flickered out in unconsidered solitude. From her refuge at Calais in the summer of 1814 she wrote to Sir William Scott[1]: "Lord Sidmouth is a good man and Lord Liverpool is also an upright Minister, pray and if ever Sir William Hamilton's and Lord Nelson's services were deserving ask them to aid me." It is doubtful whether the appeal ever reached its intended audience; at all events within a few months she was dead and could plague no more those who had been proud to describe her lover as their friend.

*　　*　　*　　*　　*

In September, 1812, Liverpool decided to go to the country so as to take advantage of the good harvest, military successes and industrial peace at home. In the ensuing election the Tories gained some sixty seats and, perhaps still more important, Canning's semi-detached wing of the party was greatly weakened. Sidmouth's own position was hardly affected. With the reintegration of their leaders in the Tory Party there was no part for the Addingtonians to play as an independent group. If they still sat together in the Commons it was for old times' sake, not because they promoted a separate policy. Sidmouth continued to take an avuncular interest in their doings and noted with approval that almost all his protégés survived the election. But there were no more anxious calculations as to whether he could muster forty, fifty or sixty votes in the lobby. Sidmouth as a party leader had virtually ceased to exist.

Though the results of the election gave him little to support his view, the Prince Regent was still anxious that Wellesley and Canning should join the Government. Sidmouth found, almost to his own surprise, that he was inclined to agree. Certainly he had no wish to fight against such a move. His feelings towards Canning had changed considerably in the past few months. In May, when the Prince Regent had circularised the Cabinet asking each member why he had refused to treat further with Wellesley and Canning, Sidmouth had answered that he could never accept their condition that Roman Catholic claims should be considered by Ministers.[1] While paying a tribute to "Mr Canning's splendid talents in debate" he stated flatly that Canning would never agree to serve under Castlereagh and that Castlereagh must, in honour, be given the lead in the House of Commons. Since then, however, all sides had agreed to a tacit truce on the Catholic question and Canning, chastened by his recent disasters, seemed ready to modify his pretensions. Sidmouth certainly was not prepared to go far out of his way to help his old foe but he was perfectly ready to call off the quarrel and do nothing to stand in Canning's way.

Shortly after the election Sidmouth called on Wellesley to explain his earlier opposition to the Prince Regent's desires. The interview seems to have gone well and sore feelings on Wellesley's part were quickly soothed. As he was about to leave Sidmouth remarked "that he had a great wish to be reconciled to Canning; that, having conceived himself treated by that gentleman with a very unbecoming levity, almost amounting to insolence, he was determined not to come into office with him; but having achieved that step by himself, all resentment in his mind had ceased, and he wished much that Lord Wellesley would bring about a meeting."[2]

As it happened, Wellesley was not to be put to the trouble of acting as go-between. A little while afterwards Canning had cause to call at the Home Office with several friends. Sidmouth received them civilly, then, after they had gone to another room, sent a messenger to ask Canning to come back for a moment. Both men made records of their conversation, reasonably similar in detail though Canning's, not surprisingly, better written.

"I found him alone," wrote the latter to Granville Leveson-Gower.[3] "He showed considerable agitation and evidently knew not how to begin, but after a short pause he came up to me, holding out both his hands, and said: 'Mr. Canning, will you allow me to avail myself of the chance which has thrown us

330

together to say how much I wish that the very unpleasant personal relation in which we have so long stood towards each other may cease?' He went on to say that he had long felt this relation of ours to be a weight upon his mind; that he had never been so situated with respect to any other persons, and that he declared with the utmost sincerity that he had not a shadow of ill-will or unkindness towards me upon his mind, and had earnestly longed for the opportunity of making this declaration to me: that he had been thinking, and had almost determined upon the necessity of calling upon me to seek this opportunity: that if he had met me in the street or the park he should have gone up to me to offer his hand; that this unlooked for chance had relieved his difficulties, and that he hoped there was no feeling in my mind towards him to prevent me from taking the hand he offered. All this spoken with great appearance of sincerity, and strong indications of feeling. I need not tell you that I took both the poor Doctor's hands, and shook and squeezed them with perfect cordiality. He really moved me; considering, too, that it may be *at least* a question whether he be not the party that has a right to complain.

"After exchanging general professions of mutual oblivion of the past, and goodwill for the future, he said how much he regretted the failure of the late negotiations, and how much he hoped that I had given him credit for being no obstacle, etc.—to which I had only to answer that I hoped he also knew that *he* had been no obstacle to my acceptance. And so we parted, exceeding good friends, and I have instigated Sheridan to ask him to dinner on Friday.

"Whether there be any, and what, hidden sense in all this, I do not know; but if there is, I own I am a dupe, for I never was more sincerely affected or gave more implicit credit to an appearance of frankness in my life. Had Castlereagh had half the Doctor's art (if it be art) or his nature (as I take it to be), *his* point would have been carried in our tête-à-tête; but (luckily perhaps for me) *he* can neither feel nor feign."

It is impossible to doubt Sidmouth's sincerity. He had nothing, save his own peace of mind, to gain from a reconciliation and could, if he had wished, have made it extremely difficult for Liverpool to admit Canning to the Government. Whatever the political rights or wrongs there can be no doubt that, on the per-

sonal plane, it had been Sidmouth who had been sinned against
That it should nevertheless be he who sought to re-establish
friendly relations illustrates admirably his basic decency and
generosity. It is these qualities that make him likeable in spite
of his many and obvious defects of personality.

No reconciliation, however sincere, could make close friends or
political allies out of two men so dissimilar in habit, character
and convictions. But the bitterness never returned. Four year
later Lord Lyttelton was to write[1]: "By the bye, Canning is now
very intimate with this self-same Doctor, which gives one a
strange notion of the shortness of their memories or the excellence
of their tempers. We are, however, not without our hopes that
your old friend is collecting fresh material for epigrams and i
reconnoitring in disguise." But though the old friends hopefully
waited Canning honoured the peace. The epigrams never came
in public and rarely even in his private letters. The two men
continued to differ. Their relationship in Cabinet was rarely
harmonious. But they treated each other's views with respect and
for the rest of their political lives, kept head-on clashes to a decent
minimum.

*   *   *   *   *

Since the so-called Delicate Investigation in 1806, the Prince
Regent and the Princess of Wales had been living contemptuously
apart. They might have continued thus, with some vestiges of
dignity, if Whitbread and Brougham had not picked upon the
miserable Princess as a suitable weapon with which to batter the
Crown and Government. Backed by these champions the Princess
began to press for the revision of the agreement by which she
could see her daughter, Princess Charlotte, only once a week
The Prince Regent returned her letter unopened, whereupon she
promptly had it published in the *Morning Chronicle*. Angrily, the
Prince appealed to the Privy Council to justify his conduct and to
condemn the Princess; in particular to confirm that the Princess
should only be given access to her daughter under strict super
vision and at weekly intervals.

Lord Sidmouth was anxious not to involve himself in the
vulgar squabble. With the final incapacity of the King he had
transferred to the Prince Regent some at least of the automatic
reverence which was inspired in him by the idea of monarchy

But reverence for the office was one thing; respect or affection for the man another. Sidmouth was to grow into a genuine attachment to the future King George IV but in 1813 he felt towards him a suspicion, even a distaste, which was only surpassed by his disapproval of the Princess of Wales. The prospect of adjudicating between them dismayed him and it was only under protest that he agreed to preside over a Committee of the Privy Council to inquire into the whole, murky affair.

The task proved no more congenial than he had expected. A great deal of dirty linen was washed in public, most of it for the second time at least, but nothing conclusive was arrived at. Lord Eldon refused to sign anything which implied the Princess's guilt, Lord Ellenborough anything which implied her innocence. The report was therefore cautious in tone but was hailed by the Prince Regent as a victory. It seems, indeed, to have been from this period that the Prince Regent began to consider whether Lord Sidmouth could perhaps be less of a poltroon than he had previously believed him. He started to treat the Home Secretary with greater respect and soon graduated to positive politeness. He discovered that Sidmouth possessed qualities which could be as valuable to him as they had been to his father. It was not long before he began to ask his advice on subjects remote from the death penalty or the security of the realm and even, sometimes, to follow the advice once it had been given. It would have been truly remarkable if this new deference which the Regent showed for him had not found its reflection in a new appreciation on Sidmouth's side of the virtues and dignity of the heir to the throne.

The next round between the estranged couple was provoked by the Lord Mayor of London. Once again Sidmouth found himself unwillingly involved. The Lord Mayor presented an adulatory address to Princess Caroline, carefully phrased so as to cause vexation to her husband. The Princess of Wales replied in gracious formulae suggested to her by Brougham and both parties then awaited with relish the reactions at Court when the correspondence was published in the *London Gazette*. Contrary to precedent, however, nothing appeared. When the Lord Mayor appealed to the Home Secretary to arrange for its publication, Sidmouth replied tersely: ". . . in the exercise of the discretion which belongs to my official situation, I do not think it proper to

cause the Address and answer above-mentioned to be inserted
. . ."[1] The Radicals, who had adopted Princess Caroline as their
cherished if ill-favoured protégée, were outraged at the Home
Secretary's failure to advance their cause. "This Secretary of
State . . ." wrote Cobbett in splendidly inaccurate disgust,[2] "was
the son of what was called a Doctor; he had been a practising
barrister of very inferior note; Pitt found it convenient to make
him speaker of the House of Commons; it was found convenient
to make him Prime Minister for a short time in order to keep the
Whigs out of power; upon the death of Pitt, he had formed a sort
of coalition with those Whigs who had had the meanness to permit it as a condition to be allowed to share in the public money.
. . . A very fit person for carrying on the work that was now to be
performed . . ."

Defence of the Prince Regent's reputation was an arduous and
sometimes hopeless task. In June, 1814, came the end of the war
and the victory parade through England of the Emperor Alexander
and the King of Prussia. Sidmouth who, as Home Secretary, was
required to dance constant attendance on the visitors, noticed
with dismay the contrast between the enthusiasm which greeted
them everywhere and the blend of tepid fervour and out-and-out
hostility which the Prince Regent inspired in his disapproving
subjects. Only in royalist Oxford did the Prince encounter an
unequivocally becoming welcome.

The visit, however, still had certain consolations for a conscientious Home Secretary keen to do his best by his country.
Sidmouth passed several enjoyable and instructive hours com-
paring notes with the Emperor on the criminal codes in Britain
and in Russia. In Britain, the Emperor obligingly explained, the
wide freedom of action given to the individual meant that crime
could only be restrained by harsh penalties once it was detected.
"In Russia we can interfere to prevent the commission; severe
punishments, therefore, are not so essential."[3] Sidmouth, like
most romantics, was deeply impressed by the Emperor's personality and good intentions. He also found much to attract him
in Alexander's exposition of the Russian law. The argument in
favour of anticipating rather than avenging crime was one which
appealed both to his humanity and his instinct for economy. It
was in the same spirit that he approved the sending of spies to
the disaffected areas of Britain in order to report on what dis-

orders were being planned and thus allow authority to nip them swiftly in the bud.

During the visit of these potentates England presented an air of unusual tranquillity and content. "The public and parliament are highly elated," wrote Vansittart to Castlereagh,[1] "and I think still more *satisfied* than elated; and indeed if they were not satisfied they must be the most unreasonable people the world has ever produced." A bumper harvest, record exports and a healthy revenue indeed added up to a comfortable picture of England's condition; a picture which the continued war with the United States could mar but by no means spoil. But the very success of the harvest was to be the cause of unrest in a different quarter. A glut of corn at home and still cheaper imports from abroad led to a sharp drop in prices and an anguished appeal for protection from the British farmers. They advanced the familiar and perennially persuasive argument that otherwise they would be forced out of business and the country left to starve in the event of another war. The Government found their case a good one and agreed that corn should only be imported if the price of home-grown wheat reached 80s. a quarter.

The measure did something for agriculture but, of course, could not guarantee that the local farmer would receive a reasonable price for his corn in case of glut. "Never," wrote Cobbett,[2] "was infatuation equal to that which now took possession of the minds of these stupid and powerful men; who . . . really thought that they had passed a law which would always secure the price of ten shillings a bushel . . ." But though the farmers were barely satisfied, the poor, in particular of London, were outraged that their hopes of cheap bread should be frustrated. On the day of the debate in the Commons they massed in Westminster and assaulted Members who seemed likely to vote the wrong way. The same night they attacked the house of the more obnoxious Ministers; their anger can hardly be called unbridled since they did little more than shatter a few windows but the apparition of a mob in the streets of London was enough to cause panic in every prosperous citizen.

Sidmouth was an ardent advocate of protection. "My apprehension and conviction," he wrote,[3] "is, that the protecting price, as fixed by the bill, is not sufficient to give that confidence to the corn-grower which is essential to the attainment of the great

object of the bill, namely, an ample and independent supply . .
Any reduction of that price I should therefore consider as im
provident and hazardous."

So staunch a defence of governmental interference with th
free course of trade comes oddly from a convinced disciple c
laissez-faire. But Sidmouth had persuaded himself that the issu
was one of property. The land-owners had built up their estate
into a valuable source of income; to their own benefit certainly bu
also to the benefit of the country. This property it was the dut
of the State to protect; to do otherwise would infringe the right
of the farmer. A failure to limit imports would be as offensiv
an action on the part of the State as, for instance, the passage c
a law designed to limit the farmer's freedom to grow as muc
corn as he thought fit. The argument that the consumer also ha
rights would have been dismissed by Sidmouth as remote meta
physics. There was no property involved and only in the defenc
of property could action be forgiven which might otherwise see
unwarrantable interference on the part of Government.

Even though he had been opposed to the Corn Laws he woul
have had no hesitation in repressing the movement of protes
against them. After the first night of rioting London was ringe
by troops of the regular army, a proclamation demanding ord
was published in the name of the Regent and Sidmouth himse
issued a circular calling on citizens to band together for their ow
protection. The more-or-less accidental shooting of a rioter ou
side the house of Frederick Robinson, future Viscount Goderic
and one of the chief protagonists of the new law, completed th
work of disenchanting the London mob. Order was soon restore
In fact, the continued surplus of corn at home ensured that brea
remained cheap for a while at least. By February, 1816, the pric
had dropped to 43s. a quarter and it was the farmers, not th
urban working-classes, who bemoaned the failure of the Goverr
ment to protect their interests.

At the start of 1815, therefore, all seemed set fair for Englanc
Sidmouth looked forward to a tranquil period in office durin
which he would be able to rule the interior with the benevoler
disinterest which seemed to him appropriate. The fighting wa
over, and the return to Britain of so many able-bodied and dis
ciplined workers could only increase still further the prosperit
of the country. It had not occurred to Sidmouth, or indeed t

any other Minister, that there might be a problem in finding anything for the returned soldiers and sailors to do: work, they vaguely supposed, would expand to accommodate the available labour force. Exports were booming; and there was no economist to warn the governmental optimists that the end of the war was likely to lead to a harsh recession. Lapped in the comfortable conviction that all was for the best, Sidmouth and his colleagues settled back to enjoy the fruits of victory. It was to be comical, or perhaps tragic, to observe their surprise and disillusionment when they discovered that most of the fruits were sour and that such as remained were quite inadequate to satisfy the hungry mouths that clamoured for a share.

On the 1st of March, 1815, Napoleon landed in France. Within three weeks he was in Paris, the French, apparently, united once more behind him. "Prinny, of course, is for war," wrote Bennet to Creevey,[1] "as for the Cabinet, Liverpool and Lord Sidmouth are for peace, they say the Chancellor is not violent the other way, but Bathurst, Castlereagh etc. are red-hot." For once Creevey was misinformed rather than himself misinforming others. Sidmouth never had the slightest doubt that the return of Napoleon must mean the resumption of the war and that this time it must be continued until the Emperor had been expelled from his territories for ever. To Cam Hobhouse, who called on him at the Foreign Office where he was standing in for Castlereagh, he spoke of acting with energy and rejoiced that Britain was in a stronger position than at the start of the previous war.[2]

Even after Waterloo, Sidmouth remained dubious about the future in Europe. "The volcano is not burnt out," he wrote in August, 1815,[3] "and even with the allied armies in France, there are evident indications of fresh convulsions." As remedy he believed whole-heartedly in the prescription of Castlereagh; the rule of law and order under the hereditary monarchs of old Europe. The same fatal madness which had overwhelmed France might strike as well at any other country. This must at all costs be guarded against, even if it meant sustaining in power unattractive despots with no apparent understanding of the British Constitution. As for the French, they had proved themselves untrustworthy. The Allies must remain united and constantly vigilant.

"It is . . . necessary to seize the moment for affording to the Continent protection, as far as possible, against the consequences which are to be apprehended from a weak government and an irritated and distracted people; for experience has shown that internal agitation is far indeed from being any security against

...e spirit of foreign conquest, a spirit which must now be ...eightened by that of revenge, and which, as the government is ...ot likely to prove strong enough to control it by authority, can ...ly be kept under by the hopelessness of success."

With some complacency he compared the state of France with ...at of his own country. In that happy land there was no question ...the Government being too weak to control unrest. But, con-...dent though he was, he still felt that the present tranquillity ...ould be used to advantage by doing something to relieve the ...t of the new industrial classes. There was not much that could ...done. Government could not make them rich, build them ...uses or improve their sanitation. But at least it was within the ...wer of Ministers to bring to the new cities the multifarious ...nefits of the Established Church. He found Lord Liverpool ...ready thinking along the same lines and in November, 1815, ...as able to inform Lord Kenyon that a Bill would shortly be laid ...fore Parliament for the building of a large number of churches ...the industrial areas.[1]

Lord Sidmouth now consulted the Dean of Bocking on the ...st way to make this scheme known to the public. The two men ...cided that the most effective means would be by commissioning ...original essay on the subject to be written by some author of ...stinction. Sidmouth suggested that the Dean's brother William ...gether with another friend should undertake the essay. Unfor-...nately for posterity the Dean thought otherwise. "However ...mpetent Mr. Coleridge or my own brother might be to the pro-...ction of a popular essay on the subject," wrote Dr. Words-...orth,[2] "neither of them is possessed of that knowledge in detail ...ecclesiastical matters which would be requisite to meet your ...rdship's purposes." He put forward Southey as a counter pro-...sition but the whole subject lapsed when the Prime Minister ...cided that the country could not afford the building programme ...er all.

Such peaceful pursuits were sadly disturbed in February, 1816, ...en Lord Buckinghamshire fell off his horse in St. James's Park ...d died shortly afterwards. Buckinghamshire had often proved ...uncomfortable ally but he had been an ally for all that since ...e days of Sidmouth's own Administration. Sidmouth missed ...n, both as a friend and as a sure support in Cabinet debate. His ...ath made room in the Government for Canning; a promotion

which Sidmouth had no wish to oppose but which still seeme
a poor exchange for his old friend. With Huskisson gainin
confidence and making his reputation as a departmental Ministe
the weight of influence in the Government shifted towards i
liberal wing. In all essentials the Cabinet was still an inert an
conservative body but at least the case for reform was no
occasionally voiced and Liverpool, for one, proved disconcerting
ready to pay attention to what was said.

* * * * *

In 1816 England found itself assailed by economic ills which
had not expected and which it felt it had done nothing to deserv
With the end of the war government spending dropped by mo
than £40 million in a single year. The demand for iron fe
dramatically and its price was halved. As industry began
move again on the shattered Continent British merchants foun
tariff barriers everywhere springing up. Instead of a growin
manufacture anxious to absorb them, the returning soldier foun
that the factories were already laying off many of their worke
and that jobs were almost impossible to find.

Certainly agriculture could not absorb the surplus. By th
beginning of the year wheat prices had fallen to 52s. 6d. Lan
put to cultivation during the war was allowed to lie fallow, labou
was laid off, wages cut among those lucky enough to remai
employed. "The alleviation of the difficulties arising from th
diminished value of agricultural produce," wrote Sidmout
ponderously,[1] "is not to be looked for from the intervention
government and parliament, but must be derived from th
adaptation of rent to the price of produce, and from the approx
mation which must take place of the price of all other articles
consumption to that of grain." If this observation meant anythin
it must have been that the country landlords, themselves im
poverished, should reduce the rents of their tenants and th
manufacturers lower the price of their products in sympathy wi
their country neighbours. Even Sidmouth can have felt litt
surprise when his compatriots failed to respond enthusiastical
to this call to enlightened self-help.

The countrymen were not disposed to sit and starve while th
Government deplored its inability to act. In May disorder bro
out in East Anglia. The shops of butchers and bakers were loote

magistrates forced to reduce the price of flour and a rabble of rioters congregated at Ely with the vague project of holding the town until something was done to satisfy their complaints. Lord Sidmouth personally instructed Sir Henry Dudley, an Ely magistrate who happened to be in London, on how to deal with the trouble and sent him hurrying back home with a band of eighteen regular soldiers and a few constables and militia-men. In the face of this far from formidable force the insurrection faded away. One rioter was killed, another five convicted and hanged for their part in the rising. A sullen peace fell on East Anglia.

Within a few months the position had been dramatically and disastrously reversed. A summer and autumn of ceaseless rain ruined the harvest and sent the price of corn leaping back to 117s. the quarter. Imports from the Continent were inadequate to meet the need. In many parts of the country the potato crops failed completely. The industrial poor, already gripped in the horrors of a recession, now found the price of their staple food doubled almost overnight. "Of the state of the country I cannot report favourably," wrote Sidmouth lugubriously.[1] "The distress is extreme; the indications of a disposition to disturbance less general than might have been expected. But it is to the autumn and winter that I look with anxiety." As the year wore on and the tide of alarmist reports from the provinces grew deeper upon his desk, so he became more convinced that a worse crisis than 1812 was in the offing.

He had some justification for his fears though this does little to excuse his misjudgment of the situation. Danger there was, but it was danger of a new and far more formidable nature. Almost imperceptibly the character of the British radical movement had altered. Under the inspiration of leaders such as Cobbett the British working-man had proved himself wiser than his employers or his Ministers. He had begun to escape from obsessive preoccupation with the symptoms of his misery to an attack upon its sources. Those sources lay in the very structure of society and this structure could only be modified by the action of Parliament. The first and great objective of the working classes must therefore be the control of Parliament. Between 1812 and 1816 there was a gradual shift from machine breaking, rick-burning and other miscellaneous demonstrations of a will to revolt to a mighty clamour for parliamentary reform.

The evolution was barely understood even by those who directed and inspired it; by Sidmouth and his like it passed at first unnoticed. Long after the change had been observed it was still largely discounted as a ploy to conceal the essential destructiveness of a revolutionary movement. Yet even if Sidmouth had appreciated the full purport of what was going on, he would not have felt that it called for modification of his policy. Agitation for parliamentary reform might be less immediately mischievous than out-and-out revolution but in the end both would prove equally disastrous for the proper government of the State and the happiness of its peoples. Both must have as their ends the upsetting of the Constitution and disturbance of the established order. Both he would oppose so long as his power remained.

He still could not accept that Government could properly occupy itself with the economic misery of the country. "I am concerned to think that the prevailing distress is so severely felt in your county," he wrote to one of the Members for Nottingham,[1] "but I see no reason for believing that it would or could be alleviated by any proceedings at a public meeting, or by parliament itself." In a short time he was to show himself eager that Parliament should reassemble but by then new legislation was needed to help him suppress disorder. This was the proper function of Parliament; to preserve order, not to waste time and raise false hopes by discussing conditions quite outside their power to heal.

As a palliative he was prepared to support a scheme of government-assisted emigration for the distressed. "The parts of the world to which the views of such persons should be directed are Upper Canada, Ceylon and the Cape of Good Hope," he told the future Bishop of Bristol.[2] But when it came to supporting emigration at the expense of British industry, his enthusiasm was quickly tempered. A party of Yorkshire shearmen, forbidden to emigrate by an Act of 1719, appealed for help to send them to North America. Lord Lascelles supported their plea but Sidmouth, backed by Liverpool, refused to act. "Machinery could not be stopped in the woollen trade," he commented curtly, and that was that.[3]

There was rioting in Birmingham, trouble around Manchester and Nottingham. But Sidmouth kept his main attention on the metropolis. On 15th November, the two radical leaders Burdett nd Hunt had held an open-air meeting at Spa Fields to gain upport for a petition to be presented to the Prince Regent. The petition called for universal male suffrage, annual parliaments nd vote by ballot; meat too strong for the genteel and wealthy Burdett who rapidly quarrelled with his colleague and withdrew rom the operation. Orator Hunt was delighted to be left alone n the limelight. A flamboyant demagogue of dashing appearance nd talents which, though considerable, were less remarkable than his vanity, Hunt was loved by the mob but distrusted by most of his close associates. ". . . really as inoffensive as Pistol or Bardolph," Creevey wrote of him contemptuously[1] and certainly o one can doubt his patent inadequacy to control or even direct he forces which he worked so hard to create.

Twice Hunt beat upon the Prince Regent's door with the etition and twice he was turned away. In his totally unreliable memoirs he recalls that he then called on Sidmouth at the Home Office.[2] ". . . his Lordship received me with all that parade of ver-strained politeness which belongs to a finished courtier." He read the petition with care and commented that "it was a most mportant paper and was couched in such proper language, that e should feel it his duty to lay it before his Royal Master the ery first thing on the following morning . . ." Sidmouth conratulated Hunt on being responsible for the moderate tone of he petition and added: "His Majesty's Ministers are greatly ndebted to you, and they are fully sensible that you have been he cause of preventing a great public calamity; you have preented the spilling of human blood."

There is no evidence, either among the Sidmouth papers or in he Home Office records, that this interview ever took place. It eems unlikely that Hunt would have invented it altogether and, ertainly, if Sidmouth had received him it would have been with ourtesy. But the details of the conversation are incredible; Sidmouth could never have expressed the thanks of Ministers to a man whom he regarded as a dangerous revolutionary or have raised as moderate a petition which he must have considered reasonable in its proposals. It is possible that Hunt's vanity was uch that he imagined Sidmouth had been won over by his charm nd eloquence. If so he was quickly disillusioned for it was made lear to him within a day or two that the petition had been rejected ut of hand. A second monster rally was called for the 2nd

December at Spa Fields to protest against this brusque rejection of the workers' plea.

Blithely Hunt set off to repeat his popular success of a few weeks before. But to his dismay he arrived to find his platform stolen and the crowd already being harangued by a group of fanatics from an extremist group, the oddly called Spencean Philanthropists. At their head was Doctor Watson, his lunatic and, on this occasion at least, drunken son, "The Younger Watson," and the already notorious Arthur Thistlewood. Egged on by their oratory the crowd was growing restless; shortly after his arrival it broke and surged away, Watson at their head, *en route* to overthrow the Government. "Plans were laid," said the report of the Secret Committee,[1] "for surprising the soldiers in their barracks, seizing the artillery, stopping the bridges, taking possession of the Tower and Bank, and liberating the inmates of the prisons." "Plans" is a grandiose word for the crazed delusions which flitted through the minds of the so-called leaders but certainly the Watsons had boasted to everyone who would listen, Government spies among them, of their intent to take London by force. Certainly, too, Lord Sidmouth had at first taken intent for ability and had prepared to meet a serious and well contrived revolution. In fact the mob disappeared in confusion when confronted by an alderman and a handful of constables, leaving their leaders to be arrested meekly and committed to the Tower which they had planned to storm. When the elder Watson was acquitted on a charge of high treason the Government did not put forward evidence against the other prisoners. Sidmouth would have preferred a prosecution but contented himself with the reflection that this farcical rising had at least shown both the alertness of the authorities and the futility of those who would oppose them.

But though Sidmouth was satisfied with the outcome of the affair, he was far from confident that all would go as easily in future. He resolved to act more rapidly next time:

"I do not hesitate to tell you," he wrote to the Speaker,[2] "that the connexion between the harangues in Spa Fields and the riot in London being completely established, the next meeting, if allowed to assemble at all, shall only assemble to hear the reading of the Riot Act, and then be dispersed immediately. Parliament must, indeed, interpose to prevent altogether these self-appointed meetings for the public discussion of alleged grievances; and the mischief which may be done in the meantime, from the want of such a legal restraint, is to me a subject of most painful reflection."

The words foreshadowed the panic legislation which Sidmouth was to push through Parliament in a few months. His point of view was sensible enough if it were assumed that every crowd assembled only to be seduced by the ravings of demented demagogues like the Younger Watson. The tragedy began with the failure of authority to distinguish between such circuses and those massively moderate, formidably respectable assemblies which were to argue the case for parliamentary reform. In Sidmouth's eyes most grievances were "alleged" and all public discussion of them likely to be mischievous. Ideally, therefore, all public meetings should be suppressed except those organised by accredited patriots serving the ends of the régime. Even these were liable to be misused and should preferably be avoided.

The speed with which the Spa Fields rioting had been quelled won Sidmouth much approval from Whigs as well as Tories. Only the radicals were left to mutter angrily of the Home Secretary's ruthless tyranny. Indeed, a more common criticism was that Sidmouth had not been stern enough or would not be so in future. "Everybody agrees," wrote Lord Lyttelton,[1] "that the Doctor has done his part well, and as that venerable old statesman when actual Prime Minister piqued himself upon repealing the Suspension and being constitutional, it is not unlikely he may still have the same laudable pride, especially as he is brave as foolish, and fears danger even less than the Regent."

If Lord Lyttelton had known a little more about Sidmouth's thinking he would have realised that his worry was unnecessary. The calm which hung uneasily over the opening weeks of 1817 did not for a moment seduce the Home Secretary into the belief that the crisis was less desperate than he feared. The Prince Regent wrote[2] to congratulate him on his "ceaseless vigilance" by which "the general quiet of the country" had been happily restored. Sidmouth knew better. He accepted the compliment gracefully and took time off for a week-end at the Pavilion—a dowdy figure among its garish splendours—but, once the feast was over, hastened back to his office to re-read his collection of lamentations from the provinces. Among the most sinister was one from Mr. Bootle Wilbraham at Manchester. "The lower

345

orders," he wrote,[1] "are everywhere meeting in large bodies, and are very clamorous. Delegates from all quarters are moving about amongst them, as they were before the last disturbance, and they talk of a general union of the lower orders throughout the Kingdom."

The report was not entirely exaggerated. There was indeed "a general union of the lower orders"; little though it had in the way of organisation or of coherent plans. But neither Mr. Bootle Wilbraham nor Lord Sidmouth had any idea what it was all about. The evolution from spasmodic industrial unrest to massive pressure for parliamentary reform had by now far advanced and all over England the radical members of the Hampden Clubs were seeking ways to persuade the legislature that their opinions were too rational to be discounted and too widely held to be ignored. Even among the members of the Hampden Clubs there were some who believed that the established order could only be overthrown by violence and others who longed for disorder, whether necessary or not, for the sake of loot and revenge on their more fortunate fellows. But the general mood was one of sobriety and determination. Few of the Radicals who converged on London in January, 1817, for the great rally at the Crown and Anchor had any thought in their heads save that of formulating their demands for parliamentary representation in a balanced, dignified and, above all, convincing way.

It is conceivable, though unlikely, that if there had been complete unity in the Radical camp the Government might have been sufficiently impressed to give its pretensions serious consideration. But the behaviour of the leading Radicals was perfectly calculated to convince their enemies that the movement was without purpose save that of mischief-making and fomenting revolution. Vanity, suspicion, jealousy, lust for the limelight: these were the hall-marks of the men who should have been dedicated solely to the cause of liberty. Of Sir Francis Burdett, Cobbett wrote: "I impute to him no crimes; I charge him with no perfidy . . . It is of his indecision, and his inconsistency, of his jealousies and of his envies, I complain."[2] Writing of Cobbett, Hunt complained of "his cowardice, his supineness . . . his treachery"[3]; while Burdett, addressing Hunt, protested angrily that he was not disposed to be made into a cat's-paw.[4] Led by such warring prima donnas, Government could be excused for doubting the

briety of the Radical movement and assuming that, whatever
e intentions of the chiefs, the rank-and-file would soon get out
hand.

The culmination of the current exercise was to have been the
esentation of a monster petition to the Houses of Parliament
the Member for Westminster, Sir Francis Burdett. But
urdett, nervous at Hunt's authority in the movement, had chosen
boycott the meeting at the Star and Garter. His preference for
limited household suffrage was swept aside and a petition
lling for universal suffrage triumphantly adopted. Hunt carried
e petition to the door of the Palace of Westminster and it was
e gallant and spectacular Lord Cochrane who received it in the
ace of Burdett.

The day could hardly have been worse chosen. On his way
ck from opening the parliamentary session the Prince Regent
d had a window of his coach shattered by some projectile. No
e seemed very clear whether a bullet or a stone had done the
mage but Sidmouth, at least, was in no doubt that a dastardly
sault on the Prince's life had miraculously failed. He broke the
ws to the House of Lords, reported Lord Holland maliciously:[1]
"with more than his usual solemnity (sufficient though it be
to that or almost any occasion) . . . Lord Sidmouth, to vent his
feelings of indignation and alarm with an equal attention to
pathos and precedent, had the journals of 1795, when a
similar event had occurred, spread out before him; and bade
the clerk, when one question was disposed of, *look out what
was to be done next*. He was disconcerted at finding that the
absence of the Masters-in-Chancery would compel us to convey our horror to the Commons by an inferior servant of the
House."

With this new tit-bit to quicken their craving for sterner
easures, it was not surprising that Ministers had little time for
titions demanding parliamentary reform. A few days later
cret Committees of both Houses were again set up to consider
e parlous state of the nation. A mountain of documents was
d before them; almost all of them indicating that England was
the brink of revolution and that, to save her, action must be
th quick and resolute.

It would be wrong to assume that the Committees were packed
th ferocious die-hards or that Sidmouth and his fellow reac-

347

tionaries were alone in predicting peril for the country. Wilbe
force for one was a member of the Committee of the Commo
and, though far from being a Radical, his moderation, fai
mindedness and dislike of repression were rarely questioned. Y
he was convinced by the evidence and was among the most dete
mined in pressing for firm measures. "It has been a very gre
mortification to me," he wrote in March,[1] ". . . that I cann
attend the House to support the measures . . . for preserving t
public peace. I assure you that in my judgment they are absolute
needed if we would not incur the danger of bloodshed a
conflagration."

There was, indeed, a great deal of evidence that bloodshed a
conflagration were being planned. A fair amount of it w
genuine. Where Sidmouth erred was in believing that a lar
number of plots or projects, few of which would ever have cor
to anything, when taken together must add up to a nation-wi
conspiracy, centrally controlled and organised with demoni
skill by cold-blooded revolutionaries. In this error, to-d
obvious yet in the context of 1817 by no means unnatural, he w
joined by virtually the whole of the English aristocracy a
middle-classes. "They sigh for a PLOT," wrote Cobbett.[2] "O
how they sigh! They are working and slaving and fretting a
stewing; they are sweating all over; they are absolutely pini
and dying for a plot!" Cobbett underestimated the goodwill a
reluctance to resort to violence which was felt by most of Britai
rulers. Both Wilberforce and Sidmouth would have been p
foundly relieved if it could have been proved to them that
plot existed. But both were determined that there was one a
the massive dossiers from the provinces were treated not
material to be sifted, analysed and largely discarded but
evidence to illustrate an already established thesis. The repo
of the Secret Committees justified almost any repressive legislati
that Sidmouth might think necessary.

Of these the first was the suspension of Habeas Corpus. S
mouth introduced the second reading of the Bill on 24th Fe
ruary. After a typical reference to "a traitorous conspiracy .
for the purpose of overthrowing . . . the established governmen
he went on to refer to "a malignant spirit which had brought su
disgrace upon the domestic character of the people," a spi
which "had long prevailed in the country, but especially since

commencement of the French Revolution." This spirit once postulated, Lord Sidmouth went on to endow it with the ability to tackle a remarkable range of subversive activities. "It" had beilttled our victories, exalted the prowess of our enemies, then, at the end of the war, redoubled its activities, fomented discontent, exaggerated calamities, encouraged violence and generally conducted itself in a way of which any decent spirit would have been ashamed. Recently it had sought to cloak its real wickedness. But Sidmouth was not to be taken in. "An organised system has been established in every quarter, under the semblance of demanding parliamentary reform, but many of them, I am convinced, have that specious pretext in their mouths only, but revolution and rebellion in their hearts."

In his peroration, Sidmouth called for "the immediate suspension of the Habeas Corpus Act for the security of his Majesty's peaceable subjects, the protection of parliament, the maintenance of our liberties and the perpetuation of the blessings of the constitution." He had little doubt that Parliament would respond to his call but the easiness of his victory surprised him. He had feared that the Opposition would remain united; instead, while the Whigs were firm to their principles and opposed the measure, Lord Grenville and his followers concluded that the country was in danger and voted for suspension. The breach between the two wings of the Opposition had already made itself apparent. After this it was never to heal.

The attitude of the Whigs was no real sign of sympathy with the causes or methods of the Radical movement. On the contrary, Grey was far closer to Sidmouth than to Hunt or Cobbett and the Radicals at this moment were isolated from all respectable political forces within the governing classes. "Is there one among them with whom you would trust yourself in the dark?" Grey haughtily asked Sir Robert Wilson.[1] ". . . Look at the men, at their character, at their conduct. What is there more base, more detestable, more at variance with all taste and decency, as well as morality, truth and honour . . ." And Cobbett, who would have been delighted to find that Grey found him lacking in taste, returned the compliment: ". . . while they pretended to oppose the measure," he wrote of the Whigs,[2] "this perfidious faction—this base and detestable and cowardly and cruel faction, represented the persons against whom it was directed in such a

light, and represented their designs as so full of horrible wickedness, that everyone who read their speeches, and who believed
what they said, must have regarded the measure as necessary to
the safety of the country . . ."

The suspension of Habeas Corpus alone was held inadequate
to secure the defeat of the revolutionaries. Bills to prevent
seditious meetings and to penalise any attempt to seduce the
loyalties of the armed forces were rushed through the alarmed
Houses. But Sidmouth went even further by executive action.
He was convinced that much of the unrest was caused by the
circulation of cheap Radical tracts, in particular Cobbett's
Political Register which, at twopence a copy, was selling the
fantastic number of 40 to 50,000 a week. After consulting with
the Law Officers Sidmouth now issued a round robin to all the
Lords Lieutenant.[1] There had, he observed, been some doubt
whether Justices of the Peace could issue a warrant for the arrest
of persons selling seditious literature. Let this doubt now be
put aside, he instructed their Lordships, and let Justices be
instructed that it was not only their right but their duty so to act.

Sidmouth's instructions were much criticised both in Parliament and in the country. Romilly and Erskine attacked them as
an unwarrantable extension of the Minister's prerogative while
The Times boomed disapprovingly: "We say that no writing is a
libel till it is found such, and that the ultimate finders of a libel
are now declared by law to be the jury that has found it." Little
use was made of the letter by magistrates and at least one Chair-
man of Quarter Sessions dismissed it curtly with "Let us not be
troubled with such trash as this."[2] But neither Sidmouth nor his
colleagues doubted that his action was wise and beneficial. "I
stand before your Lordships," he declared when the crisis was
debated,[3] "charged with having used my best endeavours to stop
the progress of blasphemy and sedition. To that charge I plead
guilty, and while I live I shall be proud to have such a charge
brought against me."

Even before Sidmouth's new instructions had been issued to
the Lords Lieutenant, William Cobbett had taken fright. He
resolved to take refuge in America. It seems unlikely that his
person was in danger but certainly he would have found it ever
more hard to continue his journalistic work without interference.
He claimed[4] that, before he sailed, he was approached by an

intermediary of Lord Sidmouth and offered compensation for loss of income if he would give up writing and return to the country. He gave no answer since he was determined not to accept and certain that refusal would be followed by arrest. It is ironic that one of the first effects of Sidmouth's new measures should have been the exile of the man who, by his emphasis on parliamentary reform and the futility of violence, had perhaps done more than any other individual to switch the British working-classes from the ill-co-ordinated and illegal excesses of machine-breaking and rick-burning to a comparatively well disciplined and constitutional crusade.

In the melancholy social history of these years it is often hard to decide whether repressive legislation did more to foment discontent and unrest or whether it was the unrest which provoked the legislation. Certainly Lord Sidmouth's new powers failed signally to restore tranquillity. On 18th April, in the same letter as he reported the execution of six Luddites at Leicester, the Home Secretary wrote optimistically to the Regent[1]: "It is highly satisfactory to me to be able to inform your Royal Highness that the accounts received at this office . . . describe the country as in a state of quiet, occasioned unquestionably by the improved conditions of its agricultural interests, and an increased demand for various articles of domestic manufacture as well as by the measures which have been necessarily adopted by the Government." Yet within a few weeks, prosperity or no prosperity, the pathetic march on London of six or seven hundred hungry weavers had confirmed the Government in all its fears.

The "March of the Blanketeers" petered out before it had got more than a few miles; viewed in retrospect it is clear that it never had the remotest chance of attaining anything except the discomfort and discomfiture of its participants. And yet in the tense and plot-ridden atmosphere of 1817 it was inevitable that Sidmouth should have seen the incident as part of a nation-wide scheme to overthrow the Government and that the Duke of Northumberland should have written to him speaking darkly of "foreign propagandists" and drawing an obvious though misleading analogy with the march of the Marseillais on Paris in 1792.[2]

The Duke was not altogether a fool. Thompson has recently done much to establish the existence of a strong and reasonably coherent covert Radical organisation operating on a national scale. Sidmouth was contending with a real enemy. But the futil splutterings in Lancashire did neither justice to the strength of th Radicals nor bore any serious relation to their aims. Their abjec failure proved that the real weight of the English working-classe was not behind them.

Yet even more surprising than the moderation of the so-calle revolutionary movements was the restraint, almost diffidence with which the Government used the repressive powers witl which they had been so handsomely endowed. The Radical pro pagandist's vision of Ministers as a gang of horrendous ogres utterly indifferent to human life or the rights of the individua does not stand up to serious examination. An illuminating com mentary is provided by Samuel Bamford, a hand-loom weave turned Radical politician and political journalist.[2] Shortly afte the March of the Blanketeers Bamford was arrested and haule before the Privy Council on suspicion of fomenting the rising which, in fact, he had done his best to check. In his memoirs h left a full account of his examination and treatment while i prison. Thoughts of the Inquisition ran through his mind as h was ushered, apprehensive, into the Council Chamber. Th Grand Inquisitor opened by informing him that he was there o suspicion of high treason, that he would not be examined for week and that he need not say anything if he did not wish:

The person who addressed me was a tall, square, and bony figure, upwards of fifty years of age, I should suppose; and with thin, and rather grey hair: his forehead was broad and prominent, and from their cavernous orbits looked mild and intelligent eyes. His manner was affable, and much more encouraging to freedom of speech than I had expected. On his left sat a gentleman whom I never made out; and next him again was Sir Samuel Shepherd, the attorney general, I think, for the time; who frequently made use of an ear trumpet. On Lord Sidmouth's right, for such was the gentle-man who had been speaking to me, sat a good-looking person in a plum-coloured coat, with a gold ring on the small finger of his left hand, on which he sometimes leaned his head as he eyed me over: this was Lord Castlereagh.

"My Lord," I said, addressing the President; "having been brought from home without a change of linen, I wish to be informed how I shall be provided for in that respect until I can be supplied from home." The council conferred a short time, and Lord Sidmouth said I should be supplied with whatever was necessary. I next asked, should I be allowed freely to correspond with my wife and child, inform them of my situation, and to receive their letters, provided such letters did not contain political information?

"You will be allowed to communicate with your family," said his Lordship, "but I trust you will see the necessity of confining yourself to matters of a domestic nature. You will always write in the presence of a person who will examine your letters; you will therefore do well to be guarded in your correspondence, as nothing of an improper tendency will be suffered to pass. I speak this for your own good."

"Could I be permitted to have pen, ink, and paper in prison?" I asked, "and could I be allowed to keep a small day-book or journal for my amusement?"

"It is an indulgence," was the reply, "which has never been granted to any state-prisoner; and as I do not see any reason for departing from the established rule, I should feel it my painful duty to refuse it."

I said I had heard that the suspension act contained a clause securing to state prisoners the right of sending petitions to parliament; and I wished to be informed if there were such a clause.

His Lordship said the suspension act did not contain any such clause, but the power to petition would be allowed by His Majesty's Ministers, and I should have the liberty whenever I thought proper to use it. I bowed and retired.

While the Home Secretary was wondering what to do with his prisoners Bamford and his fellows lived excellently, were given much to eat and free porter and tobacco. On 9th April Bamford saw the Privy Council again and gave its surprised but unprotesting members a lecture on parliamentary reform. Magistrates visited the prisoners from time to time to listen to their complaints. On 23rd April Bamford instructed the Privy Council on the state of the poor. Finally, on 29th April, he was called once more before the Council.

Lord Sidmouth said:

"Mr. Bamford, I hope you are now before me for the last time.

You will be discharged on conditions which will be read over to you; the same conditions which others of your fellow prisoners who have been discharged have accepted. I assure you I feel great pleasure in thus restoring you to your family." I said I hoped nothing would be proposed to me which was at variance with my political principles, as I could not consent to forgo my rights to which, as an Englishman, I was entitled. His Lordship could not desire me to give up the only right I had exercised; namely, the right of petition.

His Lordship said: "Nothing will be proposed to you, which an honest and good man need object to. We are not averse to the subject petitioning for a redress of grievances; it is the manner in which that right has been exercised which we condemn; a right may be exercised in such a way that it becomes a wrong, and then we must object to it. Mr. Bamford, there are three things which I would have you impress seriously on your mind. The first is, that the present distress of the country arises from unavoidable circumstances; the second that his Majesty's ministers will do all they can to alleviate such distress; and, thirdly, no violence, of whatever description, will be tolerated, but it will be put down with a very strong hand. I wish you well; I assure you I wish you well; and I hope this is the last time I shall ever see you on an occasion like the present."

I sincerely thanked his Lordship for his good wishes and condescension, and expressed my gratitude for the kindness I had experienced while his Lordship's prisoner; and having asked and very obligingly obtained permission to have my liberty the following morning, until the coach started, I bowed to his Lordship and the Council and retired.

This picture of courteous old gentlemen, armed with ear trumpets, muttering together about the state of a prisoner's linen, is not necessarily inconsistent with the inexorable application of harsh, even inhuman laws. But the care which Sidmouth showed for the rights of the prisoners, the readiness of the Council to listen to all Bamford might want to say and the cheerfulness with which they freed him as soon as they had convinced themselves that he was no danger to the State are hard to reconcile with the characteristics of totalitarian rule as made manifest in the twentieth century.

Bamford was not the only witness to testify to the moderation and humanity which Sidmouth showed in carrying out his functions. Elizabeth Fry, the Quaker and reformer, who saw much of him over her work for women prisoners, testified[1] that he had "been very kind to us when ever we have applied for the mitigation of punishment." Shortly afterwards the two fell out. "I felt much too low at heart," she wrote to Lady Harcourt,[2] "and too much grieved at the misunderstanding with Lord Sidmouth, to be capable of much pleasure, as he is one that I have really esteemed. . . . From my peculiar situation, I have had it in my power with numbers of people, to strengthen his reputation as to his having much mercy mixed with his views of justice . . . I hope that it will be in my power once more to obtain his regard and confidence."

Sidmouth, as Home Secretary, did little to alleviate the lot of the poor and distressed. His measures to repress the discontent which followed were harsh, viewed in retrospect unnecessarily harsh. He may be accused of short-sightedness and lack of imagination. But with all this it cannot be denied that he, personally, was kind, tolerant and scrupulously fair. Though there was much to criticise in his laws, his execution of them was admirable in its temperance and humanity.

*   *   *   *   *

So a summer of discontent followed this unpropitious spring. Agitation spluttered on, every now and then erupting into visible life. The most formidable—if formidable is the right word for such a pitiful squib of a rising—was the so-called Pentrich Revolution. Jeremiah Brandreth raised a group of Derbyshire peasants to march on Nottingham. An unfortunate man-servant was shot dead as he was lacing his boots in the kitchen, a murder which by its pointless wastefulness symbolised the whole spirit of the affair. Many of the revolutionaries were discouraged by the long walk and vanished into the night, the rest were dispersed in the traditional way by a handful of dragoons. It was a futile display; irrelevant to the movement headed by such men as Bamford or Cobbett and childishly inefficient even by its own out-of-date standards. "I cannot discover," reported Lord Fitzwilliam,[3] "that in this Riding any one man, above the rank of a very inferior mechanic or shop-keeper, has been suspected of a party in these plans of insurrection. Here it is considered as the war of No Property against Property, and on this ground all of the latter description shew themselves eager and anxious to resist their assailants." In 1817 it was already too late for such a war; Brandreth and his yokels had no place in an age when the Industrial Revolution was far advanced and the capture of Westminster by reform and not revolt the object of every serious Radical. But it would have been too much to expect the House of Commons to perceive or take account of this evolution. For them Brandreth and his followers were the real threat and anything else irrelevant. In such an atmosphere it was inevitable that Members should endorse Lord Sidmouth's proposal to renew the suspension of Habeas Corpus for a further period.

The autumn of 1817 saw things once more quietening down. Sidmouth took advantage of the lull to go through the list of all those detained under the Suspension Act and release as many of them as his conscience would allow. He interviewed most of the prisoners himself and in at least one case authorised a release on no grounds except that he thought the prisoner had an honest face.[1] Perhaps surprisingly his trust was not abused. He also did something to mitigate the misery of those who were still detained. "Solitary confinement," he ruled,[2] "will not be continued except under special circumstance."

Apart from a bafflingly irrational attempt to storm the Tower of London the year ended quietly. Only the antics of Arthur Thistlewood disturbed the Home Secretary's calm. Thistlewood, a blood-and-thunder revolutionary who had won some slightly shoddy spurs at the time of Spa Fields, had been imprisoned under the Suspension Act. His release did not relieve his rancour against authority. In January, 1818, he elected to send Lord Sidmouth a challenge "to fight him with sword or pistol." In heavy-handed manner the Cabinet insisted that Sidmouth should swear the peace against Thistlewood and that the latter should be indicted. Sidmouth protested strongly; the procedure would involve his deposing that Thistlewood had put him in bodily fear, this was false and would therefore involve him in perjury. The point was a fair one but pressure from the Prince Regent and his colleagues induced him to accept that the deposition was a mere form of words and carried no imputation against his courage.

Thistlewood's gesture of defiance cost him a year's imprisonment; time which he spent in nurturing his grievances against society in general and the Home Secretary in particular.

So improved was the state of the country that in February, 1818, Sidmouth felt able to introduce a Bill for repealing the Suspension Act. An automatic corollary to this was a Bill to indemnify all those who had acted to arrest or detain suspects while Habeas Corpus was suspended. This relatively unimportant postscript earned more abuse from the Radicals than the original measure. "Talk not to me of the cruelties and ferocity of those who destroyed the *noblesse* of France," fulminated Cobbett.[1] "After this, talk not to me of any such things. Talk not to me of constitution and order and the laws: show me something equal to this, done by any other people in the world, calling themselves a government and legislative assemblies."

The result in the lobbies was, of course, a comfortable victory for the Government. But the debate was of particular interest for the discussion about the role of government spies in the recent disorders. In terms of their influence on the course of domestic politics the little band of government-sponsored spies and informers deserves scant attention. Little if anything would have been different if they had never existed. But the ethics of their employment by the Home Office has been the subject of so much debate, both at the time and subsequently, and their feats have been so vastly exaggerated by propagandists and sensation-mongers, that it is impossible to deal with them in accord with their real importance. Above all is this true in a biography of Lord Sidmouth. Fairly or unfairly, Sidmouth's spies have become the best remembered feature of his tenure of the Home Office. His reputation has become inextricably involved with the doings of these few and insignificant incompetents. If only to put their activities back into proportion it is necessary to treat them at what otherwise might fairly be considered disproportionate length.

* * * * *

Close by the ever-burning brimstone beds,
Where Bedloe, Oates and Judas hide their heads,
I saw great Satan like a sexton stand
With his intolerable spade in hand

Digging three graves. . . .

                . . . all about the detestable pit
Strange headless ghosts and quartered forms did flit;
Rivers of blood from dripping traitors spilt
By treachery slung from poverty to guilt.
I asked the fiend for whom these rites were meant?
"These graves" quoth he "when life's brief oil is spent,
When the dark night comes, and they're sinking bedwards,
I mean for Castle, Oliver and Edwards."

Lamb's doggerel expresses admirably the intellectual level at which the debate about Sidmouth's use of spies has usually been conducted. To the British the word spy is a violently emotive word. The trade is felt to be detestable and the domestic government spy, the spy of authority on indiscipline, of strength on weakness, the most repulsive of its exponents. The saint, the sentimentalist, the sturdy British countryman; all joined in deprecating the devious means by which Government sought to maintain the country's safety. "I am astonished," said Wilberforce in the House of Commons,[1] "that honourable gentlemen do not see that these are crooked paths. Certainly the employment of such engines cannot be justified upon religious principles. All the ways of falsehood and deceit are hateful to the God of truth."

Luckily for Sidmouth and perhaps the country, most people at or near the centre of power realised the alarming weakness, almost the non-existence of the official security services and the inadequacy of the reports that flowed in from the misinformed, credulous and panic-stricken Justices. Certainly the Whigs were not disposed to attack the principle of using spies to supplement the regular sources of information. It was Fitzwilliam, later to be outspoken in his denunciations of Oliver the Spy, who wrote in July, 1812,[2] to ask what rewards should be paid for information leading to the arrest of ". . . a person administering unlawful oaths or endeavouring to induce others to take them—Will Government give from £100 to £200—less is thought useless? Should the country have assumed a new tone, it is possible, under that promised protection, informers may step forth, if allure sufficient is held out. Certainly it is most desirable to show that, sooner or later, the perpetrators of violent outrages are detected: a contrary example will be very mischievous."

Nor did Sidmouth's successors find it possible to dispense with the system. In spite of the comfortable theory that Peel, once installed as Home Secretary, set to work to "clean out the mystery of iniquity in the Home Office,"[1] the records show[2] that he long continued to make use of spies. So, indeed, he or any other Home Secretary would have had to do until a regular police force had removed the need to depend on amateurs.

". . . it can be satisfactorily shown," claimed Canning in the debate in the House of Commons,[3] "that government, instead of outstripping the informations they have received, has rather lagged behind them. It is clear that governments can not go on, if they refuse to receive information of plots formed against the security of the state. . . . I agree that that information is the best which comes under the sanction of established authority, or from an unsuspected channel; and if the noble Lord or his friends can prove that ministers have, by option and preference, accepted the communications of obscure agents in lieu of regular reports from established authorities, then they would make out a real case against them. But this has not happened."

Canning was being disingenuous. Lord Sidmouth may not actually have accepted the reports of Government spies "in lieu of regular reports from established authorities," but he certainly had some profound and well-justified doubts about the value of the latter. If his spies could supplement or verify the wilder rumours then they would be well worth their microscopic pay, worth even the disesteem in which they were likely to involve their employers. An efficient intelligence service, closely in touch with the disaffected, able to open the eyes of Government to their real strength and real objectives, would have been as valuable to the Radicals themselves as to Ministers. Nothing else, perhaps, could have dissipated the clouds of panic-stricken misapprehension which hung between the Government and the politically unprivileged. The charge against Government should not be that they employed spies but that they employed such bad ones; that there was no intelligence system in any proper sense; that they recruited casual amateurs, without inquiring into their background, and sent them forth, untrained and politically naïve to study situations which only long experience and good judgment could properly have evaluated.

The inefficiency and gullibility of many of the Government

spies is perpetually astonishing. Ministers were not entirely promiscuous in their recruitment. "As I rather think that Mrs. Biggs is offering her services in the shape of a regular spy," wrote a Treasury official to Vansittart,[1] "I think it right to tell you not only that I am quite satisfied that she is—what I think Lord Sidmouth called her, and what I am sure Jonathan Wild called his wife, but that she is moreover what renders her much more unfit for such a service, a blab, and goes about boasting of being in the confidence of the government." Mrs. Biggs was not employed. But such moments of prudence proved rare. The Home Office Records show vividly that almost any out-of-work incompetent had only to present himself and claim acquaintance with a troubled area to be accredited as an agent and immediately dispatched there to report on what was going on.

Such agents were often not merely useless but positively mischievous. If they wanted their employment to continue it was essential that the crisis should continue too. Professional vanity, if the word professional may be so misused, as well as self-interest encouraged them to ferret out non-existent plots and to inflate the dangers of quite trifling movements of discontent. From this it was but a step to the most heinous crime of all; that of deliberately fomenting insurrection and egging on to violent action men who otherwise would have done no more than grumble and bear their sorrows passively.

This charge, that Sidmouth's spies were not mere informers but *agents provocateurs* as well, is the most damaging that can be levelled against the Home Department's activities in the field of intelligence. Though their success in this direction was limited by the same inefficiency as made their political reporting of such little value, there can be no doubt that, on certain occasions, spies in the employ of the Home Office did step across the line between espionage and active encouragement to revolt. There are several well-authenticated instances; for example the efforts of an unidentified agent to induce Bamford to join in a march on Manchester designed to sack the town and liberate the imprisoned Blanketeers.[2] But the *locus classicus* is that of W. J. Richards, alias Oliver the Spy, who earned more notoriety than all his fellows, whose case was angrily debated in Parliament and whose evil reputation has done so much to taint the good name of his employer.[3] "This is all Oliver and the Government . . ." cried

William Turner of the Pentrich Revolution as he awaited his turn upon the scaffold. The cry echoed down the ages and has balefully reverberated through the pages of innumerable social histories bent upon establishing the iniquities of Government and the innocence of their victims.

Like most last words, Turner's were, at the best, an over-simplification, at the worst, grossly misleading. Oliver was a failed builder of some plausibility whose minimal talents were later directed towards accountancy. While thus occupied he met Joseph Mitchell, a Liverpool Radical, and somehow won his confidence. Finding himself out of work again he decided to turn his new friendship to account and called at the Home Office to offer his services. On 28th March, 1817, he saw Lord Sidmouth and was recruited as a spy. A month later he was sent off on a fact-finding mission to the Midlands and the North. It is certain that, on this tour, he represented himself sometimes as a friend of Burdett and sometimes as leader of the physical force party in London. Given his notorious vanity it is likely that he made out this movement to be more important and better organised than in fact it was.

In May Oliver reported back to the Home Office. He must have impressed the authorities with his usefulness for, on 23rd May, Hiley Addington sent him forth again armed with a letter to various magistrates attesting "He is an intelligent man, and deserving of your confidence."[1] Though he had several anxious conferences with Sir John Byng he did not make much other use of this letter and in Sheffield was himself busily spied on by a local government agent. It was reported that he was boasting he could raise 70,000 men in East London and another 70,000 in West London. "He was considered by all the party as the man who communicated and directed things from London, and as he directed, so they acted."[2] A Sheffield Justice reported that he had so far failed to arrest Oliver but felt sure he would be caught at Leeds. In dismay Sidmouth wrote back telling the Justice that ". . . O. is employed by me, that he is travelling under my directions at this time, and that I have reason to confide in his disposition and ability to render himself eminently useful, under present circumstances. I accordingly shall be anxious till I hear again and should be much relieved by hearing that he had not been apprehended."[3] On 6th June he actually was arrested at

Thornhill Lees. His immediate release destroyed his cover and, staying only to attend one final meeting at Nottingham, he moved rapidly back to London. From that date he retired from active spying.

While in Sheffield it seems that his main preoccupation was to postpone the date of any rising. This he did successfully; his insistence that London was not yet ready was at least a contributory cause of the Pentrich Revolution petering out without a hand being raised to help the rebels in any other part of the country. Nor does it seem that he was directly responsible for the so-called Revolution itself; on balance it is at least probable that something similar would have happened even though he had never left London.[1] But it cannot be disputed that Oliver's self-importance, his boasts about the strength of the movement in London, his attempt to win information by himself proffering inaccurate statistics from other parts of the country; all contributed to the atmosphere in which Brandreth could delude himself that the violence of a few hungry peasants would bring Government and Crown tumbling to the ground.

Fremantle in his careful study of Oliver's unsavoury career stated as his conclusion: "It was Oliver's primary object, in accordance with his instructions, to convey information to his superiors and not to influence events. So far as he did the latter, it was his desire to obtain the postponement of the threatened rising for as long as possible, so as to give time for the force collected against the King's peace to fall to pieces by the weight of growing discord and mutual suspicion. . . . In the difficult part which he had to play, he was on one occasion at any rate—in Sheffield—tempted to offer undue encouragement . . ."

So prosaic and, perhaps, unduly charitable a judgment would have had little appeal for those convinced of the black malignancy of Sidmouth and all his servants. Fitzwilliam reported[2]: "There certainly prevails very generally in the country a strong and decided opinion that most of the events that have recently occurred in the country, are to be attributed to the presence and active agitation of Mr. Oliver. He is considered as the mainspring from which every movement has taken its rise . . ."

That Oliver, an untrained hack with no assets except plausibility and a vivid imagination, in two short tours should so have imposed himself upon the country is, of course, incredible. That he should even have tried to achieve the results with which Fitzwilliam credits him would argue an audacious wickedness far beyond the limits of his personality. Oliver was certainly base, treacherous, unscrupulous. He was also irresponsible in that, in seeking to win the trust of others, he urged them into action that was bound to lead to their destruction. But the higher flights of villainy were outside his range. He did much harm by his ill-judged efforts to glean intelligence and win confidence, but the harm was incidental and not the real object of his activities.

Sidmouth's association with Oliver has perhaps done more than anything else to damage his reputation in the minds of decent men. It has been popularly assumed, not only that Oliver fomented revolution, but that Sidmouth encouraged him or, at least, accepted all that he was doing as necessary and desirable. A lampoon among the Broughton papers[1] purporting to be a letter to Lord Sidmouth from Oliver, recently arrived in hell, displays well the indignation with which the enemies of the Government greeted the public exposure of Oliver's activities:

> Styx I have past,
> My Lord, at last,
> And can no great encomium,
> Bestow on it
> Or that famed *Pit*
> By man called—"Pandemonium."

> At every place,
> I showed my face,
> On *Earth*, was I rejected!
> Rejected—why?
> I was a Spy!
> By *you*, my Lord, protected.

When he arrived in hell he found that he received no better treatment.

> One single friend,
> Has never deigned,

To speak, my Lord, unto me,
And that old Scrub,
Black Beelzebubb!
Pretends he never knew me.

Unto your Spy
My Lord, reply,
To me in *Hell* direct it
And, Worthy Peer,
Let's know when here
You are to be expected!

Though Oliver's activities as *agent provocateur* were incidental
to his real role and did less mischief than has often been asserted,
it is true that the smoke of abuse which hung around him, true
to the habit of its kind, concealed a small but still genuine fire.
Even of this Sidmouth was ignorant. When Fitzwilliam wrote to
tell him of the general rumours, he replied in dismay[1]: "The
statement is to me incredible but I think it so important as to
require immediate and minute investigation. It is directly at
variance with the instructions given to Oliver and with his communications to Sir John Byng, as well as to myself." There is no
reason to doubt that this is the exact truth. The Government's
public statement of their attitude was categoric. Their object in
employing Oliver was to "obtain information of what was the
real disposition of the people. . . . it would have been entirely
inconsistent with the instructions given him by Government if
he had in any instance fomented or encouraged the disaffected
to proceed with greater activity or to greater lengths than they
were themselves inclined to do."[2]

Such an overt profession of faith does not prove that no hidden
understanding existed between Oliver and the Government. But
there was nothing in his reports to the Home Office to suggest
that he was acting as more than an informer. On the contrary,
when he wrote to Beckett[3] to suggest that an energetic man
should be sent to Wakefield to play a leading part among the
conspirators, he was careful to define the new spy's function as
being no more than "ascertaining the extent they possibly have
in their view to go." The reports[4] which he submitted to the
Home Office on his return allude continually to his caution and
reticence. In Middleton, when he was asked if the people in the

"upper parts" were prepared for the struggle, he replied that "he could not tell them in reality their state." In Nottingham he went further and told the disappointed conspirators that "the Manchester people would not act." On several occasions, even though strongly pressed, he refused to give any opinion on the state of mind in London or the chances of an effective rising. To-day it is clear that his words in the provinces were decidedly less innocuous than he reported to his masters in London but, at the time, the Home Office had little reason to distrust his account. "I am obliged to appear as a Liberal Patriot," he explained to Beckett,[1] and neither Beckett nor Sidmouth suspected that he had said more than was strictly necessary to sustain the role.

It can thus be accepted that, in so far as Oliver instigated violence, he acted in a way flatly contrary to his own instructions, to professed Government policy and to the constantly reiterated views of Sidmouth on what was decent and honourable conduct. To suggest that Sidmouth approved or condoned such conduct is to accuse him of great—and, incidentally, pointless—wickedness, and hypocrisy so consummate that he deluded all his closest friends. Only the strongest evidence could justify such an accusation; no such evidence exists. All, indeed, points the other way; that Sidmouth was ignorant of Oliver's activities and incredulous to the point of naïvety when they were pointed out to him.

To say this does not acquit him of negligence in employing agents as unreliable and ill-trained as Castle, Edwards or Oliver. If Oliver were plausible enough to convince the Radicals of Sheffield that he was an important revolutionary from London he may also have been plausible enough to convince Sidmouth that he was a safe man, fit to be employed in such delicate work. But a Home Secretary should not be as gullible as ill-educated peasants and artisans. Sidmouth should either have insisted that he be given enough money to run a proper intelligence service or have abandoned the effort altogether. The haphazard selection of casual volunteers, though sanctioned by tradition, inevitably produced more mischief than information. The counsel is perhaps too much one of perfection; it is highly unlikely that the extra money or the consent of the rest of the Cabinet would have been forthcoming and, failing that, Sidmouth can be forgiven for feeling that even the reports of amateurs were better than nothing. But though there may be many excuses, the system failed. The Government spies produced little of value and, though they may also have done little real harm, the damage to the nation's morale and the Government's reputation had been considerable. For this, though for no more, Sidmouth must bear the main responsibility.

14

"I am sorry to say that our situation continues to be in many respects a melancholy one," wrote Liverpool to Sidmouth in the summer of 1818.[1] Income was barely balancing expenditure and "A debt of between 7 and 8 hundred million without any Sinking Fund or at best with a Sinking Fund of a million constitutes a state of things too appalling to be presented to the new Parliament: and too critical with a view to the permanent welfare of the country to be permitted to continue without an endeavour to improve it." New taxes would be abortive, nothing remained except to reduce expenditure.

The main object of Liverpool's letter was to win Sidmouth's consent to cutting the regular army. This was forthcoming, though with the reluctance to be expected from a Home Secretary painfully alive to the threat of civil disorder. He could not in conscience claim that the arguments for a large army were as strong as a year or so before. 1818 was a tranquil year. The price of wheat fell and of Consols rose. Exports soared and demands for our manufactures remained firm on the home market. Only in a few isolated industries was there serious hardship and even in these the malcontents were quickly forced to come to terms. On the political front the pressure for parliamentary reform seemed to have slackened. In retrospect it is easy to see that this was no more than a lull, a period of consolidation while the movement regrouped itself and prepared for fresh battles. At the time, however, Sidmouth was not the only statesman misguided enough to imagine that, so long as the proletariat had enough to eat, there was no need to feel concern about their political ambitions.

The respite was well timed for Sidmouth, for the summer of 1818 had brought him yet another domestic sorrow and this time one which was to affect him deeply in his work. Hiley, who had cried wolf over his health so often, now fell ill in earnest. Early in the year he announced that he could go on with his work no longer. Sidmouth was deeply distressed. He told his brother that he would not be able to carry on without his help and, in so saying, he did not overdramatise his feelings.[1] But reluctantly he had to accept that this time his brother's threat was not one which he could be laughed or cajoled into withdrawing. In mid-April Hiley resigned and retired in great pain to his country home.

"I need not tell you how much you are in my thoughts," Sidmouth wrote to him.[2] "It is grievous that we are not nearer to each other . . . Your separation from us is felt with real regret by every individual (I am convinced) in this office." He wrote to notify the Prince Regent of his brother's resignation.[3] Henry Clive was to be the successor. ". . . a sensible, well-informed man and a barrister . . . I think he will do very well; but I have lost a limb which cannot be replaced." It would not have been difficult to find an incumbent more assiduous at least than his predecessor. But this was not what Sidmouth asked. Sadly though Hiley might have idled, he had still worked with his brother for many years. They understood each other's minds and each other's methods. Sidmouth was now more than sixty years old. His dependence on established friendships had been fortified with the years. The pain at seeing his brother retire into ill-health was redoubled by the thought that he would have to learn to work with a stranger.

It was not long before he had to learn to do without his brother in life as well as in the office. Hiley's condition deteriorated rapidly, inflammation of the bladder arose in an aggravated form, and on 12th June, 1818, Sidmouth arrived in haste at Langford Court to find that he was too late and that his brother had died the night before.

"Good-sense, knowledge of mankind and suavity of manner" were those of Hiley's virtues which the official obituary chose particularly to laud. They were an odd selection to apply to a man whose judgment, tactlessness, intemperance and indifference to the feelings of others had done so much to mar his brother's career. Hiley was one of the most self-centred men to have played a part even in that playground for egocentrics, the House of Commons. He was vain, indolent and malicious; proud of his own slight talents and quick to denigrate the powers of those immeasurably more worthy. Yet at the same time he was oddly unambitious, prepared, if sometimes reluctantly, to serve his brother in relatively menial roles and completely loyal in that service. His penchant for needless intrigue and political skull-duggery made enemies of many who might otherwise have been neutrals or even friends. But his talent for organisation and parliamentary guerrilla warfare should not be underestimated. It was partly his fault that the Addingtonians found themselves so largely isolated between 1806 and 1812; his brother might have been distrusted by the Pittites, Hiley was loathed. But it was also to a great extent his doing that the little group of Addingtonians held together during these difficult years. He acted as an unpaid and unofficial parliamentary Whip; in this pursuit he proved himself zealous and indefatigable. He also made himself thoroughly unpopular; but only the most consummate artist can be both lovable and a successful party manager. Hiley never rated highly the affection of his fellow politicians. He sacrificed it to what he considered the good of the Addingtonians and, on the whole, in so doing gave his brother reason to be grateful.

By 1818 need for this kind of party manipulation was over. Hiley, in political terms, was expendable. But to Sidmouth, as well as being a dearly loved brother, he was a political confidant and counsellor. Only in Bragge-Bathurst did Sidmouth have comparable trust and even that relationship lacked the almost empathic intimacy which linked the two brothers. The death of Hiley did not cripple Sidmouth politically but it removed one of the main factors which had made politics tolerable. From this period Sidmouth thought more and more of retirement and withdrawal from the struggle; not just as a means of securing an agreeable rest but in recognition of the fact that, physically and psychologically, he no longer felt himself fit for office.

*   *   *   *   *

There were plenty to concur with this opinion and to write off Sidmouth as already half-way out of the Cabinet chamber. "The general notion," wrote Thomas Grenville in January, 1819,[1] "is that the leaders in the Ministry are doing all they can to oust Sidmouth in order to make room for Peel, and Peel seems so well satisfied of this that he is making quite common cause with them in that hope." Grenville was deceived both as to the attitude of Peel, who had little wish for promotion at that moment, and, still more, as to that of Sidmouth's colleagues. The "leaders in the Ministry" were perfectly content with Sidmouth's handling of the internal situation and asked nothing better than that he should continue to grapple with it. So long as a policy of repression was deemed essential by the Tory leaders, Sidmouth was held to be the man best qualified to apply it. Only the growing strength of the liberals within the Government and the new respectability of the movement for parliamentary reform gave any hint that this might one day change.

In 1819 it did not seem that such a change could be around the corner. A bad harvest in 1818 and difficult conditions in some of the more vulnerable industries gave fresh stimulus to the agitation for reform. Radical meetings were held in many parts of Britain and would-be voters revived and refurbished the traditional technique of the "mock-election." In July a vast crowd of—from the point of view of the Government—embarrassingly sober and well-ordered protestants triumphantly elected Sir Charles Wolseley as their representative for Birmingham. Sir Charles had been present at the taking of the Bastille and was apt to speak as if he personally had stormed the ramparts. That such a man should be "elected" Member, however unofficial the election, was more than Ministers could stomach. A fortnight earlier Wolseley had spoken with even more than his usual indiscretion at a meeting at Stockport. Now he was hurriedly arrested on a charge of sedition and sentenced to eighteen months' imprisonment. When the constable who had arrested him was shot outside the court-house Lord Sidmouth was once more convinced that England stood on the verge of revolution.

It is a mark of his alarm that even in mid-August he did not feel it safe to be away from his office for more than a few days. When he did escape to his favourite resort of Broadstairs it was only to write anxiously[1]: ". . . the laws are not strong enough for the times, but they must be made so, if it is meant to afford the country a reasonable hope of permanent tranquillity." With Parliament in recess and few members of the Cabinet imitating the assiduity of the Home Secretary, he knew there was no hope for legislative reform in the near future. Instead he applied himself to stiffening the morale of the forces of order so that they would do their best with the inadequate weapons at their disposal. An occasion to show their mettle was quick in coming.

Manchester was next to attempt what Birmingham had done and elect its own "legislatorial attorney." Henry Hunt was selected to play the part of Wolseley; a chance to occupy the limelight which he found irresistibly enticing. The meeting at which he was to be elected representative was first fixed for 9th August; then, on the advice of lawyers who told the sponsors that the purpose might be unconstitutional, deferred to 16th August and assigned the new task of considering "the propriety of adopting the most legal and effectual means of obtaining Reform of the Commons House of Parliament." When the first meeting was projected Sidmouth, who had been thoroughly alarmed by stories of nocturnal drilling in the countryside around Manchester, wrote to the magistrates to encourage them to face revolution boldly. He told them that he expected occasion to arise "for their energy to display itself" and assured them that they would not lack "the cordial support of the government."[1] The change in the published aims of the meeting may have reassured him a little but treason was hardly less malevolent because hidden under some milk-and-water guise. He knew there was a risk of trouble but faced the outcome of the meeting with no more trepidation than he had shown on a hundred such occasions in the past. Certainly there was no reason for him to suspect that the display of energy which he had called for from the magistrates was to reverberate down the ages and damn his own name to posterity.

The events at Peterloo have entered into British folk-lore. The name itself, like Amritsar or Buchenwald, has acquired a rich and emotive significance, so that merely to mention it can be to declare loyalty to an ideology and to denounce a form of government. It has become the symbol of the struggle of the British working-classes for parliamentary reform and the savage repression of that movement by a reactionary oligarchy. The image it invokes is one of charging dragoons and butchered babes, a spectacular hecatomb in which the flower of progressive England was ruthlessly put to the sword. On the whole, the symbolic importance of Peterloo has proved justified. Whether in the occurrence itself or in the gloss which has been put upon it, Peterloo was a watershed in British political history. The movement for parliamentary reform gained its maturity under the sabres of the Dragoons. Yet the image of Peterloo far transcends reality and its significance, though in essence merited, is altogether unjustified in detail. For there was little fodder for romantics in the prosaic doings of that mournful day.

Not that what happened was not bad enough. On 16th August, 1819, a vast but orderly crowd of men and women converged on St. Peter's Fields on the edge of Manchester. Among those present were undoubtedly a handful of would-be revolutionaries ready to incite anyone to violence and a rather larger group of rowdies eager for a fight or for a chance to break a few windows. But the prevailing tone of the crowd was one of sobriety and decorum; decent and diligent citizens in their Sunday best come to hear their betters explain to them what should be done to put things right at Westminster.

Henry Hunt was neither sober nor decorous and it was not entirely foolish of the magistrates to assume that any meeting addressed by him was likely to end in tears. For the Manchester Justices to have arrested him on arrival and declared the meeting disbanded might have been high-handed but would at least have reduced the likelihood of violence. For them to have allowed him to speak would have involved some risk but, given the temper of the crowd, would probably not have led to trouble. The disastrous compromise which the magistrates adopted was to dither uncertainly until Hunt had reached the platform and begun his speech and then to decide that the meeting was illegal and that the orator must be arrested.

Six troops of the 15th Hussars were lurking in the background but the magistrates were anxious to avoid invoking the help of the regulars unless all other measures failed. They therefore compounded the mischief which their hesitation had already caused by sending in the Yeomanry. These incompetent amateurs may possibly have had their value as week-end soldiers but had no inkling how to control their horses or themselves when driving through the midst of a hostile mob. Within a few minutes they had lost their formation and were scattered, helpless, among the audience they had hoped to disperse. Their position was more one of indignity than danger but this was not apparent to the magistrates. Belatedly, they called in the Hussars. The evidence suggests that all, or almost all the soldiers were at pains to avoid bloodshed where possible. But cavalry armed with sabres could not ride down a crowd of 60,000 and that crowd could not flee in panic through the narrow entrances of St. Peter's Fields without there being many casualties. Nor could the Yeomanry resist the urge to expunge the memory of their humiliation by recklessly lashing out at any victims within their range. In the circumstances it is, indeed, remarkable that only eleven participants were killed.

At first Sidmouth hardly seemed aware that anything serious had happened. "The proceedings," he wrote the day after he received the news,[1] ". . . . were not of an ordinary character, but they will, I trust, prove a salutary lesson to modern reformers. Hunt and his associates are in custody, and their flags etc. have been seized or destroyed by the special constables and soldiery, all of whom behaved with the greatest spirit and temper, but forbearance became impossible."

But it was not long before he realised that, by some at least, the proceedings were deemed to be most extraordinary. The Whigs seized on the chance to attack the Government and demands were made for a judicial inquiry and the punishment of those responsible for the massacre. It is doubtful if Sidmouth ever felt that there was much wrong in principle with the activities of the magistrates; the most that he would have been likely to charge them with would have been a certain inefficiency. But even if he had been beset by doubts, the uproar from the Opposition would have compelled him to stifle them. As a Minister he felt it his duty to defend all those who acted in general pursuit of his directives. As the Minister charged with the security of the nation he believed that if the magistrates were now disowned no others would be ready to risk their position by resolute action against the forces of disorder. "We all felt sure, Lord Sidmouth," remarked one of the magistrates, "that if you thought we had done *right* you would uphold us."[2] They had acted in good faith and in defence of the Constitution; that was right enough for Sidmouth and he upheld them without hesitation and without restraint.

His first step was to solicit from the Prince Regent a letter approving the action of the magistrates. This was quickly forthcoming; the Prince highly commended the part which everyone in authority had played and spoke warmly of the "forbearance" which the commander of the regular soldiers had displayed.[3] Promptly Sidmouth wrote to the Earls of Derby and of Stamford instructing them to convey the thanks of the Prince Regent to the magistrates and yeomanry.

Sidmouth's action in thus championing the perpetrators of Peterloo caused almost more uproar than the massacre itself. "Lord Sidmouth," said the Duke of Wellington in admiration, "The Radicals will impeach you for this, by God they will!"[1] They did their best and his impeachment has been upheld in the pages of history if not the Palace of Westminster. He did little to make their task more difficult. Obviously Sidmouth could not have condemned the magistrates but he could still have played his hand more cautiously. Indeed, the way had been left open for an honourable retreat. At almost the same moment as he urged energy on the Manchester magistrates Hobhouse had written[2] to them on his behalf to lay down the limits within which such energy could properly be displayed. The right course for the authorities to follow, said Hobhouse, was to record what happened and only to consider subsequently whether a prosecution would be in order. ". . . even if they should utter sedition or proceed to the election of a representative, Lord Sidmouth is of the opinion that it will be the wisest course to abstain from any endeavour to disperse the mob, unless they should proceed to acts of felony or riot." The magistrates, therefore, had acted in defiance of Sidmouth's instructions. He could at least have hinted publicly that this was so. He could have made some concession to the genuine sense of outrage felt by many who otherwise had nothing good to say for the activities of the radicals and the reformers. The fact that he did not shows insensitivity, lack of political acumen and an underdeveloped social conscience. It also shows a characteristic loyalty to his subordinates and indifference to his own popularity. Ignoble though the cause may have been, his behaviour was that of a man who did not lack integrity, dignity or a sense of what was honourable. It lifted him from the ranks of time-servers who infest the parliaments of every land. For that very reason it is perhaps an explanation of why he was not more successful as a politician.

There is another, less charitable explanation of Sidmouth's attitude.[3] According to this orders would have been issued by the Home Office subsequent to Hobhouse's letter of 4th August which instructed the Manchester magistrates, with considerable precision, both to allow Hunt to take his place in the crowd and then to arrest him. Any theory propounded by so considerable an authority as Thompson deserves careful study but, as he himself admits, no direct evidence to support it exists in the Home Office papers. It could be, as he suggests, that such incriminating documents have been destroyed but it is surely easier to believe that they were never written? The Home Office can fairly be criticised for the looseness with which they habitually supervised the local magistrates. Lack of detailed directions was a constant complaint. It seems unreasonable to suppose that, in this one instance, their control was strict enough to dictate the whole pattern of blunders which led to disaster. "Peterloo," concluded Read in his detailed study of the massacre,[1] ". . . was never desired or precipitated by the Liverpool Ministry . . . If the Manchester magistrates had followed the spirit of Home Office Policy there would never have been a 'massacre'. " In the circumstances this seems the fairest verdict. Certainly it is more in line with Sidmouth's aversion to violence and his determination, wherever possible, to take the heat out of every conflict. His own assertion, that the news of the bloodshed at Manchester came as a complete surprise, can be accepted. The reasonable ground of criticism remains that the surprise, when it came, should have seemed a great deal more unpleasant than it did.

The rest of the Government, including even such a comparative liberal as Canning, were whole-heartedly behind him. "To let down the magistrates," wrote the latter,[2] "would be to invite their resignations and to lose all gratuitous service in the counties liable to disturbance for ever. It is, to be sure, very provoking that the magistrates, right as they were in principle, and nearly right in practice, should have spoilt the completeness of their case by half an hour's precipitation." It is hard to see what an extra half-hour would have achieved but there were anyhow few observers ready to copy Canning's calm and faintly cynical detachment. The riding down by the dragoons of decorous and defenceless citizens, even without the embellishments of drawn sabres and fatal casualties among the women and children, was admirably designed to disquiet the public conscience. The Whigs and Radicals had no intention of letting it rest again. With Parliament in recess they relied on county meetings to stir up indignation and exploit the Government's failings to the uttermost.

The first meeting of protest was held by the always turbulent Common Council of London. The Mayor and Aldermen, cheerfully prejudging the finding of the courts, concluded that the meeting at Manchester was undoubtedly legal and petitioned the Prince Regent to institute an immediate inquiry and bring the "guilty perpetrators" of the assault "to signal and condign punishment." The Regent was scandalised by their impertinence and Sidmouth more so. In the speech from the throne which the latter drafted the Regent expressed his deep regret at the tone of the petition and lauded the magistrates for their "firm, faithful and active discharge of their duty." "With the circumstances which preceded the late meeting," commented the Regent coldly on the Common Council's memorandum, "you must be unacquainted; and of those which attended it you appear to have been incorrectly informed." The petition of the Common Council was certainly more concerned with dramatic effect than prosy accuracy. But with all its hyperbole it still reflected the feelings of the people more faithfully than the robust defence of Sidmouth or the modulated regrets of George Canning.

Yorkshire followed London and in turn petitioned the Regent to avenge the martyred saints of Peterloo. To make matters worse, the meeting was convened, addressed and presided over by Earl Fitzwilliam, His Majesty's Lord Lieutenant for the West Riding. Fitzwilliam was a Whig but, though he had often differed from the Government, had so far kept his opposition within the bounds of decorum. He had also been one of Sidmouth's most able and enthusiastic collaborators in the suppression of Luddism. But not even such good service could excuse this act of independence. Sidmouth quickly convinced Liverpool that Fitzwilliam must go and the Lord Lieutenancy was placed in the safely Tory hands of the young Lord Lascelles.

The county meetings went on in other parts of England. Counter-petitions sponsored by friends of the Government did something to reduce their potency but the current of opinion still ran high against the men of Peterloo. Sidmouth took events more tragically than most of his colleagues. He was convinced that the morale of the nation was being subverted. The public, he wrote,[1] "has been more inflamed and misled by unfounded assumptions and false statements than upon any other occasion within my recollection." He misinterpreted strong disapproval of authoritarian methods and a growing demand for constitutional reform as support for revolution and a lust to destroy the ruling classses. The peril which faced the country was, he was convinced, more urgent than at any time in the last few years, perhaps, indeed, than ever in Britain's history. It was far from being the first time that Sidmouth had misjudged the situation but, for perhaps the only time in his career, he was near to having lost his head.

It was his conviction that England could only be saved by the immediate convening of Parliament and the strengthening of the forces of authority by new laws and a larger army. His faith in the power of his fellow Members to dispel danger was touchingly complete. "Before the meeting of parliament was announced, all was terror," he wrote of 1792,[1] "as soon as the proclamation appeared, the loyal were animated and the disaffected abashed . . . Such will be the case at the end of this month." But to his dismay he was unable to communicate his sense of urgency to Lord Liverpool and his other colleagues. Liverpool agreed that new laws would probably be needed but blandly argued that this was all the more reason for keeping the meeting of Parliament to the usual date since the preparatory work would take so long. In the meantime he and the other Ministers continued in the pastoral pursuits appropriate to an English summer. Bitterly Sidmouth complained that it was a fortnight since he had seen any of his colleagues.[2] On 1st October[3] he wrote to Liverpool to express his:

. . . deep regret that the determination to assemble Parliament has been so long delayed.

The existing means of stopping the progress, not merely of sedition, but of treason, not merely insurrection but rebellion, have long since proved to be utterly insufficient, but hitherto my colleagues have remained unconvinced of the imperious and urgent necessity of advising the adoption of the only measure, which would of itself, animate the loyal and awe the disaffected, and by which alone effectual means can be provided to meet and overcome a danger greater, as I am firmly and deliberately convinced, than any to which the country has been exposed since the accession of the present Royal Family to the throne.

I write to you on this subject, as I have repeatedly spoken, in the fulness of my heart—Health and comfort I have willingly sacrificed to a sense of private honour and public duty; and there is no further sacrifice, be it what it might, that I an not ready and determined to make, if required by such considerations—But I feel, and have felt for some time past, that whilst the country is suffering from the want, as I conceive, of those decisive and efficient measures, which the crisis calls for, my reputation is suffering also; though I trust there has been no want of vigour or promptitude in the employment of the inefficient and inadequate means, which the existing laws have placed in my hands.

Sidmouth was by no means alone in believing that an emergency of unparalleled danger was upon the country. The Grenvilles, that "select band of moderate Whigs," as the second Duke of Buckingham was sometimes pleased to call them, communicated anxiously with each other about the inertia of the Government and the need to raise more yeomanry,[1] while the Marquis of Huntly[2] wrote to pledge that "Plenty of Highlanders will follow me to the foot of the throne and bleed with me to the last in defending and protecting it." As Home Secretary, Sidmouth was uniquely exposed to the full blast of alarmist reports from the provinces which, as in every period of tension, poured in from the panic-stricken, the self-important and the mischief makers. Plumer Ward, then Clerk of the Ordnance, called on Lord Sidmouth on 27th October after a visit to the North.[3] He found him:

. . . up to the eyes in papers . . . We immediately fell upon affairs. The designs of the Radicals of course. I told him I had just been through their country, as well as all over the north, which for the most part I found very peaceable, and even civil, and very *anti-Radical*. He shook his head, and pointing to volumes of papers, said, if I knew their contents, I would not say so, for the pictures were frightful . . .

Those volumes of papers, neatly labelled "Disturbances," now rest in the Public Record Office. Even with the benefit of hindsight the picture which they conjure up is frightful enough. To the unfortunate Sidmouth, already conditioned to believe the worst, they spelt the imminent end of civilisation in England. At least, he was resolved, it was not going to end through fault of his.

378

Liverpool eventually succumbed and agreed that Parliament should be opened a few weeks early. Sidmouth was left a month in which to prepare new laws to protect the State. "Better late than never," commented Lord Eldon, and laid at the disposal of the Home Secretary his massive experience in the drafting of illiberal legislation. With the Duke of Wellington urging them on from the background it seemed that here were assembled in their richest form all the fears, inhibitions and prejudices which had ever obsessed the British reactionary. No excess might have been beyond them. The chief surprise about the Six Acts, as the legislation which Sidmouth introduced in Parliament in November, 1819, is usually known, is their moderation. There was no suggestion that Habeas Corpus should once more be suspended and the only Bill which threatened directly the liberty of the individual was that relating to seditious meetings. This Bill, which simultaneously defined in restrictive terms what could constitute a "legal meeting" and gave the authorities greater powers to break up those which were illegal, could only have been justified by circumstances of the most imminent peril. It is highly unlikely that such circumstances in fact existed; it is certain that Lord Sidmouth believed they did and that he was sincerely convinced he was asking for no more than the minimum essential to prevent bloodshed and probably the overthrow of Government.

Two other Bills were aimed at the Press: one imposing heavy penalties on the publisher of a seditious libel, the other subjecting pamphlets to the same fourpenny tax as applied to newspapers. The latter would have done considerable harm to the forces pressing for orderly and constitutional reform and benefited only whatever anarchic elements existed in the country; luckily for the reformers, Sidmouth and England it was in practice put to little use. The remaining Bills, respectively forbidding unlawful drilling, allowing Justices in certain circumstances to search private property for arms and speeding up the administration of justice, did not give much cause for complaint even to the inveterate enemy of authoritarian Government.

The debate on Peterloo and on the Six Acts should have given the Whigs a matchless opportunity to destroy the Government's reputation and establish themselves as an honourable alternative, intent on justice and equity yet, in the long run, more able to protect the interests of property than those who relied solely on ferocious reaction to achieve their ends. The fact that they failed was partly due to the weakness of Tierney, the parliamentary leader, but even more to the deep lack of conviction of many of the Whig leaders in the doctrines to which they paid lip service. They were committed to parliamentary reform but had the gravest doubts about the morals and motives of those who would benefit by their success. Their spirit was to change but, at the end of 1819, the Whigs for the most part conducted their affairs with the gingerly half-heartedness of one sowing dragons' teeth in the secret hope that nothing would come up.

But though the proceedings in Parliament may have had the atmosphere of a charade, there can be no doubting the sincerity of the handful of upper and middle-class Radicals and the politically conscious among the working classes. Their denunciations of Sidmouth were as ferocious as they were frequent, only Castlereagh was able to match the richness of his unpopularity. In that magnificent piece of invective "The Masque of Anarchy" Castlereagh, indeed, came off the worse, being cast for Murder, while Sidmouth on his crocodile escaped with the title of Hypocrisy. But Shelley struck a better balance in his "Similes for two Political Characters."

> As from an ancestral oak
> Two empty ravens sound their clarion,
> Yell by yell and croak by croak,
> When they scent the noonday smoke
> Of fresh human carrion:
>
> As two gibb'ring night-birds flit
> From their bowers of deadly yew
> Through the night to frighten it,
> When the moon is in a fit
> And the stars are none, or few:
>
> As a shark and dogfish wait
> Under an Atlantic isle
> For the negro ship whose freight
> Is the theme of their debate,
> Wrinkling their red gills the while:

Are ye, two vultures sick for battle,
Two scorpions under one wet stone,
Two bloodless wolves whose dry throats rattle,
Two crows perched on the murrained cattle,
Two vipers tangled into one.

Such venomous, if unsophisticated abuse caused Sidmouth little concern. Almost he revelled in his unpopularity, convinced that it sprang only from those whom he sought to hold in check and was therefore a tribute to his success. Thoughts of his personal security rarely concerned him. His utmost concession to prudence was to carry a loaded pistol on the seat beside him when he drove himself late at night and in an open carriage from the centre of London to his home in Richmond Park. A few months after Peterloo, when the trial of the Queen had raised his unpopularity still higher, he found himself alone with Lord Castlereagh in the middle of an angry mob. "Here we go," he remarked blandly, "the two most popular men in England." "Yes," replied his companion with equal calm, "through a grateful and admiring multitude." Sidmouth would no doubt have resented it if he had been physically assaulted and his life endangered, but he would also have greeted the occurrence with the mild satisfaction of a man who sees events about to prove his point.

Events were indeed about to prove his point, or perhaps to prove that a policy of repression can only lead to further violence. In February, 1820, came the Cato Street Conspiracy, that strange mixture of the macabre, the farcical and the pathetic which enjoys in the esteem of the English schoolboy a place second only to that of the Gunpowder Plot. A group of conspirators, some reluctant, some deranged, all credulous, ill-informed and impracticable, met in what should have been the darkest secrecy to plot the murder of every member of the Cabinet. The leader was Arthur Thistlewood, who had already served a year's imprisonment for challenging Lord Sidmouth to a duel; in his case at least rancour against Sidmouth was one of the driving forces. "I will enter the room first," declared James Ings,[1] "I will go in with a brace of pistols, a cutlass and a knife in my pocket, and after the two swordsmen have despatched them, I will cut every head off that is in the room and Lord Castlereagh's head and

Lord Sidmouth's I will bring away in a bag. For this purpose I will provide two bags."

The police were forewarned, a false Cabinet dinner arranged to bring the conspiracy to a head, and the conspirators arrested as they met above a stable in Cato Street. By some bungle the soldiers who should have supported the police were late in arriving and some of the would-be murderers escaped. All, however, or anyway all of any prominence, were arrested the following day. At least one conspirator, George Edwards, had been in the service of the police from the start, and two other members of the gang had betrayed their fellow plotters. The incompetence and incoherence of the organisation had not been such as to tax the police severely but what they had had to do, they had done well. Sidmouth, who had personally supervised the operation, showed patience, calm and his usual courage. "The Duke of Wellington upon home service,"[1] was the comment of King George IV, as the Regent had just become.

It is beyond question that these unfortunates were driven to their ghastly yet futile enterprise by the injustice of a social system which they could see no other way to rectify. Murder, still more mass murder, can hardly be approved as a means of achieving even the most desirable political ends, but it is hard to know where, in such a case, the blame can most fairly be laid. Even from the Olympian heights of the twentieth century it would be rash to attempt any moral judgment or to weigh the guilt of society against the guilt of its victims.

There remains the question whether, within the framework of the plot itself, the Government had abided by the unwritten rules for proper conduct. It has been argued that, since they had ample warning of the existence of a plot, they should have checked the conspirators at an early stage before their plans had matured and so many others became deeply implicated. More damagingly it has been suggested that the informers who kept the police posted on day-to-day events were themselves no better than *agents provocateurs*, whose active participation turned the plot from an idle dream into an active nightmare.

The first charge is hardly serious; only when the conspiracy had advanced almost to the point of action could authority be sure that evidence sufficient to win a conviction would be available. The lives of all the Ministers were at stake and, in the circumstances, the police would have been grossly irresponsible to run the risk that the principal conspirators might escape and renew their plans in greater secrecy.

The second charge is graver. It is clear from the Home Office Records that Edwards had been implicated in the plot from the earliest stages. The question is whether he positively egged on his fellow conspirators into violent action beyond that which they anyway intended; whether, on the contrary, he sought to restrain them; or whether he played a passive role. Stanhope, in his stimulating account of the Conspiracy,[1] settles on the whole for the first solution. His main argument, as he states it in a sentence, is: "If you are going to employ a spy to mix with conspirators, he must show enthusiasm for the conspiracy; and he will have to contribute ideas and acts towards its contrivance. A silent, inactive spy would soon be suspect."

The argument does not seem conclusive. In every group of men bent on a common enterprise there will be those who lead, those who hang back and a majority who tamely follow. Certainly this is true of the Cato Street conspirators. It would have been indiscreet of Edwards to associate himself too obviously with the second group but equally he would have been bungling his job if he had appeared too often among the leaders. Unobtrusiveness is an essential prerequisite for successful spying and the task of informer can rarely be combined with that of leader. At their trial the accused naturally sought to prove that Edwards had egged them on to new excesses, indeed that he had been one of the moving forces behind the project. Their evidence was neither consistent nor convincing. Edwards may on occasion have gone too far in encouraging his co-conspirators[2] but most of the time encouragement would have been superfluous. Sidmouth knew well that Thistlewood would hang himself and the rest of his gang if left to his own devices and the sensible instructions to have given his spy would have been to hold his peace and let things take their course.

"What have we found?" concluded Stanhope. "That Lord Sidmouth endeavoured to combat evil with evil. What statesman has ever done otherwise?"[3] The comment is fair enough; spies are a dirty and a dangerous weapon and whoever employs them must accept the responsibility for their misdeeds. But though Edwards was undoubtedly unscrupulous and indiscreet he does not seem to have sought systematically to push the conspirators towards violence. There is no evidence at all that such a course would have been approved or even tolerated by the Home Secretary. Of that crime at least Sidmouth must be acquitted.

Sidmouth was convinced that the Conspiracy, like every similar incident, was part of a nation-wide intrigue. "It is certain,' he wrote to Bloomfield, the King's secretary,[1] "that the Committees of the Disaffected in Leeds, Manchester, Carlisle and Glasgow expected to hear of a blow having been struck last week in London." Certainly Thistlewood tried to persuade his followers that the country stood ready to leap to arms at the first news that the coup had succeeded. But it was remarkably naïve of Sidmouth to be taken in. The trial produced nothing to support his fears. Indeed, it revealed only the depths of despair and impotent resentment into which these men had been degraded. In his defence at the trial Thomas Brunt declared: "Lord Castlereagh and Sidmouth have been the cause of the death of millions. I conspired to put them out of the world, but I did not intend to commit high treason. In undertaking to kill them and their fellow ministers, I did not expect to save my own life but I was determined to die a martyr in my country's cause and to avenge the innocent blood shed at Manchester."

He did not conspire and die entirely in vain. The Cato Street Conspiracy had an almost traumatic effect upon the England of 1820. Suddenly there were many, hitherto unconscious, who realised that there must be something violently wrong with social system which could drive a man like Brunt to such a declaration. The macabre folly of the 23rd February had a sharply sobering effect on reactionaries and radicals alike. "From that day," wrote Cobbett,[2] "the tone of the sons of corruption became less insolent and audacious." But so also did the tone of the sons of liberty become less truculent. When a dead end is reached one can either batter one's head against it until extinction or pause and seek a way round. It is the peculiar wisdom of the British that they habitually choose the latter course. Peterloo had been a warning light, Cato Street continued the enlightenment of the people. Imperceptibly a new course was set, a course which was to lead directly to the Reform Bill of 1832.

To Sidmouth the political lull which followed the conspiracy was proof that repression had succeeded. The walls of the citadel were inviolate and it was he who had saved them. To-day one can see that the citadel was crumbling from within. While Sidmouth fought his rearguard action the England which he defended was quietly preparing to negotiate peace with the future. It is undoubtedly true that, left to Sidmouth, such a peace would never have been negotiated but before he be condemned outright it should also be considered that, but for his rearguard action, there might never have been a breathing space in which the negotiations could take place. In the beech woods of the New Forest it is part of the cycle of nature that the unsightly holly should dominate the scene while the old tree falls and the new beech grows to take its place. Few people may positively like the holly but only the most ill-informed of foresters would deny that, in its graceless way, it plays a useful role.

* * * * *

By the summer of 1820, civil disorder in England seemed at an end. "To London, and wasted my day sadly," wrote Wilberforce in his journal.[1] "Castlereagh in Kent; Sidmouth, Devonshire; Bathurst, Gloucestershire—curious that all absent, and, I fear, most improper." He would not have found so relaxed an atmosphere a year before.

But any peace which Sidmouth might have earned was quickly imperilled by the sordid antics of the royal family. Since 1814 the Princess of Wales had been leading a life of flamboyant frivolity in Italy and Germany. The Prince Regent, while conducting his own life with equal lack of dignity, spied busily on his wife and accumulated a massive dossier of gossip about her amatory and other adventures. From the moment that their daughter, Princess Charlotte, died in 1817 he began to agitate for a divorce. His Ministers played for time and only the death of George III in January, 1820, forced them finally to commit themselves. They were in little doubt what their attitude must be. The standing of the royal house was already weak, the fresh scandal of a divorce could finally try too high the patience of the new King's ever less faithful subjects. After long discussion the Cabinet agreed unanimously on a Minute advising against further action so long as the Queen remained abroad. On 11th February Liverpool, Sidmouth and the Lord Chancellor were received in audience to hear the King's comments. George IV greeted them cordially[1]: "He expressed himself with a particular warmth of affection to Lord Sidmouth, and assured him that he had long considered him as his truest and most sincere friend." But no amount of affability could alter the fact that he was still bent on divorce. Only a battle of several days with his Ministers and the promise that the Queen's name would be excluded from the Liturgy induced him temporarily to change his mind.

"They have bound themselves to ask for a divorce if the Queen comes to England," wrote Princess Lieven.[2] "They are confident of preventing her from coming. We shall see." Her scepticism was justified. Incensed by the contemptuous treatment given her by the courts of Europe, the Queen resolved to return to London and to claim, not a restitution of conjugal rights—a prospect as appalling to her as to her husband—but at least the perquisites of her position. She landed in England on 5th June and every enemy of Government surged to her defence in delighted anticipation of the embarrassment that would be caused to King and Ministers. In retort the King sent to the House of Lords a green bag containing all the evidence which he had accumulated to inculpate his wife. A Secret Committee was set up to examine the papers and to report what action was desirable.

Sidmouth, like every other Minister, wanted only to remain detached from this distasteful affair. As Home Secretary he could hardly avoid membership of the Secret Committee but it was his hope that he need play no larger part. His hope was swiftly proved illusion. Sidmouth's influence with the King was far too valuable for his colleagues willingly to do without it. If the King were allowed to play his hand in his own way he could be relied on to destroy the Government and imperil the very existence of the throne. Every weapon must be used which might help to check a destructive show of royal recalcitrance.

Given the history of the relationship between Sidmouth and King George IV, it may seem ironic that the influence of the Home Secretary should now prove to be the most effective weapon of which Ministers disposed. By the Prince of Wales, Sidmouth had been denounced as an upstart and derided as a prosy bore. By the Prince Regent he had been gradually accepted as a safe, loyal and conscientious servant. Now, by the King, he found himself valued above all the other Ministers. He could not fail to be gratified by this *volte-face* in the royal affections yet showed little wish to render them warmer still. The relationship was close but it was the King who sought to make it closer and Sidmouth who contrived to keep the courtship within the bounds of propriety.

At times, indeed, the King's obvious predilection for his Home Secretary caused embarrassment to Lord Sidmouth and chagrin to Lord Liverpool. When Canning resigned it was Sidmouth, not the Prime Minister, who was sent for to advise the King.[1] Sidmouth, in fact, was punctilious in referring the question to his colleagues, but the slight was still unpleasant for Liverpool to swallow. In June, when Liverpool was threatening resignation, the King went so far as to send for Sidmouth and press him strongly to become Prime Minister.[2] Sidmouth refused even to consider the possibility and, when the King asked him where else he could look, merely advised him to stick to the Minister he had got.

But though the King's partiality for Lord Sidmouth might occasionally be galling to Lord Liverpool, he did not hesitate to make use of it. Sidmouth was enlisted as a reluctant go-between; the Cabinet's representative specially charged with breaking disagreeable news to the King and bringing him to reason in times of crisis. When the King became overexcited by a friendly reception which had been given him on his way to the Chapel Royal and wove fantasies based on his resurgent popularity, it was Sidmouth who was sent to undeceive him. In terms that, though polite, were brutally frank the King was told that he was still execrated by the lower classes and that there was no reason to expect a change of heart in the foreseeable future. With equal insouciance Sidmouth would cross the King in his most cherished projects. When George IV resolved to appoint Lord Conyngham, husband of his latest love, Master of the Horse, Lord Liverpool failed to make him change his mind. Sidmouth was then called in and argued that the appointment would have a bad effect on public opinion and give credence to much gossip which was not generally believed.[3] "Lord Sidmouth strongly urged the necessity of the King maintaining in the view of the people an exterior correctness of deportment, which if maintained leads away the people from enquiring minutely into what passes within . . ."[4] When the King wanted to dismiss Lord Grosvenor as Lord

Lieutenant of Flintshire, Sidmouth went even further and flatly refused to obey, stating[1]: "that if he remained in office it could only be carried into effect through himself, and that he never would put his hand to the letter . . ."

In spite of these rebuffs the King remained convinced that Sidmouth was the most valuable and trustworthy of his Ministers. Liverpool continued to use him whenever it was essential to bring pressure to bear at Court. Such occasions were to arise frequently as the Queen's trial unwound its sordid course through the second half of 1820. The King consistently overestimated the strength of his own position and discounted the popularity of the Queen. He was convinced that every delay and set-back stemmed from the feebleness or incompetence of his Ministers and he relentlessly harassed them in his efforts to force events to a satisfactory conclusion.

Before the Secret Committee had reported, indeed almost before the Queen was well ashore, the London mob had given a taste of the troubles that were in store. On three successive nights they stoned Lord Sidmouth's London house. The second night was something of a debacle. A large family party was dining in the house and, with Lord Exmouth at their head, surged out in counter-attack and put the startled rioters to rout. Next night the mob gathered in greater strength. Before the attack had well begun Sidmouth drew up in a carriage in the company of Lord Eldon and the Duke of Wellington. "Let me out; I must get out!" cried Sidmouth. "You shall not alight; drive on!" replied Wellington. The case for a tactical withdrawal was strengthened a moment later when the window of the carriage was shattered and the party dashed on to safety; returning a few minutes later with a party of the Life Guards.[2]

Such incidents were not to be taken tragically but Sidmouth had good reason to wonder what might happen if public excitement were to go on mounting. On 17th August the Queen's trial, as it can most conveniently be described, began in the House of Lords. For eighty days London endured the monstrous spectacle of the royal family washing its dirty linen in public. Few people were less deserving of sympathy than Queen Caroline nor was the feeling for her in London genuinely deep, yet how could anyone justifiably condemn her "licentious, disgraceful and vicious" conduct without doing the same by her still more licentious, disgraceful and vicious spouse? Every day angry crowds gathered outside the House of Lords to cheer the Queen and jeer at every-one believed to favour the King. "The Metropolis remains quiet," reported Sidmouth on 22nd September,[1] "nor is there any reason to suppose that there is any intention, *at present*, to disturb the public peace." But such a guarantee, he knew too well, was barely valid for twenty-four hours ahead.

It was indeed a moment for despondency. The obscene antics of the royal family had involved in their disgrace all the traditional elements of the country. Church, aristocracy, country gentlemen alike seemed tarnished, somehow belittled, by the public vilifica-tion of what shreds were left the King of his dignity and his reputation. To Sidmouth the corner-stone of British life was threatened; ". . . all that just and honest pride which once gave comfort and dignity to a state of existence in this country, is nearly cancelled and obliterated."[2]

To make matters worse the brilliant defence of Brougham and the unreliability of the King's witnesses made a conviction ever more uncertain. "Matters here are in a critical state," wrote Sid-mouth on 27th October.[3] "Fear and faction are actively and not unsuccessfully at work; and it is possible that we may be in a minority, and that the fate of the government may be decided in a very few days." But unlike some of his colleagues he was con-vinced that the matter must be fought through. "Defeat itself is better than retreat"[4]; the Ministry was so far pledged to this unsavoury measure that they could not now abandon it.

On 6th November the majority in the House of Lords fell to a mere twenty-eight. Lord Grenville, formerly a champion of the trial, wrote to Liverpool to recommend that it be abandoned. The Prime Minister and several of his colleagues were ready to agree but Sidmouth objected strongly. Eventually a compromise was accepted; if the majority fell below ten then the Bill would be withdrawn.[5]

When a vote was taken on 10th November the majority for Ministers fell to nine. Lord Liverpool thereupon proposed that consideration of the Bill should be postponed for six months; a tactful euphemism to conceal its final demise. As London pre-pared to celebrate in an orgy of illuminations and window-breaking, Lords Liverpool and Sidmouth went sadly round to Carlton House. When Liverpool left the King refused to let

Sidmouth follow him, and "with the strongest expressions of reliance on Lord Sidmouth's friendship, told him that he found his body, his nerves and his spirits so shattered that he was unfit to cope with the difficulties of his station, and that he had serious thoughts of retiring to Hanover, and leaving this Kingdom to the Duke of York."[1] In the meantime he was reluctant to agree to the prorogation of Parliament and it took another visit from Sidmouth to convince him that this was necessary.

The long drawn out affair produced its strains inside as well as outside the Government. Canning's close friendship with Queen Caroline had made his position in the Cabinet unpleasant over the previous few months, it took the end of the trial to convince him that it was untenable. "It is a most unfortunate circumstance and involves us in very serious difficulties,"[2] wrote Sidmouth of Canning's resignation. "He means to go abroad. It appears to me to be very doubtful, . . . whether the Government will hold together. It is agreed to keep Canning's resignation a secret, if possible, till some arrangements can be made in consequence of it. I am sick and tired but I shall not shrink."

There is no reason to think that Sidmouth felt even a momentary satisfaction at this discomfiture of an old enemy. On the contrary, he genuinely regretted the loss which Canning's going inflicted on the Government. Filling the gap was the most urgent problem and he was anxious that Peel should be appointed. When this proved impossible he reluctantly sacrificed Bragge-Bathurst to fill the vacancy at the India Board. "I have cited your health and total want of familiarity with East Indian subjects, but in vain," he wrote in apology.[3] Bragge-Bathurst accepted the draft with dismay; he had never been among the more acquisitive of Sidmouth's friends and now his only ambition was for a quiet life. But Sidmouth's influence was still great and dutifully he consented to take the vacant office.

Though the Opposition did its best to keep the ill-treatment of the Queen before the public's eye, the public was disappointingly ready to let it drop. Both within Parliament and without there seemed a determination to forget the past and to let Ministers get on with governing the country. In the debate in February, 1821, in which the Opposition challenged the whole conduct of Government towards the Queen, Ministers stood firm on their principles and refused either to provide her with a palace or to put her name in the liturgy. They won an overwhelming majority of a hundred and forty-six. In the streets of London Queen Caroline was almost ignored and the King even greeted with occasional half-hearted cheers.

"Throughout the country the prospect is rather improving," wrote Sidmouth in nautical vein.[1] ". . . the weather has moderated, the wind is not so loud and violent, and our good old sea-boat is likely to ride out the storm without any damage to her hull, and with very little to her sail and rigging." Some praise, he may have felt, was due to the good old chief mate. At all events he was sure that the latter deserved a rest. As the crisis subsided Sidmouth looked more and more anxiously towards the time when he could give up office. Reluctantly he recognised that the moment might not yet have come but at least he was resolved to do all in his power to bring it nearer.

It was, indeed, not unreasonable of Sidmouth to think that he had earned his rest. He had now been Home Secretary for nearly ten years during a period of intense and almost continual disturbance. Throughout it his colleagues had given him their sympathy, encouragement and generalised support but had done remarkably little to make his burden lighter. He had spent his time cooped up in his offices in Whitehall immersed in a mass of indigestible and usually misleading papers. His health had survived the ordeal remarkably well; in the mid-sixties he still tumbled off his horse and held his own at table with the vigour of a man twenty years younger. But the pressure had been unremitting and was beginning to tell; he was painfully conscious of his age and more and more resolved to renounce the struggle.

Oddly enough he was now a more effective departmental minister than at any other period. Within the limits laid down by his personality he understood his job thoroughly and performed it well. The exaggerated fears which had swayed him after Peterloo had quickly subsided; he felt on top of the situation and armed to meet any threat to the internal security of the nation. The Cato Street Conspiracy had not revealed to him any fresh depths of wickedness which he had not already believed existed and had confirmed his confidence that his police and intelligence system were fully equal to what he asked of them. At the Home Office relaxed vigilance was the order of the day.

He was also a much more satisfactory member of the Cabinet. Ten years of working with fellow Ministers whom he found sympathetic and who trusted him, enjoying the enthusiastic backing of the King and with no aspirations to higher office, had made him at once more self-confident and less self-assuming. He was less ready to look for affronts to his dignity, less suspicious that every conclave among his colleagues was encompassing his downfall. In short he was ready to trust the other Ministers even though he knew that he might differ from them on certain subjects. Nor did he allow such differences to concern him gravely. Few of them related to his conduct of the Home Office and, provided he was left to run his department according to his own ideas, he was disposed to let the rest of the Cabinet proceed as they thought most fit. He would still assert his views but no longer treated it as a deliberate affront if the counsels of others won the day.

But while Lord Sidmouth had been immersed in his disturbances, the nature of the Cabinet had, almost imperceptibly, begun to alter around him. Under the influence of Canning, Lord Liverpool had learned to question some of the basic tenets on which conservative policy had for so long been based. The progress was not yet far advanced; the influence of Eldon, Sidmouth, Londonderry, as Castlereagh had now become, and the Duke of Wellington still predominated and even the small advance which the cause of reform had made was endangered when Canning temporarily disappeared from office. But the possibility of change was in the air. Sidmouth was disconcerted by the readiness of the Prime Minister to listen to the heresies of Canning. If the latter were to return he could foresee the power of his own friends being gradually eroded and their preserves encroached on by upstart radicals from the wrong end of the party. He was not yet seriously alarmed but was still conscious of a vague unease. Ten years before this might have thrown him back on the defensive, now it merely made him still less inclined to cling to office.

As early as May of 1820 Sidmouth had written[1]: "It has been a sense of honour and duty solely, which, for a considerable time past, has kept me in my present official situation; and I indulge the hope of being, ere long, released from that obligation, by a happy change in the internal state of the country." For the next twelve months he continued to talk on these lines to his friends but did little to achieve the hoped-for release. Then, towards the middle of 1821, he took up the question again with Lord Liverpool. He found Liverpool disconcertingly ready to see his point. The Prime Minister was quite ready to agree to a change provided it could be contrived without too much disturbance. The two men had never been particularly close and, in recent

393

years, the relationship had become tinged with something not far from dislike. Liverpool resented Sidmouth's special position at Court, thought anyway that his day was done and hoped that, if Sidmouth left the Home Office, the rearrangements that must follow would allow him to bring Canning back into the Government. Sidmouth would have preferred to see Peel given the preference but had no wish to block Canning's return. He made it clear that he would not interfere in the choice of his successor.

Unfortunately Liverpool had misjudged the feelings of the King. George IV was most reluctant to see Lord Sidmouth go and ill-prepared to forgive Canning for his championship of the Queen. "Lord Liverpool," he observed,[1] "was labouring to make him discard the individual of his Ministry for whom he had the greatest regard, and to introduce a man whom he loathed." The first point Liverpool was, a little reluctantly, prepared to meet by keeping Lord Sidmouth in the Cabinet without specific office[2] but, on the second, it quickly seemed that deadlock had been reached. Sidmouth called twice on the King and, according to Hobhouse, besought him to change his mind[3]. Hobhouse's account of the interviews almost certainly came from Sidmouth himself but, even so, there is no reason to doubt that the latter genuinely did his best to render Canning a little less distasteful to the King and to point out the false importance which the would-be Minister would gain if he were known to be proscribed at Court.

He was, however, singularly unsuccessful. George IV received with equanimity Lord Liverpool's threats of resignation and urged Sidmouth to become Prime Minister in his place: "telling him that he was assured no man in England could form so strong a Government as he."[4] Sidmouth knew better. He refused the offer out of hand and reverted to the need to admit Canning. Meanwhile Ministers anxiously conferred on what best to do if Liverpool should carry out his threat to resign. Most were prepared to carry on but it was not a prospect which any of them could relish, least of all Sidmouth who foresaw that he would be condemned to a term of office indefinitely prolonged and acrimonious warfare where he had sought only for a peaceful retreat.

In the event matters never came to a head. The death of Lady Liverpool did something to ease the bitterness of the dispute and

Canning, once rid of his illusion that the King would welcome his return, handsomely withdrew his claim to office. The King, too, retreated a little way and hinted that he would not object to Canning for ever but was merely loath to take him at the moment. Liverpool therefore decided to play for time. It was his turn to urge Sidmouth to remain at the Home Office, an appeal to which the latter gloomily acceded. All question of a Cabinet reshuffle was tacitly shelved, at least until after the Coronation and the projected royal visit to Ireland.

* * * * *

Given the intense dislike which the people had so recently shown for their sovereign, the Coronation passed off remarkably well. Only the Queen, petulantly beating at the doors of the Abbey, disturbed the harmony of the day and her rebuff, underlined as it was by the contemptuous amusement of the crowd, was in its way the highest point of the royal triumph. Sidmouth, who had had serious doubts about the King's reception, was relieved and moved by the enthusiasm of those who lined the way to the Abbey.

The state visit to Ireland promised to be more complicated. The King looked forward with special enthusiasm to the expedition because it would take him to the home-country of his beloved Lady Conyngham. His enthusiasm was not shared by Lord Sidmouth. As the senior Minister accompanying the King and, worse still, as the tacitly nominated watchman of the royal reputation, he foresaw a cycle of irritations and embarrassments. George IV would certainly wish to dally with his mistress when he should have been attending to his Irish subjects and the Irish could be relied on to feel themselves gravely slighted if he did. Prospects for a smooth or useful visit seemed alarmingly remote.

The visit, in fact, had to be halted when it had scarcely begun. The Queen, who during her life had done so much to plague His Majesty's Ministers, scored a final triumph with her death. The King had barely sailed from Portsmouth before the news came that Caroline was dangerously ill. Even George IV could hardly relish making his triumphal entry into Dublin at the moment of his wife's extinction. He put into Anglesey to await developments. The unfortunate Sidmouth, who had gone ahead to Dublin to prepare the royal entry, now hurried back to find out what was going on. Londonderry and he conferred and agreed that the King should proceed to Ireland but that, if the Queen died or grew worse, the entry should be informal and the state visit proper postponed for a little while. Sidmouth then hustled back to Ireland. The day after his departure a letter arrived for him from Henry Hobhouse in London. Londonderry opened it, hoping it would give news of the Queen. It did, the Queen was worse. Londonderry read the letter aloud, began a sentence "The Duke of York . . ." then stopped in dismay. The King told him to go on. "The Duke of York," read Londonderry nervously, "is in despair at an event which so much diminishes his chance of the Crown."[1]

Next day came the news of the Queen's death. The inefficiency of the police and the determination of the Radicals to extract the last drop of political advantage from the miserable Caroline turned her funeral into a saturnalia. Rioting, demagoguery and an indecent game of shuttlecock with the royal corpse provided an appropriate end to a career which had been as turbulent as it had been sordid. Save by a handful of friends and would-be mischief-makers the Queen died unlamented; to Sidmouth and the other Ministers the news could only come as a deep relief. Sidmouth could, too, be forgiven a mild satisfaction at the crumbling of public order which supervened as soon as he was not there to oversee the work. "Your Lordship may be assured that you are not blamed in the least," wrote Lord Stowell,[2] "for the universal remark from every mouth is, that, if Lord Sidmouth had been there, no such disgraceful scene would have happened."

In spite of its unpropitious start the visit to Ireland was an unexpected success. The Irish seemed genuinely pleased to see their King and George IV, unused to such affection, in his turn revealed a warmth and charm which had all too rarely appeared in recent years. "I can truly say," wrote Sidmouth in delight,[3] "that I have not heard an unpleasant word nor seen a sullen look since I came into the country." Some part at least of the Irish enthusiasm may have been due to their belief that the visit would be followed by concessions to the Catholics. Certainly everything possible was done to convince Sidmouth of the need for reform. But the Irish sadly misjudged their man if they imagined that his mild manner and readiness to listen to argument heralded a change of heart. "He was satisfied," he told Pellew,[4] "that it was possible to make determined resistance to the Roman

Catholic claims perfectly consistent with kindness and conciliation." If the Irish chose to interpret "kindness and conciliation"
as proof that concessions were on the way, then that was their
own affair; he could fairly claim that he had done nothing to
mislead them. In the course of a conversation[1] with a Roman
Catholic during the visit the latter observed: "The truth is, my
Lord, that your constitution does not suit our religion." "Yes,"
replied Sidmouth dryly. "But there is another truth. I believe
that your religion does not suit our constitution."

Sidmouth was prudent enough largely to discount the froth of
sentimentality and self-delusion which had lent such ebullience
to their welcome in Ireland. All was well as far as it went but it
would have been a grave mistake to assume that it would go
much further. "It is very important," he wrote to Lord Bathurst,[2]
"that his [the King's] visit should not be protracted. He attended
the installation ball last night, and was in good looks, temper and
spirits. There is, however, a deep-rooted dissatisfaction which is
continually showing itself, and which places us all in a painful
and irksome situation." "Old Sidmouth was never sober," wrote
Lady Glengall cheerfully of the visit,[3] "the newspapers are perfectly accurate on this, as on many other occasions." In his judgment of the political situation, at least, he showed most judicial
sobriety.

But though Sidmouth was not inclined to overrate the success
of the visit he was equally disinclined to write it off as a failure.
His views of and hopes for Ireland were summed up in the letter
which he drafted for the King and addressed, in his name, to the
Lord Lieutenant[4]:

... I am further commanded to state, that the testimonies of
dutiful and affectionate attachment, which His Majesty has
received from all classes and descriptions of his Irish subjects, have made the deepest impression on his mind; and
that he looks forward to the period when he shall revisit them
with the strongest feelings of satisfaction. His Majesty trusts
that, in the meantime, not only the spirit of loyal union,
which now so generally exists, will remain unabated and unimpaired, but that every cause of irritation will be avoided
and discountenanced, mutual forbearance and goodwill
observed and encouraged, and security be thus afforded for
the continuance of that concord among themselves which is

not less essential to his Majesty's happiness than to their own
and which it has been the chief object of his Majesty during
his residence in this country, to cherish and promote.

The sentiments were admirable but Sidmouth was more disap
pointed than surprised when widespread and violent disturbance
broke out in Ireland within two months of the royal visit. Lor
Talbot, the Lord Lieutenant, was somewhat unfairly made the
scapegoat. Sidmouth, who had found Talbot easy to work with
and believed him to be competent and reliable, did his best t
defend him. But the feeling in the Government was too strong
and Talbot was forced to resign. As successor Sidmouth sup
ported the Duke of Wellington. Once again he was overruled, on
the grounds that to send the Duke to Ireland would suggest tha
recourse to arms was in the air. Wellesley was next canvassed a
a possibility. The Duke of Wellington fraternally remarked tha
"he never was diligent, and that his indolence has increased wit
his years"; if a strong and diligent Chief Secretary could b
found, however, he saw no objection to the appointment.[1] Thi
tepid recommendation was considered adequate and Wellesle
took the job without demur.

Sidmouth had some doubts about the appointment to Dubli
of a convinced advocate of Catholic emancipation but believed
as it turned out correctly, that Wellesley could be relied on t
keep his principles comfortably in check. The Lord Lieutenant'
slogan, Sidmouth persuaded his friend, should be that "he cam
to Ireland to administer the laws, and not to change them."
With such an attitude, and under the supervision of the strongl
Protestant Goulburn as Chief Secretary, Sidmouth felt satisfie
that little harm could come. The two men had many conference
together, not all of them entirely business-like. "H.M. has a fable,
wrote Wellesley after his final interview with the King,[3] "tha
you and I sat hand to fist and drank *six* bottles of claret at Rich
mond Park the other night. He is much amused by this tale:
assured him, however, that the quantity of wine did not amoun
to *two* bottles, and that you told me it was *pectoral* claret, an
would relieve my cold. I expect that you will hear much of th
affair of the said *pectoral claret*."

*   *   *   *   *

The winter of 1821 found Sidmouth still in office. As usual h colleagues took advantage of his amiability and his conscientiousness. "How good it is of you to pull the oars, and send us all a-pleasuring," wrote Londonderry cheerfully from Blickling.[1] But the oarsman had almost reached the limit of his patience if not of his endurance. It was time, he felt, that others sacrificed their convenience to his. To Huntingford, still one of his most regular correspondents, he confided:[2]

> That I should be desirous of a life of less confinement and restraint (to say nothing of fatigue and anxiety) than that which I have led for ten years, cannot, I think, be considered by anyone as strange or unbecoming. Most people, I believe, are surprised that after sixteen years previous service in office, I should have been induced to hold my present situation so long. I am now weary of it; and at this period of internal quiet, I feel that I have satisfied all the just claims upon such services as I was capable of rendering; and that the proper time for my retirement from my present office is arrived.

Once again he announced his intentions to his King and his colleagues and once again met with a crescendo of dismay. To George IV he was the most diligent and trustworthy of his ministers; to Eldon, Londonderry and the like he was a champion of the established order whose departure would disastrously weaken the right wing of the Government; to Liverpool he was a convenience whose presence in office at least postponed a showdown with the King over the pretensions of Canning. But in the past twelve months the fact that Sidmouth must leave the Home Office had tacitly been accepted on every side. The chorus of disapproval quickly subsided. All that remained was to fix the timing and, far trickier, to settle the problem of the succession. All the usual permutations were canvassed and the old names examined; all the old grudges disinterred and the old jealousies refurbished. Finally a compromise was worked out, agreeable to few but intolerable to none. Canning was fobbed off with a promise that he would be appointed Governor-General of India and Huskisson induced to stay without his master. The Grenvilles were admitted to the Cabinet and Buckingham at last given his precious Dukedom. And the new Home Secretary was to be Robert Peel.

To Sidmouth this last appointment was, except for his own

retirement, the best part of the arrangement. "I am sure there is no one so well qualified for the office," he wrote to Bragge-Bathurst.[1] "Nothing could have been more becoming and creditable than his conduct." Peel on his side spared no pains to pay tribute to his predecessor's work. In part this may have been good nature or diplomacy but in part, too, it was based on genuine respect. The two men shared certain prejudices and certain qualities and, in their long association, Peel had learned to admire the integrity, determination and assiduity of the older man.

"For Lord Sidmouth," he wrote to Lord Stowell,[2] "I have long entertained not only the highest respect but a strong personal regard. I had the satisfaction, for a considerable period, of standing in a relation to him, which led to confidential and unremitted intercourse; and it is gratifying to me now to remember how completely free it was from the slightest difficulty or misunderstanding. I am as confident that his friendship will induce him to give me all the assistance in his power, as I am firmly persuaded that it will be of the utmost value to me."

But Sidmouth was not to escape entirely from the responsibilities of office. The King insisted that, even though he left the Home Office, he should keep his place in the Cabinet. Sidmouth disliked the idea. He would have preferred to quit public life altogether. But he could not help being flattered and touched by the determination of George IV not to lose his services. He gave in without much demur. The Prime Minister was equally unenthusiastic but, like Sidmouth, not disposed to argue. Sidmouth's remaining in the Cabinet, emphasised Lord Londonderry,[3] was "not a point ever made by Lord Sidmouth but one desired by the King and wished by the rest of the Cabinet as a mark of respect to Lord Sidmouth." It was eventually decided that he would hold no office, even titular, but attend meetings of Cabinet and give the other Ministers the benefit of his experience.

In principle the concept of an elder statesman is attractive; a wise old man with no responsibility but to be wise and old should be an embellishment to any Government. In practice, however, the position is rarely either comfortable or useful. However well disposed his colleagues, they are bound to treat him to some extent on sufferance, without the responsibility of office to vest him with influence, palpably fading from the public eye, a waning power to be handled with courtesy but little real respect. In such an atmosphere the elder stateman will tend to degenerate into elderly buffoon; a Polonius perpetually proffering unwanted counsels or, worse still, a Lear bewailing the ingratitude of his successors.

In Sidmouth's case he was not even sure that his colleagues would be well disposed. The Prime Minister certainly would have been happy to shed him and the Grenvilles, too, were known to be disgruntled.[1] Sidmouth had little hope that he would meet with that enthusiastic deference which alone could have made his position useful to others or satisfying to himself.

Lord Liverpool's coldness had been well illustrated in the matter of Sidmouth's pension. Sidmouth was far from being a rich man. Public life had cost him as much as he had put into it, his estate in Somerset was a financial liability, his eldest son was never likely to earn a penny, his wife's fortune had largely vanished in dowries for their daughters. The loss of his salary as Home Secretary was a serious blow and, without a supplement from some other source, he would have found it difficult to meet the commitments in which his continued service in the Cabinet was certain to involve him.

Early in June the King had broached the question with Liverpool. The Prime Minister pointed out that Sidmouth's son was already in possession of the Clerkship of the Pells; a sinecure worth nearly £3,000 a year. One such perquisite, he implied, was quite enough.[2] Indiscreetly the King passed on Lord Liverpool's views to Sidmouth. The latter was hurt and angry. Lord Liverpool's father had been one of the first to reproach him with improvidence when he had refused a pension on retiring in 1804 and at that time Liverpool himself had seemed to feel the same. To see impropriety in his accepting a pension now, when he was worse off financially and had added another ten years to his ministerial service, seemed to argue an exaggerated scrupulousness somewhat out of place in the son of the notoriously acquisitive first Earl of Liverpool. To the King he pointed out that the Clerkship lapsed with the death of his son—an event that could not be long delayed—and that anyway half the income was committed to the maintenance of the unfortunate invalid.

The King now wrote to Liverpool to state his intention of granting Sidmouth £3,000 a year under an Act passed in 1817 by which he could assign up to a total of six such pensions to the former holders of certain offices under the Crown. Of such offices Sidmouth had held no less than five. Without much enthusiasm Liverpool conceded that this might be done.[1] When the Ministerial Pensions Act was debated in the House of Commons in June, 1822, Creevey cited Sidmouth's pension as an illustration of the sort of abuse to which the Act gave rise. But the concept of the austere old Doctor as a greedy place-seeker did not really carry conviction and all the malignant bile of Creevey could not put much fire into the discussion. On the whole, the debate was more remarkable for the tributes paid to Sidmouth than for the rancour shown against him.

Not even forty years in politics had hardened Sidmouth against personal attacks. Liverpool's detachment and Creevey's lighthearted accusations of avarice hurt him deeply. Himself, he was convinced that his probity was beyond cavil, but the fact that others seemed to doubt it offended his pride and disturbed his peace of mind. The criticisms rankled and he was never able to enjoy his £3,000 a year in tranquillity. When he remarried a wife with a fortune of her own he hastened to resign the pension; only by such a gesture, he felt, could he demonstrate that he sought nothing for himself save what he needed to live in the modest respectability which his place in the public eye demanded.

But in spite of such unpleasantness, the moment of his retirement was a happy one for Sidmouth. The usual welter of adulatory letters arrived to stiffen his morale, a few at least of which stood out above the ruck of polite platitudes. A letter from the Rev. Mr. Edwards, chaplain of the convict hulks at Sheerness, must have given him especial pleasure. "Whatever good may hereafter be effected among the convicts," wrote Mr. Edwards,[2] "one thing is certain, that more has been achieved during your Lordship's administration, than at all previous periods put together. Very many of those, who received mitigation of sentence through your Lordship's recommendation, are now, to my certain knowledge, living honestly, and are (I hope) praying God to bless your Lordship for your goodness towards them."

Sidmouth felt that he was cruelly misunderstood by those who accused him of harshness or indifference to the sufferings of others. The reassurance that, by some at least, his good will and good intentions were appreciated did much to console him for the misinterpretations of the Whigs and the hatred of the Radicals. Comforted by such testimonials and his own bland conviction of his rectitude, Sidmouth sailed comfortably on into a vista of ease and liberty to be terminated only by the grave.

Bishop Huntingford, at seventy-four still urging on his charge to fresh endeavour, encouraged Sidmouth to sacrifice a little of his liberty to writing a history of his times. "Your letter," replied Lord Sidmouth,[1] "gave *stimulos volenti*. At all events, I shall arrange my papers, and from time to time my recollections." Since Sidmouth's "arrangement" of his papers, at least in the case of his correspondence with Pitt, involved the burning of almost every letter likely to cause embarrassment, the historian can only be grateful that the promise was never kept in full. Nor is the absence of any "recollections" a subject for unmixed regret. They would certainly have been tedious reading; pompous, prolix and obscuring every point at issue under a thick layer of sanctimonious equivocation. But there would still have been much value in Sidmouth's considered judgment on certain passages of his life, written at a time when all immediate bitterness had faded and something approaching objectivity achieved. It is possible that such a memoir would have thrown little new light on the past but it could have provided a most illuminating portrait of Sidmouth's mind in 1822.

*   *   *   *   *

Sidmouth's last years in the Cabinet were marked by the gradual disappearance of his friends and the evolution of new policies until at last he was left isolated on a promontory from which his eventual disappearance was to cause little comment and less regret. Yet for the first six months or so after his resignation it seemed as if things would go on much as they had before. Canning's standard-bearer Huskisson soldiered reluctantly on but Canning himself appeared destined for glorious isolation in the Indian Empire and the old triumvirate of Londonderry, Sidmouth and Eldon continued to command the confidence of the King.

Then, in August, 1822, while Sidmouth was holidaying in Yorkshire, came the news that Londonderry had killed himself. Sidmouth had known that his friend was "disturbed and agitated." ". . . The most generous and intrepid of mankind also was harassed by suspicion and alarm";[2] but he had never conceived that Londonderry might be driven to such a point. The tragedy, removing as it did a close personal friend and his most effective ally, both weakened Sidmouth's political standing and, at the same time, his enthusiasm for the fight. With "the right arm of the administration gone," wrote Liverpool,[1] only a complete refurbishing could save the Government. Sidmouth was too discouraged to do other than acquiesce.

He was still sufficiently interested in what transpired to suggest that Peel should take the lead in the Commons and Canning proceed as planned to India.[2] But he can never have had much hope that this solution would be acceptable; Liverpool and Wellington were convinced that the Government could only stand if Canning were inside it and Peel himself seemed in no hurry to thrust himself forward. In mid-September the King reluctantly agreed that Canning should be his Foreign Secretary and Leader of the House of Commons.

The mere inclusion of Canning was not enough. "A propos of the House of Coms," wrote Canning to Bagot,[3] "we are working to some changes there which will alter the face of Treasury Bench—very much for the better. What think you of Bragge and Van retiring? Hush! not a word to any human being. For it is a great secret yet—known only to Liverpool and me and Sidth (the negotiator of the whole) and the Twins."

It was an unkind twist which left Sidmouth to "negotiate" the removal from the Cabinet of his two friends and thus the erosion of what was left to him of his influence. But Bragge-Bathurst, he knew well, was old, ill and almost useless as a Minister, while Vansittart could not be expected to remain at the Exchequer in a Government increasingly dominated by Canning. He decided that it would be best for his friends to yield gracefully and concentrated all his efforts on gaining them favourable terms.

Bragge-Bathurst was no problem; he was anyhow anxious to retire and stood out merely for a pension for his wife if she survived him and "something for his daughters." This Sidmouth easily secured. Vansittart proved more recalcitrant. Liverpool tried to fob him off with Bragge-Bathurst's old place at the Duchy of Lancaster. Vansittart argued that this would make it obvious that he was being discarded and held out for a pension of £3,000 a year or a peerage. Sidmouth loyally stood up for his claims and Liverpool, who was anxious not to upset the balance of the Cabinet too rapidly by shedding Sidmouth as well as his friends, reluctantly settled for the peerage.

The changing face of the Cabinet was not the only factor which urged Sidmouth towards retirement. In the summer of 1823 he had startled and slightly shocked his friends by marrying for the second time. His bride was Maria Anne Townsend, the widowed daughter of his old friend William Scott, Lord Stowell. She was nearly thirty years younger than her new husband and Sidmouth had every reason to dread the derision which traditionally greets this kind of marriage. Luckily for him, however, the seventy-six-year-old Lord Fitzwilliam had taken the same step himself only a week before. The sensation which this had caused still lingered in the public memory and Sidmouth, ten years Fitzwilliam's junior, escaped more or less unscathed with his romance.

Lady Sidmouth was gentle, kindly and intelligent; a more sophisticated figure than her predecessor but in many ways of a similar nature. Mary Russell Mitford, who knew her well, wrote to a friend after her death[1]:

I have seldom known anyone more thoroughly awake and alive to all that was best worth knowing. She had an enlightened curiosity, a love of natural history, of antiquities, of literature, of art; was herself full of talent, intelligence and gaiety, and had a quick and peculiar humour, . . . such was her sweetness that Lord Sidmouth told me that some sculptor (I think Behnes) earnestly wished to be allowed to model her face for the expression, which, as he said, was more full of lively sweetness than any he ever saw. . . .

All her dealings about money were munificent in themselves and most graceful in the manner. She gave to the Berkshire Hospital six acres of land (valued at a thousand pounds an acre for building leases), standing on the finest situation on the outskirts of Reading, and told everybody that it was Lord Sidmouth's gift! And in the same way she built a new market cross in his name in the town of Devizes, of which he is High Steward.[2]

At Stowell . . . is a hazel coppice of such extent that all the fairs of the south of England are supplied from it with cobnuts—the favourite present of a country lad to his sweetheart. Gipsies and other wanderers pitch their tents around it in the nutting season; and for three weeks the coppice is as populous as a vineyard or a hop-garden in their gathering time. Poor dear Lady Sidmouth! How fond she was of distributing little bags of her own nuts, purchased from the licensed plunderers! You would have liked Lady Sidmouth!

Sidmouth was not to be allowed the pleasures of a honeymoon. Only a week before his wedding he had written to Bragge-Bathurst to say that the state of his son Harry was causing some alarm. He did not foresee any immediate crisis and so had decided neither to advance nor defer the ceremony.[1] Yet within twenty-four hours of its taking place a message was sent after him to urge his return and by the time he reached White Lodge on 31st July Harry was already dead.

"It is, indeed, a most afflicting, may I not add, a most mysterious dispensation!" William Wilberforce had written to Sidmouth some time before when it was evident that Harry could never be well again.[2] "But I really have no doubt whatever . . . that it will appear hereafter to have been for the party's real good, and if so, how little will it signify, or rather, how little will it appear to have signified some few thousands of ages hence, whether the progress of this particular specimen of moral vegetation was suddenly chilled and arrested, or whether it had been suffered to proceed from the interesting beauty of its early bloom to the rich maturity of its fruitage . . ." He may thereby, Wilberforce suggested, have been saved from "some unforeseen evil which might have befallen him, to his grievous suffering at least—perhaps to the impairment of his moral principles."

Curious consolation, to draw comfort from the death of a loved one by reflecting on hypothetical pitfalls into which otherwise he might have fallen. Yet to Sidmouth the concept was in no way unnatural. A man of profound and unquestioning faith he never for one moment doubted that his son's intellectual and now physical destruction had been brought about for some proper end. He described himself[3] as "Calm, under the perfect conviction that the wound had been inflicted by a merciful hand." If the hand were indeed merciful, what could be more natural than to congratulate oneself on the still more ugly fate from which the victim had been spared? In spite of the long dulling misery of Harry's illness the end, when it came, was a shock and the cause of much unhappiness. Yet never for an instant did it lead him to question the well-ordered excellence of the universe or to challenge the justice of a system which could impose such protracted and hopeless suffering upon an apparently innocent child.

*   *   *   *   *

Preoccupied alike by his new commitments and his old sorrows, it was inevitable that Sidmouth's role in politics should seem less and less important. He began to miss meetings of the Cabinet, stayed silent when he did attend and made it clear, so far as his determined courtesy allowed, that he found the atmosphere uncongenial and the policies increasingly ill-conceived. No one doubted that he would soon retire altogether; all that was in question was when and on what occasion. If no grounds had been forthcoming he would probably have found it necessary to contrive them. With Canning in the Government, however, it was certain that any such effort would be superfluous, some reason for a breach would arise whether he wanted it or not.

The cause turned out to be Canning's wish to recognise certain South American Republics which had broken away from Spain. It would not be true to say that for Sidmouth this was no more than an excuse; he felt strongly that recognition would be premature and would encourage republican ideas in Europe and the worst kind of radicalism at home. But he had worried little about foreign policy over the last twelve years and it seems most unlikely that he would suddenly have taken so determined a line if the issue had not acted as a catalyst for his vague resentment of Canning's growing influence and his reluctance to continue in the Cabinet. As it was, he, Eldon and the Duke of Wellington, the last and doughtiest warriors of the old brigade, banded together to oppose Canning's liberal adventures.

The crisis rapidly grew more embroiled. Canning pressed the King to let him enter into commercial treaties with Mexico and Colombia, giving in his minute no hint that all his colleagues were not behind him. The King reluctantly agreed, expressing some surprise at "the apparently unanimous opinion" of his Ministers.[1] This put Liverpool in a quandary; Canning was too far committed to withdraw, yet to press on with his projects might involve losing the whole right wing of the Government and what was left of the confidence of the King. Intensive diplomacy eventually persuaded Wellington and Eldon to withdraw their opposition but Sidmouth retreated to the country and stoutly refused to yield. In the end Liverpool won at least part of his point. He persuaded Sidmouth that he should not stand out alone from the now united Ministry. But this was to be Sidmouth's last sacrifice. Whatever debt of loyalty might be owing to his former colleagues he felt to be requited. Before the Cabinet could meet to discuss Lord Liverpool's triumph, Sidmouth's letter of resignation was in the hands of the Prime Minister.

Hobhouse[1] attributes Sidmouth's hurry at least in part to his fear that the Government was on the point of disintegration. He suspected that the King, discovering how deeply Ministers were divided, might play with the idea of dismissing Liverpool and calling on Wellington or some other hero of the right to form an alternative Government. His own retirement, if it came quickly, might discourage the King from such a hazardous scheme. Even if it did not, he could at least plead that the ill-health and fatigue which had forced him to resign now precluded him from coming to the rescue by taking an important office in a right-wing Government.

Such calculations may have played some part in Sidmouth's mind but they cannot have been decisive. Sidmouth would have seized the opportunity to retire even though he had known that the King would be ready to struggle on with Liverpool for ever. He would, for that matter, still have made a bolt for freedom even though the administration would have crumbled with his going. He had had enough. He viewed the prospect of a Cabinet meeting with a mixture of ennui and distaste; he was tired, ill and preoccupied with his domestic life, his last ambitions had faded; it was time that he was gone.

His letter of resignation to Lord Liverpool made no reference to differences of opinion within the Cabinet but merely alluded to the difficulty he found in reconciling attendance at meetings with his health and private commitments.[2] Lord Liverpool's reply was equally discreet.[3] "Whilst I must lament any circumstances," he wrote, "that can interrupt, in any degree, those confidential communications on public affairs which have now for so many years existed between us, I feel it due to you to say, that if your domestic arrangements would not admit of your being a regular attendant at the cabinets and in the House of Lords, I cannot blame your decision." No one of any importance was taken in by this exchange; indeed the general tendency of the informed was to overrate the importance of the breach over Latin America. At least, however, everyone agreed that the matter had been handled with dignity and a certain grace.

It is a mark of how far Sidmouth's standing had deteriorated in the two years of his semi-retirement that his final departure caused no more than a ripple of interest on the political scene. In the Cabinet the weight shifted yet a little further towards the progressive wing, but it was only one more stage in a slow and relentless process. In the country at large the change was hardly noticed. The King was one of the few to show sorrow. Liverpool wrote to him[1] in terms of formal regret which did little to hide his satisfaction. ". . . There always exists," he remarked bluntly, "more or less objection to any person being a member of your Majesty's Cabinet without holding a Cabinet office, the inconvenience is greatly increased if the individual is not a constant attendant." George IV swallowed the unappetising pill but wrote[2] with real pain of his grief in losing this "most excellent servant of the Crown and of the public." For the rest there was only Eldon[3] to mutter balefully at the evil consequences if the gallant few were now to be unkindly deserted in their last redoubt. It was as if all England had realised that Sidmouth's day had gone; that he could not contribute any more in the conditions of 1824. He was not defeated by any upsurge of resentment or sudden will to defeat the forces of reaction; instead he had been allowed imperceptibly to drift into the position of the ignored and forgotten man of politics. His resignation was not an event in itself, merely formal confirmation of a proceeding which, in all but name, had quietly culminated months before.

It would be tedious and unprofitable to chart in detail Lord Sidmouth's placid progress into the mists of oblivion which customarily envelop the erstwhile politician. It is true that in his case the mists seemed to come up unusually thick and fast, but then they had begun to gather even before his resignation. There had been nothing extraordinary about Sidmouth in office and the same was to prove true of his retirement. The only striking feature, indeed, was that the transit from one state to the other was made with unusual speed and with a degree of acquiescence rare on the part of a retreating Minister.

Not that Sidmouth retired altogether from public life. Shortly after his resignation Lord Colchester asked him what he planned to do and where he would sit in the House of Lords.[1] He replied that "he should certainly attend there frequently, and not sit upon the Treasury Bench, but either on the bench below the fire, or perhaps on the cross-bench as heretofore." A general support of Government with the right to criticise when the mood took him had at several times of his life been Sidmouth's favourite posture. Now it seemed that he could occupy it in permanence or at any rate until the Tory Government was overthrown. He did not keep to his promise of frequent attendance but at first rarely missed a debate of importance. Though he preserved his independence of action he was considered by Ministers to need only a little management to make him one of their most reliable supporters.

Someone whose whole life has been obsessed with politics cannot lose all interest by an act of renunciation, however sincerely meant. But for almost the first time since he had accepted the Speakership thirty-five years before, Sidmouth had time for other things. His family took first place. With his wife his relationship was close though unexacting, unlikely to cause excitement or distress. His eldest daughter had assumed proprietorial rights over her father after the death of his first wife. She cannot have found it easy to adapt herself to a step-mother but she was a good-natured girl, sincerely devoted to her father and ready to welcome anything which might make him happier. The inner circle of the family remained harmonious. His second daughter Frances similarly did her duty. In 1820 she had become Mrs. Pellew and presented her father with a model son-in-law and future biographer; orthodox, obsequious and intent to please. The two younger daughters seemed set to follow this admirable example. Only his heir, William, gave some cause for alarm. William had entered the Church and was rapidly fathering a properly parsonical family of twelve. But more philoprogenitive than sapient, he had deserted the well-trodden ways of the Anglican Church to adhere first to the Clapham sect and later to the Irvingites. Of this last group he became an angel, a promotion hardly likely to prove pleasing to his sternly canonical father. But though Sidmouth disapproved he was ready to make allowances for sincerity and a life of obvious virtue. He was never to grow close to his son, yet the two got on comfortably together and their occasional meetings seem to have given pleasure to both.

For the first time in his life Sidmouth now found time to travel. His father had had neither the money nor the inclination to send his son on the Grand Tour prescribed for the sons of noblemen, the Napoleonic wars had then supervened and the duties of a senior politician had finally checked any urge to see the world. Now he made expeditions to Holland, France and Germany. It comes as no surprise to find that, in Pellew's words,[1] his journeys "served principally to strengthen Lord Sidmouth's devoted attachment and deeply-rooted preference for the habits and institutions of his own country." It is doubtful if at any time Sidmouth could have conceived that foreign ways might hold something for an Englishman to admire or imitate. By the age of seventy the last chinks had been sealed in what had never had many claims to be considered an open mind. He judged every continental institution by its approximation to an idealised portrait of its English equivalent. In so far as it differed, it fell short; only the most assiduous aping of the English model could earn it a word of qualified approval.

In England he divided his time principally between White

Lodge and Erleigh (or sometimes Early and occasionally Earley) Court, the home of his father-in-law, Lord Stowell. The Sidmouths made it their business to persuade this formidable octogenerian to retire from the Admiralty Court which he had dominated for nearly thirty years. Though almost blind and unable to speak above a whisper, Lord Stowell nevertheless clung on until the end of 1827. When finally induced to yield he complained of loneliness and lack of occupation. His daughter thought it her duty to look after him. Lord Stowell was not an easy companion: glum, crotchety and even in senility obsessed with the virtues of economy and "the elegant simplicity of the three percents." But the Sidmouths bore with him bravely and, when he died in 1836, could feel that they had done all in their power to make his last years contented.

But to Sidmouth his Devonshire home of Up Ottery was still where he felt most at ease and he assured Bragge-Bathurst[1] that it was ". . . quite in as high favour with Lady Sidmouth as with any of the family." Together they engaged in the good works becoming to a Lord of the Manor; bullying or cajoling their tenants into a proper state of spiritual and material well-being. "You will . . ." he wrote to a friend,[2] "I trust remark an air of general improvement in the whole parish. I am desirous now of establishing a school at the hamlet of Smeath . . . and look forward to the erection, please God, during my lifetime, of a chapel of ease in that remote and neglected corner of the parish."

So far as Sidmouth was concerned, the betterment of his tenants and other bucolic pursuits were enough to pass the time. But he could not altogether ignore what happened at Westminster. In 1827 Liverpool fell ill and receded gradually from office. After prolonged and bitter wrangling Canning came to power, pledged to progress on the Catholic question. Within a few months he was dead. Goderich failed to hold his Government together. "So the ill-constructed and weak fabric has fallen to pieces!" wrote Sidmouth to Colchester.[2] "How is it to be replaced?" Within a few days he had his answer. The Duke of Wellington was in charge with his "reunion of the old Party" and a restoration of sane Tory principles. But it was the old Party with a difference, disturbingly well disposed towards the Catholics and leaving Eldon, Westmorland and Vansittart, now Lord Bexley, resentfully to one side. "It grieves me to think," commented idmouth,[1] "that an opportunity of forming an Administration which would have given entire satisfaction to the country has been lost. It must now be very imperfect . . ."

"I wish you would consider this matter a little more seriously," wrote Stowell to his son-in-law.[2] "——I mean the matter of your returning to office. I do not mean to any office of a laborious nature, but to such a one as would give you a right of interfering in the councils of state, which do not appear to me to be going on in a salutary manner and of which no man can yet foretell the result—these results are of a most serious nature and embrace the most serious consequences which alarm the whole nation. . . . Is not a time for you to depart from these Resolutions of consulting your own ease and endanger the public safety? [sic]. It is the wish of all your friends, not merely for their own private interest, but for the great object of the public safety. Can there be a doubt that the Duke of Wellington, yourself, and my brother would come into office with the acclamation of the general public and would be hailed as the restorers of public tranquillity after kicking out a few of those who have been introduced into the present government to the entire dissatisfaction of all the well-affected. I write this *ex animo* most sincerely and devoutly; I am sure that would be the most popular act of your life."

Lord Stowell was in his dotage, but he was by no means alone in dreaming that Sidmouth might yet be summoned to restore reason to the Cabinet. Ellenborough reported a rumour that he was to be offered a place as Privy Seal.[3] "I hope not," he commented. "It would show the Duke despaired of bringing the King round upon the Catholic question." Even Huskisson pondered whether the King might not fall back on Sidmouth as the last line of defence against the encroachments of the Catholics.[4] But Sidmouth himself never took seriously the well-meant suggestions of his friends and relatives. Consistent to a lifetime's principles, he was determined to oppose Ministers if they made concessions to the Catholics, but he would not put himself at the head of a faction, still less offer himself as a rival head of government. Nothing, not even the urgings of all his friends or the direct application of the King himself, would have induced him to change his mind.

By October, 1828, it became clear that Wellington could no longer be counted among the old guard on the Catholic question.

He had overcome his conviction that emancipation would be measure of extreme peril to the country. More contentiously he had convinced himself that such a step would satisfy th ambitions of the Irish. With neither opinion could Sidmouth agree. In a letter to Lord Bexley[1] he stated his view in word which form the epigraph to this book and, read in the wide context, sum up succinctly a political philosophy to which he ha devotedly adhered during more than fifty years of public life.

"It appears to me to be of the greatest importance that th proceedings in Ireland should not be brought forward as, in an degree, the grounds of our objection to the Catholic claims though, combined with other circumstances, they impose upo us the duty and necessity of a public declaration of our sentiment at this time. . . . The basis of Protestant Union, and the materia of all public declarations against further concession should be a unshaken and inviolable attachment to the Constitution as estab lished at the Revolution, and a determination to uphold it again innovation, as the best security of our civil and religious liberty.

Not only did Sidmouth feel that concessions to the Catholic would be dangerous and useless, he believed that "an immens and undiminished majority" of Englishmen would share hi view.[2] Firm in this belief, in February, 1829, Sidmouth attende the Duke of Wellington's ministerial dinner at which the comin session's Speech from the Throne was to be discussed. Th Duke told him that the Speech would contain a recommendatio for a Roman Catholic Relief Bill. "It is a bad business," said th Duke,[3] "but we are aground." "Does your Grace think, then, asked Lord Sidmouth, "that this concession will tranquilize Ire land?" "I can't tell; I hope it will." Sidmouth, with no suc hope, told Wellington that he would have to oppose the bil "I cannot . . . sacrifice principle to expediency," he wrote Exmouth,[4] "nor become a party in attempting to avert immedia difficulties at the expense of an irremediable, a permanent, an I fear, a fatal blow to the Protestant constitution of the country

In spite of Lord Sidmouth's efforts the Bill passed in the Hou of Lords by the overwhelming majority of 213 to 109. He w already resigned to defeat. "For the first time in my life," wrote to Pellew a few days before.[5] "I am disheartened. We see to be in a shattered boat, and in a strange and agitated sea, witho pilot, chart or compass." It was not so much that his enemi were triumphing as that those who should have been his friends and allies seemed to betray everything for which they stood. Sadly he withdrew still further from public life.

It was almost inevitable that one who saw the destruction of Church and State in the giving of votes to Catholics should view the Reform Bill of 1832 as a calamity without precedent. In October, 1831, he made one of his now rare visits to the House to vote against the first version of Grey's Bill. Assiduously he had worked on his speech; assiduously he attended every night of the debate. It is a pathetic commentary on the way his fame had faded that he was never called upon to speak and a speech which would have been to some extent an apologia for his whole career remained undelivered, a little bundle of notes to act as monument to a lifetime's service.

Between the rejection of the first Reform Bill and the presentation of the second, Lord Sidmouth considered the possibility of a compromise. "Until it is proved," he wrote,[1] "that some great practical evil is justly attributable to the present structure of that House, and that it would admit of a remedy which would not be productive of some evil of equal or greater magnitude, my objections to a general reform will remain unshaken." But, in the circumstances, he was reluctantly prepared to accept that some small concessions might be made, sufficient "to satisfy the more temperate and conscientious reformer."

It is hard to conceive that any reformer, conscientious or not, could have been sufficiently temperate to find grounds for compromise with Lord Sidmouth. When the revised Reform Bill came for its second reading to the House of Lords in April, 1832, it found Sidmouth still in inveterate opposition. There he was to remain, urging on the little band of die-hard Tories to obstinate, gallant and blindly irrational opposition, until long after the battle was over and lost. At last the King himself accepted that reform must come. He expressed his wish that the peers should allow the Bill to pass. But even the King's command could not induce Sidmouth to vote against his conscience. With a handful of the old brigade he went into the lobbies to register one final protest against the destruction of his country, then withdrew from the debate for ever. "I hope," he said to Grey,[2] "God will forgive you on account of this bill: I don't think I can." "Mark my words," replied the Prime Minister cynically, "within two years you will find that we have become unpopular, for having brought forward the most aristocratic measure that ever was proposed in parliament."

The passage of the Reform Bill marked the end of Sidmouth's public life. He still appeared occasionally in the House of Lords, but only so as to qualify for a proxy. He never attempted to speak and only on one or two minor occasions bothered personally to register his vote. It was not so much that reform had made the Palace of Westminster disagreeable; even Sidmouth had to admit that things seemed perplexingly the same. But at the age of seventy-six, growing deaf, his friends departed, he found the House of Lords a dreary and depressing spot. He never lost interest in what was going on but the interest was academic; all urge to play a part himself had gone.

*   *   *   *   *

Sidmouth's friends and contemporaries were a long-lived lot. Of those who still survived in 1832 Bragge-Bathurst lived to seventy-eight, Wellesley to eighty-two, Huntingford, eighty-four, Eldon, eighty-seven, and Stowell ninety-one. One by one Sidmouth outlived them all. As the news of their passing was brought him, so he seemed increasingly cut off from the period of his struggles, his victories and his setbacks. Yet, paradoxically, each new death seemed rather to bind him more firmly to the past than to leave him isolated in the present. Through the obituary notices of his friends he clambered peacefully backward into a twilight world where life and death had no existence and past and present were consolingly confused. More and more he spent his days brooding, thinking, dreaming in a study lined with pictures of his friends; an antique figure, greyed but still unbowed, communing tranquilly with the ghosts of his vintage years. An advantage of ghosts is that they cannot answer back and it is not too cynical to hazard that Sidmouth, in these satisfactorily one-sided colloquies, achieved a relationship with his companions as happy as any he had known on earth.

"Here you find me," he told a friend of the family who invaded his study,[1] "surrounded by my early friends and valued contemporaries. There is the Bishop of Hereford, my first tutor at Winchester College, whose correspondence I enjoyed until he was removed from the earth—there hangs Lord Ellenborough—

416

there Lord Stowell—Pitt—Perceval—Lord Nelson—Lord Hood—Lord Exmouth—Windham—Sir William Grant, and many other faces and names which can never be obliterated from my mind." He paused a moment. "But they are all gone—all passed away except myself. And I too shall soon be remembered but in name . . ."

Living thus contentedly in his personal cemetery he little by little ceased altogether to venture out. Ability was fading as well as inclination. In July, 1838, he wrote to Bexley to announce that he would not be attending a Committee of the House of Lords.[1] "In fact I am totally unfit for the discharge of any of my public duties; and it is possible that my increased and increasing languor and infirmities, including deafness, will ere long disqualify me for the enjoyment of private society, except on a very limited scale." To Wellesley he wrote concisely, "I am gradually wearing out,"[2] and in truth the body which had served him so well in the past was now at last beginning to disintegrate.

Yet even at the age of eighty-four he could still emerge from the shadows and hold his own in society. Sir Thomas Martin lunched with him in September, 1840,[3] "and was much entertained with his lively conversation, and the powers of his memory. . . . He said Geo. III told him he knew who was the author of Junius and so did Lord Grenville but both said they could not name him. Lord Sidmouth had no doubt Sir P. Francis was the man. . . ." Nor did he look exclusively to the past; in the same year he startled another visitor with his knowledge of a wrangle that was then going on between the House of Commons and the Law Courts.[4] "The fine old gentleman . . . still takes the most lively interest in the question and, strange for an old Speaker, is on the side of the law." "He was in raptures with my speech," the letter continued, a piece of self-satisfaction perhaps not surprising given that the visitor was Benjamin Disraeli.

But such ventures from the past were rare and soon they were to cease entirely. In April, 1842, Lady Sidmouth died and with her passed Sidmouth's last interest in the business of staying alive. It was not that he had loved her with passion; passion had never been prominent in his personality and such as there was had long been spent before he married his second wife. Nor did the event even come as a surprise; Lady Sidmouth had been ill for years, half paralysed and in severe pain for many months. But his preoccupation with her health had retained his attention in spite of all the counter-attractions of eternity. Now the last anchor was hauled up and he was left free to drift aimlessly, impelled only by the slight winds of his imagination and his memory. Mary Anne, his eldest daughter, "a very cultivated and excellent person," as Miss Mitford fairly described her, was still left him as nurse-secretary, but the role of secretary scarcely now counted and the nurse's patient became ever more comatose and inattentive.

From the time of his wife's last illness Sidmouth never left White Lodge. His sight failed rapidly and even a few shuffling steps on to the terrace became a major expedition. "In youth," he remarked as old age lapped around him,[1] "the absence of pleasure is pain, in old age, the absence of pain is pleasure." The final crumbling of his faculties removed him to a limbo where pain and pleasure were equally remote. Day after day he would keep his study, staring blankly before him, impervious to all around, beyond speech, beyond thought, perhaps even beyond dreams.

In February, 1844, he developed what seemed to be a trivial cold. It turned into influenza. The illness, slight in itself, was more than his enfeebled body could bear. It was quickly apparent to everyone that the end must be near. The crisis strangely restored him to animation. In the last few feverish days he began again to take an interest in what went on around him; his spirit seemed to gain in strength as his body weakened. With it all, he was cheerful, tranquil and without a trace of fear. His son-in-law[2] asked him how he felt[3]:

"Breaking up and breaking down, my dear Horace, but that gives me no disquietude."

"You put your whole trust in the merits of your Saviour?"

"I hope I may say I do."

"This has not come upon you unawares, I think."

"No; I have had many warnings, and I look forward to be re-united with all those I love, in a blessed immortality."

The scene of his death has been recorded by his daughter, Mary Anne, in the correct and lifeless phrases which he would undoubtedly have used himself[4]:

All his children now knelt weeping around his bed. I held his right hand in mine, and once, when I wiped his brow, he faintly said, "Who?" Day, his faithful attendant, replied, "Miss Addington, my Lord." He with difficulty articulated "Mary Anne," and that was the last word he ever uttered. The breathing now gradually became fainter: the dear hand began to lose its vital warmth, and at 7 o'clock p.m. of Thursday, the 15th of February, with one or two deep sighs, the earthly tie was severed, and the pure and noble spirit soared into the blessed presence of its God.

Thus Sidmouth died as he had lived: conventional, dignified and with infinite propriety.

* * * * *

The news that Sidmouth was dead passed almost unnoticed by the great mass of Britons and provoked only a slight flicker of interest even among those to whom the obituary columns were essential reading. Raikes, the diarist, was one of the few who found the matter worth recording[1]: "His talents were moderate, but his good luck was great," he noted laconically. He quoted a derisive epitaph which was to be heard in London drawing-rooms:

> *Sous ce marbre, passant le Sieur Addington gît,*
> *Ministre soi-disant, Médécin malgré lui.*

Thus, with a few covert sniggers and the usual sententious paragraphs in the leading newspapers, Sidmouth sank into oblivion. There he has remained. In eighteen hundred pages of unexampled flatness his son-in-law, George Pellew, sought to resurrect his name and enshrine it for ever in the pantheon of British history. He succeeded only in burying it still deeper. The public had long suspected that Sidmouth was among the dullest of statesmen. Pellew's biography confirmed them in their view. Gratefully he was forgotten; to be revived only as a butt for epigrams or to be compared derisively with his great contemporary William Pitt. Even the serious historian has hardly found him worthy of attention. He has remained, neglected and forlorn, in the back ranks of British politicians, a figure so deeply cloaked in dust that even the careful observer could hardly tell whether the hidden features were those of saint or sinner, emperor or clown.

The public had, of course, a fair amount of justice on its side. Sidmouth, in many ways, was a dull man. He had no wit and little humour. His private life was decorous to the point of suffocation. His talk was drab and his writing doubly so. A career devoid of panache and eccentricity; responsible, sober and prosaic; may fairly be said to lack the more obvious kind of popular appeal. But glamour is not all, and many men with no more in the way of colour and of brilliance are still allowed to have played a great and honourable part in Britain's history. Sidmouth's virtual extinction, after three years as Prime Minister and almost thirty in high office, is a fate which few have shared. It cannot be wholly explained by an unalluring personality or a shortage of dramatic incidents.

In part a solution may be looked for in the timing of his life and of his death, in part in his own character and political philosophy. When Sidmouth was born, George II had still three years to reign; when he died the future King Edward VII was already six years old: the age of Sterne and Hogarth had become the age of Tennyson and Winterhalter. Even the span of his public life seems extravagantly long. When his thoughts first turned to a career in Parliament, Bute, North and Rockingham held the scene; when he finally withdrew Gladstone and Disraeli were already prominent. Between these limits there seemed mysteriously to have been compressed developments which, in another age, might comfortably have been spread over a period twice as long.

To say that Sidmouth failed to change with the times is to say little more than that he was human. To be old is not necessarily to be out of touch but there can be few men who have been perfectly attuned to the spirit of their age at every stage of their career. In Sidmouth's case every factor seemed so contrived as to exaggerate his maladjustment. By temperament he was destined to be out of date, the circumstances of his time determined that what might have been a trivial misfortune should become the predominant feature of his career.

Few statesmen who were established before the French Revolution and the Napoleonic Wars found themselves at ease in the years that followed. Sidmouth had learned his trade under Pitt the repressive, at a time when all that mattered was to hold the line at home and allow the military to get on with the war. Temperamentally, the course suited him too well. What should have been emergency measures, devised to meet an extraordinary crisis, instead came to be considered as part of the ordinary machinery of government and a sufficient answer to any problem. By the time that the battlefield had shifted to the new industrial centres of the country he had grown beyond hope rigid, incapable of the effort of imagination and of will which might have led him to revise old dogmas and to propound new solutions.

It can be said of Sidmouth, as of many of his contemporaries, that he was an eighteenth-century statesman unable to cope with the problems of an industrial era. But Sidmouth's outlook was also timeless, that of the reactionary throughout the ages; a mind immutably opposed to change, blind to the realities of the present, blind to the possibilities of the future, blind to everything except the sanctity of the established order and the overriding need to defend it against every onslaught. It was because these personal principles contrasted so strongly with the political fluidity of his age that Sidmouth and his times were so conspicuously out of joint.

The effectiveness of a reactionary can only endure for a limited period after the moment of his final petrification. Once events have flowed too far beyond his chosen standpoint then he becomes no longer dangerous, merely absurd. Already in 1815 Sidmouth was an anachronism; by the time of his death he had become a dodo. The disappearance of an animal already believed to be extinct cannot be considered so much an item of news as the correction by nature of a regrettable anomaly. In this way was Sidmouth's death accepted. It did not put an end to anything for all that his life stood for had already passed away. It was no more than a reminder of a period too remote to be of urgent interest and yet too near to be historically appealing. It is hardly surprising that it was ignored and that there has been little since in the way of revived attention.

Yet it does not follow that Sidmouth deserved no better than extinction. As a Minister, above all as Prime Minister, his deficiencies were obvious. He lacked imagination and a broad grasp of policy; he lacked flexibility; he lacked enterprise; above all he lacked grandeur and the art of kindling enthusiasm in the public. But he had qualities too. He was determined; he was courageous; he was thorough; he was indomitable in the defence of what he believed to be the right; he could command the devoted loyalty of his followers; the very prudence which betrayed him when bold measures were called for from the Prime Minister was to be among his strongest points when the most important thing asked of the Home Secretary was that he should not lose his head. Given a job to do, clearly defined and soluble by conventional techniques, Sidmouth would see it through against all difficulties and opposition. Only in the uncharted fields of wider policy did he begin to flounder; only when new problems arose and new solutions were demanded did he conspicuously fail.

Sidmouth, in short, was a competent and conscientious executor of accepted policy but unable himself to challenge the dogmas on which that policy was based or to formulate new lines for action when the need arose. He was a capable Minister when the way was clear ahead of him, a disastrous Prime Minister in times of stress. There is less to be said for many men whose reputations now stand higher than Lord Sidmouth's. It is his peculiar misfortune that his blunders and inadequacies should have lived after him while his qualities remain interred with his bones.

Among those qualities were several which are not invariably associated with the trade of politician; qualities, indeed, which contributed in no small measure to his failures. Integrity can be a dangerous asset, and Sidmouth's inability either to conceal or to compromise his strong, if often wrong-headed principles, won him many enemies and little respect. Courtesy is often taken as the defence of the feeble and Sidmouth, deeply reluctant to cause offence to anyone, was dismissed as a flatterer, a hypocrite and a weakling. Consideration for others is a grave handicap for the ambitious, yet when Sidmouth claimed, "I am not aware of having ever wilfully injured or given pain to any human being," his conscience was justifiably at rest.

His achievements were the more remarkable for the insignificance of his family. In an age when every dice was loaded heavily in favour of the aristocrat, Sidmouth was uncompromisingly from the middle-class. Nor did he seek to evade the handicap. He was proud of his background, proud that he was a doctor's son; not with the pride of the vainglorious surveying the obstacles over which he has climbed but the pride of a good citizen who knows that his ancestors have done well by society and asks only that he should be allowed to do the same. He never sought to rise above his father to higher things for the place in life which he had inherited seemed to him entirely honourable

422

and in no need of betterment. He cared little for great wealth and the lure of titles and high places. Sidmouth, perhaps, was a vain man but he also possessed the genuine humility of one who knows that he is on earth to serve and strives for nothing that will not help him in that service.

Modest boasts, perhaps, and yet by no means commonplace. Nor can they be dismissed as the negative virtues of a man who lacked the will to fight. Sidmouth's was a life of self-discipline and self-restraint, a spirit small, humble even, yet not without nobility. If needs must he would accept abuse, mockery, hatred; he would assume any responsibility that might be thrust upon him, he would make any sacrifice that he believed was called for. Failure is hard to face, yet Sidmouth could bear it with almost undiminished self-esteem. So long as his faith in his own probity was unshaken then, come the three corners of the world in arms, he would outface them. Through all the embittered warfare of a parliamentary life he never lost that faith or lowered his standards in quest of power, revenge or easy popularity. If Sidmouth has any claim to greatness, it lies in this.

NOTES
BIBLIOGRAPHY
INDEX

Notes

CHAPTER I

p. 13   1   Roll of the Royal College of Physicians.
        2   Munk. Life of Sir Henry Halford. (London, 1895), pp. 41-2.
   14   1   Belfield. Annals of Addington Family. pp. 21-2.
        2   Public Characters of 1801-2.
   15   1   Highway Manor mss. Note on Dr. Addington by Dr. Thomas.
   16   1   Sidmouth mss.
   17   1   Memoirs of Dr. Richard Gilpin, p. 123 *et seq.*
   18   1   Sidmouth mss. Gilpin to Dr. Addington, 15th July, 1762.
        2   Sidmouth mss. Gilpin to Dr. Addington, 12th December, 1764.
   20   1   Sidmouth mss. Huntingford to Addington, 1770.
   21   1   Sidmouth mss. Huntingford to Addington, 1772.
        2   Sidmouth mss. Huntingford to Addington, 5th October, 1780.
        3   Sidmouth mss. About 1777.
   22   1   Add mss. 32,575, J. Mitford's notebook. "Sayings of Lord Sidmouth."
        2   Sidmouth mss. Mrs. Addington to Addington, 1st September, 1769.
   23   1   Sidmouth mss. Warton to Dr. Addington, 16th May, 1770.
        2   Sidmouth mss. Huntingford to Addington, 26th May, 1772.
        3   Sidmouth mss. Addington to Hiley Addington, 22nd February, 1798.
   24   1   Gilpin, p. 135.
        2   Sidmouth mss. Huntingford to Addington, 6th May, 1773.
   25   1   Sidmouth mss. Addington to Dr. Addington, 29 Aug., 1774.
        2   Sidmouth mss. Dr. Addington to Addington, Oct., 1774.
        3   Sidmouth mss. Addington to Dr. Addington, end of 1774.
   26   1   Sidmouth mss. Sutton to Addington, 17th Oct., 1774.
   27   1   Sidmouth mss. Mrs. Addington to Addington, undated.
        2   Sidmouth mss. Bragge to Addington, undated.
   28   1   Sidmouth mss. Addington to Dr. Addington, 21st Oct., 1774.

p. 28 2 Sidmouth mss. Addington to Dr. Addington, 6th Nov., 1774.

     3 Add mss. 19,696.

29 1 Pellew, vol. I, p. 21.

     2 Tresham Lever. House of Pitt, p. 170.

30 1 Chatham mss. Dr. Addington to Lady Chatham, undated.

     2 Walpole's Correspondence. Walpole to Mann, 5th April, 1767.

     3 Chatham mss. Chatham to George III, 15th June, 1767.

     4 "An authentic account of a transaction which passed in the beginning of the year 1778." London, 1778. See also "Another account . . ."

31 1 Add mss. 41,357. Martin papers, vol. XII.

     2 Pellew, vol. I, p. 28.

     3 Broughton, Recollections of a Long Life, 9th Jan., 1813.

     4 Wilberforce. Life, vol. III, p. 211.

     5 Sidmouth mss. Huntingford to Addington, 3rd June, 1772.

33 1 Chatham mss. Dr. Addington to Lady Chatham, 3rd Nov., 1778.

CHAPTER 2

34 1 Sidmouth mss. Huntingford to Addington, 1st July, 1780.

35 1 Pellew, vol. I, p. 15.

36 1 Sidmouth mss. Dr. Addington to Addington, undated.

     2 Sidmouth mss. Dr. Addington to Addington, 8th Aug., 1781.

     3 Sidmouth mss. Huntingford to Addington, 25th Oct., 1781.

37 1 Diaries of George Rose. 30th Sept., 1804.

     2 Sidmouth mss. Mrs. Addington to Addington, 26th Sept., 1792.

     3 Sidmouth mss. Mrs. Addington to Addington, undated.

     4 Sidmouth mss. Addington to Dr. Addington, 15th June, 1787.

40 1 Rosebery. Pitt, p. 5.

42 1 Bathurst mss. George III to Bathurst, 26th Feb., 1783.

     2 Russell. Memorials of C. J. Fox, vol. II, p. 253.

43 1 Chatham mss. Dr. Addington to Lady Chatham, 31st Jan., 1777.

45 1 Sidmouth mss. Bragge to Addington, 30th Dec., 1784.

     2 Sidmouth mss. Hiley Addington to Addington, undated.

     3 Sidmouth mss. Addington to Pole-Carew, April, 1784.

46 1 Pellew, vol. I, p. 38.

p. 47   1   Diaries of Sylvester Douglas, Lord Glenbervie, 2nd Sept., 1802.

48   1   Sidmouth mss. Huntingford to Addington, Jan., 1785.

      2   Sidmouth mss. Pitt to Addington, 4th Jan., 1786.

      3   Wraxall Memoirs, Jan., 1786.

      4   Sidmouth mss. Hiley Addington to Dr. Addington, 24th Jan., 1786.

      5   Chatham mss. Dr. Addington to Lady Chatham, 9th Feb., 1786.

50   1   Sidmouth mss. Bragge to Addington, 20th Dec., 1787.

51   1   Sidmouth mss. Addington to Dr. Addington, 9th Sept., 1786.

      2   Sidmouth mss. Addington to Dr. Addington, 12th Sept., 1786.

      3   Sidmouth mss. Bragge to Addington, Nov., 1787.

52   1   Stanhope. Life of Pitt, vol. 1, p. 362.

53   1   Holland. Further Memoirs of the Whig Party, vol. II, p. 214.

      2   Sidmouth mss. Addington to Dr. Addington, 29th March, 1788.

54   1   Sidmouth mss. Grenville to Addington, 7th Nov., 1788.

      2   Dropmore mss. Buckingham to Grenville, 8th Dec., 1788.

      3   Connell. Portrait of a Whig Peer, p. 182 (London, 1957), 4th Dec., 1788, though dated 4th Nov. by Connell.

      4   Sidmouth mss. Addington to Dr. Addington, 20th Feb., 1789.

55   1   Pellew, vol. 1, p. 62.

CHAPTER 3

56   1   Journal of Lord Auckland. Liverpool to Auckland, 4th April, 1807.

57   1   Pellew, vol. 1, p. 56.

58   1   Dropmore mss. Grenville to Buckingham, 1st June, 1789.

      2   Life and letters of Sir Gilbert Elliot. Elliot to Lady Elliot, June, 1789.

      3   Elliot. Lady Elliot to Elliot, Jan., 1789.

59   1   Elliot. Elliot to Lady Elliot, Jan., 1799.

      2   Sidmouth mss. Gilpin to Addington, June, 1789.

      3   Porritt. Unreformed House of Commons, vol. 1, p. 452.

      4   Wraxall's Memoirs, vol. v, p. 246.

60   1   Pellew, vol. 1, p. 65.

      2   House of Commons, 10th March, 1790.

      3   Farington Diary. 21st Feb., 1799.

p. 60   4   House of Commons, 10th Feb., 1801.

61   1   House of Commons, 8th June, 1789.

     2   Sidmouth mss. Pole-Carew to Dr. Addington, 12th Mar., 1790.

62   1   House of Commons, 10th March, 1790. Hussey.

     2   Pellew, vol. I, p. 75.

     3   Diary of Lord Colchester, 18th July, 1803.

63   1   Colchester, 20th Feb., 1796.

     2   Life of William Wilberforce, 17th April, 1798.

     3   Wilberforce, 5th May, 1798.

64   1   Sidmouth mss. Addington to Hiley Addington, 26th May, 1786.

65   1   Sidmouth mss. Addington to Dr. Addington, 9th Feb., 1787.

66   1   Elliot. Elliot to Lady Elliot, 18th Dec., 1790.

     2   Sidmouth mss. Burke to Addington, 7th Mar., 1796.

67   1   Sidmouth mss. Addington to Pole-Carew, 22nd Mar., 1790.

68   1   Sidmouth mss. Addington to Hiley Addington, 8th July, 1798.

     2   Sidmouth mss. Addington to Huntingford, 5th April, 1795.

     3   Sidmouth mss. Huntingford to Addington, 15th Aug., 1795.

     4   Sidmouth mss. Huntingford to Addington, 6th Jan., 1799.

70   1   Pellew, vol. I, p. 91.

     2   Pellew, vol. I, p. 152.

     3   Farington Diary, 30th Oct., 1800.

71   1   Wilberforce, 12th Feb., 1795.

     2   Sidmouth mss. Mornington to Addington, 5th May, 1794.

     3   Sidmouth mss. Huntingford to Addington, 14th Nov., 1793.

72   1   Sidmouth mss. Addington to Abbot, 3rd July, 1799.

73   1   Colchester, vol. I, p. 76.

     2   Parliamentary Register XXXIV, p. 558.

     3   Sidmouth mss. Addington to Hiley Addington, 11th Nov., 1794.

     4   House of Commons, 2nd April, 1792.

75   1   Holland. Memoirs of Whig Party, p. 264.

77   1   Sidmouth mss. Addington to Pitt, 8th Oct., 1797.

     2   J. Steven Watson. Reign of George III, p. 357.

p. 79   1   House of Commons, 3rd Dec., 1798.

       2   Parliamentary Papers (1806), vol. III, p. 205.

       3   Colchester, Jan., 1798.

       4   Dropmore mss. Grenville to Buckingham, Dec., 1797.

80   1   Add mss. 37416, 8th Dec., 1798.

       2   Sidmouth mss. Addington to Hiley Addington, 8th May, 1798.

       3   "Poems spoken on public occasions at Reading school." Ed., Dr. Valpy, Reading, 1804.

81   1   Trevelyan. Grey of the Reform Bill, p. 130.

       2   Tomline's Pitt. Chapters XXIII, XXIV and XXVII printed for private circulation. John Murray, 1903, p. 101.

83   1   Pellew, vol. I, p. 205.

       2   Add mss. 37,416, 8th Dec., 1798.

       3   Sidmouth mss., 23rd Jan., 1797.

84   1   Stanhope, vol. III, p. 4.

85   1   Add mss. 37,416, 13th June, 1799.

       2   Sidmouth mss. Copy of speech transcribed for Pellew.

87   1   Sidmouth mss. Pitt to Addington, 4th Jan., 1800.

88   1   Sidmouth mss. Addington to Hiley Addington, 9th Jan., 1800.

       2   Sidmouth mss. Addington to Hiley Addington, 13th Sept., 1800.

       3   Pellew, vol. I, p. 263, Pitt to Addington, 8th Oct., 1800.

89   1   Sidmouth mss. Addington to Hiley Addington, 19th Oct., 1800.

       2   Colchester. Addington to Abbot, 9th Nov., 1800.

       3   Add mss. 37,416, Addington to Wellesley, 5th Oct., 1800.

90   1   Castlereagh Memoirs, vol. IV, p. 8 *et seq.*

       2   Dacres Adams mss. 31st Jan., 1801.

91   1   Campbell's "Lives of the Chancellors," vol. VI, p. 297.

       2   See, e.g., Stanhope, vol. III, p. 269.

       3   Stanhope, vol. III, p. 273.

92   1   Rose, 13th Feb., 1801.

       2   Wilberforce, vol. III, p. 7.

       3   Sidmouth mss. George III to Addington, 29th Jan., 1801.

93   1   Sidmouth mss. George III to Addington, 31st Jan., 1801.

       2   Stanhope, vol. III, Appendix p. xxx. Pitt to George III 3rd Feb., 1801.

       3   Pellew, vol. I, p. 287.

       4   Sidmouth mss. Mary Anne Addington's Notebook.

94   1   *The Times*, 9th and 10th Feb., 1801.

p. 94   2   Sidmouth's mss. Mary Anne's Notebook.

       3   Sidmouth mss.   Mrs. Bragge to Mrs. Goodenough, undated.

95   1   Colchester, 9th Feb., 1801.

     2   House of Commons, 17th Feb., 1801.

     3   Ashbourne. Pitt to Chatham, 5th Feb., 1801.

96   1   Rose. 13th Feb., 1801.

     2   Malmesbury's Diary. 14th Mar., 1801.

     3   Stapleton. Canning to Lord Boringdon, 29th Oct., 1801.

     4   Sidmouth mss. Mary Anne's Notebook.

     5   Rose. 13th Feb., 1801.

     6   Dacres Adams mss. Mitford to Pitt, 6th Feb., 1801.

97   1   House of Commons, 16th Feb., 1801.

98   1   Bagot. Canning to Sneyd, 14th Feb., 1801.

     2   Glenbervie. 17th Feb., 1801.

     3   Memoirs of Court and Cabinets of George III.   Tom Grenville to Buckingham, 27th July, 1801.

     4   Rose. 6th April, 1801.

     5   Colchester. 8th Feb., 1801.

99   1   Stanhope, vol. III, p. 291.

     2   Campbell. "Lives of the Chancellors," vol. VI, p. 327, Addington to Loughborough, 25th April, 1801.

     3   Feiling. Second Tory Party, p. 170.

     4   Chatham mss. Chatham to Pitt, 6th Feb., 1801.

     5   Colchester. 18th Feb., 1801.

     6   Colchester. 5th Feb., 1801.

100   1   Ashbourne. Duchess of Devonshire to Pelham, 9th Feb., 1801.

      2   Twiss. Lord Eldon, vol. I, p. 251.

      3   Granville Leveson-Gower. Correspondence, vol. I, p. 329.

101   1   Letters of Lord St. Vincent. St. Vincent to Keith, 21st Feb., 1801.

      2   *The Times*, 19th Feb., 1801.

      3   Campbell. Lives of the Chief Justices, vol. III, p. 143.

102   1   Glenbervie. Nov., 1801.

103   1   e.g. Trevelyan. Grey. Grey to Wyvill, 11th Feb., 1801.

      2   Dropmore mss. Wellesley to Grenville, 8th June, 1802.

      3   Colchester. 9th Feb., 1801.

      4   Sidmouth mss. George III to Addington, 15th Mar., 1801.

      5   Wilberforce. Wilberforce to Muncaster, 7th Feb., 1801.

104   1   Stanhope, vol. III, p. 303.

      2   Dacres Adams mss. Willis to Pitt, undated.

105   1   Rosebery. Pitt, p. 226.

      2   Ashbourne. Canning to Pitt, 8th Mar., 1801.

      3   Malmesbury. 9th Mar., 1801.

CHAPTER 5

p. 124   2   House of Commons, 3rd Nov., 1801.

3   Pellew, vol. 1, p. 451, Macpherson to Addington, 14th Aug., 1801.

125   1   Windham Papers. Windham to Addington, 1st Oct., 1801.

2   Stapleton. Canning to Boringdon, 29th Oct., 1801.

3   Dacres Adams mss. Spencer to Pitt, 3rd Oct., 1801.

4   Dacres Adams mss. Villiers to Pitt, 5th Oct., 1801.

5   Dacres Adams mss. Dundas to Pitt, 6th Oct., 1801.

6   Dacres Adams mss. Grenville to Pitt, 6th Oct., 1801.

7   Russell. Memorials and Correspondence of C. J. Fox. Fox to Grey, 12th Oct., 1801.

126   1   St. Vincent Letters. St. Vincent to Uxbridge, 12th Oct., 1801.

2   Sidmouth mss. Nelson to Addington, 4th Oct., 1801.

3   Dacres Adams mss. Grenville to Pitt, 2nd Oct., 1801.

4   Sidmouth mss. Addington to Pitt, 18th Oct., 1801.

5   Pitt and Wilberforce. 1st Oct., 1801.

6   Bathurst mss. Pitt to Bathurst, 18th Oct., 1801.

7   House of Commons, 3rd Nov., 1801.

127   1   Glenbervie. 31st Oct., 1801.

2   Windham Papers. Cobbett to Windham, 20th Oct., 1801.

3   Colchester. Legge to Abbot, 31st Oct., 1801.

4   Holland. Memoirs of Whig Party, vol. 1, p. 185.

128   1   Sidmouth mss. George III to Addington, 14th June, 1801.

129   1   Glenbervie. 16th July, 1801. Pellew, vol. 1, p. 409.

2   Glenbervie. 14th April, 1801.

3   Rose. 30th Sept., 1804.

130   1   Pellew, vol. 1, p. 413.

2   Add mss. 33,108. Addington to Pelham, 8th Oct., 1801.

131   1   See, in particular, Aspinall, Politics and the Press.

2   Aspinall. Ibid. Grenville to Carysfort, 16th Dec., 1800.

3   History of *The Times*, vol. 1, pp. 120-1.

4   *The Times*, 19th June, 1819.

5   See Belfield, p. 58, for a careful study of Hiley Addington's journalistic efforts.

132   1   Festing. Canning to Frere, 21st Nov., 1801.

2   Olphin. Tierney to Moira, Nov., 1801.

3   Festing. Canning to Frere, 21st Nov., 1801.

4   Olphin. Grey to Tierney, 28th Dec., 1801.

133   1   Trevelyan. Grey, p. 127.

2   Cornwallis' Correspondence. 15th Nov., 1799.

134   1   Ashbourne. Clare to Pelham, 5th Sept., 1801.

2   Colchester, vol. 1, p. 280.

3   Pellew, vol. 1, p. 435. Littlehales to Abbot, 16th Sept., 1801.

435

p. 149 2 Festing. Canning to Frere, April, 1802.

151 1 Wilberforce. Wilberforce to Addington, 2nd Jan., 1802.

      2 Wilberforce. Pitt to Wilberforce, 4th Feb., 1802.

152 1 Festing. Canning to Frere, 7th Mar., 1802.

      2 Dacres Adams mss. Canning to Pitt, 13th May, 1802.

      3 Festing. Canning to Frere, 7th June, 1802.

      4 House of Commons (Committee of Supply). 20th Nov., 1801.

153 1 Holland. History of Whig Party, vol. II, p. 214.

      2 Southey. Letters from England. April, 1802.

154 1 House of Commons. 24th Nov., 1801.

      2 Malmesbury. 12th April, 1802.

155 1 Add mss. 41,378. Martin's Biographical Notes.

156 1 Sidmouth mss. Wellesley to Addington, 13th Mar., 1802.

      2 Sidmouth mss. Addington to Wellesley, 28th Sept., 1802.

      3 Sidmouth mss. Wellesley to Addington, 12th Feb., 1803.

157 1 Hobhouse Diary. 20th Aug., 1822.

      2 Castlereagh. Castlereagh to Addington, 21st July, 1802.

      3 Glenbervie. 2nd Sept., 1802.

158 1 Wellesley Papers. Wilberforce to Wellesley, 3rd Sept., 1801.

      2 Furber, p. 274. Dundas to Pitt, 5th Feb., 1802.

      3 Add mss. 35,708. Addington to Hardwicke, 29th June, 1802.

159 1 Pellew, vol. II, p. 72.

      2 Feiling, Second Tory Party, p. 227.

      3 Rogers, M. S., B.Litt., d. 97, whose analysis of Addington's parliamentary strength has been of the greatest value.

      4 Sidmouth mss. Addington to Pole-Carew, 1st Aug., 1802.

CHAPTER 7

162 1 Hol'and Rose, p. 477.

163 1 Glenbervie. 27th Aug., 1802.

      2 Croker Papers, vol. II, p. 339.

      3 Rose. 26th Dec., 1802.

      4 Wellesley Papers. Wellesley Pole to Wellesley, 28th Sept., 1802.

164 1 Fairburn's "Whole Correspondence . . ." Merry to Hawkesbury, 4th June, 1802.

      2 Fairburn. Hawkesbury to Merry, 24th May, 1802.

      3 Sidmouth mss. Glenbervie to Addington, 24th May, 1802.

      4 Fairburn. Hawkesbury to Merry, 28th Aug., 1802.

p. 165 1 Aspinall, "Politics and the Press." Heriot to Addington, 10th Aug., 1802.

      2 Sidmouth mss. Addington to Heriot, 12th Aug., 1802.

166 1 Add mss. 35,708. Addington to Hardwicke, 30th Oct., 1802.

      2 Sidmouth mss. Pitt to Addington, 10th Nov., 1802.

      3 Dacres Adams mss. Addington to Pitt, 12th Nov., 1802.

167 1 Creevey Papers. Creevey to Dr. Currie, 8th Nov., 1802.

168 1 Leveson-Gower. Lady Bessborough to Leveson-Gower, 23rd Dec., 1802.

      2 Holland Rose. Rose to Tomline, 24th Dec., 1802.

      3 Stanhope, vol. III, p. 426.

169 1 Sidmouth mss. Farquhar to Addington, 12th Dec., 1802.

      2 See, for example, Farington Diary, 13th Feb., 1803.

      3 Tucker. Memoirs of St. Vincent, p. 156.

170 1 Malmesbury. Canning to Malmesbury, 23rd Dec., 1802.

      2 Creevey. Creevey to Dr. Currie, 25th Nov., 1802.

      3 Russell. Memorials. Fox to Grey, 12th Dec., 1802.

      4 Pellew, vol. II, p. 105.

171 1 House of Commons. 8th Dec., 1802.

      2 Malmesbury. Canning to Malmesbury, 20th Oct., 1802.

172 1 Malmesbury. 21st Nov., 1802.

173 1 Rose. 5th Dec., 1802.

      2 See Belfield, p. 61.

      3 22nd Dec., 1802.

174 1 e.g. Dropmore mss. Buckingham to Grenville, 1st Nov., 1802.

      2 Dropmore mss. Grenville to Pitt, 8th Nov., 1802.

      3 Stanhope, vol. III, p. 406. Rose to Tomline, 21st Nov., 1802.

      4 Sidmouth mss. Pitt to Addington, 30th Dec., 1802.

      5 Pellew, vol. II, p. 108. 31st Dec., 1802

      6 Sidmouth mss. Addington to Hiley Addington, 8th Jan., 1803.

      7 Yonge. Earl of Liverpool. Hawkesbury to Liverpool, 9th Jan., 1803.

175 1 Stanhope, vol. III, p. 434. Pitt to Rose, 28th Jan., 1803.

      2 Rose. 21st Feb., 1803.

      3 Plumer Ward. Mulgrave to Pitt, 28th Feb., 1803.

176 1 Sidmouth mss. Melville to Addington, 22nd Mar., 1803.

177 1 Stanhope, vol. IV, p. 28. Long to Pitt, 3rd April, 1803.

      2 Grenville. Court and Cabinets of George III, vol. III, p. 282 *et seq.*

178 1 Pellew, vol. II, p. 120. Addington to Pitt, 12th April, 1803.

      2 Sidmouth mss. Pitt to Addington, 13th April, 1803.

p. 178   3   Pellew, vol. II, p. 125. Addington to Pitt, 18th April, 1803.
179   1   Malmesbury, vol. IV, p. 187.
      2   Dacres Adams mss. Canning to Pitt, 3rd May, 1803.
      3   Dacres Adams mss. Melville to Pitt, 16th June, 1803.
181   1   Dropmore mss. Tom Grenville to Grenville, 8th April, 1803.
      2   Olphin, p. 85.
      3   Malmesbury. 30th May, 1803.
      4   Russell. Memorials. Fox to Grey, 16th April, 1803.
      5   Trevelyan. Grey. Grey to Lady Grey, April, 1803.
      6   Brock. Lord Liverpool and Liberal Toryism, p. 13.
      7   Letters of Lord St. Vincent. St. Vincent to Addington, 30th Mar. and 19th May, 1803.
182   1   Fairburn. Whitworth to Hawkesbury, 21st Feb., 1803.
      2   Fairburn. Whitworth to Hawkesbury, 5th Mar., 1803.
183   1   Malmesbury. 19th Feb., 1803.
      2   Malmesbury. Feb., 1803.
      3   Barker. Thomas Coutts. Fox to Coutts, 22nd July, 1803.
      4   Russell. Memorials. Fox to Lauderdale, 2nd April, 1804.
184   1   Fairburn. Whitworth to Hawkesbury, 14th Mar., 1803.
      2   Sidmouth mss. Nelson to Addington, 9th Mar., 1803.
185   1   Pellew, vol. III, p. 470.
186   1   Horner, vol. I, p. 221.
      2   Malmesbury. 24th May, 1803.
187   1   Pellew, vol. II, p. 138.
      2   Sidmouth mss. Mary Anne's Notebook.
      3   Sidmouth mss. George III to Addington, 4th June, 1803.
      4   Russell. Memorials. Fox to Holland, 6th June, 1803.
188   1   Cobbett. Political Register, 7th May, 1803.

CHAPTER 8

189   1   Sidmouth mss. Private Memoir on Finance, June, 1803.
190   1   Malmesbury. 13th June, 1803.
      2   See Farnsworth, op. cit., for an elaboration of this theme.
191   1   House of Commons. 5th July, 1803.
      2   House of Commons. 13th July, 1803.
      3   Stanhope, vol. IV, p. 65.
192   1   House of Commons. 13th July, 1803.
193   1   Farnsworth, chap. VI.
      2   Minutes of Evidence. Cmd. 288-1 of 1919, App. no. 1.
      3   Cmd. 7362 of 1948, p. 549.
194   1   Colchester. 27th May, 1803.
195   1   Festing. Canning to Frere, 23rd Nov., 1802.

438

p. 195   2   Russell. Memorials. Fox to Grey, 19th Oct., 1803.

         3   Rose. 2nd Oct., 1803.

  196   1   Malmesbury. Jan., 1804.

  197   1   Pellew, vol. II, p. 310.

  199   1   House of Commons. 6th June, 1803.

         2   House of Commons. 20th June, 1803.

  200   1   Malmesbury. 19th Feb., 1804.

         2   Wilberforce. Private Papers. Windham to Wilberforce, 18th Aug., 1803.

         3   Fortescue. County Lieutenancies and the Army, p. 73.

         4   House of Commons. 27th July, 1807.

         5   See, in particular, Professor Glover's expert defence of Addington's policy in his recent "Peninsular Preparation: The Reform of the British Army 1795-1809," pp. 230-3.

         6   Sidmouth mss. Addington to Simcoe. 4th Sept., 1803.

         7   Fremantle. England in the Nineteenth Century, vol. I, p. 382.

         8   Sidmouth mss. 19th Sept., 1803.

  201   1   Russell. Memorials. Fox to Grey. Aug., 1803.

         2   House of Commons. 9th Dec., 1803.

         3   Add mss. 37,846 Grenville to Windham, 15th July, 1803.

         4   Wilberforce, vol. III, p. 120.

  202   1   Sidmouth mss. Addington to Hiley Addington, 12th Oct., 1803.

         2   Glover, pp. 233-8.

         3   Ross. Cornwallis Correspondence, vol. III, p. 509, cited by Glover.

         4   Sidmouth mss. Addington to Hiley Addington, 12th Oct., 1803.

         5   Sidmouth mss. Redesdale to Addington, 26th Aug., 1802.

  203   1   Add mss. 33,112. 24th Oct., 1803.

  204   1   Sidmouth mss. Addington to Hiley Addington, 19th Aug., 1803.

         2   Elliot. Elliot to Lady Elliot, 16th July, 1803.

         3   Leveson-Gower. Lady Bessborough to Leveson-Gower, 17th Oct., 1803.

         4   Add mss. 35,702. Yorke to Hardwicke, 2nd Aug., 1803.

         5   Add mss. 35,702. Yorke to Hardwicke, 21st Sept., 1803.

         6   Add mss. 35,702. Yorke to Hardwicke, Oct., 1803.

         7   Add mss. 35,702. Yorke to Hardwicke, 18th Oct., 1803.

  205   1   Court and Cabinets of George III. T. Grenville to Buckingham, 25th Nov., 1803.

         2   Dropmore mss. Buckingham to Grenville, 25th Dec., 1803.

p. 206	1	Colchester. 25th Dec., 1803.
	2	Sidmouth mss. Addington to Hiley Addington, 10th Nov., 1803.
	3	Auckland. Auckland to Beresford, 19th Dec., 1803.
	4	Creevey. Creevey to Currie, 29th Dec., 1803.
207	1	Add mss. 37,416. Wellesley to Hobart, 31st Dec., 1803.
	2	Add mss. 37,416. Wellesley to Grenville, 1st Jan., 1804.
	3	Pitt and Wilberforce. Pitt to Wilberforce, 5th Jan., 1804.
	4	Court and Cabinets of George III. Grenville to Buckingham, 10th Jan., 1804.
208	1	Trevelyan. Grey. Fox to Grey, 29th Jan, 1804.
	2	Russell. Memorials. Fox to Fitzpatrick, 27th Jan., 1804.
	3	Stanhope, vol. IV, p. 115. Grenville to Pitt, 31st Jan., 1804.
209	1	Sidmouth mss. Addington to Hiley Addington, 24th Jan., 1804.
	2	House of Commons. 27th Feb., 1804.
	3	Secret Correspondence at Melville Castle. Hope to Melville, 22nd Mar., 1804.
	4	Malmesbury. 19th Feb., 1804.
	5	Secret Correspondence. Pitt to Melville, 29th Mar., 1804.
210	1	Secret Correspondence. Pitt to Melville, 29th Mar., 1804.
211	1	Secret Correspondence. Pitt to Melville, 17th April, 1804.
	2	Add mss. 35,702. Yorke to Hardwicke, Jan., 1804.
	3	Creevey Papers. Creevey to Currie, 21st June, 1804.
212	1	Osler. Exmouth, p. 225.
	2	House of Commons. 19th Mar., 1804.
	3	Ashbourne. 11th April, 1804.
213	1	Add mss. 35,702. Yorke to Hardwicke, 14th April, 1804.
	2	Sidmouth mss. Hiley Addington to Mrs. Goodenough, 24th April, 1804.
214	1	Malmesbury. May, 1804.
	2	Moore. Sheridan, vol. II, p. 323.
	3	e.g. Donoughmore mss. Hutchinson to Donoughmore, undated. ". . . It is now rather supposed that we should have beat them in the Lords. Certain it is they would not have had a majority of more than two or three . . ."
	4	Stanhope, vol. IV, p. 151. Grenville to Buckingham, 19th April, 1804.
	5	Stanhope, vol. IV, App. p. iii. Pitt to George III, 21st April, 1804.
215	1	Stanhope, vol. IV, p. 155. Eldon to Pitt, 22nd April, 1804.
	2	House of Lords. 30th April, 1803.

p. 216   1   Stanhope, vol. IV, App. p. viii. George III to Pitt, 5th May, 1804.

2   Sidmouth mss. Hastings to Addington, undated.

217   1   Sidmouth mss. Mary Anne's Notebook.

2   Malmesbury. 8th May, 1804.

3   Glenbervie. 19th Aug., 1804.

218   1   Colchester. 29th April, 1804.

2   Sidmouth mss. Addington to Pole-Carew, May, 1804.

219   1   Farington Diary. 19th May, 1803.

220   1   Rosebery. Pitt, p. 230.

CHAPTER 9

222   1   Sidmouth mss. George III to Addington, 9th May, 1804.

2   Sidmouth mss. Addington to George III, 9th May, 1804.

223   1   Sidmouth mss. Mary Anne's Notebook.

2   Sidmouth mss. George III to Addington, 14th May, 1804.

3   Secret Correspondence. George III to Eldon, 18th May, 1804.

4   Sidmouth mss. George III to Bragge, 11th May, 1804.

224   1   Glenbervie. 19th Aug., 1804.

2   Leveson-Gower. Lady Bessborough to Leveson-Gower, Aug., 1804.

225   1   Sidmouth mss. Addington to Harry Addington, 8th Oct., 1803.

2   Sidmouth mss. Addington to Hiley Addington, 7th Sept., 1805.

3   Colchester. 8th May, 1803.

226   1   Sidmouth mss. Nelson to Addington, 30th June, 1804.

2   Stanhope. Castlereagh to Wellesley, 18th May, 1804.

3   Yonge. Liverpool to Bishop of Hereford, 16th July, 1804.

4   Rose, vol. II, p. 119.

5   Add mss. 31,229. Beeke to Vansittart, 11th May, 1804.

227   1   Trevelyan. Grey. Grey to Lady Grey, 8th May, 1804.

2   Sidmouth mss. Addington to Hiley Addington, 1st Nov., 1804.

228   1   Sidmouth mss. Addington to Hiley Addington, 6th Oct., 1804.

2   House of Commons. 18th June, 1804.

3   Sidmouth mss. Addington to Hiley Addington, 13th June, 1804.

4   Sidmouth mss. Addington to Hiley Addington, 20th June, 1804.

p. 228   5   Dropmore mss. Buckingham to Grenville, 23rd Sept., 1804.

229   1   Pellew, vol. II, p. 320.

    2   Wilberforce. 27th June, 1804.

    3   Wilberforce. Wilberforce to Muncaster, 6th July, 1804.

    4   Dropmore mss. Buckingham to Grenville, 30th Sept., 1804.

230   1   Colchester. 29th Oct., 1804.

    2   Sidmouth mss. Addington to Hiley Addington, 3rd Dec., 1804.

    3   Colchester. 20th Jan., 1805.

231   1   Sidmouth mss. Addington to Bragge-Bathurst, 12th Dec., 1804.

    2   Sidmouth mss. Addington to Hiley Addington, 22nd Dec., 1804.

    3   Sidmouth mss. Addington to Bragge-Bathurst, 3rd Jan., 1805.

    4   Sidmouth mss. Hawkesbury to Addington, 19th Dec., 1804.

232   1   See, e.g., Porritt. The Unreformed House of Commons, vol. I, p. 452.

    2   Sidmouth mss. Addington to Pitt, 28th Dec., 1804.

233   1   Yonge. Hawkesbury to Liverpool. Early Dec., 1804.

    2   Windham Papers. Windham to Mrs. Crewe, 6th Jan., 1805.

    3   Holland Rose. William Pitt and the Great War, p. 517.

    4   Stanhope, vol. IV, p. 245. Canning to Lady H. Stanhope, 1st Jan., 1805.

234   1   Donoughmore mss. Hutchinson to Donoughmore, 1st Jan., 1805.

    2   Sidmouth mss. Addington to Bragge-Bathurst, 3rd Jan., 1805.

    3   Sidmouth mss. Addington to Hiley Addington, 24th Dec., 1804.

    4   Sidmouth mss. Addington to Ellenborough, 24th Dec., 1804.

235   1   Wilberforce, vol. III, p. 211.

236   1   House of Commons. 6th Mar., 1805.

237   1   Sidmouth mss. Steele to Addington, Sept., 1804.

    2   Colchester. 7th April, 1805.

    3   Letters to Ivy. 2nd April, 1805.

238   1   Sidmouth mss. Sidmouth to Hiley Addington, 16th April, 1805.

    2   Sidmouth mss. Sidmouth to Hiley Addington, 22nd April, 1805.

p. 238   3   Creevey Papers. Creevey to Currie, 11th May, 1805.

239   1   Sidmouth mss. Sidmouth to Hawkesbury, 27th April, 1805.

      2   Sidmouth mss. Sidmouth to Hiley Addington, 28th April, 1805.

240   1   Dropmore mss. Buckingham to Grenville, 28th June, 1805.

      2   Sidmouth mss. Sidmouth to Hiley Addington, 1st July, 1805.

      3   Dropmore mss. Buckingham to Grenville, 12th July, 1805.

241   1   Pellew, vol. II, pp. 371-2. Sidmouth to Hiley Addington, 1st July, 1805.

      2   Sidmouth mss. Mary Anne's Notebook.

242   1   Donoughmore mss. Hutchinson to Donoughmore, 21st May, 1805.

      2   Auckland. Henley to Auckland, 9th July, 1805.

      3   Auckland. Henley to Auckland, 11th July, 1805.

      4   Malmesbury, vol. v, p. 339.

      5   Sidmouth mss. Sidmouth to Hiley Addington, 7th July, 1805.

      6   Malmesbury, vol. v, p. 339.

      7   Sidmouth mss. Bond to Sidmouth, 12th Sept., 1805.

243   1   Sidmouth mss. Sidmouth to Hiley Addington, 19th July, 1805.

      2   Sidmouth mss. Sidmouth to Buckinghamshire, 19th Sept., 1805.

      3   Russell. Memorials. Fox to Grey, 12th July, 1805.

244   1   Russell. Fox to O'Brien, 17th July, 1805.

      2   Pellew, vol. II, p. 382.

      3   Sidmouth mss. Sidmouth to Hiley Addington, 12th Nov., 1805.

245   1   Sichel. Lady Hamilton to Addington, 1803.

      2   Sidmouth mss. Lady Hamilton to Sir W. Scott, undated, probably late 1805.

      3   Sidmouth mss. Sidmouth to Hiley Addington, 4th Sept., 1805.

246   1   Dropmore mss. Thos. Grenville to Grenville, 7th Oct., 1805.

      2   Sidmouth to Hiley Addington, 5th, 6th, 15th Nov., 1805.

      3   Sidmouth mss. Mary Anne's Notebook.

247   1   Sidmouth mss. Ellenborough to Sidmouth, 4th Oct., 1805.

      2   Sidmouth mss. Sidmouth to Hiley Addington, 12th Nov., 1805.

p. 247 3 Sidmouth mss. Hiley Addington to Sidmouth, undated, probably 7th or 8th Jan., 1805.

248 1 Pellew, vol. II, p. 406. Bishop of Lincoln to Sidmouth, 22nd Jan., 1805.

2 Sidmouth mss. Sidmouth to Bragge-Bathurst, 22nd. Jan., 1805.

CHAPTER 10

250 1 Russell. Memorials. Fox to Lauderdale, 17th Dec., 1805. See also Donoughmore mss. Hutchinson to Donoughmore, 26th Jan., 1806.

2 Sidmouth mss. St. Vincent to Sidmouth, 25th Jan., 1806.

3 Dropmore mss. Buckingham to Grenville, 25th Jan., 1806.

4 Dropmore mss. Thos. Grenville to Grenville, 23rd Jan., 1806.

5 Donoughmore mss. Hutchinson to Donoughmore, 26th Jan., 1806.

251 1 Donoughmore mss. Hutchinson to Donoughmore, 4th Feb., 1806.

252 1 Pellew, vol. II, p. 415. Sidmouth to Dunstanville, 31st Jan., 1806.

2 Pellew, vol. II, p. 417.

3 Colchester, 4th Feb., 1806.

4 Sidmouth mss. Sidmouth to Bragge-Bathurst, 31st Jan., 1806.

253 1 Sidmouth mss. Sidmouth to Buckinghamshire, Aug., 1806.

2 Wilberforce. Private Papers. Ellenborough to Wilberforce, 4th Feb., 1806.

3 Sidmouth mss. Sidmouth to Ellenborough, Feb., 1806.

254 1 Sidmouth mss. Sidmouth to Bragge-Bathurst, 20th Feb., 1806.

2 Leveson-Gower. Lady Bessborough to Leveson-Gower, 5th Feb., 1806.

3 Leveson-Gower. Lady Bessborough to Leveson-Gower, 24th Feb., 1806.

4 Sidmouth mss. Sidmouth to Bragge-Bathurst, 20th Feb., 1806.

255 1 Add mss. 37,883. Minute of 4th Feb., 1806.

256 1 Pellew, vol. II, p. 425.

2 Sidmouth mss. Grenville to Sidmouth, 1st June, 1806.

257 1 Pellew, vol. II, p. 429.

2 House of Lords. 5th Feb., 1807.

258 1 Pellew, vol. II, p. 435.

p. 258 2 Sidmouth mss.   Sidmouth to Hiley Addington, 14th
            Sept., 1806.

        3 Sidmouth mss. Sidmouth to Hiley Addington, 28th July,
            1806.

    259 1 Sidmouth mss. Sidmouth to Hiley Addington, 13th Aug.,
            1806.

        2 Feiling. Second Tory Party, p. 249. Ryder to Harrowby,
            5th July, 1806.

        3 Sidmouth mss. Sidmouth to Bragge-Bathurst, 6th Sept.,
            1806.

        4 Sidmouth mss.   Sidmouth to Hiley Addington, 18th
            Sept., 1806.

    260 1 Sidmouth mss. Sidmouth to Hiley Addington, 21st Sept.,
            1806.

        2 Sidmouth mss.   Sidmouth to Hiley Addington, 29th
            Sept., 1806.

        3 Leveson-Gower. Lady Bessborough to Leveson-Gower,
            27th Sept., 1806.

    261 1 Holland. Memoirs of Whig Party, vol. II, p. 92.
        2 Add mss. 38,737. Canning to Huskisson, 26th Nov., 1806.
        3 Roberts. Whig Party, 1807-12, p. 339.
        4 Presumably the Clerk of the House who, though as in-
            fluential as any Member and a staunch Addingtonian,
            can hardly be counted as a voter.

    262 1 Rogers, who has analysed the strength of the Addingtonians
            with great care, puts the total at the end of 1806 at
            50.

    263 1 Holland. Memoirs of Whig Party, vol. II, p. 181.
    264 1 Colchester. 1st March, 1807.
        2 House of Commons. 26th March, 1807.
        3 Holland. Memoirs of Whig Party, vol. II, p. 193.
    265 1 Colchester. 2nd March, 1807.
        2 Colchester. 14th March, 1807.
        3 Dropmore mss. Buckingham to Grenville, 19th Feb.,
            1807.

        4 Dropmore mss. Holland to Howick, March, 1807.
    266 1 Sidmouth mss. Grenville to Sidmouth, 11th March, 1807.
        2 Walpole. Perceval to Sidmouth, 11th March, 1807.
        3 Gray. Perceval, pp. 74-5.
    267 1 Walpole, vol. I, p. 231.
        2 Dropmore mss.   Temple to Buckingham, 20th March,
            1807

    268 1 Lord Grenville, Thomas Grenville, Moira and Petty for;
            Holland, Howick and Windham against. Fitzwilliam
            and Spencer were both ill.

p. 268   2   Colchester. Grenville to Abbot, 18th March, 1807.

269   1   Lord Melbourne's Papers, ed. Lord Cowper.

      2   Based on opinions such as Moira's, who wrote to Hutchinson (Donoughmore mss, 5th April, 1807), stating: "our removal is the result of an intrigue long carried on by Lord Melville through the agency of a personage whom you will readily guess."

270   1   Stapleton. Canning to Boringdon, 15th March, 1807.

      2   Pellew, vol. II, p. 470.

271   1   Dropmore mss. Howick to Grenville, 7th April, 1807.

      2   Sidmouth mss. George III to Sidmouth, 25th March, 1807.

272   1   Leveson-Gower. Lady Bessborough to Leveson-Gower, 20th May, 1806.

      2   Holland. Memoirs of Whig Party, vol. I, p. 209.

CHAPTER II

274   1   Sidmouth mss. Sidmouth to Hiley Addington, 29th Nov., 1808.

275   1   Sidmouth mss. Sidmouth to Hiley Addington, Sept., 1807, to May, 1811.

      2   Sidmouth mss. Sidmouth to Hiley Addington, 5th July, 1808.

276   1   Sidmouth mss. Sidmouth to Hiley Addington, 13th Nov., 1807.

      2   Sidmouth mss. Sidmouth to Hiley Addington, 7th Jan., 1810.

278   1   Sidmouth mss. Sidmouth to Buckinghamshire, 22nd March, 1807.

      2   Sidmouth mss. Sidmouth to Buckinghamshire, 3rd July, 1807.

      3   Sidmouth mss. Sidmouth to Dunstanville, 5th April, 1807.

280   1   Sidmouth mss. Sidmouth to Hiley Addington, 3rd Oct., 1807.

      2   Sidmouth mss. Sidmouth to Hiley Addington, 24th Sept., 1807.

281   1   Sidmouth mss. Sidmouth to Hiley Addington, 10th Sept., 1807.

282   1   House of Lords. 27th May, 1808.

      2   Sidmouth mss. Sidmouth to Hiley Addington, 29th May, 1808.

283   1   Sidmouth mss. Sidmouth to Hiley Addington, 9th June, 1808.

p. 283 2 Sidmouth mss. Sidmouth to Hiley Addington, 29th July, 1808.

3 Sidmouth mss. Sidmouth to Hiley Addington, undated, probably Dec., 1807.

284 1 House of Lords. 17th Feb., 1809.

2 Sidmouth mss. Sidmouth to Hiley Addington, 3rd April, 1809.

3 Sidmouth mss. Sidmouth to Hiley Addington, 10th Aug., 1808.

4 Sidmouth mss. Sidmouth to Hiley Addington, 4th Sept., 1808.

285 1 Sidmouth mss. Sidmouth to Hiley Addington, 18th Sept., 1808.

2 Sidmouth mss. Sidmouth to Hiley Addington, 27th Sept., 1808.

3 Pellew, vol. II, p. 505.

4 Wellesley Papers. Brougham to Wellesley, Oct., 1837.

286 1 Sidmouth mss. Sidmouth to Hiley Addington, 30th Sept., 1809.

287 1 Sidmouth mss. Buckinghamshire to Sidmouth, 23rd Sept., 1809.

2 Sidmouth mss. Sidmouth to Buckinghamshire, 24th Sept., 1809.

288 1 Colchester, vol. II, p. 215.

2 Sidmouth mss. Sidmouth to Bragge-Bathurst, 12th Oct., 1809.

3 Sidmouth mss. Perceval to Sidmouth, 7th Oct., 1809.

4 Sidmouth mss. Sidmouth to Hiley Addington, 8th Oct., 1809.

5 Walpole. Eldon to Perceval, undated.

289 1 Walpole. Sidmouth to Perceval, 7th Oct., 1809.

2 Sidmouth mss. Vansittart to Sidmouth, Oct., 1809.

3 Sidmouth mss. Sidmouth to Buckinghamshire, 18th Oct., 1809.

4 Sidmouth mss. Buckinghamshire to Sidmouth, 14th Oct., 1809.

5 Sidmouth mss. Ellenborough to Sidmouth, 1st Nov., 1809.

290 1 Dropmore mss. Grenville to Grey, 27th Oct., 1809.

2 Dropmore mss. Grey to Grenville, 3rd Nov., 1809.

3 Dropmore mss. Grenville to Grey, 28th Oct., 1809.

4 Sidmouth mss. Sidmouth to Hiley Addington, 30th Oct., 1809.

5 Pellew, vol. III, p. 12.

6 Sidmouth mss. Sidmouth to Buckinghamshire, undated.

p. 291 1 Sidmouth mss. Sidmouth to Bragge-Bathurst, 1st Dec., 1809.

       2 Hastings mss. Moira to Hastings, 24th Jan., 1810.

292 1 Sidmouth mss. Sidmouth to Hiley Addington, 26th Jan., 1810.

       2 Sidmouth mss. Sidmouth to Grenville, 18th Feb., 1810.

       3 Dropmore mss. Auckland to Grenville, 25th Feb., 1810.

       4 Walpole. Perceval to Rutland, 30th April, 1810.

293 1 Walpole. Perceval to Castlereagh, Aug. (?), 1810.

       2 Gray. Perceval. Perceval to Dundas, 15th April, 1810.

294 1 Sidmouth mss. Sidmouth to Bragge-Bathurst, 27th April, 1810.

       2 Auckland. Cooke to Auckland, Sept., 1809.

       3 Add mss. 38,738. Canning to Huskisson, 5th July, 1811.

295 1 Sidmouth mss. Sidmouth to Hiley Addington, 31st. Oct., 1810.

296 1 Fulford. George IV.

       2 Dropmore mss. Buckingham to Grenville, 9th Jan., 1811.

298 1 Sidmouth mss. Sidmouth to Hiley Addington, 20th April, 1811.

       2 Edinburgh Review, no. xxxiv of 1811.

299 1 Sidmouth mss. Sidmouth to Perceval, 20th May, 1811.

       2 Sidmouth mss. Sidmouth to Hiley Addington, 16th May, 1811.

       3 Holland. Further Memoirs of Whig Party, p. 101.

       4 Sidmouth mss. Sidmouth to Hiley Addington, 22nd May, 1811.

300 1 Belfield, p. 92.

301 1 Sidmouth mss. Sidmouth to Bragge-Bathurst, 23rd June, 1811.

       2 Add mss. 31,229. Vansittart to Miranda, 19th Aug., 1811.

       3 Highway Manor mss. Sidmouth to Buchan, 1st March, 1812.

302 1 Auckland. Grenville to Auckland, 15th Feb., 1812.

303 1 Cornwallis mss. Bishop of Lichfield to Cornwallis, 17th Jan., 1812.

       2 Walpole. Perceval to Lonsdale, Feb., 1812.

       3 Pellew, vol. iii, p. 85. Plumer Ward. Melville to Ward, 8th March, 1812.

       4 Gray, p. 449. Lonsdale to Perceval.

304 1 Walpole. Perceval to Lonsdale, Feb., 1812.

       2 Dropmore mss. D—— to Buckingham, 1st Feb., 1812. (D—— has been identified by Sir G. Lewis as Mr. Dardin, a confidant of Wellesley's.)

       3 Dropmore mss. Buckingham to Grenville, 2nd Feb., 1812.

p. 304   4   Sidmouth mss. Sidmouth to le Mesurier, 22nd Feb., 1812.
305   1   Twiss, vol. I, p. 494.
306   1   e.g. Memoirs of the Court of England. Thos. Grenville to Buckingham, 28th May, 1812.
     2   Sidmouth mss. Sidmouth to Hiley Addington, 23rd May, 1821.
     3   Memoirs of Thomas Moore (ed. Lord John Russell). Lady Donegal to Moore, May, 1812.
307   1   Sidmouth mss. Mary Anne's Notebook.

CHAPTER 12

311   1   Thompson. Making of the English working-class. See, in particular, pp. 573-602.
312   1   See especially Darvall. Public Order and Popular Disturbance in Regency England.
     2   Introduction to "The Liberal Awakening," p. vi.
     3   Sidmouth mss. Sidmouth to Babington, 13th Nov., 1812.
313   1   H.O. 40, 1. 11th April, 1812.
     2   H.O. 42, 197. cf. Hammond, Skilled Labourer, p. 91.
315   1   Imperial Calendar.
     2   1st July, 1812.
316   1   Later, as Sir John Beckett, Permanent Under-Secretary at the Colonial Office.
     2   Cmd. 309 (1806). Report of Royal Commission.
     3   Strutt. Home Office: Peeps into Past.
     4   Imperial Calendar.
317   1   Sidmouth mss. Sidmouth to Hiley Addington, 7th Jan., 1817.
318   1   6th Jan., 1812. Halévy, England in 1815, p. 44.
319   1   Parker. Peel. Sidmouth to Peel, 19th Jan., 1814.
321   1   Pellew, vol. III, p. 84. Seale to Sidmouth, 30th June, 1812.
322   1   H.O. 42, 125.
     2   House of Lords. 29th June, 1812.
     3   H.O. 42, 125. Sidmouth to Maitland, 20th July, 1812.
323   1   Sidmouth mss. Sidmouth to Maitland, 13th Jan., 1813.
     2   Pellew, vol. III, p. 85.
     3   Sidmouth mss. Sidmouth to Maitland, 16th Jan., 1813.
324   1   Sidmouth mss. Mary Anne's Notebook.
     2   Add mss. 40,182. Sidmouth to Peel, 23rd Sept., 1812.
     3   Add mss. 40,182. Peel to Sidmouth, 24th Sept., 1812.
     4   Add mss. 40,182. Sidmouth to Peel, 13th Jan., 1814.
     5   Gash, p. 179.

p. 325   1   Add mss. 34,458. Auckland to Sidmouth, 25th Aug., 1812.

326   1   Hobhouse Diary, p. 17.

     2   Add mss. 33,544. Bentham to Sidmouth, 13th June, 1812.

     3   H.O. 42, 124. Bentham to Sidmouth, 20th June, 1812.

327   1   Cole. Robert Owen, p. 115; Podmore. Owen, pp. 124-5.

     2   Cole, p. 124.

328   1   Aspinall. Letters of George IV. Lady Hamilton to Sidmouth, 28th Feb., 1813.

     2   Add mss. 41,378. Sir T. Martin's Biographical Notes.

     3   Aspinall. Letters of George IV. Lady Hamilton to Sidmouth, 28th Feb., 1813.

     4   Sidmouth mss. Sidmouth to Lady Hamilton, 6th March, 1813.

329   1   Sichel, Lady Hamilton. Lady Hamilton to Scott, 12th Sept., 1814.

330   1   Aspinall. Letters of George IV. Minute of Sidmouth, 28th May, 1812.

     2   Buckingham. Regency. Dardin to Temple, 4th Sept., 1812.

     3   Leveson-Gower. Canning to Leveson-Gower, 18th Aug., 1812. C.f. Pellew, vol. II, p. 301.

332   1   Bagot. Lyttelton to Bagot, 30th Dec., 1816.

334   1   Cobbett. History of Regency, chap. IV, p. 191. Sidmouth to City Remembrancer, 7th April, 1813.

     2   Cobbett. Regency, chap. IV, p. 192.

     3   Pellew, vol. III, p. 120.

335   1   Add mss. 31,230. Vansittart to Castlereagh, 20th April, 1814.

     2   Cobbett. Regency, chap. VII, p. 387.

     3   Sidmouth mss. Sidmouth to Coker, 15th March, 1815.

CHAPTER 13

338   1   Creevey Papers. Bennet to Creevey, 3rd April, 1815 .

     2   Broughton. Recollections of Long Life, 28th March, 1815.

     3   Pellew, vol. III, p. 132. Sidmouth to Maitland, 30th Aug., 1815.

339   1   Sidmouth mss. Sidmouth to Kenyon, 20th Nov., 1815.

     2   Sidmouth mss. Wordsworth to Sidmouth, 26th Sept., 1815.

340   1   Sidmouth mss. Sidmouth to Sheffield, 21st Jan., 1816.

341   1   Sidmouth mss. Sidmouth to Hiley Addington, 24th July, 1816.

342   1   Sidmouth mss. Sidmouth to Frank, 16th Sept., 1816.

p. 342   2   Pellew, vol. III, p. 155. Sidmouth to Grey, 29th Oct., 1816.
      3   H.O. 79, 3. 12th Oct., 1817.
343   1   Creevey Papers. Creevey to Fawkes, 12th Nov., 1822.
      2   Memoirs of Henry Hunt, vol. III, pp. 360-2.
344   1   Report of Secret Committees of Houses of Lords and
         Commons presented to Parliament, 18th and 19th
         Feb., 1817.
      2   Sidmouth mss. Sidmouth to Abbot, 8th Dec., 1816.
345   1   Bagot. Lyttelton to Bagot, 30th Dec., 1816.
      2   Sidmouth mss. Prince Regent to Sidmouth, 5th Jan.,
         1817.
346   1   Pellew, vol. III, p. 166. Report of Nadin, Deputy Con-
         stable of Manchester.
      2   Political Register, 23rd July, 1817.
      3   See Bamford, vol. II, p. 308, as illustration of mutual dis-
         likes.
      4   Patterson. Burdett. Burdett to Hunt, 9th Nov., 1816.
347   1   Holland. Further Memoirs, p. 251.
348   1   Wilberforce. Wilberforce to Simeon, 3rd March, 1817.
      2   Political Register. 14th Dec., 1816.
349   1   Grey. Grey to Wilson, Oct., 1819.
      2   Cobbett. History of Regency, chap. VII, p. 392.
350   1   For full text see Memoirs of Life of Sir Samuel Romilly,
         vol. III, p. 302.
      2   Aspinall. Politics and the Press, pp. 53-54.
      3   House of Lords. 12th May, 1817.
      4   Cole, p. 217.
351   1   Sidmouth mss. Sidmouth to Prince Regent, 18th April,
         1817.
      2   Pellew, vol. III, p. 178.
352   1   Thompson. See, in particular, pp. 649-651.
      2   Bamford, vol. II, p. 95 *et seq.*
355   1   Memoirs of Life of Elizabeth Fry. Feb., 1818.
      2   Fry. May, 1818.
      3   H.O. 42, 167. Fitzwilliam to Sidmouth, 14th June, 1817.
356   1   Sidmouth mss. Mary Anne's Notebook.
      2   Sidmouth mss. Sidmouth to Hiley Addington, 20th July,
         1817.
357   1   Cobbett. Regency, chap. VII, p. 393.
358   1   House of Commons. 11th Feb, 1818.
      2   Sidmouth mss. Fitzwilliam to Sidmouth, 13th July, 1812.
359   1   Trevelyan. Grey, p. 198.
      2   See, e.g., Gash's Peel, p. 361. Add mss. 40, 388 ff. 21,
         60, 215.
      3   House of Commons. 11th Feb., 1818.

p. 360   1   Add mss. 31, 231. Rosenhagen to Vansittart, 15th Jan., 1816.

2   Hammonds. Skilled Labourer, pp. 350-3.

3   The account of the Hammonds in "The Skilled Labourer" (chap. XII) and of A. F. Fremantle in the English Historical Review (XLVII, 1932, p. 601) are the two leading contributions to the history of Oliver the Spy. The first is the more circumstantial, the second the more dispassionate. See also Thompson, pp. 650-69.

361   1   H.O. 42, 165.

2   H.O. 40, 10.

3   H.O. 79, 3.

362   1   Though cf. Thompson, op. cit.

2   H.O. 42, 167.

363   1   Add mss. 36, 464.

364   1   H.O. 42, 167.

2   H.O. 40, 9.

3   H.O. 40, 10. Richards to Beckett, 9th May, 1817.

4   H.O. 40, 9. Oliver's Narrative.

365   1   H.O. 40, 10. 25th April, 1817.

CHAPTER 14

367   1   Add mss. 38,273. Liverpool to Sidmouth, 6th Aug., 1818.

368   1   Sidmouth mss. Sidmouth to Hiley Addington, 4th April, 1818.

2   Sidmouth mss. Sidmouth to Hiley Addington, 18th April, 1818.

3   Sidmouth mss. Sidmouth to Prince Regent, 22nd April, 1818.

369   1   Dropmore mss. Thos. Grenville to Grenville, 26th Jan., 1819.

370   1   Sidmouth mss. Sidmouth to Exmouth, 15th Aug., 1819.

371   1   Pellew, vol. III, p. 252.

373   1   Sidmouth mss. Sidmouth to Mary Anne Addington, 18th Aug., 1819.

2   Sidmouth's mss. Mary Anne's Notebook.

3   Sidmouth mss. Bloomfield to Sidmouth, 19th Aug., 1819.

374   1   Sidmouth mss. Mary Anne's Notebook.

2   H.O. 79, 3. Hobhouse to Norris, 4th Aug., 1819.

3   e.g. Thompson, p. 683.

375   1   Read, p. 207.

2   Add mss. 38,741. Canning to Huskisson, wrongly dated 14th Aug., 1819.

p. 376   1   Pellew, vol. III, p. 277. Sidmouth to Wodehouse, 3rd Oct., 1819.

377   1   Sidmouth mss. Sidmouth to Yorke, 7th Nov., 1819.

     2   Sidmouth mss. Sidmouth to Bragge-Bathurst, 14th Sept., 1819.

     3   Sidmouth mss. Sidmouth to Liverpool, 1st Oct., 1819.

378   1   e.g. Buckingham. Regency. Thos. Grenville to Buckingham, 1st Oct., 1819.

     2   Sidmouth mss. Huntly to Sidmouth, 7th Nov., 1819.

     3   Memoirs of Plumer Ward. 27th Oct., 1819.

381   1   Stanhope. Cato Street Conspiracy, p. 87

382   1   Sidmouth mss. Bloomfield to Sidmouth, 12th March, 1820.

383   1   Stanhope, p. 162.

     2   See, in particular, H.O. 44, 4 ff. 9 and 10.

     3   Stanhope, p. 169.

384   1   Sidmouth mss. Sidmouth to Bloomfield, 3rd March, 1820.

     2   Cobbett. Regency, chap. VII, p. 400.

385   1   Wilberforce. 28th July, 1820.

386   1   Hobhouse. 12th Feb., 1820.

     2   Lieven-Metternich Letters. Princess Lieven to Metternich, 16th Feb., 1820.

387   1   Hobhouse. 20th Dec., 1820.

     2   Hobhouse. 19th June, 1820.

     3   Bathurst mss. Goulburn to Bathurst, 2nd Aug., 1821.

     4   Hobhouse. 1st Aug., 1821.

388   1   Hobhouse. 26th Feb., 1821.

     2   Pellew, vol. III, p. 328.

389   1   Sidmouth mss. Sidmouth to George IV, 22nd Sept., 1820.

     2   Pellew, vol. III, p. 333.

     3   Sidmouth mss. Sidmouth to Bragge-Bathurst, 27th Oct., 1820.

     4   Sidmouth mss. Sidmouth to Bragge-Bathurst, 29th Oct., 1820.

     5   Hobhouse. 8th and 10th Nov., 1820.

390   1   Hobhouse. 10th Nov., 1820.

     2   Sidmouth mss. Sidmouth to Bragge-Bathurst, 20th Dec., 1820.

     3   Sidmouth mss. Sidmouth to Bragge-Bathurst, 20th Dec., 1820.

391   1   Sidmouth mss. Sidmouth to Bond, 14th Feb., 1821.

p. 393   1   Sidmouth mss.   Sidmouth to Exmouth, 11th (?) May, 1820.

394   1   Hobhouse. 4th June, 1821.

2   Yonge, vol. III, p. 142.

3   Hobhouse. 8th June, 1821.

4   Hobhouse. 9th June, 1821.

396   1   Fulford. George IV, p. 234.

2   Pellew, vol. III, p. 365.

3   Bathurst mss. Sidmouth to Bathurst, 26th Aug., 1821.

4   Pellew, vol. III, p. 368. Cf. Hobhouse, 14th Sept., 1821.

397   1   Sidmouth mss. Mary Anne's Notebook.

2   Bathurst mss. Sidmouth to Bathurst, 31st Aug., 1821.

3   Creevey Papers. Countess of Glengall to Mrs. Taylor, Sept., 1821.

4   Sidmouth mss. Sidmouth to Talbot, 3rd Sept., 1821.

398   1   Hobhouse. 28th Nov., 1821.

2   Pellew, vol. III, p. 378.

3   Pellew, vol. III, p. 379.

399   1   Pellew, vol. III, p. 387.

2   Sidmouth mss. Sidmouth to Huntingford, 11th Nov., 1821.

400   1   Sidmouth mss. Sidmouth to Bragge-Bathurst, 29th Nov., 1821.

2   Sidmouth mss. Peel to Stowell, 4th Dec., 1821.

3   Yonge. Londonderry to Liverpool, 5th Dec., 1821.

401   1   Add mss. 38,273. Arbuthnot to Liverpool, 5th Dec., 1821.

2   Hobhouse. 2nd June, 1821.

402   1   Yonge. Liverpool to George IV, 10th June, 1821.

2   Pellew, vol. III, p. 401.

403   1   Sidmouth mss. Sidmouth to Huntingford, 11th Nov., 1821.

2   Pellew, vol. III, p. 409.

404   1   Add mss. 38,291. Liverpool to Melville, 25th Aug., 1822.

2   Hobhouse. 9th Sept., 1822.

3   Bagot. Canning to Bagot, 3rd Jan., 1823.

405   1   Dormer. Erleigh Court and its Owners.

2   The Cross still stands. On the back, is to be found the cautionary tale of Ruth Pierce who asked that she might be struck dead if she lied. Heaven obliged and she fell dead in the middle of Devizes market-place.

p. 406 1 Sidmouth mss. Sidmouth to Bragge-Bathurst, 24th July, 1823.
2 Sidmouth mss. Wilberforce to Sidmouth, 14th Dec., 1816.
3 Sidmouth mss. Sidmouth to Bragge-Bathurst, 31st July, 1823.
407 1 Colchester. 2nd Dec., 1824.
408 1 Hobhouse. 20th Dec., 1824.
2 Sidmouth mss. Sidmouth to Liverpool, 26th Nov., 1824.
3 Sidmouth mss. Liverpool to Sidmouth, 29th Nov., 1824.
409 1 Letters of George IV. Liverpool to George IV., 26th Nov., 1824.
2 Letters of George IV. George IV to Liverpool, 30th Nov., 1824.
3 Letters of George IV. Eldon to Sidmouth, Dec., 1824.

CHAPTER 16

410 1 Colchester. 2nd Dec., 1824.
411 1 Pellew, vol. III, p. 417.
412 1 Sidmouth mss. Sidmouth to Bragge-Bathurst, 4th Sept., 1823.
2 Highway Manor mss. Sidmouth to Mrs. Valentine, 22nd Sept., 1833.
3 Colchester. Sidmouth to Colchester, 11th Jan., 1828.
413 1 Colchester. Sidmouth to Colchester, 25th Jan., 1828.
2 Sidmouth mss. Stowell to Sidmouth, 24th Nov., 1828.
3 Ellenborough. Political Diary, 26th Nov., 1828.
4 Letters of Elizabeth, Lady Holland to her Son, 6th March, 1829.
414 1 Add mss. 31,232. Sidmouth to Bexley, 11th Oct., 1828.
2 Colchester. Sidmouth to Colchester, 18th Nov., 1828.
3 Pellew, vol. III, p. 425.
4 Pellew, vol. III, p. 425.
5 Sidmouth mss. Sidmouth to Pellew, 5th April, 1829.
415 1 Sidmouth mss. Sidmouth to Pole-Carew, 12th Dec., 1831.
2 Pellew, vol. III, p. 439.
416 1 Pellew, vol. III, p. 459.
417 1 Sidmouth mss. Sidmouth to Bexley, 11th July, 1838.
2 Sidmouth mss. Sidmouth to Wellesley, 10th Oct., 1839.
3 Add mss. 41,378. Sir T. Martin's Notes, 10th Sept., 1840.
4 Moneypenny and Buckle. Disraeli. Disraeli to Sarah Disraeli, Jan.-Feb., 1840.
418 1 Pellew, vol. III, p. 475.

p. 418   2   The Rev. Horace Currie, who had married Charlotte
                  Addington in 1838.
         3   Pellew, vol. III, p. 477.
         4   Sidmouth mss. Mary Anne's Notebook.
   419   1   Raikes. Journal, 19th Feb., 1844.

Bibliography

MANUSCRIPT SOURCES

Incomparably the most important is the collection of Sidmouth family papers now lodged in the County Archives at Exeter. Pellew used many of these in his biography of 1847 but only after severe editing in the interests of grammar, prudery and the feelings of descendants. I have used the originals in every case where it seems that they are still in the collection. I say "seems" since the family collection is a m·.ssive one and as yet (1962) uncatalogued and in disorder. My search was reasonably thorough but I cannot guarantee that some letter appertaining to Henry Addington may not have slipped into other boxes and escaped my notice. Because of this lack of a catalogue I have given details of dates, etc., for letters of even trivial importance.

Certain family papers, for the most part of minor importance, are not with the main collection. I have referred to these as Highway Manor mss. as opposed to Sidmouth mss. in the case of papers in the Exeter archives.

The Home Office papers in the Public Record Office are of great value for the later stages of Sidmouth's career and I have also found material of considerable relevance and importance in the Dacres Adams mss. at the P.R.O. and the Hardwicke papers (add mss. 35,678; 35,690; 35,707-8) at the British Museum. Other collections which contained a certain amount of interest are those of Auckland (add mss. 34,455; 34,458), Bentham (add mss. 33,544), Bexley (add mss. 31,229-32), Broughton (add mss. 36,464), Chatham (P.R.O., vols. xv and xvi), Colchester (P.R.O.), Donoughmore (Knocklofty, Clonmel), Grenville (add mss. 41,855), Huskisson (add mss. 38,741), Liverpool (add mss. 38,241; 38,249; 38,261-2; 38,273; 38, 289-90), Martin (add mss. 41,357) and Sir T. Martin's Biographical Notes (add mss. 41,378), Mitford (Notebook, add mss. 32,575), Peel (add mss. 40,182; 40,190; 40,239; 40,388 and 40,489), Pelham (add mss. 33,108-9; 33,111-12), Wellesley (add mss. 37,416), Willis (add mss. 41,694), and Windham (add mss. 37,880; 37,883).

I have been fortunate in seeing the unpublished M.A. thesis of Mr. D. A. Schofield of Southampton University, "Henry Addington as Speaker of the House of Commons," and the B.Litt. thesis of Mr. J. G. Rogers of Oxford University, "Addington and the Addingtonian interest in Parliament 1801-12." (M.S. B.Litt cl. 97) The latter, in particular, was invaluable for its excellent bibliography. I have also been allowed to see the text of a lecture on Home Office History entitled "The Home Office: Peeps into the Past," delivered in 1961 by Sir Austin Strutt and printed for limited circulation.

Among the publications of the Historical Manuscripts Commission by far the most useful were the mss. of J. B. Fortescue, Esq., at Dropmore (Report of 1892), which are referred to in the notes to this book as Dropmore mss. Other collections of value in this series are those of Bathurst, Cornwallis, Hastings and Knox.

PUBLISHED SOURCES

The only book covering the whole of Addington's career is the three-volume life by Pellew published in London in 1847. Other works which deal directly with aspects of the life of Addington or his family are:

BELFIELD, E. M. G. *Annals of the Addington Family* (Winchester, 1959).

BUCHAN, JOHN. *Brasenose College Quatercentenary Monographs* (Oxford, 1909).

DASENT, A. I. *Speakers of the House of Commons* (London, 1911).

DORMER, C. *Erleigh Court and its Owners* (Reading, 1912).

FARNSWORTH, A. *Addington, Author of the Modern Income Tax* (London, 1951).

MANNING, J. A. *Lives of the Speakers of the House of Commons* (London, 1851).

With the exception of Mr. Belfield's family history and Dr. Farnsworth's monograph, these essays contain little of substance. More solid accounts of Addington's career are contained in the long reviews of Pellew's biography to be found in the Edinburgh Review (July, 1847, vol. 86) and the Quarterly Review (March, 1847, vol. 79).

Among the many general works dealing with the period as a whole or more specialised aspects of it I have found of particular value Professor Aspinall's *Politics and the Press* (London, 1949), Professor Feiling's *Second Tory Party* (London, 1938), and, with reference to Sidmouth's period as Home Secretary, F. O. Darvall's *Popular Disturbances and Public Order in Regency England* (Oxford, 1934), J. L. and Barbara Hammond's *The Skilled Labourer* (London, 1919), and E. P. Thompson's *The Making of the English Working Class* (London, 1964). Sir Arthur Bryant's trilogy, *The Years of Endurance*, *The Years of Victory* and *The Years of Elegance* (London, 1942-6) provide an unequalled background to the period. Other works in this category which I have drawn on for more than a minor reference are listed below. The name of the author in each case comes first.

ASHTON, J. *The Dawn of the XIXth Century in England* (London, 1906).

ASPINALL, A. *The Early English Trade Unions* (London, 1949).

BUCKINGHAM, Duke of. *Memoirs of the Court and Cabinets of George III* (London, 1855).

Memoirs of the Court of England during the Regency (London, 1856).

CAMPBELL. *Lives of the Lord Chancellors.* In particular *Lords Thurlow and Loughborough,* vol. VII (London, 1868).

Lives of the Lord Justices. Lord Ellenborough, vol. IV (London, 1874).

COBBETT, WILLIAM. *History of the Regency and Reign of King George IV* (London, 1830).

Rural Rides (London, 1830).

COLERIDGE, S. T. *Essays on his Own Times* (London, 1850).

FAIRBURN. *Edition of the whole Correspondence between the United Kingdom and France since the signing of the Definitive Treaty at Amiens. Presented to Parliament 13th May,* 1803.

FORTESCUE, SIR JOHN. *County Lieutenancies and the Army* (London, 1909).

FREMANTLE, A. F. *England in the 19th Century* (London, 1929-30).

GLOVER, RICHARD. *Peninsular Preparation: The Reform of the British Army 1795-1809* (Cambridge, 1964).

HALÉVY. *England in 1815* (London, 1924).

The Liberal Awakening 1815-1830 (London, 1926).

HOLLAND, HENRY, LORD. *Memoirs of the Whig Party* (London, 1852). *Further Memoirs of the Whig Party* (London, 1905).

LEWIS, SIR GEORGE. *Essays on the Administrations of Great Britain from 1783 to 1830* (London, 1864).

MUNK, WILLIAM. *Roll of the Royal College of Physicians* (London, 1878).

NAMIER, SIR LEWIS. *England in the Age of the American Revolution* (London, 1961).

READ, DONALD. *Peterloo: the Massacre and its Background* (Manchester, 1958).

ROBERTS, M. *The Whig Party, 1807-12* (London, 1939).

SMART, WILLIAM. *Economic Annals of the 19th Century, 1801-20* (London, 1910).

SOUTHEY, ROBERT. *Letters from England* (London, 1807).

STANHOPE, JOHN. *The Cato Street Conspiracy* (London, 1962).

TROUP, SIR EDWARD. *The Home Office* (London, 1925).

TURBERVILLE, A. S. *The House of Lords in the Age of Reform* (London, 1958).

WATSON, J. STEVEN. *The Reign of George III* (Oxford, 1960).

WHITE, R. J. *Waterloo to Peterloo* (London, 1957).

Finally there is a great mass of biographical and autobiographical material. Some, of no more than marginal relevance, I have referred to only in the notes. Of the others, I have marked with an asterisk the half-dozen or so on which I have drawn most heavily. The name of the subject in each case comes first.

AUCKLAND: *Journal and Correspondence of William, Lord Auckland* (London, 1862).

BAMFORD, SAMUEL: *Passages in the Life of a Radical* (London, 1844).

BROUGHTON: *Recollections of a Long Life* (London, 1909).

BURDETT, SIR FRANCIS: M. W. Patterson (London, 1931).

CANNING: *George Canning and his Times*. A. G. Stapleton (London, 1859).

Political Life. A. G. Stapleton (London, 1831).

Life of Canning, Sir Charles Petrie (London, 1930).

George Canning and his friends. Josceline Bagot (London, 1909).

CASTLEREAGH: *Memoirs and Correspondence of Viscount Castlereagh.* Edited by Lord Londonderry (London, 1849).

Life of Castlereagh. Ione Leigh (London, 1951).

COBBETT: *The Life of William Cobbett.* G. D. H. Cole (London, 1861).

*COLCHESTER: *Diary and Correspondence of Lord Colchester* (London, 1861).

CORNWALLIS: *Correspondence of Charles, 1st Marquis Cornwallis.* Ed. C. Ross (London, 1859).

COUTTS: *Life of Thomas Coutts.* E. H. Coleridge (London, 1920).

CREEVEY: *Papers.* Ed. Sir Herbert Maxwell (London, 1903).

Life and Times. Ed. John Gore (London, 1934).

CROKER: *Papers.* Ed. Louis Jennings (London, 1884).

DUDLEY: *Letters of Earl of Dudley to Bishop of Llandaff* (London, 1841).

Letters to Ivy (London, 1905).

ELDON: *Life of Lord Chancellor Eldon.* Horace Twiss (London, 1844).

ELLENBOROUGH: *Political Diary of Lord Ellenborough*, 1828-30 (London, 1881).

ELLIOT: *Life and Letters of Sir Gilbert Elliot, 1st Earl of Minto* (London, 1874).

EXMOUTH: *Life of Admiral, Viscount Exmouth.* Osler (London, 1835).

FARINGTON: *Diary.* Ed. J. Grieg (London, 1922-6).

FOX: *Memorials and Correspondence of Charles James Fox.* Ed. Lord John Russell (London, 4 vols., 1853-7).

Life and Times of Charles James Fox. Lord John Russell (London, 1859).

FOX: *Journal of Henry Edward Fox* (London, 1923).

FRY: *Memoirs of the Life of Elizabeth Fry* (London, 1847).

GEORGE IV: *Life of George IV.* Roger Fulford (London, 1935).

Correspondence of George, Prince of Wales. Ed. Aspinall; vol. 1 (Cambridge, 1963).

Letters of George IV. Ed. Aspinall (Cambridge, 1938).

GILPIN: *Memoirs of Dr. Richard Gilpin* (London, 1879).

GLENBERVIE: *Diaries of Sylvester Douglas, Lord Glenbervie* (London, 1928).

GREVILLE: *Diary*. Ed. Philip Wilson (London, 1927).

GREY: *Lord Grey of the Reform Bill*. G. M. Trevelyan (London, 1920).

HAMILTON, EMMA, LADY.

Lady Hamilton. Sichel (London, 1905).

Life and Letters of Lady Hamilton. Tours (London, 1963).

*HOBHOUSE: *Diary of Henry Hobhouse*. Ed. Aspinall (London, 1947).

HOLLAND: *Journal of Lady Elizabeth Holland*. Ed. Lord Ilchester (London, 1908).

Letters of Lady Elizabeth Holland to her son (London, 1946).

HOOKHAM FRERE: *John Hookham Frere and his friends*. Festing (London, 1899).

HUNT: *Memoirs of Henry Hunt* (London, 1820).

HUSKISSON: *Huskisson and his Age*. C. R. Fay (London, 1951).

KNIGHTON: *Memoirs of Sir William Knighton*. Lady Knighton (London, 1838).

LEVESON-GOWER: *Private Correspondence of Lord Granville Leveson-Gower* (London, 1916).

LIVERPOOL: *Life and Administration of the 2nd Earl of Liverpool*. Yonge (London, 1868).

Life of Lord Liverpool. Sir Charles Petrie (London, 1954).

Lord Liverpool and Liberal Toryism. Brock (Cambridge, 1941).

MACKINTOSH: *Life of Sir James Mackintosh*. Ed. by his son (London, 1836).

*MALMESBURY: *Diaries and Correspondence of 1st Earl of Malmesbury* (London, 1844).

MELVILLE: *Henry Dundas*. Furber (Oxford, 1931).

NELSON: *Life of Nelson*. A. T. Mahan (London, 1897).

OWEN: *Life of Robert Owen*. G. D. H. Cole (London, 1930).

PEEL: *Sir Robert Peel, from his Private Papers*. Ed. Parker (London, 1891).

Mr. Secretary Peel. Gash (London, 1961).

PERCEVAL: *Life of Rt. Hon. Spencer Perceval*. Walpole (London, 1874).

Life of Perceval. Gray (Manchester, 1963).

PITT: *Some Chapters of his Life and Time*. Ashbourne (London, 1898).

The House of Pitt. Tresham Lever (London, 1947).

Life of Pitt. Rosebery (London, 1891).

William Pitt and the Great War. Holland Rose (London, 1911).

**Life of Pitt*. Stanhope (London, 1862).

Life of Pitt. Tomline (London, 1821) and chapters XXIII, XXIV and XXVII, privately printed for Lord Rosebery (London, 1903).

Pitt and Wilberforce (Edinburgh, 1899).

Secret Correspondence Connected with Mr. Pitt's return to office in
1804. Ed. Lord Mahon. (Privately printed, London, 1852.)

PLUMER WARD: *Memoirs of the Political and Literary Life of Plumer Ward* (London, 1850).

RAIKES, THOMAS: *Journal 1831-47* (London, 1856).

ROMILLY: *Memoirs of the Life of Sir Samuel Romilly* (London, 1840).

*ROSE: *Diaries and Correspondence of George Rose.* Ed. Harcourt (London, 1860).

ST. VINCENT: *Life and Correspondence of Earl St. Vincent.* Brenton (London, 1838).

Memoirs of Earl St. Vincent. Tucker (London, 1844).

Letters of Earl St. Vincent 1801-4 (Navy Records Society, 1922).

SHELLEY: *Diary of Frances, Lady Shelley.* Ed. Edgcumbe (London, 1912).

SHERIDAN: *Life of Sheridan.* Sichel (London, 1909).

TIERNEY, *Life of George Tierney.* Olphin (London, 1934).

WELLESLEY: *The Wellesley Papers* (London, 1914).

WELLINGTON: *Supplementary Despatches,* etc. (London, 1871).

WILBERFORCE: *Life of William Wilberforce.* By his sons (London, 1839).

Correspondence of Wilberforce. Ed. by his sons (London, 1840).

Life of Wilberforce. Sir R. Coupland (London, 1945).

Private Papers of Wilberforce (London, 1897).

WINDHAM: *The Windham Papers* (London, 1913).

The Windham Diary. Ed. Mrs. Baring (London, 1866).

WRAXALL, SIR N. W.: *Posthumous Memoirs of his own time* (London, 1836).

Index

227–8; reconciles Pitt and Addington, 230–2; 234; 238; 242; 250; after Pitt's death, 254; 269; 271; and Catholic Emancipation, 281–2; 305; Prime Minister, 306–7; remoteness from Sidmouth, 320; 322; 324; and Lady Hamilton, 328–9; 331; 338–40; 342; 367; 375–7; 379; and Queen Caroline, 385; 387–8; and Queen's trial, 389; moves towards liberalism, 393; and Sidmouth's resignation, 394–5, 399–400; opposes pension for Sidmouth, 401–2; reshuffles Government, 404–5; 407; and Sidmouth's retirement, 408–9; retires, 412

Heriot, John, 165

Hertford, Francis Seymour, Marquis of, 306

Hobart, Robert, Lord, Earl of Buckinghamshire, 101; 130; 135; 204; 211; becomes Buckinghamshire, 231; 238–9; excluded from Talents' Cabinet, 252–3, 259–60; leads splinter-group, 262, 273, 278; 287; 289; joins Perceval's Government, 303; 305; dies, 339–40

Hobhouse, Benjamin, 28; 76

Hobhouse, Henry, 157; 374; 394; 396; 408

Hobhouse, John Cam, 338

Holland, Henry Fox, Lord, 53; 75; 110; 123; on Addington's domestic policy, 153; 217; Privy Seal, 260; 261; fall of Talents, 263–6; 272; 296; opposes licensing of Dissenting Ministers, 299; 347

Home Office, The, 100; 203; organisation in 1812, 315–17; inadequacy of means at disposal, 318–20; 343; employment of spies, 357–66; 375; in 1822, 392

Hood, Samuel, Lord, 238; 416

Hope, Charles, 209

Horne Tooke, John, 73

Horsfall, William, 321; 323

Howick, Lord, see Grey

Hulse, Sir Edward, 13

Hunt, Henry, at Spa Fields, 343–4; 346–7; 349; at Peterloo, 371–5

Huntingford, George Isaac, influence on Addington, 19–22; 23–4; 26; 31; injunctions to virtue, 34; on marriage, 36; 48–9; and Harry Addington, 68; 71; 121; Bishop of Gloucester, 139; 225; 245; 275; interrogates Grenville, 290; 399; urges Sidmouth to write memoirs, 403; 416

Huntly, Alexander Gordon, Marquis of, 378

Huskisson, William, 340; 399; 403; 413

Hutchinson, John Hely-Hutchinson, Lord, 234; 250–1

Income Tax, abolished by Addington, 148–9; 167; remodelled, 189–94; 215

Ings, James, 381

Ireland, 51; Union with England, 84–7, 90; 121; in 1801, 133–5; 157; 198; Emmet's rising, 202–3; and the Talents, 262–4; under Peel, 324–5; royal visit, 395–8; 414

Jefferson, Thomas, 283

Jenkinson (or "Jenky"), see Hawkesbury

Jernegham, Dr., 13

Junius, Letters of, 417

471

Morning Chronicle, The, 70; 131; 318; 332
Morning Herald, The, 131
Mornington, Lord, see Wellesley
Morpeth, George Howard, Lord, 172
Mulgrave, Henry Phipps, Lord, 123; 175; 227; 288; at death of Perceval, 305

Naval Commission of Enquiry, 169–70; 236–40
Navy, The Royal, Addington's interest in, 52; cut by St. Vincent, 155; Commission of Enquiry, 169–70; 182; 206; debate on, 211–12
Nelson, Admiral, Lord, 52; at Copenhagen, 119–21; 124; support of Peace, 126; 184; 198; regrets at Addington's fall, 226; Trafalgar, 244–5; 284–5; 328–9; 416
North, Frederick, Lord, 40–2; 44; 102; 255; 420
Northern League, The, 88; 117; 120–1
Northumberland, Hugh Percy, Duke of, 351
Norton, Fletcher, 59

Oliver the Spy, 358; 360–5
Onslow, Arthur, 59
Oracle, The, 115
Orders in Council, 283–4; 303
Otto, Monsieur, 119; 122; 127; 150–1; 164
Oudh, Begums of, 64
Owen, Robert, 153; Sidmouth's support for projects of, 327–8

Paine, Thomas, 313

Palk, Lawrence, 75
Parker, Sir Hyde, 120
Parliamentary Reform, in 1785, 49; abandoned by Pitt, 77–8; 132; adopted by Radicals, 341–7; Reform Bill, 415–16
Patten, Colonel, 187
Peel, Sir Robert, 153
Peel, Robert, 319; Chief Secretary in Ireland, 324–5; and Government spies, 359; 369; 390; 394; succeeds Sidmouth as Home Secretary, 399–400; 404
Pelham, Thomas, Earl of Chichester, 100; 105; on fall of Pitt, 107–8; 130; opposition to Treaty of Amiens, 146; 179; move to Duchy of Lancaster, 203
Pellew, Edward, 1st Viscount Exmouth, 52; 212; 388; 414; 417
Pellew, George, 83; 139; 323; 396; 411; 414; 419
Pells, Clerkship of the, 141–2; 225; 401
Peltier, Jean, 164–5
Peninsular Campaign, 279; championed by Sidmouth, 284–6, 291–2
Pentrich Revolution, 355–6; 361–2
Pepys, Sir Lucas, 276
Perceval, Spencer, 101–2; 213; after Pitt's death, 254; negotiations with Sidmouth, 266–7; forms ministry, 269–70; 278; 281; succeeds Portland, 287; overtures, to Addingtonians, 288–90, 292–5; supported by Prince of Wales, 296–7; 299; 302–3; includes Sidmouth in Government, 304; assassinated, 305; 416
Peterloo, 371–6; 379; 381; 384; 392